International Business and Culture

International Business and Culture: Challenges in Cross-Cultural Marketing and Management explores the intricate relationship between culture and business, offering valuable insights for both practitioners and scholars. The authors delve into the profound impact of cultural dimensions on various aspects of international business, marketing, human resource management, and organisational structure. They examine the theoretical frameworks underpinning these studies through a meticulous narrative literature review and case studies.

The significance of understanding cultural influences on business decisions becomes paramount in an increasingly interconnected world. The book addresses challenges faced by companies operating across diverse cultures, emphasising the need for adaptation in international marketing and management. Based on practical examples, the research focuses on identifying the most culturally sensitive areas in international business and explores the crucial cultural determinants influencing engagement with foreign markets.

The book's theoretical background spans international business, marketing, and management, and it is intertwined with cultural concepts from Hofstede and Hall. It consists of 16 chapters covering marketing and communication strategies across cultures, cultural aspects of international business and cross-cultural management based on practical examples of Duracell, Inc., PepsiCo, Volkswagen, VELUX Group, and Amica Group, among others.

The book highlights the undeniable interconnectedness of culture and business. As businesses expand internationally, the symbiotic relationship between culture and business remains a pivotal factor influencing success and growth.

Małgorzata Bartosik-Purgat, Professor in the Department of International Management at Poznań University of Economics and Business, Poland. Her research addresses cultural aspects in international business, cross-cultural communication, cross-cultural consumer behaviour, consumer ethnocentrism, acceptance of innovations in the consumers' decisions, and the significance of new media in marketing and personal communication. Member of EIBA – European International Business Association, IAIR – International Academy for Intercultural Research, ABC – Association for Business Communication, SIETAR Poland – Society for Intercultural Education, Training and Research, IT&FA – International Trade and Finance Association, and AIB – Academy of International Business. Author and co-author of publications in International Journal of Emerging Markets, European Journal of International Management, Technology Analysis & Strategic Management, Entrepreneurial Business and Economics Review, and Economics and Business Review.

Monika Guzek, Assistant and Ph.D. candidate in the Department of International Management at Poznań University of Economics and Business, Poland. Her research encompasses diversity management, cultural aspects in international business and management, age diversity management, cross-cultural communication, cross-cultural consumer behaviour, and organisational culture. She also holds the esteemed position of President of the Society for Intercultural Education, Training and Research in Poland (SIETAR Polska) and is a member of SIETAR Europa and EIBA – European International Business Association.

Routledge Studies in International Business and the World Economy

83. International Entrepreneurship in Emerging Markets
Contexts, Behaviours, and Successful Entry
Edited by Vahid Jafari-Sadeghi and Léo-Paul Dana

84. Management Research, International Business, and National Culture
Evaluating Hofstede and GLOBE
Sunil Venaik, Paul Brewer and David Midgley

85. Business Impacts of COVID-19
International Business, Crisis Management, and the Global Economy
Edited by Tomasz Bernat and Joanna Duda

86. Global Mindset and International Business
Driving Process Outsourcing Organizations
Magdalena Kossowska and Jerzy Rosiński

87. The Consumer Co-operative Sector
International Perspectives on Strategic Renewal
Edited by John F. Wilson, Anthony Webster, Espen Ekberg and Samuli Skurnik

88. Mergers and Acquisitions
The Pharmaceutical and Biotechnology Industries
Edited by Mark Thomas and Janna L. Rose

89. International Business and Culture
Challenges in Cross-Cultural Marketing and Management
Edited by Małgorzata Bartosik-Purgat and Monika Guzek

For more information about this series, please visit: www.routledge.com/Routledge-Studies-in-International-Business-and-the-World-Economy/book-series/SE0358

International Business and Culture

Challenges in Cross-Cultural Marketing and Management

Edited by Małgorzata Bartosik-Purgat and Monika Guzek

Routledge
Taylor & Francis Group
NEW YORK AND LONDON

First published 2024
by Routledge
605 Third Avenue, New York, NY 10158

and by Routledge
4 Park Square, Milton Park, Abingdon, Oxon, OX14 4RN

Routledge is an imprint of the Taylor & Francis Group, an informa business

Library of Congress Cataloging-in-Publication Data
Names: Bartosik-Purgat, Małgorzata, editor. | Guzek, Monika, editor.
Title: International business and culture : challenges in cross-cultural marketing and management / edited by Małgorzata Bartosik-Purgat and Monika Guzek.
Description: New York, NY : Routledge, 2024. | Series: Routledge studies in international business and the world economy | Includes bibliographical references and index.
Identifiers: LCCN 2023059302 | ISBN 9781032633893 (hbk) | ISBN 9781032636955 (pbk) | ISBN 9781032636962 (ebk)
Subjects: LCSH: International business enterprises. | Management. | Marketing.
Classification: LCC HD62.4 .I5475 2024 | DDC 658/.049—dc23/eng/20240220
LC record available at https://lccn.loc.gov/2023059302

ISBN: 978-1-032-63389-3 (hbk)
ISBN: 978-1-032-63695-5 (pbk)
ISBN: 978-1-032-63696-2 (ebk)

DOI: 10.4324/9781032636962

Typeset in Times New Roman
by Apex CoVantage, LLC

International Business and Culture

Challenges in Cross-Cultural Marketing and Management

Edited by Małgorzata Bartosik-Purgat and Monika Guzek

Routledge
Taylor & Francis Group
NEW YORK AND LONDON

First published 2024
by Routledge
605 Third Avenue, New York, NY 10158

and by Routledge
4 Park Square, Milton Park, Abingdon, Oxon, OX14 4RN

Routledge is an imprint of the Taylor & Francis Group, an informa business

Library of Congress Cataloging-in-Publication Data
Names: Bartosik-Purgat, Małgorzata, editor. | Guzek, Monika, editor.
Title: International business and culture : challenges in cross-cultural marketing and management / edited by Małgorzata Bartosik-Purgat and Monika Guzek.
Description: New York, NY : Routledge, 2024. | Series: Routledge studies in international business and the world economy | Includes bibliographical references and index.
Identifiers: LCCN 2023059302 | ISBN 9781032633893 (hbk) | ISBN 9781032636955 (pbk) | ISBN 9781032636962 (ebk)
Subjects: LCSH: International business enterprises. | Management. | Marketing.
Classification: LCC HD62.4 .I5475 2024 | DDC 658/.049—dc23/eng/20240220
LC record available at https://lccn.loc.gov/2023059302

ISBN: 978-1-032-63389-3 (hbk)
ISBN: 978-1-032-63695-5 (pbk)
ISBN: 978-1-032-63696-2 (ebk)

DOI: 10.4324/9781032636962

Typeset in Times New Roman
by Apex CoVantage, LLC

Contents

Contributors

Editors

Małgorzata Bartosik-Purgat, Poznań University of Economics and Business, Poland

Monika Guzek, Poznań University of Economics and Business, Poland

Chapters' authors (in alphabetical order)

Klaudia Bączyk-Lesiuk, Collegium Da Vinci

Małgorzata Bartosik-Purgat, Poznań University of Economics and Business

Joanna Bednarz, University of Gdańsk, Faculty of Economics

Katarzyna Chojnowska, Poznań University of Economics and Business

Aleksandra Cybulska, Petro Mohyla Black Sea National University

Nela Filimon, University of Girona, Spain

Francesc Fusté-Forné, University of Girona

Tomasz Grzegorczyk, Poznań University of Economics and Business

Monika Guzek, Poznań University of Economics and Business

Alicja Hadryś, Poznań University of Economics and Business

Barbara Jankowska, Poznań University of Economics and Business

Alina Jankowska-Brzóska, Amica

Patrycja Kasprzyk, Volkswagen

Agnieszka Klimczak, Iddeni

Maria Kubala, Poznań University of Economics and Business

Dorota Malicka, Zanglory – Investments

F. Xavier Medina, Universitat Oberta de Catalunya

Aleksandra Myszk, University of Gdańsk

Agata Nikonowicz, Poznań University of Economics and Business

Paweł Nowakowski, Duracell Inc.

Łukasz Puślecki, Poznań University of Economics and Business

Wiktoria Rakowska, Poznań University of Economics and Business

Michał Staszków, Poznań University of Economics and Business

Magdalena Steier, VELUX

Marek G. Tomalak, PepsiCo

Figures

Tables

Instead of introduction

Culture and business – are they interdependent?

Małgorzata Bartosik-Purgat and Monika Guzek

In our increasingly interconnected world, the relationship between culture and business has gained paramount importance (Caligiuri, 2021). Globalisation processes and the internationalisation of businesses in the twenty-first century influence the need to learn not only about financial, economic, and management issues but also about different cultures and cultural factors, which are involved in these micro- and macroeconomic processes and function as the background of many strategic decisions made by international companies and institutions (Gibson, 2022; Lee et al., 2023). As globalisation continues to dissolve geographic boundaries and facilitate international trade, the intricate interplay between cultural dynamics and business practices becomes not only a matter of academic inquiry but a pressing concern for companies seeking success on the global stage. In order to be competitive in the international market, companies go beyond their domestic markets with their activities in order to gain a number of benefits in the form of entering new markets, gaining supplies, international recognition of the company, and increasing revenues in general (Cuervo-Cazura et al., 2015). However, these activities are also associated with many challenges, which can sometimes be a significant barrier to international operations. A major challenge for foreign companies is often the cultural environment (Ahsan & Sinha, 2022).

Culture, a complex of beliefs, values, traditions, and behavioural norms, exerts a profound influence on every facet of human interaction, including commerce (Gong, 2009). Cultural determinants are usually sensitive and sometimes challenging to recognise. These aspects impact not only the people's behaviour but also the international functioning of organisations concerning at least two areas concerning marketing and management activities. First, the consumers and their needs, preferences, behaviours, beliefs, values, and decisions usually depend on their cultural traits. Sometimes, consumers do not even realise that their behaviour and reactions are linked to their cultural features (Nahavandi, 2021; Bartosik-Purgat & Filimon, 2023). Consumer decisions depend on their cultural traits because these elements are interdependent. Companies aspiring to enter a particular foreign market must gather information about its environment (including cultural aspects) and try to adapt their products and services to local

DOI: 10.4324/9781032636962-1

preferences. These modifications are typically integrated during the product preparation phase, before entering a new market or in anticipation of launching marketing initiatives targeted at the respective region (Bartosik-Purgat, 2019; Hall et al., 2019; Lee et al., 2023). Second, different sources of employers in international companies and their subsidiaries (usually from the local market – host country nationals, but also from the headquarters' home country nationals and other nationalities) impact the companies' organisation, including management style. The management and other processes which contain a human factor became more challenging in such a culturally differentiated environment (Barmeyer et al., 2021; Thomas & Inkson, 2021; Mahadevan, 2023). Consequently, acknowledging and comprehending this symbiotic relationship between culture and business (e.g. marketing and management) is essential for any company aspiring to thrive in the multifaceted landscape of international trade.

According to the significance of the aspects presented earlier, the primary purpose of the research presented in the monograph concerns the identification of the influence of cultural traits in different aspects of conducting business in culturally differentiated environments with an emphasis on two main areas. The first one focuses on the international marketing activities of companies whose products and services meet the requirements of their potential clients in diverse markets. The second area places a particular emphasis on the management aspects, such as the organisational culture of a company, communication process (internal and external), negotiations, internationalisation, remote working, and others.

To examine the primary purpose of the research presented in the monograph, the authors are seeking for answers to the following threefold research questions:

- First: what are the main areas in doing business internationally that are the most dependent on the foreign environments (focusing on the cultural aspects)? The answer to this question will support the indication of the most "sensitive" areas in international business because of cultural influences.
- Second: what are the most essential cultural determinants that impact various aspects of international companies' engagement? What should companies know about their actual and potential clients and different local suppliers (e.g. their values, attitudes, behaviour, and expectations) to be able to adapt decisions or strategies in order to match their needs and expectations? An answer to this question will expose the most significant and challenging cultural factors that should not be neglected when trying to identify and analyse foreign markets, where companies operate or want to expand into new markets.
- Third: what are the practical solutions to the expected challenges in running cross-cultural business?

Presented above considerations related to cultural aspects, international marketing and management offer a broad scope of challenges companies face while running cross-cultural business worldwide (Ahsan & Sinha, 2022; Lee et al.,

2023; Thomas & Inkson, 2021). This book is a compendium of knowledge on the interaction between the business world and culture. The research presents not only the theoretical underpinnings of this relationship but also concrete examples and cases that illustrate the challenges and opportunities of international cooperation. In other words, the authors link the theoretical aspects of acting and managing across cultures with their adaptation in particular companies (Amica Group, Codorniu, Duracell, Inc. IKEA, Duracell, Inc., McDonald, PepsiCo, Piel de Toro, Unilever, VELUX Group, Volkswagen Group, and Zanglory Investments Ltd.). They present theoretical concepts, models, and strategies widely found in the literature, together with their practical adoption in international companies.

The main research methods used in the studies presented in the chapters combine a mix of various techniques and approaches. Authors use different analytical methods based on both primary and secondary resources related to the issues described in the particular chapters. The research methods used in almost all chapters are both a narrative literature review and a case study. The scientific validity of the case study method is evidenced by objectified, rational, organised, systematic, and structured activities, ensuring the conclusion's reliability (Ellet, 2018; Yin, 2018). The most important principle is the triangulation method, understood as obtaining data from several independent sources. Such a research method focuses more on an in-depth understanding of the phenomenon than the statistical analysis of variables. According to Glaser and Barney (2001), anything can constitute data: not only what, how, and under what circumstances something is said in an interview but also the documents that address an issue, newspaper articles, observation results, and audio and video recordings. For exploratory problems, these research methods allow authors to answer the question of why the phenomenon under study occurs. Based on the collected data, the case study method allows for an in-depth analysis of the problem and describes its specifics in a particular company.

The theoretical background of the research can be divided into two main parts. The first focuses on international business (including internationalisation in general, marketing, and management). The second theoretical concept concerns cultural aspects (definitions, cultural models and classifications, intercultural competence, and cross-cultural management).

The main reason for the linkage between business and cultural diversity is associated with running a business outside of the home market. This requires a lot of analysis and strategic decisions about motives and forms of entry into foreign markets (Ahsan & Sinha, 2022; Cuervo-Cazura et al., 2015). These elements in the context of companies' entry into foreign markets became the basis for the considerations in the sections of the monograph on internationalisation. Various internationalisation theories and strategies for entering international markets (e.g. direct investments, and acquisitions) are presented in the monograph.

In the context of cultural influences on company decisions, strategies for standardising and adapting activities in foreign markets are presented (Gao et al., 2022). Due to the need to consider cultural differences, companies often decide to implement an adaptation strategy, which, in its assumptions, differentiates activities in foreign markets (Vrontis et al., 2009; Gao et al., 2022; Vescovi, 2022). As a next step, concerning the theoretical foundations of international business, marketing concepts and selected elements of management are also indicated. Product strategies (including packaging strategies, branding, and other elements of the product structure) and communication are most often discussed within the marketing framework. Further, regarding management fundamentals, the theoretical frameworks most often considered in research presented in the monograph are international human resource management (IHRM) and creating the organisational culture of international subsidiaries. These areas are highly dependent on cultural factors because, firstly, IHRM is concerned with managing people from different cultural backgrounds (Dasgupta et al., 2022; Tarique et al., 2022) and secondly, organisational culture is a carrier of national culture. It is often largely a reflection of the characteristics and values recognised by employees or the parent company (headquarters) in the case of subsidiaries (Jung et al., 2008; Rottig et al., 2014; Wiengarten et al., 2015). Furthermore, the evolving nature of global markets accentuates the continuous need for scientific discourse to transmit ideas, data, and observations, and opens research to understand practical aspects to refine the understanding and application of these management frameworks in an ever-changing international business landscape.

The theoretical framework used in the studies presented in the monographs also touches on cultural issues. The main cultural concepts that are the base for discussion refer to Hofstede's cultural model (Hofstede, 2001; Hofstede et al., 2010) and Hall's (1989). Within the framework of Hofstede's classification, the following cultural dimensions are presented: individualism–collectivism, power distance (high and low), uncertainty avoidance (high and low), masculinity/femininity (nowadays replaced by the name of motivation towards achievement and success) (Hofstede Insights.com, 2023), time orientation (long and short), and restraint/indulgence (Hofstede et al., 2010). Cultural dimensions, proposed by the American anthropologist Hall, refer to intercultural communication, which is the main field of the author's interests. Describing intercultural communication, Hall (1989) distinguished the cultural groups by considering two fundamental criteria of divisions: the degree of using context in communication and the approach to time. Additionally, the incorporation of cultural dimensions as presented by Meyer (2014) allows the reader to understand how to make decisions and build authority as well as provide feedback in a multicultural environment. Also, an appreciation of cultural diversity through Gibson's (2022) perspectives further enriches the theoretical foundation, contributing to a comprehensive understanding of the intricate interplay between culture and business in the international context. Gibson's approach goes beyond traditional frameworks, emphasising the dynamic nature of cultural diversity and its impact on organisational dynamics.

The structure of the monograph is subordinate to its main purpose. It is divided into two parts including 16 chapters in total. The first part is dedicated to marketing and communication strategies across cultures, and the second includes chapters related to cultural aspects of international business including issues of cross-cultural management. Almost every chapter contains theoretical aspects of international business and examples of companies that face these problems in culturally diversified markets. The case studies present the companies, their bios, international expansions, and the manners of overcoming cultural barriers. The theoretical aspects concern, for example, marketing strategies (Chapters 1–6), management aspects (Chapters 9–12 and 14), internationalisation process (Chapters 7–8), ESG processes (Chapter 13), and others. In addition, the authors provide discussion points and the practical implications of the analyses in particular chapters. The countries and their cultural backgrounds presented in chapters and cases are Denmark, Poland, Ukraine, Germany, China, Canada, Japan, India, Singapore, Israel, Nigeria, Morocco, Egypt, Sweden, Tanzania (Zanzibar), and others.

Concluding, the interconnectedness of culture and business is undeniable. Companies that acknowledge and embrace cultural diversity, foster inclusivity, and adapt their strategies accordingly are more likely to thrive in the globalised marketplace. As businesses continue to expand their horizons, the synergy between culture and business will remain a pivotal factor influencing success and growth in the international marketplace. In the future, the imperative for companies to take into account cultural diversity, both in the creation of strategies, adaptation of products and services to local preferences or the management of international human resources, becomes increasingly apparent. This awareness and commitment to action not only enhance cultural competence within the workforce but this knowledge also serves as a proactive measure against potential cultural pitfalls in the ever-evolving global business landscape. Furthermore, fostering strong partnerships with local communities and stakeholders emerges as a strategic necessity, ensuring that businesses not only understand but actively contribute to the diverse tapestry of cultures they engage with.

The symbiotic relationship between culture and business underscores the need for continuous research and refinement of management approaches, facilitating a more profound understanding of the dynamic interplay between cultural factors and organisational success. Consistent exploration and consideration of practical insights from companies actively operating in the global markets will undoubtedly lay the foundation for a business environment that can consciously develop its intercultural competence and adapt its business practices in a culturally intelligent and globally competitive way.

Bibliography

Ahsan, F.M., & Sinha, A.K. (2022). Internationalization motives, location advantages and performance: The case of Indian firms from knowledge-intensive industries. *Cross Cultural & Strategic Management, 29*(3), 516–551. https://doi.org/10.1108/CCSM-07-2021-0119

Barmeyer, C., Bausch, M., & Mayrhofer, U. (2021). *Constructive Intercultural Management*. London: Edward Elgar Publications.

Bartosik-Purgat, M. (2019). *New Media in the Marketing Communication of Enterprises in the International Market*. Warsaw: PWN Publications.

Bartosik-Purgat, M., & Filimon, N. (2023). *European Consumers in the Digital Era: Implications of Technology, Media and Culture on Consumer Behavior*. London: Routledge Publications.

Caligiuri, P. (2021). *Build Your Cultural Agility: The Nine Competencies of Successful Global Professionals*. New York: Kogan Page Publications.

Cuervo-Cazura, A., Narula, R., & Un, C.A. (2015). Internationalization motives: Sell more, buy better, upgrade and escape. *Multinational Business Review, 23*(1), 25–35. https://doi.org/10.1108/MBR-02-2015-0009

Dasgupta, P., Carbery, R., & McDonnell, A. (2022). Human resource management in multinational corporations. In P. Holland, T. Bartram, T. Garavan & K. Grant (Eds.), *The Emerald Handbook of Work, Workplaces and Disruptive Issues in HRM* (pp. 67–86). Bingley: Emerald Publishing Limited.

Ellet, W. (2018). *The Case Study Handbook: A Student's Guide*. Brighton, MA: Harvard Business Review Press.

Gao, J., Wang, T., Jia, Y., & Wang, C.L. (2022). How and when do exporters benefit from an international adaptation strategy? The moderating effect of formal and informal institutional distance. *International Marketing Review, 39*(6), 1390–1416.

Gibson, R. (2022). *Bridge the Culture Gaps: A Toolkit for Effective Collaboration in the Diverse, Global Workplace*. London: Nicholas Brealey Publication.

Glaser, B., & Barney, G. (2001). *The Grounded Theory Perspective: Conceptualization Contrasted With Description*. Mill Valley: Sociology Press.

Gong, W. (2009). National culture and global diffusion of business-to-consumer e-commerce. *Cross Cultural Management: An International Journal, 16*(1), 83–101. https://doi.org/10.1108/13527600910930059

Hall, B.J., Covarrubias, P.O., Kirschbaum, K.A., & Rapaille, C. (2019). *Among Cultures: The Challenges of Communication*. London: Routledge Publications.

Hall, E.T. (1989). *Beyond Culture* (2nd ed.). New York: Anchor Books.

Hofstede, G. (2001). *Culture's Consequences: Comparing Values, Behaviors, Institutions, and Organizations across Nations* (2nd ed.). Thousand Oaks, CA: Sage Publications.

Hofstede, G., Hofstede, G.J., & Minkov, M. (2010). *Cultures and Organizations: Software of the Mind* (3rd ed.). New York: McGraw-Hill.

Hofstede Insights.com. (2023). *Country Comparison Tool*. www.hofstede-insights.com/country-comparison-tool?

Jung, J., Su, X., Baeza, M., & Hong, S. (2008). The effect of organizational culture stemming from national culture towards quality management deployment. *The TQM Journal, 20*(6), 622–635. https://doi.org/10.1108/17542730810909374

Lee, J.A., Usunier, J.C., & Taras, V. (2023). *Business & Marketing across Cultures*. London: Sage Publications.

Mahadevan, J. (2023). *Cross-Cultural Management: A Contemporary Approach*. London: Sage Publications.

Meyer, E. (2014). *The Culture Map: Breaking Through the Invisible Boundaries of Global Business*. New York: Public Affairs.

Nahavandi, A. (2021). *The Cultural Mindset: Managing People across Cultures*. London: Sage Publications.
Rottig, D., Reus, T.H., & Tarba, S.Y. (2014). The impact of culture on mergers and acquisitions: A third of a century of research. In *Advances in Mergers and Acquisitions (Advances in Mergers and Acquisitions, Vol. 12)* (pp. 135–172). Bingley: Emerald Group Publishing Limited. https://doi.org/10.1108/S1479-361X(2013)0000012009
Tarique, I., Briscoe, D.R., & Schuler, R.S. (2022). *International Human Resource Management: Policies and Practices for Multinational Enterprises*. London: Routledge Publications.
Thomas, D.C., & Inkson, K. (2021). *Cross-Cultural Management*. London: Sage Publications.
Vescovi, T. (2022). *Cross-Cultural Marketing: European Perspectives*. Camberley: Edward Elgar Publications.
Vrontis, D., Thrassou, A., & Lamprianou, I. (2009). International marketing adaptation versus standardisation of multinational companies. *International Marketing Review*, *26*(4/5), 477–500.
Wiengarten, F., Gimenez, C., Fynes, B., & Ferdows, K. (2015). Exploring the importance of cultural collectivism on the efficacy of lean practices: Taking an organisational and national perspective. *International Journal of Operations & Production Management*, *35*(3), 370–391. https://doi.org/10.1108/IJOPM-09-2012-0357
Yin, R.K. (2018). *Case Study Research and Applications: Design and Methods*. London: Sage Publications.

Part I

Cross-cultural marketing challenges

1 McDonald's cross-cultural product strategy

Małgorzata Bartosik-Purgat and Katarzyna Chojnowska

Introduction

Globalisation processes and business internationalisation in the twenty-first century influence the need to learn about economic and management issues and different cultures (Coucher, 2019; Kotabe & Helsen, 2022; Usunier & Lee, 2012). They are involved in these processes and become a background of many strategic decisions made by international institutions.

In the 1980s, the development of globalisation and convergence influenced marketers to assume often that consumers around the world were becoming increasingly alike – as if they were living in a "global village" – and that it would be possible to advertise, promote, and sell the same products, under the same name, and in the same way almost all over the world (Kotabe & Helsen, 2022). This would also mean that the cost of entering and successfully operating in a new market would not be high, thanks to economies of scale (Guedes et al., 2022). These assumptions are general principles of global marketing. However, it turns out that establishing a company and successfully selling its products in a culturally different market is much more demanding (Brodowsky & Schuster, 2020; Gibson, 2022; Vescovi, 2022). Not only are the conditions and requirements of different markets more demanding than many thought, but individual markets also exhibit significant differences in the tastes and preferences of potential customers. These determinants relate to national cultures' elements and structures (Choo et al., 2023; Cleveland et al., 2015; Gibson, 2022; Sasaki et al., 2021). They are both compassionate and hidden (Caligiuri, 2021). Thus, it is challenging to recognise and predict their impact on consumers' behaviour in a particular culture (Kotabe & Helsen, 2022; Sobol et al., 2018; Vescovi, 2022).

Companies operating internationally face a constant dilemma regarding the standardisation and adaptation of their operations (Gao et al., 2022; Sasaki et al., 2021). On the one hand, standardisation brings many advantages, such as economies of scale, global competition, and recognition. On the other hand, it may cause low acceptance by local consumers because the offer may not suit their cultural habits. The adaptation strategy usually brings opposite consequences

DOI: 10.4324/9781032636962-3

to the standardisation. An interesting example is global restaurant chains such as McDonald's. According to popular belief and perception, they can be associated with standardising their operations internationally. They are often perceived as safe, secure, and predictable restaurants when travelling abroad, as customers generally know or guess what kind of meal they can eat there, what menu they will see, and what quality of dishes they will experience (Gao et al., 2022; Vescovi, 2022). Meanwhile, it turns out that local McDonald's restaurants often adapt the appearance of these places and promotional messages to local conditions and diversify the menu by enriching it with national dishes or flavours (Di Mooij, 2021; Usunier & Lee, 2012). Such situations occur daily in culturally diverse markets, where consumers are attached to local tastes (Gibson, 2022).

This chapter aims to identify the product strategy McDonald's uses in international activity with particular attention to the cultural background of markets. The main research methods used in this chapter are twofold: a literature analysis and a case study. The external sources used for the study were information from papers from scientific databases like Emerald, F&T, or Elsevier, along with articles on websites where product information is presented. Moreover, sources of information also included materials available on McDonald's websites in various foreign markets. The applied research methods answer the main research questions:

RQ1: To what extent does McDonald's adapt its products in culturally diverse foreign markets?

RQ2: What cultural elements influence the need to adjust product strategy at McDonald's in foreign markets?

The research method in the form of a case study is mainly used for descriptive research topics (Amadi, 2023; Wang et al., 2022). It answers what, where, and how something happened. For exploratory problems, the method allows answering why the phenomenon under study occurs. Such research focuses more on an in-depth understanding of the phenomenon than on the statistical analysis of variables (Wang et al., 2022). Compared to other research methods, the case study uses the broadest range of techniques and tools for data collection and analysis. These may include observations, interviews, surveys, documentation of the organisation under study, media sources, online sources, and available databases (Alon et al., 2020; Kumar et al., 2020; Yin, 2018). Based on the collected data, the case study method provides an in-depth analysis of the studied problem and describes its specificity (Yin, 2018).

The chapter consists of four sections. After the introduction, there will be a focus on international business standardisation and adaptation and the cultural conditions that may be of influence. In the third section, we will present the case of McDonald's in the context of international standardisation/adaptation of production activities. Finally, the last section will summarise and discuss the results' implications, limitations, and directions for possible future research.

Adaptation, standardisation, and culture in marketing strategies

International marketing represents the coordinated activities of enterprises in the international market to meet buyers' needs and preferences (Kotabe & Helsen, 2022) so that they decide to buy the product. These activities include identifying buyers' expectations, recognising the foreign environment in which the enterprise operates, designing and developing products, setting prices, and choosing distribution channels and appropriate communication methods (Barmeyer et al., 2021; Coucher, 2019; Di Mooij, 2021). This chapter then concentrates on possible solutions within the framework of international product strategy.

Product strategy is first to recognise clients' needs and then develop an offer that would satisfy these needs as much as possible. Concerning international business, identifying needs should include a detailed analysis of the foreign environment. This is a challenging but necessary activity for companies to recognise demand. After all, product strategy aims to adapt a product so the customer can purchase it. Thus, product strategy should be present at every stage of the product life cycle, from the creation of the product concept through its entry into the market to the final sale – until it is withdrawn from the market. Product strategy refers to forming the various elements that constitute product structure: core, tangible, and augmented (Kotler et al., 2021). The core product includes essential benefits linked with using a particular product (e.g. in food, these are physical and chemical characteristics). A tangible product refers to its packaging, product name, and brand or quality. Finally, the augmented product includes warranty and after-sales services (Kotler et al., 2021).

As highlighted earlier, when beginning international operations, one should recognise the foreign market in terms of its differences and diversification. The foreign business environment includes the entity (buyers, suppliers, competitors, and regulatory entities) and the macroeconomic environment (Usunier & Lee, 2012; Vescovi, 2022). Usually cultural, legal, economic, and technical factors are distinguished in the foreign environment (Alon et al., 2020; Kotabe & Helsen, 2022). Sometimes, natural and demographic factors are also emphasised. Each distinguished factor can be attributed to components affecting a company's marketing activities in foreign markets (Brodowsky & Schuster, 2020; Choo et al., 2023; Di Mooij, 2021). Due to this study's purpose and the chapter's subject matter, the following section will focus on the components of the cultural environment.

The cultural environment of a company's operations is shaped by elements of the national culture specific to a particular foreign market (Craig et al., 2009). The term "culture" was first defined and applied in 1871 by Edward Burnett Tylor in his book *Primitive Culture*: "culture includes knowledge, beliefs, arts, morals, laws, customs and other abilities and habits acquired by man as a member of society" (Tylor, 1871, p. 15).

Literature has many different interpretations of the terms "national culture" and "cultural environment". According to Adler and Gundersen (2007), culture is a way of life of a group of people, a configuration of all the more or less stereotyped patterns of learned behaviour passed down from generation to generation. On the other hand, Goodenough (1971) believes that culture is a set of beliefs and standards adopted and shared by a group of people. It helps individuals decide who they are, who they can be, how they feel, and what they do. According to this interpretation, culture significantly influences the behaviour of people living in a particular society and sets specific rules to be followed (Craig et al., 2009).

The cultural environment – which includes tradition, language, habit, customs, and religion – often affects the possibility of applying standardisation or the need to adapt marketing efforts internationally (Alon et al., 2020; Caligiuri, 2021; Gibson, 2022; Kotabe & Helsen, 2022; Sasaki et al., 2021). Cultural elements impact diverse aspects of people's lives, behaviours, and decisions. However, the cultural features of a particular nation are not easily recognisable. They require a lot of engagement and effort from companies that want to explore their potential customers' cultural features (needs, preferences, values, beliefs, etc.).

An enterprise operating in domestic and foreign markets can most often conduct marketing activities in both local and international environments. Different forms of expansion into foreign markets usually correspond to other marketing strategies (Alon et al., 2020; Cateora et al., 2021). On the one hand, an enterprise may use an international marketing strategy, most often associated with the adaptation of activities to the peculiarities of foreign markets; on the other hand, it may use a global marketing strategy and a corresponding standardisation strategy (Alon et al., 2020; Kotabe & Helsen, 2022; Vescovi, 2022).

The adaptation strategy involves modifying marketing activities in foreign markets due to differences in local conditions and buyer preferences. There are two types of adaptation: optional and isomorphic (Vescovi, 2022; Vrontis et al., 2009). Optional adaptation is implemented even though it is not necessary, seeking to reinforce the local competitive position, like the cultural traits of consumers. On the other hand, isomorphic adaptation is forced. Companies must implement it in response to different laws or technical standards. A significant advantage of adaptation is the greater acceptance of products adapted to foreign consumers' diverse needs and preferences (Usunier & Lee, 2012; Vrontis et al., 2009). Such activities involve increased costs resulting from identifying foreign markets (R&D) and modifications in marketing activities. These elements are considered among the most significant limitations of adaptation strategies (Usunier & Lee, 2012; Brodowsky & Schuster, 2020).

The opposite activity to adaptation is standardisation, namely offering buyers in different foreign markets the same or similar marketing solutions in terms of product, price, promotion, and distribution. Homogenisation of activities is associated with fundamental benefits in cost reduction, mainly thanks to economies of scale – an advantage of standardisation – and the possibility of achieving global competitiveness. At the same time, the lack of adaptation to the different needs of customers can be a fundamental limitation to the use of standardisation in marketing activities (Brodowsky & Schuster, 2020; Vrontis et al., 2009).

The decision to choose a specific product strategy for a culture of a given foreign market results from many considerations. These include, among others (Vescovi, 2022; Vrontis et al., 2009):

- product type: a greater need for adaptation is noted in the business-to-consumer (B2C) than in the business-to-business (B2B) market. Consumer products (both short-lived, e.g. food, and long-lived, e.g. furniture and cars) are more often dependent on the elements of the environment that require adaptation;
- company's international goals related to the achievement of the international competition: depending on whether the company wants the brand to be recognised globally or locally, it can use a standardisation or adaptation strategy, respectively; moreover, there is then the possibility of being globally or locally competitive;
- adaptation costs: when adaptation costs are high in the initial phase of internationalisation, the company may initially follow a standardisation strategy and then gradually adapt the offer to local conditions;
- similarity/otherness of markets and consumers: when the needs and preferences of potential buyers differ significantly from the domestic market on which the offer is available, then there is a need to adapt the request to the foreign market. In the opposite situation, when the domestic and foreign cultural environments are similar, the standardisation strategy may be internationally successful;
- economies of scale: if a company wants to achieve economies of scale in the form of reduced costs by offering the same products in more markets, then a standardisation strategy is advisable.

Due to the desire to achieve favourable effects from the advantages of both standardisation and adaptation, companies often use an indirect strategy in marketing activities, such as semi-standardisation (Usunier & Lee, 2012; Vrontis et al., 2009). This involves adapting only necessary elements in the foreign market product strategy and standardising the rest. In such a situation, economies of scale and increased acceptance of the offer by buyers in foreign markets are achievable.

The case of McDonald's

The company's history began in the 1940s when brothers Richard and Maurice (Dick and Mac) McDonald opened a roadside restaurant in San Bernardino, California, offering hamburgers, fries, and milkshakes.

Although their business was profitable, the brothers felt that running it traditionally involved too many difficulties and decided to make a few changes. First and foremost, they noticed that their establishment had become an attractive social gathering place, with customers "puzzling" the staff and not leaving the restaurant after their meal, which reduced traffic and turnover. Moreover, the McDonald brothers realised the potential of the upcoming generation of post-war baby boomers and wanted to create a more family-oriented atmosphere in their restaurant. The reorganisation of the restaurant included eliminating the positions of carhops (waiters who bring fast food to guests), limiting the menu to cheeseburgers, hamburgers, milkshakes, and sodas and developing a Speedee Service System (each person on the crew specialised in specific tasks, and most of the food was already pre-prepared, packaged, and heated with unique heat lamps). This allowed for faster food preparation (Klein, 2019). These innovations made the company more competitive in terms of price in the market. The first "mascot", also the logo of McDonald's, was Speedee – a plump chef with a head in the shape of a hamburger to symbolise the speed of order processing (Behr, 2023).

The changes were profitable, which prompted the owners to seek franchisees. Ray Kroc, a supplier of milkshake machines, became very involved in these activities (Close, 2016). Based on a partnership agreement with the McDonald brothers, Kroc formed a new franchise company in 1955 called McDonald's System, Inc. This was the beginning of McDonald's as we know it today, in the third decade of the twenty-first century ("McDonald's History (McDonald's)", n.d.). Over the next few years, a chain of 228 McDonald's restaurants was established in specially selected locations in the suburbs that were attractive to families, who were the chain's main target audience at the time (Close, 2016). A major contributor to McDonald's success at the time was the rise of the automobile in the USA, which came with the development of suburban neighbourhoods and interstate highways.

Kroc's difficult relationship with the McDonald brothers eventually led to the buyout of McDonald's along with the name (Schlosser, 2001). In 1962, McDonald's Golden Arches replaced Speedee. Furthermore, in 1965, the company introduced a new mascot: a red-haired clown named Ronald McDonald, who became the face of television commercials. The company was one of the first restaurants to introduce television commercials and spent millions of dollars to promote new products and create an image ("Reference for Business (Advameg, Inc.)", n.d.).

McDonald's became a leader in standardising American retail environments, rigorously controlling the appearance of its restaurants inside and out. Kroc developed standards for running every establishment, from food preparation to cleaning. To ensure the standardised operation of outlets, he created a programme, later known as Hamburger University, to train franchisees.

The year 1967 can be considered the beginning of McDonald's overseas expansion, because that year the first McDonald's outside the United States was opened in Richmond, Canada. In 1968, the Big Mac (a burger consisting of two patties, sauce, lettuce, cheese, pickles, and onions) was introduced and became McDonald's symbol. By 1970, McDonald's had restaurants in all 50 states and a few in Canada and the Caribbean. In the 1970s and 1980s, the company expanded to Asia, Australia, South America, and Europe. Kroc counted on the expertise of local franchisees to help adapt McDonald's offers and services to conditions in other markets. By 1992, nearly 40% of the company's sales came from overseas ("Reference for Business (Advameg, Inc.)", n.d.).

The company expanded its offer by adding some new elements to the menu. For example, in 1972, McDonald's introduced the fast-food concept for breakfast, selling the first Egg McMuffin sandwich ("Who we are (McDonald's)", n.d.). In 1979, the company introduced Happy Meals, a set consisting of a sandwich, fries, and a drink in reduced sizes packaged in a colourful cardboard box. Later, Happy Meals included an additional attraction, a toy from a regularly changing collection, not available in other stores. Moreover, many restaurants opened outdoor and indoor play areas. McDonald's also opened in new locations, such as airports, museums, and gas stations.

On 17 June 1992, the first McDonald's restaurant in Poland was opened in Warsaw. Within a dozen hours, the facility was visited by more than 45,000 customers. With 13,304 customers, the Poles set a world record for the number of transactions on the opening day. In the first months of McDonald's operation in Poland, the basic menu included hamburgers, double hamburgers, cheeseburgers, double cheeseburgers, Big Macs, fries, drinks, ice cream, and milkshakes ("Who we are (McDonald's)", n.d.). In 1993, the world's first McCafé – a separate café space within a restaurant, with separate service and tables – was opened in Melbourne, Australia ("Who we are (McDonald's)", n.d.).

During the COVID-19 pandemic, the company reduced sales of less profitable menu items, including kits and products (such as "Dollar Menus" in the USA) in favour of selling more expensive burgers and family kits. The move to cut sales of lower-priced meals (which often have slim margins) and encourage customers to more profitable menu items is nothing new, but it accelerated during the pandemic as ingredient costs rose and some restaurants struggled to find enough employees. According to Black Box Intelligence, in May 2021, chains selling new, more expensive meals raised restaurant sales by 11.5% compared to the same month in 2019 (Nesbit, 2021). During the COVID-19 pandemic, fast-food restaurants gained market share due to the closure of other restaurants; customers were even more likely to use the drive-through option.

Today, in the third decade of the twenty-first century, McDonald's operates about 38,000 restaurants in more than 100 countries around the world (39 countries in Europe, 31 in Asia and Oceania, 17 in South America, 11 in North America, and 4 in Africa ("Where we operate (McDonald's)", n.d.)), employs nearly 2 million workers, and serves 69 million customers every day ("Who we are (McDonald's)", n.d.). McDonald's restaurants are situated in different places depending on the demand and needs of customers. Some of them are connected to gas stations and grocery stores. McDonald's has several unusual types of restaurants, such as Ski Thru, a McDrive for skiers on the slopes in Lindvallen (Sweden), the only one of its kind worldwide. Next, McBarge, a floating outpost operating during the World Expo 86' in Vancouver (Canada), and McBoat, the world's only float-through restaurant, located on the Elbe River in Hamburg (Germany). This location is open 24/7 in the warmer months (usually in spring and summer) but closes for the cooler months as fewer people spend time "on the water". When employers see an order at the restaurant, they prepare it and then carry the bag to the dock (Frishberg, 2021).

Sometimes, McDonald's opens restaurants in places that had other uses in the past, such as a former tin smelter office (The Birch House in George Town, Penang, Malaysia), a former nineteenth-century Tudor-style market house (Bray, Ireland), an 1860s mansion, nineteenth-century Georgian style (Denton House in New Hyde Park, USA), an 1850s colonial mansion with elegant carved furniture and fireplaces (Gore House in Freeport, Maine, USA), a decommissioned Douglas DC-3 aeroplane (Taupo, New Zealand), or an old train station (Barstow, California, USA) that has been out of service since 1955. The restaurant in Barstow has installed several train cars with dining rooms. The central space is located in the restored station building.

In the USA, McDonald's has adapted its restaurants in a "local" way. For example, in Dallas, next to the zoo, the restaurant is decorated with animal figures both outside and inside. On the other hand, in Roswell, not far from the site of the "Roswell incident", there is a "space" at McDonald's: the exterior of a UFO-shaped restaurant. There is a play area inside with mascots in spacesuits (Racoma, 2019; Atlas Obscura, n.d.).

Another example of an uncommon location can be found in Australia. Sydney Airport has created Sky Kitchen, a McDonald's restaurant with a glass kitchen located above the order counter. The vertical design makes the most of the restaurant's small footprint while providing a glimpse into food preparation. However, the unique arrangement posed challenges in delivering food quickly and seamlessly to customers below. This was overcome by creating an order delivery system using a belt boom that moves up and down. The design drew inspiration from similar solutions in Asia, where space is at a premium (Gross, 2019). Since 2017, it has been possible to order and deliver meals to a designated address (McDelivery). Originally, the only delivery service in the United States providing McDelivery was Uber Eats; over time, McDonald's has also "opened up" to DoorDash (2019) or Grubhub (2021). In Poland, customers can place orders via Uber Eats, Pyszne.pl, Glovo, and Stava (Lucas, 2019).

The expansion of McDonald's into many foreign markets caused it to become a symbol of globalisation and the spread of the American lifestyle. McDonald's mainly offers burgers, fries, dishes prepared from chicken, soft drinks, breakfast products, and desserts (Racoma, 2019). McDonald's also sells salads, vegetarian products, wraps, and local dishes. Menus at McDonald's restaurants are typically adapted to a particular region either to respect traditions or adhere to food taboos (e.g. the ban on beef in India) or to use local/national products and create market-specific meals from them. Below are some examples of the product's strategy used in particular countries, namely African countries, Israel, India, China, Singapore, and Japan.

McDonald's in Africa

In Africa, McDonald's operates in Egypt, Morocco, and South Africa. The company tries to adapt its menu to this region's local tastes, customs, traditions, and religions. For example, McDonald's introduced the McFalafel sandwich (Falafel is a deep-fried ball or pancake of ground chickpeas and/or broad beans and it is a traditional Middle Eastern dish) at its locations in Egypt (Al Bawaba, 2001). Moreover, McArabia, a sandwich with grilled chicken and vegetables on Arabic bread, is available in Moroccan restaurants (but also in other mainly Muslim countries). Moroccan McDonald's is also adapting the architecture and design of its restaurants to the local culture. For example, McDonald's in Fez (Morocco) has a terrace overlooking the medina and is decorated with polychrome zellige tiles and carved wood, which are characteristics of the Moroccan city. McDonald's also recognises its halal meat certification (Hamid, 2008).

McDonald's in Israel

The first McDonald's in the Middle East was opened in Tel Aviv (Israel) in October 1993. In contrast, the world's first kosher McDonald's was opened in the suburb of Jerusalem in 1995. In 2022, McDonald's had 215 restaurants in Israel, about 50 of which were utterly kosher (although all subsidiaries in Israel buy only kosher-certified ingredients). This means that these locations are closed on Shabbat and Jewish holidays and have no "mixed" meat and dairy products (e.g. cheeseburgers). Moreover, on the Pesach holiday, McDonald's replaces its regular burger buns with potato starch buns, in keeping with the Jewish custom of not eating bread products on the holiday, which is a dietary commemoration of the biblical story of the exodus from Egypt when the Israelites were in such a hurry to escape that they had no time for the bread to bake (Estrin, 2016). Healthy alternatives, such as various salads with chicken, have also been added to the menu. "Regular" Israeli McDonald's menus are supplemented with kebab or falafel dishes, served in a classic roll and a pita, catering to local tastes (Estrin, 2016).

Another interesting fact connected with the McDonald's adaptation is that in 2006, under the influence of Tel Aviv's chief rabbi, the yellow and red logo was replaced in some McDonald's branches with the blue and white logo with the Hebrew word "kosher" to avoid confusion and "save religious Jews from accidentally eating a cheeseburger" (McGreal, 2006).

McDonald's in Japan

The first McDonald's in Asia was opened in a Ginza (Tokyo's district with shopping, entertainment, and dining areas) in July 1971. One of the main differences between McDonald's in the USA and Japan is Japanese consumers' perception of the restaurant. Many Japanese consumers perceive McDonald's products as snacks rather than "real" meals. The main reason is that sharing them with several people (e.g. burgers) is impossible. For Japanese consumers, the possibility of sharing a meal (lunch or dinner) is an essential aspect related to the sense of community (Onikoyi, 2020). Collectivistic values and behaviours are very crucial for Japanese society (Hofstede et al., 2010).

The McDonald's menu in Japan offers well-known products such as Big Mac, Chicken McNuggets, Happy Meal, and McFlurry. However, there are many other items in Japan that are not available in all countries, for example, Bacon Lettuce Burger or Teriyaki McBurger (Peter, 2022). Other meals that suit Japanese tastes and preferences include the Gracoro Burger with noodles, shrimp, and white sauce, available only in winter and similar to the McRib in the United States (Ashcraft, 2012). What is more, the seasoned fries are served with a mixture of cherry blossoms (sakura), dried seaweed (nori), and salt. Cherry blossom flavour is prevalent in Japan, especially during the spring when cherry trees bloom (late March, early May) (McDonald's Japan, 2015). The following example of adaptation is a Roasted Soy Sauce Double Thick Beef, which is a seasonal beef burger with cheddar, bacon, tomatoes, lettuce, onions, and the addition of roasted soybeans for an umami flavour. Moreover, a cup of edamame and corn is available as a side dish, an alternative to salads. Other trendy items are Teriyaki Chicken Fillet with teriyaki sauce and Rice Teriyaki, Rice Bacon Lettuce and Rice Fish Japanese-Style Black Pepper burgers, where the bun is replaced by grilled rice (Loew, 2021). Many Japanese restaurant products contain teriyaki sauce, rice, fish, or eggs.

Nevertheless, menus at McDonald's in Japan vary depending on the time of day. For example, after 5 p.m. restaurants sell double items, such as a double Big Mac, with four chops instead of two. Besides, the size of items also varies, and a large drink in Japan is much smaller than a large drink in America (Peter, 2022). It is connected not only with dietary restrictions but also with Japanese preferences.

McDonald's in India

In the case of India, it proved to be a significant challenge just to enter a market that was perceived as traditional and conservative – religious beliefs, customs, and value systems play an essential role in local customers' food and meal preferences. Amit Jatia, the first Indian franchisee, recalls that he "had to start with the message that a burger is also a meal", which resembles the Japanese situation. According to his research in 2003, customers in India usually ate at home, not in restaurants. However, after ten years, that number had risen to 9% of outdoor dining per month. This may indicate an increase in affluence but also changes in people's lifestyles (Kannan, 2014). Besides, the young age of the population has significantly contributed to the current success of McDonald's in India. As the role of women is also changing, and they are reorganising how they run their households, the habit of eating out is becoming more common. Restaurants with ready-to-eat meals and a family atmosphere are becoming popular (Nandini, 2014).

Another challenge that occurred at the beginning of McDonald's activity in India was connected with the availability of some products that were essential for standard meals. For example, there was no lettuce supply chain in India when McDonald's entered this market. Instead of lettuce, most people used cabbage for burgers. Thus, the entire chain had to be created from scratch (Kannan, 2014).

After overcoming initial difficulties, the company offers several fits for the Indian market. The McDonald's menu for the Indian market was prepared with the implementation of cultural and religious restrictions. For example, beef and pork were removed from the menu or replaced with other equivalents (Nandini, 2014). Many of the Indian products for McDonald's were prepared and developed locally with the help of franchisees. Moreover, they try to ensure complete segregation of vegetarian and non-vegetarian products, from food production to customer service (Nandini, 2014). The determinant that influenced this decision is the fact that half of India's population is vegetarian, and a separate menu had to be created or served. One of the first sandwiches introduced to Indian customers was the McAloo Tikki burger with a cutlet made of mashed potatoes, and peas and seasoned with Indian spices (e.g. sweet tomato mayo), which quickly became a hit in the Indian market (Kannan, 2014). Furthermore, the classic McDonald's product – the Big Mac – was replaced with the Chicken Maharaja Mac burger, which contains chicken instead of beef (McDonald's in India – Official Blog, 2016). Because of religious restrictions in India, beef is not served there (Vignali, 2001). Apart from chicken, Maharaja Mac includes tomatoes, onion, cheddar cheese, lettuce, jalapeños, and habanero sauce (Lazzarus, 2020).

The vegetarian menu is very welcome and popular in India, which is why many companies try to adapt their offer to these requirements. For example, many meals include a popular cheese paneer that is sometimes treated as an equivalent of meat in India. Because of that, McDonald's introduced the McSpicy Paneer, where the main element is paneer cheese in a crunchy coating. This meal also contains lettuce and tandoori mayonnaise. It should be underlined that in McDonald's Indian restaurants, all vegetarian products, even mayonnaise, do not contain eggs. This type of mayonnaise is also included in Big Spicy Paneer Wrap served in a wrap instead of a burger bun (Lazzarus, 2020). McDonald's in India also serves diverse rice bowls with vegetables, corn, peas, etc. It may also include chicken nuggets. Rice bowls were introduced to provide a familiar meal for Indian customers (Lazzarus, 2020). Moreover, in Indian McDonald's, Veg Pizza McPuff is a trendy dish for local consumers. It is a fried pie filled with carrots, beans, bell peppers, onions, tomato sauce, and melted mozzarella cheese (Lazzarus, 2020).

McDonald's in Singapore

In addition to classic menu items, McDonald's in Singapore offers local versions of burgers. These are, for example, the Samurai Beef Burger with beef in teriyaki sauce, the Shiok Satay Burger with peanut sauce, the Roasted Sesame Ebi Burger with shrimp cutlet and roasted sesame mayonnaise (also available in Japan), Nasi Lemak Burger (also available in Malaysia) with coconut-flavoured chicken, cornflakes, fried egg, caramelised onions, cucumber, and sambal. Originally, nasi lemak is a Malay and Singaporean dish. It is rice cooked with coconut milk and pandan, topped with cucumber, sambal sauce, fried anchovies, roasted peanuts, and hard-boiled eggs. Other products introduced in Singapore are, for example, the Chili Lime Fish Burger which is a classic fish filet with romaine lettuce, cheese, and spicy Kaffir lime-flavoured mayonnaise, and the Prosperity Burger (available with chicken or beef) with black pepper sauce. That burger was introduced for Lunar New Year celebrations in Singapore and Malaysia (EconoTimes, 2002).

Typically, McDonald's has promoted selected films by adding toys – movie characters – to Happy Meal sets. In China and Singapore, the company did something even more enjoyable. At a time of high popularity of the game and the movie Angry Birds, McDonald's decided to serve customers red and green burgers resembling Angry Birds movie characters. For example, the Naughty Green Pork Burger consisted of a pork chop, egg, lettuce, and sauce with jalapeños peppers in a green bun, while the Super Red consisted of chicken, bell pepper mayonnaise, egg, and lettuce in a red bun (Obias, 2016). The use of egg and pork instead of classic beef most likely refers to the theme of the game and movie, in which birds save eggs from pigs. Some even more elaborate items from Singapore's McDonald's include the Spicy Chicken with Apple Slaw (chicken, red apple salad, arugula, white cheddar cheese, creamy black pepper mayonnaise sauce, and a semolina bun), the Sea Salt McFlurry (previously only available at McDonald's stores in Malaysia; it resembles a galaxy, contains sea salt particles, topped with blue and purple sprinkles), or the Ninja Chicken Burger (with chicken in nanban sauce, white cabbage, and tartar sauce in a black bun) (Obias, 2016).

McDonald's in China

At the beginning of McDonald's expansion in China (1990), Chinese consumers were largely unfamiliar with Western culture and preferences. However, the fascination with the West was growing among Chinese people. Especially among young consumers, an openness to Western fashion, lifestyles and even (oddly enough given the uniqueness of Chinese cuisine, to Western cooking) was noticed. At the beginning of the Chinese McDonald's expansion, getting out of the house for a Big Mac became a way to indulge in Western consumerism (Ronggang, 2017). McDonald's became enshrined in the memories of Chinese children in the 1980s as a place they went to only when their parents decided to reward them for good grades. Some newlyweds even held their wedding receptions at McDonald's (Ronggang, 2017). In the initial phase of expansion into the Chinese market, the target segment was the Chinese middle class. At the beginning of the twenty-first century, McDonald's targeted Chinese youth through increased advertising and penetration into pop culture. The famous slogan "I'm lovin' it" also reached China. With its rapid expansion, McDonald's lost its exoticism and began to become an integral part of the Chinese cityscape. McDonald's next decision in China was to reduce American symbolism and introduce Chinese flavours to the menu, further reducing the restaurant's "Westernness". The company took several steps to appeal to Chinese customers with local touches and further reduce production costs. McDonald's restaurants in China offer several Chinese dishes, such as

- congee: a breakfast dish consisting of shredded rice cooked with a lot of water to create an oatmeal-like mixture;
- cakes with taro filling: an exotic type of sweet potato used in some countries as a flavouring for boba milk tea;
- Chicken Cola: a sweet and sour dish that includes Coca-Cola, chicken wings, ginger, soy sauce, and Sichuan pepper (CSM China Social Media, 2019);
- bubble tea or soy milk.

Moreover, McDonald's had to adapt its menus in China due to the availability of ingredients in the local market (Zhang et al., 2022). For example, Chinese hamburgers use imitation cheese due to the lack of reasonably priced cheese. Moreover, McDonald's encourages potential customers with meal boxes styled like Chinese video games.

Despite many adaptations aimed at tailoring meals to Chinese consumers at McDonald's, some elements remained unchanged due to cultural considerations. For example, the restaurant seating arrangement does not allow for the traditional Chinese hierarchical positioning of people at the table (Melosik, 2013).

Conclusions

Cultural factors are important in shaping marketing strategy in foreign markets. A particularly strong influence concerns fast-moving products offered in the B2C market. Cultural elements that should be analysed for adaptation include taste preferences, local consumers' habits, religion, language, and customs.

These elements have a great impact on food producers. These types of goods are susceptible regarding religion, customs, and tastes. McDonald's offer is particularly exposed to factors that differentiate one culture from another. Due to the nature of its products and services, McDonald's offers its customers a diverse menu worldwide. It is primarily adapted to local consumers' preferences, habits, and religions.

The most significant form of McDonald's adaptation is the introduction of "culturally localised" burger variants. As a result, McDonald's is no longer seen in the context of the "Americanisation of taste" (Melosik, 2013). Good examples of local burger variants are McFalafel in Egypt, McArabia in Morocco, vegetarian McAloo Tikki Burger in India, Japanese Teriyaki McBurger or Tsukimi Burger, Bulgogi Burger in South Korea, Croque McDo in Belgium, McCurrywurst in Germany, McAvocado in Chile, and Kiwiburger in New Zealand (one can also mention Polish WieśMac). They all use ingredients typical of the local cuisine as the main or supplementing element (Melosik, 2013).

However, McDonald's restaurants with subsidiaries in different countries of the world have many common elements. The most standardised elements in the company's product strategy include the McDonald's brand, colour scheme, logo, classic and traditional meals in the company's menu, and their quality. McDonald's represents a classic example of combining the strategy of adaptation and standardisation, which can be referred to as semi-standardisation according to the saying "think globally, act locally" (Vignali, 2001). On the one hand, the managers of this company take advantage of the benefits of standardisation in areas where you can reduce unit costs and achieve economies of scale. Thanks to the standard elements in the strategy, McDonald's achieves global competition by being recognisable around the world. On the other hand, managers reach the adaptation goals by matching their meals to local tastes, traditions, and religions. They try to identify the local needs and customs and adapt old or create new meals, especially for particular consumers. By doing this, the company avoids customer disfavour and achieves the advantages of local competition. This is one of the crucial elements of McDonald's product strategy around the world.

Trends observed in foreign markets regarding cultural diversity and the need to consider them in company strategy indicate that these trends are intensifying. Thus, foreign companies that wish to offer their food products in culturally diverse markets should first identify the needs of local consumers and then tailor their offer, especially regarding food and beverages. These types of products are very sensitive to cultural preferences. To achieve international success and become a recognisable brand almost worldwide, it is important to respect the local environment and use the standard elements worldwide.

Bibliography

Adler, N.J., & Gundersen, A. (2007). *International Dimensions of Organizational Behavior*. Mason: Thomson South-Western Publications.

Advameg, Inc. (n.d.). *Reference for Business: McDonald's Corporation*. www.referenceforbusiness.com/businesses/M-Z/McDonald-s-Corporation.html
Al Bawaba. (2001, June 1). *Falafel Becomes McFalafel in Egypt*. www.albawaba.com/news/falafel-becomes-mcfalafel-egypt
Alon, I., Jaffe, E., Prange, C., & Vianelli, D. (2020). *Global Marketing: Strategy, Practice, and Cases*. Abingdon: Routledge Publications.
Amadi, A. (2023). Integration in a mixed-method case study of construction phenomena: From data to theory. *Engineering, Construction and Architectural Management*, *30*(1), 210–237.
Ashcraft, B. (2012, November 10). *At McDonald's Japan, these Special Burgers Sure Are . . . Creamy*. https://kotaku.com/at-mcdonalds-japan-these-special-burgers-sure-are-cr-5959406
Atlas Obscura. (n.d.). *Roswell McDonald's*. www.atlasobscura.com/places/roswell-mcdonalds
Barmeyer, C., Bausch, M., & Mayrhofer, U. (2021). *Constructive Intercultural Management*. London: Edward Elgar Publications.
Behr, F. (2023, February 2). *Whatever Happened to McDonald's First Mascot, Speedee?* www.mashed.com/256435/whatever-happened-to-mcdonalds-first-mascot-speedee/
Brodowsky, G.H., & Schuster, C.P. (2020). *Handbook on Cross-Cultural Marketing*. Camberley, UK: Edward Elgar Publications.
Caligiuri, P. (2021). *Build Your Cultural Agility: The Nine Competencies of Successful Global Professionals*. London: Kogan Page Publications.
Cateora, P., Money, R.B., Gilly, M.C., & Graham, J.L. (2021). *International Marketing*. New York: McGraw-Hill Publications.
Choo, H.J., Lee, H.K., & Xie, J. (2023). Consumers' cultural identity under globalization: Vietnamese consumers' global and national identities and their cross-cultural consumption. *Asia Pacific Journal of Marketing and Logistics*, *35*(5), 1052–1074.
Cleveland, M., Laroche, M., & Takahashi, I. (2015). The intersection of global consumer culture and national identity and the effect on Japanese consumer behavior. *Journal of International Consumer Marketing*, *27*(5), 364–387.
Close, K. (2016, December 16). *The Founder and the Complicated True Story Behind the Founding of McDonald's*. https://money.com/the-founder-mcdonalds-movie-accuracy/
Coucher, S.M. (2019). *Global Perspectives on Intercultural Communication*. London: Routledge Publications.
Craig, S.C., Douglas, S.P., & Bennett, A. (2009). Contextual and cultural factors underlying Americanization. *International Marketing Review*, *26*(1), 90–109.
CSM China Social Media. (2019, July 16). *Adapting McDonald's Menu to China*. https://chinasocialmedia.net/adapting-mcdonalds-menu-to-china/
Di Mooij, M. (2021). *Global Marketing and Advertising*. New York: Sage Publications.
EconoTimes. (2002, January 19). *McDonald's Prosperity Burger is Back on the Menu in Time for the Lunar New Year*. www.econotimes.com/McDonalds-Prosperity-Burger-is-back-on-the-menu-in-time-for-the-Lunar-New-Year-1625301
Estrin, D. (2016, April 22). *Israel's Health Minister to McDonald's: "Not In Our Country"*. www.npr.org/sections/thesalt/2016/04/22/475271835/israeli-official-denounces-mcdonald-s-as-junk-food-but-chain-fights-back
Frishberg, H. (2021, October 14). This one-of-a-kind McDonald's has a "McBoat" float-thru window. *The New York Post*. https://nypost.com/2021/10/14/mcdonalds-has-a-mcboat-float-thru-window/
Gao, J., Wang, T., Jia, Y., & Wang, C.L. (2022). How and when do exporters benefit from an international adaptation strategy? The moderating effect of formal and informal institutional distance. *International Marketing Review*, *39*(6), 1390–1416.
Gibson, R. (2022). *Bridge the Culture Gaps: A Toolkit for Effective Collaboration in the Diverse: Global Workplace*. London: Nicholas Brealey Publications.

Goodenough, W.H. (1971). *Culture, Language and Society*. Reading, MA: Addison-Wesley Reading.

Gross, R. (2019, June 12). *A Study in Yellow: McDonald's in the Sky*. https://architectureau.com/articles/mcdonalds-landini/

Guedes, M.J., Fernandes Crespo, N., & Patel, P.C. (2023). When in Rome, do as the Romans do: Can international marketing adaptation improve the association between servitization and profitability? *Journal of Business & Industrial Marketing*, *ahead-of-print* (ahead-of-print). https://doi.org/10.1108/JBIM-03-2022-0145

Hamid. (2008, July 10). *Globalisation of McDonald's: Comparative Study Morocco and France*. https://halalfocus.net/globalisation-of-mcdonald-s-comparative-study-morocco-and-france/

Hofstede, G., Hofstede, G.J., & Minkov, M. (2010). *Cultures and Organizations – Software of the Mind: Intercultural Cooperation and Its Importance for Survival*. New York: McGraw-Hill Education.

Kannan, S. (2014, November 19). *How McDonald's Conquered India*. www.bbc.com/news/business-30115555

Klein, C. (2019, August 7). *How McDonald's Beat Its Early Competition and Became an Icon of Fast Food*. www.history.com/news/how-mcdonalds-became-fast-food-giant

Kotabe, M., & Helsen, M. (2022). *International Marketing*. New Jersey: Wiley & Sons Inc.

Kotler, P., Chernev, A., & Keller, K. (2021). *Marketing Management: Global Edition*. London: Pearson Publications.

Kumar, V., Leone, R.P., Aaker, D.A., & Day, G.S. (2020). *Marketing Research*. New Jersey: Wiley & Sons Inc.

Lazzarus, L. (2020, May 6). *What Does McDonald's In India Serve? Check Out These Delicious Menu Items*. www.thetravel.com/mcdonalds-india-menu-items/

Loew, C. (2021, March 23). *McDonald's Japan Offering Fish Rice-burgers*. www.seafoodsource.com/news/foodservice-retail/mcdonald-s-japan-offering-fish-rice-burgers

Lucas, A. (2019, July 16). *McDonald's Adds DoorDash as New Delivery Partner, Ending Exclusivity with UberEats*. www.cnbc.com/2019/07/16/mcdonalds-adds-doordash-as-partner-ending-exclusivity-with-ubereats.html

McDonald's Japan. (2015). *McDonald's Japan Offering New Cherry Blossom Seasoned Fries*. https://www.brandeating.com/2015/04/mcdonalds-japan-offering-new-cherry-blossom-seasoned-fries.html

McDonald's. (n.d. a). *Kim Jesteśmy*. https://mcdonalds.pl/o-mcdonalds/kim-jestesmy/

McDonald's. (n.d. b). *McDonald's History*. https://corporate.mcdonalds.com/corpmcd/our-company/who-we-are/our-history.html

McDonald's. (n.d. c). *Where We Operate*. https://corporate.mcdonalds.com/corpmcd/our-company/where-we-operate.html

McDonald's. (n.d. d). *Who We Are*. https://corporate.mcdonalds.com/corpmcd/our-company/who-we-are.html

McDonald's India–Official Blog. (2016, November 16). *Chicken Maharaja Mac: The Indian Answer to Big Mac*. https://mcdonaldsblog.in/2016/11/chicken-maharaja-mac-the-indian-answer-to-big-mac/

McGreal, C. (2006, March 13). McDonald's changes its brand to suit Kosher appetites. *The Guardian*. www.theguardian.com/world/2006/mar/13/israel.foodanddrink

Melosik, Z. (2013). *Kultura popularna i tożsamość młodzieży. W niewoli władzy i wolności*. (eng. *Popular Culture and Youth Identity: In bondage to power and freedom*). Impuls Publications.

Nandini, A.S. (2014). McDonald's success story in India. *Journal of Contemporary Research in Management*, *9*(3), 21–31.

Nesbit, J. (2021). *Fast-Food Restaurants Cut Value Menu Items, Push Meal Combos Post-Pandemic*. www.gobankingrates.com/saving-money/food/fast-food-restaurants-cut-discounts-push-value-meals/

Obias, R. (2016, May 21). *McDonald's Introduces Red and Green Burgers in China*. www.mentalfloss.com/article/80385/mcdonalds-introduces-red-and-green-burgers-china

Onikoyi, O. (2020, January 31). *Turning Things Around: How McDonald's is Addressing Its Sales and Revenue Decline in Japan*. https://medium.com/swlh/turning-things-around-how-mcdonalds-is-addressing-its-sales-and-revenue-decline-in-japan-c8f5cf6c91e5

Peter, V. (2022, November 24). *Eating McDonald's in Japan: A Comparison to American McDonalds*. https://delishably.com/dining-out/JapanMcDonalds

Racoma, B. (2019, January 4). *McDonald's International Strategy: Adapting Around the World*. www.daytranslations.com/blog/mcdonalds-international-strategy-adapting-around-the-world/

Ronggang, C. (2017, December 14). *Why Once-Loved McDonald's Now Has an Image Problem in China*. www.sixthtone.com/news/1001386/why-once-loved-mcdonalds-now-has-an-image-problem-in-china

Sasaki, I., Nummela, N., & Ravasi, D. (2021). Managing cultural specificity and cultural embeddedness when internationalizing: Cultural strategies of Japanese craft firms. *Journal of International Business Studies*, *52*(2), 245–281.

Schlosser, E. (2001). *Fast Food Nation: The Dark Side of the All-American Meal*. Boston-New York: Houghton Mifflin.

Sobol, K., Cleveland, M., & Laroche, M. (2018). Globalization, national identity, biculturalism and consumer behavior: A longitudinal study of Dutch consumers. *Journal of Business Research*, *82*, 340–353.

Tylor, E.B. (1871). *Primitive Culture: Researches Into the Development of Mythology, Philosophy, Religion, Art, and Custom* (Vol. 1). London: Murray Publications.

Usunier, J.C., & Lee, J.A. (2012). *Marketing across Cultures: Marketing across Culture*. New Jersey: Prentice Hall.

Vescovi, T. (2022). *Cross-Cultural Marketing: European Perspectives*. New York: Edward Elgar Publications.

Vignali, C. (2001). McDonald's: "Think global, act local" – The marketing mix. *British Food Journal*, *103*(2), 97–111.

Vrontis, D., Thrassou, A., & Lamprianou, I. (2009). International marketing adaptation versus standardisation of multinational companies. *International Marketing Review*, *26*(4/5), 477–500.

Wang, J., Zhang, L., Lin, K.-Y., & Feng, L. (2022). The quality of case studies on new product development: State of the art and future prospects. *Journal of Business & Industrial Marketing*, *7*, 1447–1464.

Yin, R.K. (2018). *Case Study Research and Applications: Design and methods*. London: Sage Publications.

Zhang, B., Mulhern, F.J., Wu, Y., Xu, M., Wang, W., & Gao, L. (2022). Thirty years and "I'm still lovin' it!": Brand perceptions of McDonald's among generation Y and generation Z consumers in China. *Asia Pacific Journal of Marketing and Logistics*, *34*(5), 906–921.

2 Expansion of cosmetic manufacturers to the GCC countries – challenges and cultural adaptation of products

Joanna Bednarz and Agnieszka Klimczak

Introduction

The decision to enter a foreign market may result in the need to introduce changes to the product offer, including launching new products that meet foreign consumers' specific needs and preferences. Foreign expansion may also require meeting specific quality requirements, adapting ingredients, and introducing changes to packaging and labelling. The need to implement an adaptation strategy is greater the more the foreign market differs from the domestic one.

The cosmetics market is complex and demanding, associated with solid competition, changing trends, and constantly growing awareness of buyers. It requires continuous analysis of consumer needs, searching for new solutions, and quick response to these needs through new products supported by effective promotional, pricing, and distribution policies (Bednarz, 2013).

The subject of the analysis in this chapter is the Muslim Gulf countries and cosmetic products. The Middle East is a vast geopolitical region encompassing Africa (Egypt), the Arabian Peninsula, the Levant, Turkey, Iran, and Iraq. Six Arab countries, such as the Kingdom of Saudi Arabia, Oman, Bahrain, Qatar, the United Arab Emirates, and Kuwait, formed the Gulf Cooperation Council (GCC). It is a political and economic alliance aiming to achieve unity among its members by leveraging a similar identity rooted in Arab and Islamic culture, strengthening relations between its member countries, and promoting cooperation among members (Klimczak, 2023; Britannica). All these countries also belong to the Arab League, another political and economic union of 22 Arab countries. The common elements of the GCC countries are religion and language, which leads to similarities in culture and customer behaviour. However, some differences are visible. The Kingdom of Saudi Arabia is the largest country in the Middle East, 30 times larger than the neighbouring United Arab Emirates. Over 32 million people live in the Kingdom of Saudi Arabia, of which only 60% are of Saudi origin, and the remaining 40% represent other nations. In the West, on the Red Sea coast, strong African influences are visible in the population and skin colours and types, while lighter skin tones predominate in the East. The

DOI: 10.4324/9781032636962-4

remaining GCC countries, Oman, Kuwait, Bahrain, Qatar, and the United Arab Emirates, are characterised by small populations and the dominance of foreigners (emigrants). For the GCC countries, culture and especially religion play a unique role in introducing products to the market, particularly by foreign companies. A young population and a large group of expatriates characterise them. Preparing an appropriate offer of cosmetic products is particularly demanding (Klimczak, 2023).

This chapter aims to identify the influence of religion on the behaviour and consumers' buying decisions in Muslim Gulf countries, including cosmetic products. The authors present examples of groups of cosmetic products that require unique adaptation.

This chapter used two main research methods: a literature analysis and a case study. The theoretical part was prepared on the basis of the profound literature review. The appropriate scientific articles were obtained from Web of Science, Scopus, EBSCOhost, Emerald, and Springer databases. To prepare the empirical part regarding the Muslim countries of the Persian Gulf, market and business reports and publications written by researchers from this region were used.

Based on the literature review, three research questions were formulated:

RQ1: Does Islam religion significantly influence consumer behaviour and preferences regarding cosmetics?
RQ2: What modifications must cosmetics producers make when entering Muslim Gulf countries?
RQ3: What dedicated cosmetic products are expected in the GCC countries?

The structure of the chapter consists of five sections. The theoretical part begins with a discussion of the essence of internationalisation and the motives and possibilities of foreign expansion of enterprises. Then, the consequences of implementing an internationalisation strategy for product introduction and management are discussed. Particular attention was paid to the process of introducing products to the market and the need to thoroughly identify the specific characteristics of foreign consumers, which may result in appropriate modification of products and their packaging. The empirical part consists of the specificity of the Arab societies and GCC countries and their impact on the cosmetics market. Finally, selected groups of cosmetics for face, body, and hair care, perfumes, and colour cosmetics for make-up were described.

Internationalisation of enterprises – essence and marketing consequences

Enterprises decide to expand into foreign markets, seeing it as their opportunity to develop and strengthen their competitive position. Internationalisation creates additional opportunities to increase competitiveness thanks to access to raw material resources, labour force, external sources of financing, as well as the existing infrastructure, production, and technological cooperation (scientific and research cooperation). Essential decision-making elements include the development potential of the foreign market, the stability of business operations, the policy of the host country's government, and the habits and expectations of buyers. In addition, international entities take advantage of the comparative effects of locating operations in different countries. This undoubtedly drives new opportunities for the development and creation of crucial company competencies and advantages (Autio, 2017, pp. 213–217; Bednarz, 2013, p. 40; Brouthers et al., 2015; Laufs & Schwens, 2014).

The decision to expand into foreign markets causes changes in the way of managing products (including brand, packaging, assortment, and quality level), price (discounts and sales), distribution, and promotion (advertising, personal promotion, sales promotion, public relations, etc.). This has a particular impact on the policy of creating new products. Producers must decide to choose one of two strategies for operating in a foreign market: product standardisation (global unification) and product adaptation (local adjustment) (Głodowska et al., 2023, pp. 73–74). The following arguments will support the implementation of the standardisation strategy: the possibility of achieving economies of scale, significant expenditure on research and product development, unification of technical specifications of products and service standards, as well as the mobility of consumers and their tendency to be loyal in this product group. In turn, the adaptation strategy is the only solution when deciding to enter diversified, distinct economic, technical, legal, geographical, and cultural markets (Głodowska et al., 2023, pp. 73–74; Yap & Yazdanifard, 2014; Bednarz, 2013, p. 42).

Preparation of products and packaging for the foreign market

Bednarz (2013) claims that developing new products and launching them on the market is a process consisting of several systematic stages: (1) searching and creating ideas for a new product, (2) selection of ideas, (3) economic and financial analysis, (4) production of a trial batch, (5) testing of a trial batch, and (6) commercialisation. The first stage of the process is searching for and creating an idea for a new product. New ideas can be generated by company employees from sales, marketing, R&D, and production departments, as well as by people from the company's environment, such as buyers of the manufacturer's products, competitors' customers, sales intermediaries, competitors, scientists, and industry institutes. In practice, producers collect ideas for new products as a result of surveys, observations, in-depth individual and group interviews, analysis of complaints or other business correspondence, consumer research conducted to identify market niches using the perceptual map method, and the use of heuristic techniques such as Design Thinking, Brainstorming, Synectics, or the Delphi method (Bednarz et al., 2020).

When entering foreign markets, companies should consider the need to adapt brand management elements such as the brand name and the corresponding marketing slogan (Alashban et al., 2002; Passos et al., 2018). Entrepreneurs often position their brands as global, foreign, or local. If a company is present in various foreign markets, it has several strategies to choose from. Firstly, it can use the same brand in all foreign markets (global and multinational). Enterprises that have been present on the market for a long time and have a strong position there can use the umbrella brand strategy. Another solution is a brand portfolio strategy, which is a family of brands that should provide synergy, energy, but also transparency, and product differentiation (Wiktor et al., 2008). The way consumers perceive and evaluate the international character of a brand is the result of the synergy of at least two elements: the way the brand is positioned in global markets and critical factors such as the quality and prestige of the brand (Archpru Akaka & Alden, 2010). In the case of graphic signs, it is worth paying attention to select the colours appropriately and, if any, symbols. These elements can vary significantly between the home country and the expansion country. Trademarks also need to be registered with the patent office.

Packaging is an integral part of the product. It is "the wrapping material around a consumer item that serves to contain, identify, describe, protect, display, promote, and otherwise make the product marketable and keep it clean" (Mishra & Jain, 2012, p. 48). Having a different approach, Kotler and Keller (2012, p. 368) define packaging as "all activities of designing and producing the container or a product". In the marketing literature, packaging is presented as the buyer's first encounter with the product. It can be treated as an essential marketing tool, a vehicle for consumer communication and branding, which takes a role similar to other marketing communications elements (Verguraand & Luceri, 2018, p. 219; Draskovic, 2007, p. 317). It is even called the fifth P, along with product, price, place, and promotion (Kotler & Keller, 2012, p. 368). For Keller (1998), the packaging is one of the five elements of the brand, together with the name, the logo (graphic symbol), the personality, and the slogans.

Prendergast and Pitt (1996, pp. 60–61) enumerate several functions that must be fulfilled by good packaging. These functions are related to marketing and logistics. From the marketing point of view, packaging is the most critical factor in purchasing decisions made at the point of sales and must perform many sales tasks. First of all, it should aid in product differentiation and positioning and ought to be a source of competitive advantage helping a product to be distinguished from the competitors' offer (Ford et al., 2012, p. 341). Packaging should also attract attention to a product, reinforce its image, present and describe the product's virtues, convince the customers, and make a favourable overall impression. Kotler and Keller (2012, p. 368) even call the packaging a "five-second" commercial for the product. Moreover, the package may facilitate the use of the product and influence the consumers to pay more for convenience, appearance, and prestige. Considering logistic aspects, packaging should facilitate product transportation and protection by reducing damage, spoilage, or loss. It might positively impact the overall productivity of the warehouse, assist at-home storage, and aid product consumption.

On the basis of the literature review, Verguraand and Luceri (2018, p. 219) state that the package is the first thing consumers see before making the final buying decision. This is particularly important in the current self-service economy and impulse purchase products. Kauppinen-Räisänen (2014) declares that 70% of all brand and purchase decisions are made in-store at the moment of buying, even if a consumer enters a store intending to purchase specific products based on a shopping list (Mohebbi, 2014, p. 93). Moreover, when today's consumers buy under time pressure, an attractive package as the "silent salesman" can help them to make quick decisions. It is, therefore, a critical factor in the decision-making process. Visual elements are incredibly vivid communication stimuli that may attract consumers' attention and provide information on whether a product can meet consumers' needs and expectations.

It is possible to distinguish two groups of packaging elements: visual elements, for example, graphics, pictures, letter fonts, colour, shape, size, material and informational ones like product name, brand, producer, product information (e.g. allergy and nutritional preferences), and special offers (Letona et al., 2014, p. 1). Visual attributes are associated with the affective side of decision-making, while informational elements are related to the cognitive side of determination. Products must be correctly marked by the legal requirements in force in a given country and industry. The information on the packaging must be translated into the language applicable in a given country. The manufacturer may use obligatory information (the product cannot be placed on the market without it) and non-obligatory (optional) ones which companies voluntarily use to create a specific image of the product or company. The most commonly used information, symbols, and signs on the packaging can be grouped into safety (CE, HACCP), certification (ISO), handling, advertising, environmental (recycling) signs, and barcodes.

Graphical symbols (pictograms) refer to visually perceptible figures with particular meanings that are common in global commerce across countries because they are understood regardless of the language. Compared to the text, they are distinguished by readability, transparency, and effectiveness in the transition of information, which occupies less space on products (Seo et al., 2017, p. 62). Well-designed, they can communicate large amounts of information at a glance (Wolff & Wogalter, 1998, p. 173). It is essential because consumers are primarily visual learners.

When entering foreign markets, companies must consider foreign consumers' specific needs, preferences, expectations, and behaviours. This advanced and in-depth analysis of consumers leads to the definition of buyer segments. Farah and Fawaz (2016, p. 140) point out that "culture, as a dynamic process, assumes that cultural differences instigate distinctions in consumer behaviour within and across national borders". It is essential to learn about elements of foreign culture, customs, and rituals such as values, beliefs, religion, law, social organisation, politics, education, artefacts, language, symbols, appearance, dress code, gender role, social role, food, eating, relationship, learning, mental style, time conscious, work, and leisure (Phipps & Simmons, 2008; Smyczek, 2012, p. 154; Farah & Fawaz, 2016). Ebaidalla and Malkawi (2023) claim that religion is a force and crucial factor influencing self-construal, moral judgement, consumption decisions, independent and interdependent behaviours, and everyday activities.

Specificity of the Arab societies

Islam is not only a religion but also a legal institution, a code of ethics, culture, traditions (Aljayyousi et al., 2019), and behaviour to guide individuals in life (The Arab World, 2007). It influences and enhances features of Arab culture, such as honesty, loyalty, flexibility, trust (Obeidat et al., 2012), hospitality, and generosity (The Arab World, 2007). Conservative Arab community places greater value on religious principles and shared beliefs. Reputation is one of the most critical factors for both men and women. This affects many areas of customers' lives and decision-making processes.

Hofstede characterises Arab countries as having a significant power distance, relatively strong uncertainty avoidance, high collectivism, and moderate masculinity/femininity (Obeidat et al., 2012; Hofstede Insights). Arab societies are collectivist in nature, with similar traditions, customs, cultures, beliefs, local languages, and political structures; consequently, they can be considered homogeneous (Farah & Fawaz, 2016; Semaan et al., 2019). They are more willing to make group decisions, implement consensus, and cooperate than individuals (At-Twaijri & Al-Muhaiza, 1996). A highly collectivistic society also means that, according to tradition, norms and values are passed down from generation to generation, influencing consumer behaviour (Farah & Fawaz, 2016). Moreover, Arab culture is a high-context culture with more meaning embedded in the context. This means the listener must understand contextual indications or signals to comprehend the full message (The Arab World, 2007).

Arab societies are hierarchical and patriarchal. For them, the family is the most important institution and the centre of obligations and loyalty. In this culture, living in close relationships with relatives is normal. Arab families are considered partnerships, in which the husband and wife are assigned complementary duties and responsibilities. The husband often makes important family decisions (Semaan et al., 2019) and provides the family with financial resources. The wife takes care of the family and home. Risha (n.d.) declares that a working mother is a partner in many situations and contributes to her family's expenses. On the other hand, The Arab World (2007) describes five main aspects that discriminate against women:

- seclusion and control of appearance and behaviour in public places (Semaan et al., 2019);

- significant disparities between men's and women's employment patterns and traditional views on women's roles in society and family;
- laws regarding marriage, obedience, fidelity, divorce, and inheritance are biased against women. "Women living in the Gulf Arab have a very strong cultural identity and view family traditions, religious values, and the family's position in society as significant factors in their daily lives" (Semaan et al., 2019, p. 165);
- Arab cultural norms discriminate against women, and their behaviour is strictly controlled;
- domestic violence, the criminalisation of public offences, and even the practice of mutilation.

Nevertheless, El-Bassiouny (2017) states that Arab culture combines authenticity with modernity, and cosmopolitan consumers share global values within halal parameters. Ebaidalla and Malkawi (2023) add that religion also plays an essential role in shaping people's self-awareness, which impacts attitudes towards luxury brands in the Arabian Gulf communities.

Specificity of GCC countries and its impact on the cosmetics market

Chęś (2016) states that six GCC countries have been the most dynamic part of the Middle East and Africa regions with the highest growth rates in the cosmetics and toiletries sectors from the global perspective. The Kingdom of Saudi Arabia and the United Arab Emirates have the highest expenditure on cosmetics. According to the latest study, the average Saudi woman spends over US$900 yearly on cosmetics, and Emirati women spend about US$700 (Rahul Vaimal, 2020). There are forecasts that expenditures on cosmetics will increase due to the growing purchasing power of women in these countries.

A very young population characterises the GCC countries because more than half of the inhabitants are under 25, and the average age is 27. This significantly affects the product offer because young people, paying attention to their appearance, are aware of current global trends and styles and try experimenting with cosmetics, hair colouring, and styling. For the cosmetics industry, this means modifying existing products and introducing new ones. In turn, older customers know their needs better, are more consistent in their preferences, and, therefore more loyal to their choices (Alhedhaif et al., 2016). Young people are looking for cosmetics offered at an affordable price. However, a large part of society having a high disposable income can afford to buy luxury outstanding products and brands.

The second characteristic of GCC countries is expatriates. These are representatives of other nations that live, work, and spend money in the Arabian Gulf countries. There are more foreigners living here than native residents. The United Arab Emirates is home to over 200 nations, and almost 90% of its population is of non-Emirate origins (The United Arab Emirates' Government portal). Most of them come from Asian countries "due to economic reasons and are cautious about spending and investing money" (Chęś, 2016, p. 119). Global cosmetics corporations benefit from the many expatriates and their awareness and trust in the brands they know from their home countries. This is the reason why Asian brands have a presence in the GCC countries (Chęś, 2016). Another important group of potential buyers is Muslim pilgrims and foreign tourists who, when visiting GCC countries, buy cosmetics and perfumes available only in these countries (Chęś, 2016).

The noticeable dominance of native Arabs and Asians determines the different needs of the cosmetics market. This is due to the diversity of skin tones, from very delicate and light, requiring the use of products with high sun protection factors, through darker skin tones in South Asian countries (Bangladesh, India, and Sri Lanka), to the dark skin colour of people of African origin. Due to such a mix of cultures and nationalities in the Gulf countries, it is difficult to describe a typical cosmetic customer, as differences in skin colour, needs, and economic opportunities are significant (Klimczak, 2023). This is undoubtedly a challenge for cosmetic manufacturers.

"Gender separation in the Middle East is a common experience, and women tend to spend the majority of their time with other women. Many Arab women can go shopping only when assisted by a male family member". Moreover, "women often gather together at home for beauty regimens, or they go out together to beauticians" (Chęś, 2016, p. 127). Cosmetics and fragrances are available in the GCC countries in shopping malls and beauty salons, while mass brands are offered in supermarkets, hypermarkets, and pharmacies.

"The importance of fragrances stems from long traditions, religious commandments, and rules of politeness" (Chęś, 2016, p. 126). The author adds that religious and high-society people are expected to wear perfume because it shows their social sense. On the basis of the Nielsen data, Chęś (2016, p. 126) states that "fragrance is the most important item of the beauty budget for GCC nationals (a minimum of 40%) followed by make-up (35%) and skin care products (20–25%, depending on the country)". The largest group of cosmetics and toiletries buyers are women, who especially buy skin care products, make-up, perfumes, and others. Arab females use more personal care and beauty products compared to Western ones. "Arab upper-class women are expected always to show perfect grooming; expensive clothes and golden jewellery are to be completed by expensive perfumes and perfect make-up" (Chęś, 2016, p. 127). On the basis of the results of the research, Ebaidalla and Malkawi (2023, p. 2633) claim that "the relationship between income and attitude towards the consumption of luxury goods is positive and significant. This suggests that individuals' income influences their attitudes toward luxury brands".

The Gulf Cooperation Council Standardization Organization (GSO) is responsible for the safety of cosmetic products. The organisation has led to the formation and published in 2016 the GSO 1943:2015 standards "Safe Cosmetics and Personal Hygiene Products". Cosmetics must be registered and meet all safety criteria (Shree et al., 2022). Shree et al. (2022) enumerate the list of information that all cosmetics and personal care products must contain: product name, logo, name and address of the manufacturer/distributor, country of origin of the product, nominal content, list of ingredients, batch date or lot code, labelling regulations, the role of the product, instructions for use, warnings, and precautions. This information is provided in Arabic and English. Cosmetics are registered in the responsible institution in each GCC country by the applicable procedure. Shree et al. (2022) state that the product must be safe for human health and durable, the properties of which will not change during the shelf life (if stored and used by the instructions). It must not contain pork, pork derivatives, or dirty or decaying substances. The production of cosmetic products must follow good manufacturing practices, meet certain microbiological limits, and the pH value should be within the range (4–8). The packaging or label must not contain graphics, images, or expressions that are inconsistent with the Islamic traditions and social values prevailing in the GCC countries.

Cosmetics products in GCC countries

The range of cosmetic products is vast and is divided into several segments: face and body care cosmetics, hair care products, deodorants, perfumes, women's eau de toilettes and perfumes, and men's Eau de toilettes and colognes, shaving and aftershave cosmetics, and colour cosmetics for make-up. Due to differences in brightening trends, lifestyle, climate, religion, culture, and specifics such as different types of hair and skin, the offer of cosmetic products in the Middle Eastern market requires appropriate adaptation.

An essential characteristic of the Middle Eastern market for the cosmetics industry is the climate and lifestyle. The climate varies from arid in the desert (Riyad) to humid on the coast of the Arabian Peninsula (such as Jeddah in the Kingdom of Saudi Arabia or Dubai in the United Arab Emirates). Humid conditions require lighter cosmetic formulas, usually less oily but more moisturising. However, in dry weather, offering heavier and richer moisturisers is better to help the skin gain adequate hydration levels. Moreover, residents mostly spend time in air-conditioned rooms, which are not indifferent to the skin and require additional care due to the dry air and air pollutants and protection (mainly moisturising the dry skin).

Among face and body skin care products (also for "sensitive areas"), there is an excellent demand for whitening products of high quality and effectiveness. This is a dynamically developing category in the Middle East and Asian markets that is not available in Europe. "The brighter the better" is a synonym for supremacy in Arab countries. Following the trend of lighter skin tones dominating, women in the Middle East are willing to spend a lot to achieve the desired effect, often risking their health by using strong and dangerous products. Based on this strong demand, cosmetic companies produce dedicated products such as brightening face creams, oils, scrubs, roll-ons, and pigments for biologically sensitive areas. For this purpose, unique, strong formulas that remove discolourations but do not irritate the skin are developed. These products are offered by global corporations like Eucerin, La Roche Posay, The Ordinary, Cetaphil, and Neutrogena as well as Polish manufacturers of natural and organic cosmetics, Clochee and Eveline.

On the other hand, it is worth noting that due to the covering of the face and body and the tendency to avoid the sun, women in the Middle East do not use sun protection products (SPF). Awareness of the advantages of these products in Arab countries is low.

In humid or dry climates, different types of make-up products are needed. Humidity causes immediate sweating of the entire body and drains off the make-up. In turn, dryness causes faster skin ageing and an unpleasant feeling of tightness on the face. Different styles and trends follow the diversity of skin colours in make-up. What is popular in Europe is not necessarily well received by customers in the Muslim Gulf countries. There is a tendency towards stronger and heavier make-up, with darker colours and intense shades and fragrances. On the one hand, lighter shades of foundation are needed (to brighten the skin tone), on the other hand, to match the natural skin colour, usually darker than European ones. Arab women prefer yellowish shades of foundation, while beige shades dominate the European market, all thanks to the original shade of carnation and its blending properties (beige looks artificial on darker skin, while yellowish base looks natural on darker skin). Regarding foundation shades, make-up companies have tended to offer a limited palette of shades, usually aimed at light carnation customers. They began to expand it, following Estee Lauder as the pioneer of this trend. It has also been seen in advertisements where models with different carnation colours promoted foundations and powders. Fenty Beauty by Rihanna is one of the largest cosmetics brands, offering a wide range of shades targeted for women of all skin colours. The L'Oréal True Match liquid has 48 shades, and Fenty Beauty offers 59 shades of Soft Matte Longwear foundation, from ultra-light to black.

Due to cultural differences, women in the Middle Eastern market, mainly of Arab descent (where a woman's body is covered and often only the eyes are exposed), tend to emphasise it with heavy eyeliners and mascaras or by applying fake eyelashes. This makes it necessary for cosmetic manufacturers to expand their regular product portfolio with heavier mascaras, eye pencils, and eyeliners. Furthermore, the consumption of eye make-up products is much higher in Arab countries than in other parts of the world. Here, customers are less willing to experiment with colours and most often choose black, while in Europe, women use different colours, for example, shades of brown, blue, or green, depending on the prevailing fashion trends. Arab women are more traditional in their colour choices.

Due to the diverse climate and local trends in GCC countries, women prefer matte lipsticks. The latest trend is nude tones. Recently, the make-up company

Pierre Rene from Poland introduced a new line of matte lipsticks in various shades of beige. Lip glosses, which are popular in Europe and cause glossy lips, are not fashionable in Arab countries. Arab women prefer neutral shades and tend to avoid pink.

Nail polish is another colourful product. Due to the religious obligation to wash several parts of the body five times a day before each prayer, the use of the so-called hybrid polish is not popular among Muslim females. When applied to nails, classic products create a water-impermeable layer, which does not correspond to religious requirements. INGLOT, the colour cosmetics manufacturer from Poland, invented and launched in 2009 "a breathable nail polish for conservative Muslim customers that provides better nail care combined with a perfect appearance" (Basit, 2015). It was the first such innovation globally and was a massive success in the Arab market.

In Arab countries, there are different perfumes and fragrances compared to those famous in Europe. As a rule, Arab customers prefer heavier fragrances. The most popular fragrances are those rooted in the tradition of Arab culture: oud (woody fragrances), incense, and rose water. Many Asian emigrants seek out the scents of sandalwood and turmeric. These preferences are incredibly different from the fresh, floral, or citrus scents liked in Europe. Fragrance-free products are not allowed. Due to the high demand and significant purchasing power, fragrances are dedicated to Arab customers. Typically, Arab women carry perfumes with them in their handbags throughout the day.

Hair care products also require a different approach in Arab Gulf countries. A serious problem in hair care here is excess sebum and problems with scalp irritation resulting from the veiling of the hair. The weather also plays a role, as hair behaves differently depending on humidity levels. However, women who wear the hijab (a head covering worn by Muslim women) are less affected by moisture levels. It should also be noticed that people from the Middle East usually have thicker and stronger hair. They use many oily products for hair care. Typically, these are not light oils known in European countries. This type of hair often makes it difficult to care for them independently. For this reason, Arab women commonly use hairdressing services. For cosmetics producers, it means distributing products through various channels, including professional salons.

The packaging of cosmetics intended for the Middle Eastern market often differs from those offered for other parts of the world. The colours associated with Islam are white, black, red, yellow, and green. There are many different colours on cosmetic packaging. White, black, red, and its varieties such as orange, pink, and burgundy are well perceived. Gold elements on the packaging are associated with wealth and luxury, generosity, and strength. It is still highly appreciated if the packaging is over the top and resembles luxury rather than simplicity. Sophisticated boxes with gold elements reminiscent of an "expensive look" are what Arab customers are looking for on the shelves of cosmetics and perfume stores. In contrast, mass-produced, everyday cosmetic products such as shower gels and body lotions have the same graphic design as packaging in Europe. The information on the packaging must be in Arabic. Due to the presence of non-Arabic speaking customers, English is also often used. Information should be short and precise, pointing out the benefits for customers. Notably, using natural active ingredients is essential as consumers have depended on natural ingredients since the early years of trade in the region and perceive them to be gentle and effective. For this reason, packaging brands highlight the content of products. The growing use of ingredients such as argan oil, shea butter, olive oil, almond oil, aloe vera, and musk is seen in categories such as skin care, hair care, bath and shower. Halal certification is not mandatory on the Middle East market; however, it is required that cosmetic products do not contain any ingredients of animal origin, any constituents that are Najs (filthy or unclean), and not have any chemical, biological, or microbiological hazards (Ali et al., 2016). Products labelled as halal are prioritised by consumers who are willing to pay higher for them (Hussin, et al., 2013; Ali et al., 2016).

The key to the success of the new brand in the Middle Eastern market remains, above all, an appropriate communication strategy. It should respect Muslim customs and traditions but do it modernly. Social media is one of the most powerful communication tools, however, different media are gaining popularity in the Middle East rather than Europe. In 2023, the most important and recommended social media channel for communication is Snapchat, which is not that popular in Europe. The use of photos showing nudity or tattoos is prohibited. Nevertheless, it is advisable to use models with the faces and features of Arab women and men. Influencer marketing among Arab women has a significant impact, but this activity is highly controlled because a special business license is required to promote commercial products on social media.

Conclusion

When entering a foreign market, the manufacturer must meet requirements to ensure the safety and quality of its products. They must also address their products to customers' different needs and preferences. Because there is a significant difference between the people of Europe and the Middle East, cosmetics manufacturers are forced to create, innovate, replace, or improve their products.

According to Hofstede (Hofstede Insights, n.d.), Arab countries are characterised by high power distance, relatively strong uncertainty avoidance, high collectivism, and moderate masculinity/femininity. Arab societies are hierarchical and patriarchal, in which the traditional division of roles between husband and wife is visible. Religion also plays an important role here. Islam is a legal institution, a code of ethics, culture, tradition and that guides individuals in life.

GCC countries are important to the beauty industry due to the global growth rates. They are characterised by a very young population and a large number of emigrants. Such a mixture of cultures and nationalities undoubtedly constitutes a challenge for cosmetics producers to prepare products considering differences in skin colour, needs, and economic opportunities. Climatic diversity also requires the introduction of appropriate product recipes.

Regarding skincare products, bleaching, brightening, and bleaching treatments are very popular. Various styles and trends in make-up follow the diversity of skin colours. This means that cosmetics manufacturers must expand their permanent product portfolio to include a broader range of shades of foundations and powders, heavier mascaras, black eyeliners, and matte lipsticks in various shades of beige. The use of breathable nail polish is also required. Perfume recipes need to change radically because Arab customers prefer heavier scents rooted in the tradition of Arab culture: oud (woody scents), incense, and rose water. A similar situation applies to hair care products, as different hair types require many oily products. Finally, the packaging of cosmetics intended for the Middle Eastern market often differs from the packaging offered for other parts of the world. Some colour changes are required, such as black, red, white, and gold. The information on the packaging must be translated into Arabic and English.

Bibliography

Alashban, A.A., Hayes, L.A., Zinkhan, G.M., & Balazs, A.L. (2002). International brand-name standardization/adaptation: Antecedents and consequences. *Journal of International Marketing*, *10*(3), 22–48. https://doi.org/10.1509/jimk.10.3.22.19544

Alhedhaif, S., Lele, U., & Kaifi, B.A. (2016). Brand loyalty and factors affecting cosmetics buying behavior of Saudi female consumers. *Journal of Business Studies Quarterly*, *7*(3), 24–38.

Ali, S., Halim, F., & Bt. Ahmad, N. (2016). Beauty premium and halal cosmetics. *Industry Journal of Marketing Management and Consumer Behavior*, *1*(4), 52–63.

Aljayyousi, G.F., Abu Munshar, M., Al-Salim, F., & Osman, E.R. (2019). Addressing context to understand physical activity among Muslim university students: The role of gender, family, and culture. *BMC Public Health*, *19*, 1452. https://doi.org/10.1186/s12889-019-7670-8

The Arab World. (2007, January). *An Introduction to Cultural Appreciation*. https://assets.publishing.service.gov.uk/media/5a79916340f0b642860d91ac/arab_world_introduction_cultural_appreciation_booklet.pdf

Archpru Akaka, M., & Alden, D.L. (2010). Global brand positioning and perceptions: International advertising and global consumer culture. *International Journal of Advertising*, *29*(1), s. 37–56. https://doi.org/10.2501/S0265048709201026

At-Twaijri, M.I., & Al-Muhaiza, I.A. (1996). Hofstede's cultural dimensions in the GCC countries: An empirical investigation. *International Journal of Value Based Management*, *9*(2), 121–131. http://dx.doi.org/10.1007/BF00440149

Autio, E. (2017). Strategic entrepreneurial internationalization: A normative framework. *Strategic Entrepreneurship Journal*, *11*(3), 211–227. http://dx.doi.org/10.1002/sej.1261

Basit, A. (2015, April 7). Inglot plans 200 stores in Middle East by 2020. *Khaleej Times*. www.khaleejtimes.com/local-business/inglot-plans-200-stores-in-middle-east-by-2020

Bednarz, J. (2005). *Proces wprowadzania nowych produktów konsumpcyjnych na rynek*, [w:] *Problemy współczesnej gospodarki światowej* (*The Process of Introducing New Consumer Products to the Market*, [In:] *Problems of the Contemporary World*

Economy) (pp. 80–89), red. H. Treder, Prace i Materiały IHZ nr 20. Sopot: Fundacja Rozwoju Uniwersytetu Gdańskiego.

Bednarz, J. (2013). *Konkurencyjność polskich przedsiębiorstw na rynkach europejskich na przykładzie wybranych branż (Competitiveness of Polish Enterprises on European Markets on the Example of Selected Industries)* (pp. 1–332). Gdańsk: Wydawnictwo Uniwersytetu Gdańskiego.

Bednarz, J., Pangsy-Kania, S., & Treder, H. (2020). *Ekspansja zagraniczna przedsiębiorstw w warunkach konkurencji międzynarodowej (Foreign Expansion of Enterprises in the Conditions of International Competition)*. Gdańsk: Wydawnictwo Uniwersytetu Gdańskiego.

Britannica, The Editors of Encyclopedia. (2023, October 17). Gulf cooperation council. *Encyclopedia Britannica*. www.britannica.com/topic/Gulf-Cooperation-Council.

Brouthers, K.D., Geisser, K.D., & Rothlauf, F. (2015). Explaining the internationalization of ibusiness firms. *Journal of International Business Studies*, *47*(5), 513–534. https://doi.org/10.1057/jibs.2015.20

Chęś, A. (2016). The Middle Eastern market of cosmetics and toiletries: Characteristics underlying demand and potential for growth. *Studia Ekonomiczne*, *303*, 114–133.

Draskovic, N. (2007). The marketing role of packaging: A review. *International Journal of Management Cases*. Special Issue: CIRCLE Conference 2007. https://doi.org/10.5848/APBJ.2007.00034

Ebaidalla, E.M., & Malkawi, A. (2023). The impact of religion and modernity on luxury consumption in an Arabian Gulf community: Does self-construal matter? *Journal of Islamic Marketing*, *4*(10), 2622–2643. https://doi.org/10.1108/JIMA-05-2022-0137

El-Bassiouny, N.M. (2017). The Trojan horse of affluence and halal in the Arabian Gulf. *Journal of Islamic Marketing*, *8*(4), 578–594. https://doi.org/10.1108/JIMA-12-2015-0094

Farah, M.F., & Fawaz, R.S. (2016). A comparison of the influence of personal and cultural values on the consumption of luxury goods across Arab regions: Levant versus Gulf. *Contemporary Management Research*, *12*(2). https://doi.org/10.7903/cmr.15067

Ford, A., Moodie, C., & Hastings, G. (2012). The role of packaging for consumer products: Understanding the move towards "plain" tobacco packaging. *Addiction Research and Theory*, *20*(4), 339–347. https://doi.org/10.3109/16066359.2011.632700

Głodowska, A., Wach, K., & Maciejewski, M. (2023). Does high-tech industry matter for marketing strategy selection? Adaptation vs. standardization on the international market. *Studies of the Industrial Geography Commission of the Polish Geographical Society*, *37*(1), 70–82. https://doi.org/10.24917/20801653.371.4

Hofstede Insights. (n.d.). www.hofstede-insights.com/

Hussin, S.R., Hashim, H., Raja Yusof, R.N., & Alias, N.N. (2013). Relationship between product factors, advertising, and purchase intention of halal cosmetic. *Pertanika Journal of Social Sciences & Humanities*, *21*(S), 85–100.

Kauppinen-Räisänen, H. (2014). Strategic use of colour in brand packaging. *Packaging Technology and Science*, *27*, 663–676. https://doi.org/10.1002/pts.2061

Keller, K.L. (1998). *Strategic Brand Management*. Upper Saddle River: Prentice Hall.

Klimczak, A. (2023). *Biznes po Arabsku*, (*Business in Arabic*). Gdansk: Iddeni.

Kotler, P., & Keller, K.L. (2012). *Marketing Management* (Global Edition 14e). London: Pearson Education.

Laufs, K., & Schwens, C. (2014). Foreign market entry mode choice of small and medium-sized enterprises: A systematic review and future research agenda. *International Business Review*, *23*(6), 1109–1126. https://doi.org/10.1016/j.ibusrev.2014.03.006

Letona, P., Chacon, V., Roberto, C., & Barnoya, J. (2014). A qualitative study of children's snack food packaging perceptions and preferences. *BMC Public Health*, *14*(1274). https://doi.org/10.1186/1471-2458-14-1274

Mishra, H.G., & Jain, D. (2012). Impact of packaging in consumer decision making process of namkeen products. *Journal of Marketing & Communication*, *7*(3).
Mohebbi, B. (2014). The art of packaging: An investigation into the role of color in packaging, marketing, and branding. *International Journal of Organizational Leadership*, *3*(2), 92–102. https://doi.org/10.33844/ijol.2014.60248
Obeidat, B., Shannak, R., Masa'deh, R., & Al-Jarrah, I. (2012). Toward better understanding for Arabian culture: Implications based on Hofstede's cultural model. *European Journal of Social Sciences*, *28*, 512–522.
Passos, A.R., Sousa, B., & Azevedo, A. (2018). Brand management and internationalization: A case study in the sports equipment industry. *Tékhne Published by Walter de Gruyter*, *16*(2), 19–27. https://doi.org/10.2478/tekhne-2019-0009
Phipps, R., & Simmons, C. (2008). *Understanding Customers*. Oxford: Butterworth Heinemann.
Prendergast, G., & Pitt, L. (1996). Packaging, marketing, logistics and the environment: Are there trade-offs? *International Journal of Physical Distribution & Logistics Management*, *26*(6), 60–72. https://doi.org/10.1108/09600039610125206
Rahul Vaimal, R. (2020). *Saudi Women Spent the Most on Cosmetics around the World; Picodi Study*. www.gccbusinessnews.com/saudi-women-spent-the-most-on-cosmetics-around-the-world-picodi-study
Risha, S. (n.d.). *Arab Customs and Culture*, The University of Arizona, College of Social & Behavioural Sciences, Center for Middle Eastern Studies. https://communitycollegeoutreach.arizona.edu/sites/communitycollegeoutreach.arizona.edu/files/handouts/ARAB%20CUSTOMS%20AND%20CULTURE_0.pdf
Semaan, R.W., Lindsay, V., Williams, P., & Ashill, N. (2019). The influence of gender roles in the drivers of luxury consumption for women: Insights from the gulf region. *Journal of Retailing and Consumer Services, 51*, 165–175. https://doi.org/10.1016/j.jretconser.2019.06.006
Seo, D.C., Landoni, M., Brunk, E., Becker, M.W., & Bix, L. (2017). Do healthcare professionals comprehend standardized symbols present on medical device packaging? An important factor in the fight over label space. *Packaging Technology and Science*, *30*(3), 61–73. https://doi.org/10.1002/pts.2199
Shree, G.R., Venkatesh, M.P., & Bose, P.S.C. (2022). A comprehensive outline of the Gulf nations' cosmetics review and approval process: GSO standards. *Asian Journal of Advanced Research and Reports*, *16*(5), 7–16. https://doi.org/10.9734/ajarr/2022/v16i530471
Smyczek, S. (2012). *Consumer Behavior on International Markets*. Warszawa: Placet.
UAE Government. (2022, October 18). *Population and Demographic Mix*. https://u.ae/en/information-and-services/social-affairs/preserving-the-emirati-national-identity/population-and-demographic-mix#:~:text=According%20to%20the%20World%20Bank,cent%20of%20the%20total%20population
Verguraand, D.T., & Luceri, B. (2018). Product packaging and consumers' emotional response: Does spatial representation influence product evaluation and choice? *Journal of Consumer Marketing*, *35*(2), 218–227. https://doi.org/10.1108/JCM-12-2016-2021
Wiktor, J.W., Oczkowska, R., & Żbikowska, A. (2008). *Marketing międzynarodowy. Zarys problematyki (International Marketing: Outline of the Issues)*. Warszawa: PWE Publications.
Wolff, J.S., & Wogalter, M.S. (1998). Comprehension of pictorial symbols: Effects of context and test method. *Human Factors*, *40*(2), 173–186. https://doi.org/10.1518/001872098779480433
Yap, S., & Yazdanifard, R. (2014). Comparison on the impact of standardization and adaptation on international marketing. *Journal of Research in Marketing*, *14*(4), 41–50. https://doi.org/10.17722/jorm.v3i1.83

3 Codorniu's "cava" in China

Bridging marketing strategies and cultural differences

Nela Filimon, Francesc Fusté-Forné, and F. Xavier Medina

Introduction

In the dynamic context of global business, the intersection of marketing strategies and cultural differences has become a pivotal battleground for brands seeking to establish a presence in diverse markets. They need to design market strategies to overcome cultural barriers in internationalisation processes. This chapter delves into the case study of Codorniu, a renowned Spanish producer of sparkling wine known as "cava", as it enters the Chinese market (Jiménez-Asenjo & Filipescu, 2019). The juxtaposition of the Spanish winemaking heritage with the Chinese culture presents a narrative of adaptation, innovation, and cross-cultural synergies. As Codorniu ventures into the consumer landscape of China, it faces the challenge of not merely selling a product but fostering a connection that aims to transcend borders, which are physical and symbolic. How does Codorniu, rooted in the traditions of Catalonia, engage its narrative with Chinese consumers? What marketing strategies does it employ to not only introduce "cava" but also make it a celebrated part of food consumption experiences in China? After the introduction, the chapter is divided into different sections that inform this case study, based on the literature review, the context of the Codorniu and "cava" production, results, and conclusion.

Literature review

The agricultural production as a source of local identity

Agricultural production is the foundation upon which communities build their local identities, serving also as a repository of cultural heritage and a dynamic expression of collective values (Christensen et al., 2015; Moreno & Malone, 2021). In the case of cava, a sparkling wine DO from the vineyards of Catalonia, Spain, the relationship between agricultural practices and local identity also becomes evident (Mariné-Roig, 2011; Molleví-Bortoló et al., 2020). Cava is not just a product of the land, it is a manifestation of the history, traditions, and

DOI: 10.4324/9781032636962-5

craftsmanship of the region (Duarte Alonso, 2017; Medina & Tresserras, 2008). The grape varieties, the terroir of Catalonia's vineyards, and the winemaking techniques contribute to the distinctive character of cava as part of the attraction factor (Molleví-Bortoló & Fusté-Forné, 2016).

These elements form the essence of the wine itself, making it a cultural emblem that encapsulates the spirit of Catalan places, people, and practices. The vineyards are living canvases that tell the story of generations cultivating the land (Markowska & Lopez-Vega, 2018; Planas, 2016). This cultivation process and the landscape have become a ritual expression of cultural pride (Mercer & Song, 2020; Nogué & Vicente, 2004) and differentiation. In this context, each production unit (e.g. each vine) is a conduit for transmitting the region's cultural heritage (Fusté-Forné, 2015). As knowledge and practices are passed down from generation to generation, Catalonia's landscape of vineyards serves as a testament to the agricultural skill and distinctive cultural character of the region through the continuity of agricultural traditions.

The role of cultural differences in food production and consumption

The diversity of food production and consumption practices worldwide reflects the diverse nature of culture itself (Guerrero et al., 2009; Venkatesh et al., 2016). It includes ingredients and recipes, but it also embraces rituals, traditions, and social dynamics surrounding food (Frewer & Van Trijp, 2006), with an increasing role in organic production and consumption (Seegebarth et al., 2016; Thøgersen, 2010). Cultural differences play a fundamental role in shaping the global culinary landscape, which includes the commensality of the Mediterranean area (Medina, 2021) or the tea ceremonies of China (Benn, 2015). Understanding these cultural complexities involves valorising food's emotional, historical, and social significance (Berno & Fusté-Forné, 2020).

Food is a medium through which cultural identities are expressed, communicated, and shared. Preparing and sharing a meal is a powerful means to connect with others, express cultural values, and forge social bonds (Marovelli, 2019; Purnell, 2013; Ren & Fusté-Forné, 2023). This understanding of cultural differences becomes a strategic imperative for businesses that venture into the global market because it involves appreciating and respecting the cultural context that defines how food is perceived and experienced (Ares et al., 2016; Chang et al., 2010; Fieldhouse, 2013). In this regard, businesses move beyond a transactional relationship with consumers to one rooted in cultural competence that increases consumer acceptance and trust (Altinay et al., 2014; Reidy, 2012; Sirdeshmukh et al., 2002).

The features of marketing mix in food-based businesses

Food-based businesses' marketing mix is a strategic framework influencing consumer perceptions and purchasing decisions (Praesri et al., 2022). For products like cava, where cultural associations and authenticity are integral, the marketing mix is also crucial in the internationalisation of companies (Chamorro et al., 2015), and when they enter the Chinese market (Jiménez-Asenjo & Filipescu, 2019). While the traditional 4Ps of the marketing mix are explained in the following paragraph, recent research also calls for the 4Es formula, which includes expertise, evaluation, education, and experience based on the knowledge of the consumer (Festa et al., 2016).

Starting with the product aspect, cava is a beverage that embodies a rich cultural narrative, as stated earlier. Craftsmanship, history, and regional specificity transform cava into more than just a sparkling wine: it becomes a cultural artefact (Varriano, 2022). The product's essence is based on Catalonia's cultural heritage, making it a symbol of identity and tradition. For cava, price is not only a reflection of production costs but a process of acknowledging the cultural narrative embedded into each authentic bottle (Beverland, 2005). Consumers are paying for a cultural experience, a taste of Catalonia that transcends the product's physical properties and carries its symbolic values attached to local landscapes (vineyards) and lifestyles (winemaking). The Place component of the marketing mix involves distribution channels that become conduits for cultural exchange (Clifton, 2016). Whether in local or international markets, the distribution strategy must also align with the cultural preferences of the target audiences. Lastly, effective Promotion in the food industry is not just about marketing a product, it is about creating a shared cultural experience around the product, which also includes the digital environment (Fusté-Forné & Filimon, 2021).

The designation of origin "cava"

Main categories and types

A labelling system regulates the quality of Spanish foods and wines, the so-called "designation of origin" (in Spanish, "*denominación de origen*", DO), which is assigned only to those products meeting the highest quality standards. Thus, the DO "cava" and its Regulatory Board were approved in 1991 by the ministerial order issued on 14 November 1991 by the Ministry of Agriculture, Fisheries, and Food (1991). Under this regulatory framework, in Spain, for example, "cava" can be elaborated only in the territories belonging to the DO "cava", which are classified into four main zones: Comtats de Barcelona (with five sub-zones), Ebro Valley (with two sub-zones), Viñedos de Almendralejo (Extremadura), and Levante zone, in Valencia (D.O. Cava, 2023). All in all, the DO "cava" zones are spread across seven autonomous regions, Catalonia being the region with the highest concentration of production, 132 municipalities out of 159, that is, 83% of the total (Díaz, 2019).

The elaboration of the first "cava" can be tracked down to the year 1872, in the Catalan town of the Sant Sadurní d'Anoia (a winemaking area belonging today to the Comtats de Barcelona zone), also considered the "capital of cava" (D.O. Cava, 2023). Excellence, authenticity, and versatility are only some of the attributes usually associated with "cava", combined with the production method, so-called today "traditional" or formerly the "méthode champenoise" (consisting of a second fermentation in bottle), all together contributed to help distinguish it from other sparkling wines. In this fashion, official sources classify the DO "cava", based on the ageing period, in the following four categories (Table 3.1), with Cava Rosé and the Organic Cava as more recent emerging categories. The sample of dishes recommended for each category, covering a wide range of world cuisines, shows the high versatility of the DO "cava" and its capacity to match well basically any flavour and food preferences. The amount of the added sugar allows to further classify the various categories of the DO "cava" into several types: brut nature (0–3 grams per litre), extra brut (0–6 g/l), brut (max 12 g/l), extra seco (extra dry, 12–17 g/l), seco (dry, 17–32 g/l), semi seco (semi-dry, 32–50 g/l), and dulce (sweet, more than 50 g/l) (D.O. Cava, 2023a).

Main statistics of DO "cava" in the domestic market and the foreign market

Recent statistics on the sector (D.O. Cava, 2023b, p. 11), provided in the Global Report for the year 2022, have shown its capacity of resilience to the impact of the COVID-19 pandemic, being able to recover after the slowdown observed in the production level, which decreased from 249.544 million bottles in 2019 to 215.566 million in 2020 (−13.62%). In this line, the production levels registered in 2021 (with 252.931 million bottles) and in 2022 (with 254.683 million bottles) are overpassing the historical record registered in 2017 (with 252.512 million bottles) and anticipate optimistic data for the future. Data from the same source also show that while the production of cava bottles has exhibited quite a steady increasing trend in the period 2009–2022 (with some exceptions, e.g. years 2009, 2011, 2013, and the 2020's pandemic), the number of "cava" producers went

Table 3.1 Categories of DO "cava" according to ageing period

Category of "cava"	*Ageing (months)*	*Recommended accompanying dishes*
Cava de Guarda	Min 9 months	Sushi (Japanese dish), Sea bass ceviche (Latin American dish)
Cavas de Guarda Superior (Premium cavas)		
Cava Reserva	Min 18 months	Chicken causa limeña (Peruvian dish), Tacos al pastor (Mexican dish)
Cava Gran Reserva	Min 30 months	Chifles (Peruvian/Latin American dish), Mexican chicken fajitas (Mexican dish)
Cava de Paraje Calificado (cava of qualified location)	Min 36 months	Smoked eel (Japanese dish), Mediterranean black rice (traditional Mediterranean dish)

Source: D.O. Cava (2023a)

the opposite path, smoothly decreasing, from 266 in 2009 to only 206 in 2022 (p. 10). The number of base wine producers (grapes used to make cava) followed a similar trend in the same period despite a smoother decreasing rate, going from 164 (in 2009) to 144 producers in 2022 (p. 10).

The destination of sales shows that the most significant part of the DO "cava" produced in 2022 went to the foreign market (69% of the total sales, of which 38% belong to the EU market and 31% to third countries markets) (D.O. Cava, 2023b, p. 12). It is essential to notice that while the demand from the EU market has lost 13.94% in 2022 concerning 2021, the demand from third countries has increased by around 28.9% in the same period. The same increasing trend was observed also in the domestic market, although the percentage of change was lower, of only 13.15% (D.O. Cava, 2023b, p. 12). By the same report, country statistics for 2022 show that in the EU market, Germany is leading the ranking as the main DO "cava" consumer (no. of bottles), followed by the US, Belgium, the UK, and Sweden, in the top 5 rankings; Asian countries occupy lower positions in the ranking, with Japan as top 6, South Korea top 11, and at a greater distance China top 30, Hong Kong top 40, and Singapore as top 47 (p. 12). In the case of China, in particular, the evolution of the demand for DO "cava" in the period 2015–2022 is given in Table 3.2. The data show a recovery of Spanish cava consumption in the Chinese market after the pandemic, with a pic of 0.68% of the total volume of sales in the foreign market.

In monetary terms, according to Statista (2023), the total retail sales value of Spanish "cava" in China has shown a growing trend in the last decade, increasing from US$18 million in 2013 to $38.8 million in 2017, and $41.1 million in 2018, being expected to overpass the barrier of $60 million in 2022. Specific data on the consumption of different categories of Premium DO "cava" in the Chinese market (see Table 3.3) show an increasing preference of Chinese consumers for premium cavas of higher quality and more expensive due to their longer ageing period and selected locations of the vineyards.

Table 3.2 Evolution of the demand for DO "cava" in the period 2015–2022

	2015	*2016*	*2017*	*2018*	*2019*	*2020*	*2021*	*2022*
China*	515.839	525.387	556.267	356.280	400.000	411.000	746.000	457.000
China**	0.33%	0.33%	0.34%	0.22%	0.24%	0.27%	0.68%	0.48%
Domestic market***	35%	35%	36%	32.5%	33.9%	29.5%	29%	31%
EU market***	47%	46%	44%	47.1%	45.5%	49.4%	46%	38%
Third countries***	18%	19%	20%	20.4%	20.6%	21.1%	25%	31%

Source: D.O. Cava (2023c), various reports

* Million bottles

** % in the total volume of sales in the foreign market (EU and third countries)

*** % in the total volume of sales in all markets

Table 3.3 Evolution of the demand for categories of DO "cava" in China (data represent the number of bottles)

	2022	*2021*	*2020*	*2019*	*2018*
Cava de Guarda	395.000	649.511	390.197	365.959	314.679
Premium cavas (min 18 months of ageing)					
Cava Reserva	56.000	92.692	17.449	33.748	39.425
Cava Gran Reserva	6.000	-	3.264	-	2.175
Cava de Paralaje Cualificado	360	460	121	96	-

Source: D.O. Cava (2023c), various reports

The company Codorníu SA

Brief historical perspective

The company Codorniu SA (Group Raventós-Codorníu) is one of the leading Spanish winemakers and producers of DO "cava", located in the town of Sant Sadurní d'Anoia (Penedès country, Barcelona) where its famous cellars, opened in 1915, can also be found. Designed by the modernist architect Josep Puig i Cadafalch, the cellars were declared a National Artistic Historical Monument in 1976, due to their outstanding historic, cultural, and architectural value. Apart from being the oldest wine-growing business in Catalonia and Spain, it is also among the oldest worldwide. The beginnings of the business go back to the sixteenth century, more precisely to the year 1551, when the founder, Jaume Codorniu, started his endeavours as a winemaker. An important landmark in the history of the business is the year 1872, when Josep Raventós Fatjó (Anna Codorníu, the daughter of the business founder, married a member of the Raventós family two centuries before, in 1659) created the first sparkling white wine (the Codorníu "cava"), after previous experiments with sparkling wines (other authors, such as Giralt Raventós in 1998, mark nevertheless the first production also in 1872, but in the coastal town of Blanes, in Girona, and by another company: Caves Mont-Ferrant). It is also essential to notice that "cava" eventually became the cultural symbol of Catalonia, a region which was thus assimilated as the cradle of "cava".

At present, the company has its legal headquarters located in Haro (La Rioja region), and since 2018 it has been controlled by the Carlyle Group, a US investment company, to expand its international expansion and its growth through either organic or inorganic strategies (Saborit, 2018). By June 2023, gross sales amounted to €227 million, with cava representing 54.6% of the company's business and 13% of the cava's global market volume (Alimarket Alimentación, 2023). The cava is produced in its 15 wineries and commercialised under the following brands: Anna de Codorníu, Bach, Codorníu, Codorníu Ars Collecta,

Mont-Ferrant, Parxet, Raimat, Signat, and Titiana (Raventós Codorníu, 2023). Moreover, starting with October 2023, all Codorníu's cavas are 100% ecologic, Codorníu becoming the most significant world producer of ecologic cava, with 11 million bottles per year, that is, about 35% of the world market (Alimarket Alimentación, 2023).

The internationalisation strategy of Codorniu SA

According to some sources (see Food and Wines from Spain, 2016), Codorníu apparently made its first steps in international markets already at the end of the nineteenth century (in 1894), with some exports to Cuba and Argentina. Following Jiménez-Asenjo (2016, p. 154), Codorníu entered international markets in 1940, with exports and imports to and from Cuba, Argentina, and Latin America. The author identifies several characteristics of the internalisation process followed by the company (p. 154):

- the market entry strategy gradually shifted from relying on family contacts to start operating at the early stages of internationalisation to intermediaries and later establishing overseas offices (either commercial or production subsidiaries); by 2016, the company had eight subsidiaries, the one in the Chinese market being opened in 2013. The company has a significant presence in the international markets, owning 15 wineries worldwide, and it sells its products in more than 50 countries (Raventós Codorníu, 2023);
- the business model was adapted to markets' characteristics, the differences with the domestic market playing a role in the definition of the management strategy: thus, in the European market, the management strategy was very similar to the one in the domestic market (e.g. direct management of the relationships with distributors or trading companies); in US and Argentina, the company had its own distribution channel and sales team to ensure tight control and supervision of the selling process; in Latin America and Asia, the company operated through intermediaries (e.g. trading companies);
- all in all, Codorníu's internalisation model combined networks' advantages (e.g. family contacts in some distant markets) with markets' selection strategy (based on variables such as market size and market potential), and strategic growth objectives (Jiménez-Asenjo (2016, p. 157).

About the Chinese market and the Chinese drinking culture

In a different way from other significant competitors of Codorniu in the world of cava, as is the case of Freixenet, who established, for example, an essential sparkling wine production base in Querétaro, Mexico, in the eighties, instead of focusing its action in exports from Catalonia (De Jesús et al., 2020; De Jesús & Medina, 2022), Codorníu chose historically, since the 1940s, the path of boosting its exports. Regarding the Chinese market, the company established a commercial subsidiary for the Asian region in 2012, a strategic decision meant to support the Chinese country manager based in Shanghai, whose activity started in 2011 (Jiménez-Asenjo, 2016, p. 330); some years before, in 2005, the company started introducing its brands in the Chinese market through indirect exporting, relying on trading companies (e.g. specialised importers) to ensure a good market promotion.

Research evidence (see Cateora et al., 2011; Niu et al., 2012; Niñerola, 2017) on the companies' internationalisation in China points to several key barriers, such as the competitive environment, legislation, advertising strategies, and regional differences across China (e.g. language, culture, history, traditions, religious beliefs, rituals, lifestyle, negotiation patterns, and varying consumer preferences), which need to be considered to ensure a successful market entry. In the case of Codorníu, culture, local legislation, demanding access to distribution channels, the grandness of the country, business practices, and bureaucracy were the main barriers (Jiménez-Asenjo, 2016, p. 332).

In this line, Lawati (2022) states that although Chinese consumers are more found of red wines due to the red colour's cultural significance associated with positive connotations, they are nevertheless ready to try other wines too, such as the Champagne (in 2021, the exports reached a market value of €66.7 million), the primary triggers being not only the restauration sector located in big metropolis (not completely locked down during the pandemic) but also the home consumption through online purchases, which increased significantly, especially during the pandemic. The author also points to the importance of the previous training received by consumers on the correct consumption to ensure optimal satisfaction with the drink, Chinese consumers' being sensitive to its sharp acidity, and cold temperature serving; moreover, data show that Chinese consumers are more likely to taste high-quality sparkling wines, like vintage and rosé Champagne. Thus, easy access to the product, consumers' openness to culturally different products, and a good affinity with gastronomy play a crucial role in the Chinese market (Lawati, 2022).

This evidence confirms the role of *consumers education*, a marketing strategy usually applied by companies at the *introduction* stage of a market life cycle, to increase awareness and knowledge about the product. In the case of Codorníu, being the top brand in the Spanish market was a marketing competitive advantage used by the company to position the brand in China better, and the increasing presence of the Spanish restauration sector in China also contributed to increasing the awareness about Spanish food and drinks, having a positive impact on the brand (Jiménez-Asenjo, 2016, p. 331).

The Chinese tea culture should be considered as well, Jefford (2011) argues that "there is no better way to explain fine wine to Chinese consumers than via the analogy of fine tea" (e.g. special locations, production techniques to enhance quality, and ageing over time). In this line, Decanter China (2017) focuses on four common elements: the effect of tannins (present in both Chinese tea and some red wines), which create a mouth-drying sensation; aromas associated with tea are typical to aged red wines as well; ceremonial elements (e.g. tea sets and wine glasses) enhancing the consumption experience; origins (e.g. special terraces) and the production and labelling, following strict rules (e.g. harvesting and fermentation). Similarly, Gentlemen Marketing Agency (2023), based in Shanghai, points to the prominent landmarks of the Chinese drinking culture: drinking alcohol is a lifestyle associated with sharing experiences/bonding with others; drinking rituals (etiquette and norms) are part of the Chinese hospitality, honour, and good manners being a way of showing respect and gratitude to others; it is crucial to business relationships, enhancing communication, trust, and friendship; although Chinese consumers are still very fond of local drinks, very much rooted in their culture and traditions (e.g. baijiu, rice wine, and herbal liquors), good health habits are changing consumption preferences towards drinking less alcohol, and in favour of wines and beers, which are less strong drinks, thus increasing their willingness to learn more about drinks from other countries, with a particular focus on quality.

This evidence argues in favour of the *imitation-differentiation strategy*, given that this dynamic, involving the new customers trying to imitate but also to differentiate from the predecessors and new businesses entering the market versus incumbents, is playing a pivotal role in shaping the market evolution (Troilo, 2015). By the time Codorníu entered the Chinese market, wines' quality differentiation was not well defined in the local market, and the company launched its premium and super-premium wines and cavas at a later stage.

Codorníu DO "cava": main competitors and marketing strategies in China

Recent data offered by Gentlemen Marketing Agency (2021) show that the top six suppliers of sparkling wine in the Chinese market are Australia, France, Chile, Spain, Italy, and the US. Two main groups of producers are also identified: Italy and France, old wine producers subject to paying higher VAT in the Chinese market and the new ones, integrated by Australia, Chile, Spain, South Africa, and the US. China is in the top four of sparkling wine consumers, together with France, Italy, and the US, with the increase in the demand for this type of wine being directly related to the increase observed in Chinese consumers' living standards (Gentlemen Marketing Agency, 2021).

Despite being the main competitor of the DO "cava", when the brand entered the Chinese market, the weaknesses reported by Daxue Consulting (2014), at that time, about the French Champagne served to show the difficulties faced by the businesses competing in this market: that is, unique tart flavour, not easily matching Chinese consumers' taste; prohibitive price, being perceived as a luxury drink; cultural issues (e.g. the lower degree of alcohol compared to stronger local white spirits, firmly rooted in the Chinese culture; being perceived as a drink only appropriate in special occasions); hard to differentiate from sparkling wines; consumption habits of drinking only a part of the bottle, in contrast with the Champagne's difficult long time storage were crucial elements that marked the French company's 4Ps marketing strategy, focused on reaching a segment of well-educated, high-income, socially active and open to try fresh things, consumers.

When comparing the French Champagne and the Spanish DO "cava", Decanter China Staff (2012) highlighted the softer acidity of DO "cava", its green apple, honey, and dried herbs blended flavour, and lower prices as the main strengths in the Chinese market.

In 2013, Spain was already one of the top three wine exporters to China, and the DO "cava" consumption was growing, especially in nightclubs and bars (Gentlemen Marketing Agency, 2013). In an interview published by China Daily (2013), the President of the Institute of Cava stressed the diverse personalities of the Spanish wines, personalities emanating from the wide range of Spanish DOs; furthermore, he was explaining the industry's strategy, meant to change Chinese consumers' perception about the Spanish sparkling wines, by positioning them as a daily drink, not limited only to particular dates and events, due to their appealing matching with any aspect of gastronomy.

Recent data on the Chinese market (Wang, 2023) signal a significant change in Chinese consumers' preferences, who are attracted by Italian sparkling wines (e.g. Moscato and Prosecco being preferred by the younger Chinese drinkers), which amounted to 54% of the annual imports in 2022: affordable prices, especially during the pandemic crisis, and the sweeter flavour profile which is a better match for Chinese drinkers, who prefer semi-sweet and sweet wines, are some strengths of the Italian brands. Nevertheless, while Italian sparkling wines are perceived as popular, French Champagne is still seen as a prestige brand.

In the case of Codorníu, the company applied a 4Ps marketing-mix international strategy, with the following key characteristics (Jiménez-Asenjo, 2016): (a) standard positioning, with global products and brands (e.g. classic cava and cava rosé, distributed in supermarkets, and Anna de Codorníu and cava 1551, through Horeca channel) and little local adaptations; a special meaning was developed for the brand name, presenting Codorníu as a luxury Spanish winegrowing business, with glamour and history; (b) prices adapted to the local market, higher than in the domestic market, as sparkling wines are perceived as luxury drinks, but flexible to meet consumers' expectations; (c) promotion strategies adapted to the Chinese market, through direct marketing (e.g. social media communicators, influence bloggers, and opinion leaders, all knowledgeable about wines, or supermarket in-store promotions); (d) place: differentiated distribution channels – for supermarkets and Horeca – each with a different product portfolio, managed through intermediaries, and adapted to local market's infrastructure. Codorníu's marketing strategy in the Chinese market is like other Spanish wine brands operating in China (e.g. Freixenet).

Conclusion

The decision of the Codorníu company to enter the Chinese market responds to its strategy of looking to growth opportunities in foreign markets, a business vision rooted in its history, with first exporting actions to distant markets tracked back to 1940 or even earlier, at the end of the nineteenth century, according to some sources. As highlighted by the research evidence, the entry into the Chinese market gradually followed, starting with indirect exporting through specialised importing agents and later with a country-based commercial subsidiary managed by a Chinese CEO. Previous experience in other foreign markets was an asset, allowing Codorníu better to evaluate the opportunities and threats of the Chinese market. Several key entry barriers were identified, including cultural differences, customers' drinking habits and preferences for wines and sparkling wines, and market rivalry, which were among the most challenging.

In terms of marketing strategy, Codorníu followed a 4Ps marketing-mix approach, with the following key features: (1) standardised products, brands, and labelling, with minor adaptations to the Chinese market (e.g. language), and the construction of a unique brand meaning for the Chinese consumers, to help position the brand in consumers' minds as a historic, glamorous, and luxury winemaker; (2) flexible pricing strategy, adapted to Codorníu cava's perception as a luxury drink; (3) product differentiated distribution channels, managed through intermediaries; (4) promotion strategies based on direct marketing, more suitable for the first stage of the market life cycle (e.g. wine experts' communication campaigns in social media, influencer blogs) or supermarket in-store promotions.

Cultural differences deserve a special mention, showing that the Chinese drinking culture and rituals, consumers' drink preferences, local drinks and traditions, drinking and business implications, lifestyle, and health habits are significant challenges. In this regard, Codorníu DO "cava", with a versatile and rich flavour, has eventually a competitive advantage over other brands. Consumers' awareness about the DO "cava" (e.g. served cold) remains essential, some authors invite to take advantage of the similarities between the Chinese tea culture and the European wine culture. Finally, the joint promotion of cava and gastronomy could change Chinese consumers' perception of cava (e.g. only for celebration) and incorporate it as a drink with meals.

This panorama seems to open up a range of possibilities for a company that has been committed to opening new markets for decades. Codorniu has found in Asia, especially in the Chinese market, an essential niche for international promotion and for establishing its exports. The constant growth of these seems to prove them right.

Bibliography

Alimarket Alimentación. (2023, October 18). *Codorníu anuncia que ha registrado los mejores resultados de la década*. www.alimarket.es/alimentacion/noticia/378428/codorniu-anuncia-que-ha-registrado-los-mejores-resultados-de-la-decada

Altinay, L., Saunders, M.N., & Wang, C.L. (2014). The influence of culture on trust judgments in customer relationship development by ethnic minority small businesses. *Journal of Small Business Management*, *52*(1), 59–78. https://doi.org/10.1111/jsbm.12033
Ares, G., Giménez, A., Vidal, L., Zhou, Y., Krystallis, A., Tsalis, G., Symoneaux, R., Cunha, L.M., Pinto de Moura, A., Claret, A., Guerrero, L., Cardello, A.V., Wright, A., Jefferies, L., Lloyd, M., Oliveira, D., & Deliza, R. (2016). Do we all perceive food-related wellbeing in the same way? Results from an exploratory cross-cultural study. *Food Quality and Preference*, *52*, 62–73. https://doi.org/10.1016/j.foodqual.2016.03.014
Benn, J.A. (2015). *Tea in China: A Religious and Cultural History*. Honolulu, HI: University of Hawaii Press.
Berno, T., & Fusté-Forné, F. (2020). Imaginaries of cheese: Revisiting narratives of local produce in the contemporary world. *Annals of Leisure Research*, *23*(5), 608–626. https://doi.org/10.1080/11745398.2019.1603113
Beverland, M.B. (2005). Crafting brand authenticity: The case of luxury wines. *Journal of Management Studies*, *42*(5), 1003–1029. https://doi.org/10.1111/j.1467-6486.2005.00530.x
Cateora, P., Money, R., Gilly, M., & Graham, J. (2011). *International Marketing*. New York: McGraw-Hill.
Chamorro, A., Rubio, S., & Miranda, F.J. (2015). The Region-Of-Origin (ROO) effect on purchasing preferences: The case of a multiregional designation of origin. *British Food Journal*, *117*(2), 820–839. https://doi.org/10.1108/BFJ-03-2014-0112
Chang, R.C., Kivela, J., & Mak, A.H. (2010). Food preferences of Chinese tourists. *Annals of Tourism Research*, *37*(4), 989–1011. http://dx.doi.org/10.1016/j.annals.2010.03.007
China Daily. (2013, October 28). *China, a Very Attractive Market for Spanish Cava*. https://global.chinadaily.com.cn/food/2013-10/28/content_17063752.htm
Christensen, B., Kenney, M., & Patton, D. (2015). Regional identity can add value to agricultural products. *California Agriculture*, *69*(2), 85–91. https://doi.org/10.3733/ca.v069n02p85
Clifton, N. (2016). Regional culture in the marketplace: Place branding and product branding as cultural exchange. In N. Clifton, S. Gartner & D. Rehfeld (Eds.), *Companies, Cultures, and the Region* (pp. 119–140). London: Routledge.
Daxue Consulting. (2014, October 24). *Promotion Strategy of Champagne on Domestic Market*. https://daxueconsulting.com/champagne-market-china/
Decanter China. (2017, March 13). *Wine and Tea: Four Enjoyable Elements in Common*. www.decanterchina.com/en/news/Decanter%20Features/wine-and-tea-four-enjoyable-elements-in-common
Decanter China Staff. (2012, October 4). *Spanish Sparkling Wine – Cava*. www.decanterchina.com/en/knowledge/trivia/spanish-sparkling-wine-cava
De Jesús, D., & Medina, F.X. (2022). Reflexiones etnográficas sobre la descontextualización del patrimonio alimentario en el marco de las rutas gastronómicas en Querétaro (México). *Disparidades. Revista de Antropología*, *77*(1). https://doi.org/10.3989/dra.2022.013
De Jesús, D., Thomé, H., & Medina, F.X. (2020). Enoturismo y promoción del territorio. Análisis comparativo entre el nuevo y el viejo mundo del vino. *PASOS. Revista de Turismo y Patrimonio Cultural*, *18*(3), 457–471. https://doi.org/10.25145/j.pasos.2020.18.032
Díaz, Á. (2019, December 31). Estos son los lugares de procedencia del cava con denominación de origen con el que brindaremos por un feliz año 2020. *Viajestic*. www.lasexta.com/viajestic/escapadas/estos-son-lugares-procedencia-cava-denominacion-origen-que-brindaremos-feliz-ano-2020_201912315e0b01ab0cf24af4454a3ffc.html
D.O. Cava. (2023a). *Categories of Cava*. https://www.cava.wine/en/categories-types/
D.O. Cava. (2023b). *Global Report 2022*. https://www.cava.wine/documents/515/ULTIMA_CORREC_INGLES_EDITABLE_27_04_23.pdf

D.O. Cava. (2023c). *Statistics and the Wineries*. https://www.cava.wine/en/regulatory-board/cava-designation-of-origin/statistics/

D.O. Cava. (2023d). *Zoning: The Origin of Cava*. www.cava.wine/en/origin-cava/4-zones/

Duarte Alonso, A. (2017). An exploration of Cava wineries: A resource-based approach. *International Journal of Wine Business Research*, *29*(1), 20–36. https://doi.org/10.1108/IJWBR-11-2015-0050

Festa, G., Cuomo, M.T., Metallo, G., & Festa, A. (2016). The (r) evolution of wine marketing mix: From the 4Ps to the 4Es. *Journal of Business Research*, *69*(5), 1550–1555. https://doi.org/10.1016/j.jbusres.2015.10.015

Fieldhouse, P. (2013). *Food and Nutrition: Customs and Culture*. Berlin: Springer.

Food and Wines from Spain. (2016, September 14). *Grupo Codorníu: Cava's Past and Present*. http://pre.contenidos.icex.es/spanishfoodwine/global/wine/features/feature-detail/grupo-codorniu-cava-wines-spain.html

Frewer, L., & Van Trijp, H. (2006). *Understanding Consumers of Food Products*. Sawston: Woodhead Publishing.

Fusté-Forné, F. (2015). Cheese tourism in a world heritage site: Vall de Boí (Catalan Pyrenees). *European Journal of Tourism Research*, *11*, 87–101. https://doi.org/10.54055/ejtr.v11i.196

Fusté-Forné, F., & Filimon, N. (2021). Using social media to preserve consumers' awareness on food identity in times of crisis: The case of bakeries. *International Journal of Environmental Research and Public Health*, *18*(12), 6251. https://doi.org/10.3390/ijerph18126251

Giralt Raventós, E. (1998). *Els inicis del cava: Mont-Ferrant. Agustí Vilaret I Centrich (1820–1903)*. Blanes: Caves Mont-Ferrant.

Gentlemen Marketing Agency. (2013, November 14). *Spanish Wine Market Is Developing in China*. https://marketingtochina.com/spanish-wine-market-china-developing/

Gentlemen Marketing Agency. (2021, March 22). *The Sparkling Wine Market in China*. https://marketingtochina.com/the-sparkling-wine-market-in-china/

Gentlemen Marketing Agency. (2023, November 10). *China's Drinking Culture – All You Should Know*. https://marketingtochina.com/china-drinking-culture/

Guerrero, L., Guàrdia, M.D., Xicola, J., Verbeke, W., Vanhonacker, F., Zakowska-Biemans, S., . . . & Hersleth, M. (2009). Consumer-driven definition of traditional food products and innovation in traditional foods: A qualitative cross-cultural study. *Appetite*, *52*(2), 345–354. https://doi.org/10.1016/j.appet.2008.11.008

Jefford, A. (2011, November 14). Jefford on Monday: Dragon well meets DRC. *Decanter*. www.decanter.com/wine-news/opinion/jefford-on-monday/jefford-on-monday-dragon-well-meets-drc-33895/?_ga=2.8334769.2082317606.1700566256-2019278671.1700566256

Jiménez-Asenjo, N. (2016). Estudio de los procesos de internacionalización y políticas de marketing internacional de empresas vitivinícolas catalanas de la DO cava en China. Doctoral tesis. *Universitat Internacional de Catalunya*. http://hdl.handle.net/10803/393886

Jiménez-Asenjo, N., & Filipescu, D.A. (2019). Cheers in China! International marketing strategies of Spanish wine exporters. *International Business Review*, *28*(4), 647–659. https://doi.org/10.1016/j.ibusrev.2019.01.001

Lawati, N.S. (2022, May 13). Chinese drinkers popped record Champagne in 2021, and here's why. *Vino Joy News*. https://vino-joy.com/2022/05/13/chinese-drinkers-popped-record-champagne-in-2021-and-heres-why/

Mariné-Roig, E. (2011). The image and identity of the Catalan coast as a tourist destination in twentieth-century tourist guidebooks. *Journal of Tourism and Cultural Change*, *9*(2), 118–139. https://doi.org/10.1080/14766825.2011.566929

Markowska, M., & Lopez-Vega, H. (2018). Entrepreneurial storying: Winepreneurs as crafters of regional identity stories. *The International Journal of Entrepreneurship and Innovation*, *19*(4), 282–297. https://doi.org/10.1177/1465750318772285

Marovelli, B. (2019). Cooking and eating together in London: Food sharing initiatives as collective spaces of encounter. *Geoforum*, *99*, 190–201. https://doi.org/10.1016/j.geoforum.2018.09.006

Medina, F.X. (2021). Looking for commensality: On culture, health, heritage, and the Mediterranean diet. *International Journal of Environmental Research and Public Health*, *18*(5), 2605. https://doi.org/10.3390/ijerph18052605

Medina, F.X., & Tresserras, J. (2008). Turismo enológico y rutas del vino en Cataluña. Análisis de casos: DO Penedès, DO Priorat y DO Montsant. *Pasos. Revista de Turismo y Patrimonio Cultural*, *6*(3), 493–509. https://doi.org/10.25145/j.pasos.2008.06.037

Mercer, L.K., & Song, H.R. (2020). Catalanidad in the kitchen: Tourism, gastronomy and identity in modern and contemporary Barcelona. *Bulletin of Spanish Studies*, *97*(4), 659–680. https://doi.org/10.1080/14753820.2020.1699346

Ministry of Agriculture, Fisheries, and Food. (1991, November 20). Orden de 14 de noviembre de 1991 por la que se aprueba el Reglamento de la Denominación "Cava" y de su Consejo Regulador. *BOE*, *278*, 37587–37593.

Molleví-Bortoló, G., & Fusté-Forné, F. (2016). El turismo gastronómico, rutas turísticas y productos locales: el caso del vino y el queso en Cataluña. *Geographicalia*, *68*, 25–47.

Molleví-Bortoló, G., Nicolas-Sans, R., Álvarez, J., & Villoro, J. (2020). PDO certification: A brand identity for wine tourism. *Geographicalia*, *72*, 87–109.

Moreno, F., & Malone, T. (2021). The role of collective food identity in local food demand. *Agricultural and Resource Economics Review*, *50*(1), 22–42. https://doi.org/10.1017/age.2020.9

Niñerola, M.A. (2017). Essays on the internationalisation process of Spanish companies in China. Doctoral thesis. *Universitat Rovira i Virgili*. http://hdl.handle.net/10803/440517

Niu, Y., Dong, L.C., & Chen, R. (2012). Market entry barriers in China. *Journal of Business Research*, *65*(1), 68–76. https://doi.org/10.1016/j.jbusres.2011.01.018

Nogué, J., & Vicente, J. (2004). Landscape and national identity in Catalonia. *Political Geography*, *23*(2), 113–132. https://doi.org/10.1016/j.polgeo.2003.09.005

Planas, J. (2016). The emergence of winemaking cooperatives in Catalonia. *Business History*, *58*(2), 264–282. https://doi.org/10.1080/00076791.2015.1082546

Praesri, S., Meekun, K., Lee, T.J., & Hyun, S.S. (2022). Marketing mix factors and a business development model for street food tourism. *Journal of Hospitality and Tourism Management*, *52*, 123–127. https://doi.org/10.1016/j.jhtm.2022.06.007

Purnell, D.F. (2013). *Community on the Menu: Seven Courses to Cultivate Familial Bonds, Exchange Social Capital, and Nourish Community*. Tampa, FL: University of South Florida.

Raventós Codorníu. (2023). *Wineries*. www.raventoscodorniu.com/en/wineries/abadia-de-poblet

Reidy, R.W. (2012). The role of business leadership in developing customer intimacy through cultural competence. *Journal of Intercultural Management*, *4*(4), 52–69.

Ren, C., & Fusté-Forné, F. (2023). Food, national identity and tourism in Greenland. *Food, Culture and Society*, 1–25. https://doi.org/10.1080/15528014.2023.2199667

Saborit, S. (2018, June 28). Carlyle compra Codorníu por 390 millones. *Expansión*. www.expansion.com/catalunya/2018/06/28/5b34b9b6468aeb11098b4607.html

Seegebarth, B., Behrens, S.H., Klarmann, C., Hennigs, N., & Scribner, L.L. (2016). Customer value perception of organic food: Cultural differences and cross-national segments. *British Food Journal*, *118*(2), 396–411.

Sirdeshmukh, D., Singh, J., & Sabol, B. (2002). Consumer trust, value, and loyalty in relational exchanges. *Journal of Marketing*, *66*(1), 15–37. https://doi.org/10.1108/BFJ-07-2015-0235

Statista. (2023). *Total Retail Sales Value of Cava in China from 2013 to 2018 with a Forecast for 2022* (in million U.S. dollars). www.statista.com/statistics/1013996/china-cava-retail-sales-value/

Thøgersen, J. (2010). Country differences in sustainable consumption: The case of organic food. *Journal of Macromarketing*, *30*(2), 171–185. https://doi.org/10.1177/027614671036192

Troilo, G. (2015). *Marketing in Creative Industries: Value, Experience and Creativity*. London: Palgrave Macmillan.

Varriano, J. (2022). *Wine: A Cultural History*. London: Reaktion Books.

Venkatesh, P., Sangeetha, V., & Singh, P. (2016). Relationship between food production and consumption diversity in India – Empirical evidence from cross-section analysis. *Agricultural Economics Research Review*, *29*, 139–148. https://doi.org/10.22004/ag.econ.253173

Wang, N. (2023, June 21). One in two sparkling wines opened in China is from Italy. *Vino Joy News*. https://vino-joy.com/2023/06/21/one-in-two-sparkling-wines-opened-in-china-is-from-italy/

4 The importance of communication in shaping organisational culture at Unilever Nigeria Plc

Agata Nikonowicz

Introduction

Organisational culture is the lifeblood of any successful company. It defines an organisation's values, beliefs, and norms (Schein, 2010). It also shapes how employees interact, make decisions, and work together. One of the fundamental elements in the construction and maintenance of this organisational culture is communication (Szczepańska & Kosiorek, 2017). Effective communication within a company is essential for transmitting and reinforcing its culture, fostering employee engagement, and ensuring that employees understand and internalise the organisation's core values (Kotter & Heskett, 2011). It is essential to delve into the theoretical underpinnings of organisational culture, highlighting the interconnectedness of communication and culture. When individuals within an organisation possess diverse viewpoints, there is an elevated potential for ineffective communication (Dai et al., 2022). This is not solely due to people's unique perspectives can influence their social judgements of others. If individuals within an organisation understand themselves and their interaction context from significantly diverse viewpoints, the risk of ineffective organisational dialogue is heightened (Göker, 2020). Consequently, individuals must share a reasonably consistent understanding of information that guides actions, communicative interactions, and the workplace environment (Göker, 2020).

In the case of Unilever Nigeria Plc, a multinational corporation operating in a culturally diverse and dynamic Nigerian environment, the role of communication in shaping organisational culture is pivotal. Effective communication, both formal and informal, is the catalyst that integrates local dynamics with global values. This chapter explores the magnitude of communication in shaping the unique organisational culture in the example of Unilever Nigeria.

Organisational and national culture

Organisational culture is a foundational concept in management and organisational studies, shaping a company or institution's behaviour, values, and norms. This part

DOI: 10.4324/9781032636962-6

of the chapter explores the theoretical underpinnings of national and organisational cultures, providing a comprehensive understanding of its definitions, elements, and development based on the sources and research in the field and exploring its relation to cultural differences, with insights drawn from the Hofstede model. However, it would be essential to delve into the meaning of culture itself.

Definition of national culture

The ambiguity of the term "national culture" has sparked the interest of experts from various fields, such as anthropology, history, political science, ethnology, sociology, and many others. There are numerous definitions of this concept; however, in the context of international business, the approach of anthropologists, as utilised by Hofstede, holds the most tremendous significance. Hofstede defines culture as "the collective programming of the mind that distinguishes the members of one group or category of people from others" (Hofstede et al., 2010, p. 6). National culture refers to a relatively large community like an entire nation. Unlike the state, a nation is a cultural community. Some factors within a country significantly influence the formation of a common culture and the integration of society, such as language, the political system, the education system, or mass media (Hofstede et al., 2010). Tylor presented national culture as a complex whole encompassing knowledge, belief, art, morals, law, customs, and other skills and habits acquired by a person as a member of society (Bartosik-Purgat, 2010). However, it is vital to remember that each person also possesses a personal culture, which may differ from the national culture. Common factors exist in all nations (e.g. attitudes towards time, and emotional expression) but are perceived differently depending on the culture. Many experts have taken an interest in this topic and have created models to describe the differences between people based on the culture in which they live.

Interpretations and elements of organisational culture

Organisational culture can be defined in several ways, reflecting its multidimensional nature. Schein (2004), a pioneer in organisational culture research, defines it as a pattern of shared basic assumptions that the group learned as it solved its problems of external adaptation and internal integration that has worked well enough to be considered valid and, therefore, to be taught to new members as the correct way to perceive, think, and feel concerning those problems (Schein, 2004). Hofstede (2001), known for his work on cultural dimensions, defines organisational culture as the collective programming of the mind that distinguishes the members of one organisation from others. This collective programming includes, among others, values and norms as well as the system of how they are communicated. This concept has been defined in various ways in the literature, but most interpretations fall under Schein's famous short characterisation of it as "The way we do things around here" (Schein, 2010, p. 13). Organisational culture is an integral element of any business, shaping its identity, values, and day-to-day operations. But when it comes to understanding and managing organisational culture, it's essential to recognise that it is not a one-size-fits-all concept. Organisational culture is profoundly influenced by the broader cultural context in which a company operates.

Organisational culture is a system that combines, for example, artefacts, values, and assumptions (Schein, 2004) within an organisation. It also involves the way of communication used by members of the organisation. Artefacts refer to observable or tangible elements, encompassing everything that can be perceived or sensed within the organisational context. For instance, a prominent artefact associated with a company is its logo. Beyond serving as a symbol of the organisation's presence, a logo distinguishes it from other institutions (Keyton, 2010). However, not all artefacts are as evident as logos. One particularly significant artefact is the concept of norms. Norms represent the customary behaviours practised by a collective or group of individuals. They also collectively define expectations regarding appropriate behaviour or responses to specific actions (Keyton, 2010). Consequently, a comprehensive understanding of an organisation's culture cannot solely be derived from its artefacts. Although they are readily observable, deciphering their significance within a specific group of employees can be a complex endeavour (Schein, 2004).

Values are other ingredients of organisational culture. They are defined as a broad tendency to prefer certain states of affairs over others (Hofstede, 2001) and determine our view of reality. Values encompass strategies, objectives, principles, or qualities perceived as ideal, valuable, or desirable. Consequently, they serve as a framework for guiding the behaviour of an organisation (Keyton, 2010). Organisational cultures consist of many values, often interconnected in various ways. While some values, such as independence and personal achievement, complement each other, others may conflict, for example, autonomy and teamwork (Keyton, 2010). Individual employers' values often impact a particular organisation's central values. They are culturally diverse even within one international company because of cultural differences worldwide. Particular subsidiaries located in different countries and cultures may have slightly different values and other elements of organisational cultures.

The next elements of organisational culture are assumptions underlying beliefs that are unquestioned and deeply ingrained within an organisation, to the extent that they are no longer a subject of discussion among its members. These assumptions are crucial in shaping behaviour by dictating how organisational members should perceive, think, feel, and act. Since assumptions typically remain beneath the surface and are not openly discussed, they are exceedingly resistant to change (Keyton, 2010).

Although an organisation's culture encompasses artefacts, values, and assumptions, it is a rarity for its members to engage in direct discussions about these elements. Instead, organisational members commonly unveil their values and assumptions through communication, primarily when discussing company-related topics (Keyton, 2010). Therefore, the essence of organisational culture resides in the act of communicating. It is essential to acknowledge that no single artefact, value, or assumption singularly defines or generates an organisation's culture. Instead, culture emerges from the intricate interplay of these elements of communication among all members, irrespective of their position, level, or role within the company. Consequently, culture is a highly subtle phenomenon which may not be entirely apparent (Golembiewski, 2000).

Communication

Communication is a fundamental aspect of human interaction and is pivotal in various domains, including interpersonal relationships, organisations, media, and society. It is a multifaceted concept encompassing the exchange of information, ideas, emotions, and intentions between individuals or groups. Communication can occur through various channels and mediums, including verbal and non-verbal forms, written text, visual imagery, and digital platforms. To gain a comprehensive understanding of communication, it is essential to explore its various dimensions and components, including its purpose, processes, models, and contexts.

The very concept of "communication" derives from two Latin words: *communicare*, meaning providing information, being in a relationship, making common and connecting, and *communis*, translated as striving for a state of communication and community with someone (Sharma, 2017). Engel et al. (1998) defined communication as a transaction between two or more parties consisting of the mutual transfer of content employing consciously selected symbols with a specific meaning. Therefore, communicating with someone means transferring information by transmitting and receiving certain behaviours and symbols, including words, sounds, gestures, images, or touch (DeVito, 2008).

The individual communication process comprises four key elements: *sender*, *message*, *receiver*, and *channel* (Lunenburg, 2010). The sender is the individual who initiates the communication and seeks to convey an idea, desire, or concept to others. Conversely, the receiver is the person to whom the message is directed. The sender conveys the idea by selecting words, symbols, or gestures to construct a message. This message, which can take the form of spoken, non-verbal, or written language, is the result of this encoding process. The message is then transmitted through a medium or channel, which serves as the means of communication. These channels can encompass face-to-face conversations, phone calls, emails, text messages, written letters, or various other forms. Finally, the receiver deciphers the received message to extract meaningful information from it (Lunenburg, 2010).

Communication between people is based on a multimedia message that combines "body language", that is, facial expressions and gestures, as well as sound, in the form of an articulated sequence (Paleczny, 2008). Many divide communication into two main types: verbal and non-verbal (Bartosik-Purgat,

2010). In addition, written language is considered another type of communication. Furthermore, in the 2020s, it is also necessary to discuss technology-based communication through various electronic channels. Effective communication encompasses both verbal and non-verbal forms. Understanding the nuances of these communication modes is crucial for navigating social interactions, building relationships, and interpreting meaning in diverse contexts.

Forms of communication

There are four forms of communication: *verbal*, *non-verbal*, *written*, and *via electronic channels* (Keyton, 2010). Properly using all four methods is crucial to work efficiency and success.

Verbal communication

Verbal communication employs formulated sentences as verbal messages. It is integral to an individual's functioning within society, professional settings, and family dynamics (Bartosik-Purgat, 2010). It encompasses various functions, including informing, motivating, persuading, entertaining, and more.

In this complex communication system, message senders must consider two critical attributes: content and form, which are usually constructed, invented, planned, shaped, constituted, chosen, or adopted by the message sender (Griffin et al., 2021). Each utterance should have a specific meaning and purpose. Several requirements must be met to ensure that words fulfil their intended role in communication, such as precise expression, selecting appropriate words for the recipient's understanding, and clear articulation (Kozak, 2005). At the core of verbal communication lies language, a versatile means of communication encompassing verbal and non-verbal symbols (Bartosik-Purgat, 2010). Language is the foundation of any culture, facilitating communication and reflecting the unique world views of different societies.

Non-verbal communication

Non-verbal messages, often called "body language", encompass signals originating from human body properties, sensed by conversation partners through multiple senses (Kozak, 2005). It serves as a means of conveying information without using words, essentially acting as an indirect and symbolic form of communication (Bartosik-Purgat, 2010). Non-verbal communication employs various elements, including hand gestures, posture, facial expressions, proxemics (physical distance), and more. With the considerable diversity in non-verbal cues worldwide, it's crucial to be aware of these differences to avoid misinterpreting an interlocutor's intentions, especially when interacting with individuals from different cultures. The research underscores that over half of message interpretation relies on these non-verbal signals (Bartosik-Purgat, 2010).

Written language

Written language provides a distinct mode of communication devoid of the support of facial expressions, intonation, or gestures. It allows the sender to carefully consider the message, word choice, and style. Written language comes into play when conveying information verbally is not feasible or for significant events and documents, often requiring more effort and being slower. Written communication comprises three crucial elements: content, structure, and style (Mruk, 2004). Unlike spoken communication, written messages are permanent and can be repeatedly reviewed and analysed by the recipient.

Communication via electronic channels

Communication via electronic channels refers to exchanging information, ideas, or messages using electronic devices and digital platforms. It includes an extensive array of technologies such as the Internet, social media, email, videoconferencing, digital media, and e-commerce. The significance of electronic communication lies in its ability to facilitate rapid and convenient interaction, transcending geographical boundaries. This form of communication has become increasingly integral in both personal and professional spheres, allowing for efficient collaboration and connectivity in the digital age. Electronic communication has transformed the dynamics of interpersonal relationships and organisational structures, offering new opportunities and challenges in the evolving landscape of digital connectivity (Mwiinga, 2023).

The way of communication varies across countries and cultures. Understanding and respecting cultural differences is foundational to successful cross-cultural communication. This includes awareness of diverse communication styles, nonverbal cues, and varying degrees of formality within different cultures (Sahadevan & Sumangala, 2021). Being culturally sensitive is not only a mark of respect but also a strategy for building rapport and trust.

A very important issue in communication worldwide is the high-low context presented by Hall (1976). Hall (1976) clarified that a high-low cultural context relates to whether communication in a particular culture occurs through vocally expressed messages or is intimately associated with the context in which the message is communicated (Kaynak et al., 2023). Low-context cultures focus more on the message's inherent significance. However, communication in high-context cultures is not straightforward, implicit, or verbalised; instead, it requires a closer examination of what is actually meant, understood, or interpreted. Individuals from low-context cultures may lean towards technologically advanced communication platforms, while those in high-context cultures tend to favour face-to-face interactions. This preference stems from the significance attached to spoken words and the interpretation of non-verbal cues, which holds considerable importance for those engaged in the conversation (Bakalarska et al., 2018). Relationships are valued in high-context cultures, therefore, individuals internalise the meaning of communication (Saputri & Saraswati, 2017).

Through appropriate identification and recognition of differences in cross-cultural communication and flexibility and adaptability, intercultural communication in the workplace enables companies to cooperate with people from different backgrounds and cultures.

The significance of cultural diversity and communication in organisational culture

The implications of cultural differences on organisational culture and communication

Cultural differences can have profound implications on the fabric of organisational culture, influencing how values, beliefs, and behaviours are defined and embraced within a company. These implications are crucial for understanding and managing a diverse workforce and promoting a cohesive organisational culture (Hofstede, 2001). Several scholarly sources shed light on the impact of cultural differences on organisational culture concerning some areas presented as follows:

- *Conflict Resolution:* Cultural differences can lead to organisational misunderstandings and conflicts. Recognising and respecting these differences is essential for effective conflict resolution strategies (Hofstede, 2001);
- *Leadership Styles:* Effective leadership is often influenced by the cultural context. Understanding the values and expectations of team members from diverse cultural backgrounds is crucial for adapting leadership styles (Trompenaars & Hampden-Turner, 1997);
- *Communication:* Effective communication strategies must consider the cultural context to ensure messages are accurately conveyed and interpreted. Awareness of cultural differences can help avoid miscommunication (Hofstede, 2001);
- *Team Dynamics:* Cultural diversity can enrich team dynamics, fostering innovative solutions and approaches. However, it can also introduce challenges in terms of collaboration and decision-making. Organisations need to nurture inclusive environments that harness the benefits of diversity (Cameron & Quinn, 2011).

Organisations that embrace cultural diversity and understand the implications of cultural differences on organisational culture are better positioned for success in an increasingly globalised world. Recognising the role of culture in shaping organisational culture is not just a matter of effective management; it is a vital component of fostering inclusivity and a more interconnected and culturally aware global business environment (Vveinhardt, 2018).

Communication's influence on the organisation's culture

Organisational culture is the collective personality of an enterprise, encompassing its values, beliefs, behaviours, and shared assumptions (Rita, 2022). It plays a pivotal role in defining an organisation's identity and influencing the behaviours and decisions of its members. Effective communication is the foundation that shapes and sustains organisational commitment (Ketprapakorn & Kantabutra, 2022) and, therefore, culture, and it is an integral component of every successful company in many ways.

Defining core values and beliefs

Effective communication articulates the company's core values and beliefs. Leaders and key stakeholders must communicate these fundamental principles clearly and consistently to employees. This transparency helps align the workforce with the organisation's values and promotes a shared understanding of its identity (Schein, 2004).

Reinforcing cultural norms

Consistent and clear communication reinforces cultural norms within the enterprise. When leaders communicate the expected behaviours and attitudes, employees are more likely to internalise and adhere to them. Through feedback, recognition, and performance appraisals, communication perpetuates cultural norms (O'Reilly et al., 1991).

Crisis management and adaptation

In times of crisis or significant change, communication is essential in preserving and adapting the organisational culture. Effective crisis communication can mitigate cultural disruptions, while open dialogue about change initiatives helps employees understand and adapt to new cultural dynamics (Cameron & Quinn, 2011).

Leadership as cultural role models

Leaders serve as cultural role models. Their communication styles, values, and behaviours set the tone for the entire organisation. The clarity and consistency of their communication influence the degree to which employees embrace the culture (Denison & Mishra, 1995).

Communication channels and accessibility

Effective communication ensures that employees can access the information necessary to embrace the organisational culture. Employing various communication channels and making information easily accessible are essential for fostering understanding and buy-in (Martin & Meyerson, 1988).

Organisational culture is a powerful force that influences behaviour, decision-making, and the overall success of an enterprise. Effective communication is the catalyst that shapes and sustains this culture. Clear and consistent communication of values, norms, and expectations defines the cultural identity, reinforces behavioural standards, and ensures cultural adaptability during change (Jerab & Mabrouk, 2023). As a result, communication stands as an essential component of every organisation's cultural DNA.

The link between organisational culture and communication is evident in the sense that a well-established communication network within a company plays a pivotal role in shaping a robust corporate framework (Curado et al., 2022). Organisational culture essentially represents how a company manages its internal and external affairs, serving as a blueprint for its identity and revealing the driving force behind its pursuit of objectives. The effectiveness of communication is what determines whether a company has a strong organisational culture and communication network (Ejim, 2023). In the case of companies operating in a culturally diverse environment, this issue is even more difficult. In intercultural encounters where individuals from different cultures are interdependent, miscommunication tends to happen more frequently. Individuals whose backgrounds are very different from one another frequently respond and behave in unfamiliar and confusing ways (Thomas et al., 2010). Therefore, adopting the appropriate communication style in shaping organisational culture is necessary, especially in cross-cultural enterprises.

Nigerian culture in the light of Hofstede and Hall's model

Hofstede is one of the most renowned figures in intercultural psychology. He is primarily associated with extensive research conducted in over 50 countries on the relationship between organisational and national culture (Hofstede, 2011). His work confirmed that national culture significantly influences the attitudes and values of employees, often more so than individual characteristics such as gender, age, profession, or social status. Hofstede's model will be presented on the basis of Nigerian culture in this part. Despite the significant ethnic diversity in Nigeria, most members of society share a relatively similar approach. The Hofstede model distinguishes six cultural dimensions (Hofstede et al., 2010):

- *Power distance* represents the extent of expectations and acceptance of an unequal power distribution among less influential members of an organisation (Hofstede et al., 2010). This dimension ranges from small to large power distance. In societies with a small-power distance, members treat each other as equals, reducing inequalities. Hierarchy is based solely on social or professional roles. In contrast, high-power distance cultures exhibit significant inequalities in the workplace and daily life, where employees depend on superiors, and children are expected to be obedient and respectful at home. Nigerians acknowledge a hierarchical order where each person's position is accepted without further justification. Organisational hierarchy is perceived as a reflection of inherent inequalities here. Centralisation is prevalent, and subordinates anticipate clear directives. An ideal leader in Nigeria is a benevolent autocrat (Hofstede Insights.com, 2023);

- *Individualism and Collectivism* emphasise the importance of the individual, encouraging independence, open expression of feelings and emotions, a strong sense of autonomy, loose social bonds, and early self-reliance. Work in individualistic cultures emphasises personal freedom, self-realisation, and challenging tasks. In collectivist societies, values are rooted in community life, emphasising social harmony, duty, solidarity, the "we" concept, interdependence, and group support in personal and professional life (Hofstede et al., 2010). Nigeria is characterised as a collectivist society, emphasising solid and enduring commitments to one's group, whether it is family or other relationships. Loyalty holds paramount importance here, superseding most other social norms. Strong interpersonal bonds are favoured, with each member assuming responsibility for others in their group in Nigeria. Moreover, group considerations influence decisions regarding hiring and promotion, and management is oriented towards the group (Hofstede Insights.com, 2023);
- *Masculinity and Femininity* – dimension categorises societies based on a rigid division of gender-related traits and roles or a more fluid approach where gender-based distinctions are less pronounced. Masculine societies stress qualities like toughness, courage, assertiveness, material success, and competitive skills for men while expecting women to be nurturing, modest, compromising, and focused on improving their quality of life. In contrast, feminine societies blur these distinctions, allowing for more flexibility in the roles and traits associated with both genders (Hofstede et al., 2010). Nigeria exhibits characteristics of a masculine society where individuals live to work, and managerial traits include decisiveness and assertiveness. Moreover, emphasis is placed on competition and performance, with conflicts addressed through confrontation (Hofstede Insights.com, 2023);
- *Uncertainty Avoidance* measures a culture's tolerance for the unknown, new, or uncertain (Hofstede et al., 2010). It reflects the degree of threat perceived by members of a culture when faced with new, unfamiliar, or uncertain situations. High uncertainty avoidance cultures adhere to strict rules and regulations, disapprove of unconventional behaviours and ideas, and prioritise security. Individuals in these cultures tend to be more aggressive, stressed, and nervous. In contrast, low uncertainty avoidance cultures are more relaxed, optimistic, unafraid of the future, and less bound by rules (Venaik, 2010). Nigeria leans slightly towards a higher level of uncertainty avoidance (Hofstede Insights.com, 2023). This society is relatively neutral in this aspect but

may exhibit more aggressive, stressed, and nervous behaviour. A decreased sense of security is caused by failure to comply with rigid rules, regulations, or unconventional ideas and behaviours (Venaik, 2010);

- *Long-Term and Short-Term Orientation* – Long-term orientation values traits that focus on the future, such as perseverance and thriftiness. Societies with this orientation place importance on values that bring specific advantages in the future. In contrast, short-term-oriented cultures emphasise values related to the past and present, like respect for tradition, face-saving, and fulfilling social obligations (Shetty et al., 2023). Nigeria is inclined towards a short-term orientation, preferring the maintenance of traditional norms and expressing scepticism towards social change (Hofstede Insights.com, 2023);
- *Indulgence versus Restraint* – This dimension was added to Hofstede's model in 2010 and gauges the permissiveness of a culture. Indulgence is the degree to which people allow themselves to enjoy life and have fun (Hofstede et al., 2010), while restraint reflects a belief in tightly regulated societal norms for enjoying life and having fun. These cultural dimensions provide valuable insights into the values and behaviours of different societies and help understand how culture influences organisational practices and employee behaviour. Nigeria is identified as an indulgent society. There is a positive outlook, a tendency towards optimism, and a higher value placed on free time, personal autonomy, and discretionary spending (Hofstede Insights.com, 2023).

Unilever Nigeria Plc – a case study

Unilever Nigeria Plc is a subsidiary of Unilever Plc, one of the world's leading consumer goods companies. Unilever Plc was officially established on 1 January 1930 and is now a multinational consumer goods company with a presence in over 190 countries and employs over 127,000 people (Unilever, 2023a). It is a highly successful British-Dutch FMCG company renowned for its diverse and well-known brands, including Viso, Sunsilk, OMO, P/S, Knorr, and Clear, among others. Like other multinational corporations, Unilever Plc possesses distinct advantages such as credit and stakeholder trust, abundant capital, and a wealth of experience in the market (Burns, 2008). Unilever Plc has cultivated a robust corporate culture throughout its establishment, considered a valuable intangible asset (Unilever, 2011). Nevertheless, operating a business across national boundaries poses significant challenges.

In this study, the focus is on the multinational corporation Unilever operating in Nigeria. Since 1973, Unilever Nigeria Plc has been listed on the Nigerian Stock Exchange and is recognised as a publicly traded company, with 49% of its equity currently owned by Nigerians (Murphy, 2009). Unilever Plc London has granted Unilever Nigeria Plc exclusive rights for marketing, manufacturing, and distributing their brands (Unilever Nigeria, 2017). This global network allows Unilever Nigeria Plc to leverage the expertise and resources of the parent company. Unilever's competitive edge lies in its strong customer relationships, built on a deep understanding of markets and local business culture, ensuring long-term business success (Maljers, 1997). The company maintains an unwavering commitment to high standards of productivity and performance.

To sustain its success, Unilever Plc emphasises upholding exemplary corporate behaviour concerning its customers, operating environment, communities, and employees (Unilever, 2017). The company is dedicated to meeting the daily needs of consumers throughout Nigeria, making its brands household favourites.

Unilever Plc embraces a performance-driven culture, positioning it firmly in the market. Their operational strategies not only prioritise customers but also involve employees and other stakeholders in the organisational culture, recognising that the overall success of an organisation depends on all stakeholders (Unilever, 2023b). The corporate culture has both positive and negative impacts on employee performance and the organisation as a whole. Failure to harmonise different organisational cultures into one can jeopardise the company's success (Schein, 2004).

From Unilever's perspective, upholding the highest standards of behaviour is imperative for positively impacting the lives of employees, the environment, and the communities associated with their products. The company's code of conduct underscores values such as openness, communication, integrity, and honesty concerning employees' human interests and rights. Unilever Plc respects the legitimate interests of all those connected with the organisation (Unilever, 2023c). Renowned as one of the most culturally diverse corporations globally, Unilever Plc establishes strong relationships with local communities, including labour forces, suppliers, and consumers. These relationships leverage global expertise to address local circumstances (Unilever, 2023c).

Unilever Plc strongly emphasises respecting all employees' values, regardless of their cultural backgrounds. The organisational culture of Unilever Nigeria Plc is grounded in fundamental principles that underpin success. These principles encompass employees' continuous learning and daily application of acquired knowledge, fostering a culture where individuals are encouraged to take risks and act on well-defined objectives collaboratively (Unilever Nigeria, 2022). Unilever Nigeria Plc has articulated several principles guiding its workforce, particularly concerning the organisation's cultural performance. A pivotal principle emphasises the provision of fair and equal opportunities to employees, irrespective of age, nationality, gender, marital status, or religion (Unilever, 2023c).

Another crucial facet of Unilever Nigeria's corporate culture is ensuring that all employees have the right to participate in the performance evaluation process. This commitment facilitates developing and enhancing employees' knowledge, experiences, and skills. Additionally, Unilever Nigeria Plc actively encourages employees to share their ideas and suggestions with the management or through the human resource department, valuing the commitment and care demonstrated towards the organisation's interests and the evolving demands of consumers, with a focus on improving manufacturing methods (Unilever Nigeria, 2022).

The company places significant emphasis on employee satisfaction, happiness, and a safe working environment (Unilever Nigeria, 2022), aligning well with the cultural indulgence of Nigerians, as demonstrated in Hofstede's model. Unilever Nigeria Plc believes that the success of the company is intricately tied to the commitment to productivity standards and the well-being of all employees. Employees are deemed a priority and a vital resource, playing an indispensable role in the company's overall success. Their resilience and dedication were particularly evident during challenging times, such as the economic crisis in Nigeria, where employees' hard work and intelligence propelled the company's spectacular growth after overcoming the crisis (Unilever Nigeria, 2017).

Unilever Nigeria Plc views its human capital's primary objective as enhancing the lives of consumers daily. The high levels of employee enthusiasm and loyalty are attributed to the efficacy of the corporate culture, fostering a sense of devotion to their roles within the organisation. To better understand the local business environment in Nigeria, Unilever Nigeria Plc strategically aligned with government agencies such as the Ministry of Education and the Ministry of Health (Murphy, 2009). This collaboration facilitated a nuanced understanding of the Nigerian people, their environment, and the market, which was then incorporated into the company's business strategies.

When Unilever Plc entered the Nigerian market, it had to partially adapt its organisational culture to the different local cultures. The following section will discuss the communication style in Nigeria, the cultural model of Nigeria, and a description of Unilever's adaptation to this market.

Unilever Nigeria Plc – the importance of communication in shaping organisational culture

According to Unilever's official website (2023), a company statement was published, "Global Reach with Local Roots", and the core strategy of the company states corporate reputation with local stakeholders (Unilever Nigeria, 2023b).

Prioritising harmonisation is a central focus at Unilever Plc, given its status as a large corporation operating in a diverse cultural landscape. The organisational culture underscores the need for employees to navigate potential conflicts between the company's interests and their personal activities. The company's management strictly prohibits the misuse of positions, emphasising that employees should refrain from seeking personal benefits by improperly using their roles (Unilever, 2023c).

Unilever Nigeria Plc, being a multinational company with a considerable workforce and diverse divisions, operates within a tall organisational hierarchy (Unilever, 2023d). While not directly involved in day-to-day activities, top-level managers play a crucial role in formulating strategies to enhance overall employee and organisational performance. The leadership structure at Unilever Nigeria Plc includes foreign Vice Presidents and Chairmen alongside Nigerian nationals in various roles. The organisational culture is complex, featuring numerous hierarchical layers with a significant presence of supervisory personnel. Generally, superiors expect obedience from their subordinates, creating a distinct hierarchy which is specific to Nigerian culture. This type of hierarchy makes employees feel safe and rely on their superiors (Unilever Nigeria, 2022).

Roles and tasks at Unilever Plc are well-defined by superiors, ensuring clarity and minimising role ambiguity within the company. Managers are responsible for guiding employees on routine tasks and providing clear directives for accomplishing them. This structured approach contributes to a well-defined organisational framework (Unilever, 2023d).

Unilever Nigeria Plc mandates that its employees actively contribute to team success (Unilever Nigeria, 2022). While the company does not endorse individualistic styles of risk-taking entrepreneurship, it recognises the value of taking substantial risks, albeit within a framework of centralised decision-making, to mitigate associated risks. This is another cultural dimension that coincides with the collectivism of Nigerians.

Unilever Nigeria Plc operates in a highly diverse cultural landscape, reflecting the rich tapestry of Nigerian society. With a commitment to harmonisation, the company strongly emphasises ensuring that its organisational culture aligns with the varied backgrounds of its employees. The company recognises the need to bridge potential gaps between corporate interests and personal activities through effective communication (Unilever Nigeria, 2022).

In a diverse workforce comprising both Nigerian nationals and foreign executives, Unilever Nigeria Plc navigates the complexities of communication styles. The preference for direct communication is deeply ingrained in Nigerian culture, emphasising the importance of understanding and adapting to local norms. African cultures have evolved over centuries as so-called oral cultures, relying on spoken words. Before the ability to record ethnic languages reached these cultures, verbal communication dominated. Griots were widespread in West Africa, professionals who narrated stories and transmitted generational knowledge, as well as oral and musical traditions (Tchindjang et al., 2008). In oral transmission, context holds significant importance, namely who speaks, how, and under what circumstances. A Nigerian, representative of a high-context culture, not only listens to spoken words but also "sees" beyond words, interpreting other messages like posture, facial expression, tone of voice, or gestures. In high-context cultures, non-verbal cues carry value, influencing perceptions of the other person, shaping attitudes towards foreigners, and potential collaboration (Bakalarska et al., 2018). While employees from low-context cultures may prefer advanced technological communication channels like emails and videoconferences, the high-context culture of Nigeria places a premium on face-to-face interactions (Mordi, 2017).

Unilever Nigeria Plc acknowledges the need for a harmonious and inclusive work environment. The company's commitment to clear communication channels facilitates the integration of diverse cultures within the organisation (Unilever Nigeria, 2022). Non-verbal communication can be challenging from a cultural standpoint since different cultures do not communicate non-verbally in the same way. In Nigerian culture, indirect eye contact is commonly used to show respect to others. Direct eye contact may be interpreted as intrusive unless there is a long-standing personal relationship, whereas in other countries, refraining from direct eye contact may be seen as a sign of guilt (Mordi, 2017). By recognising the value of non-verbal cues, such as body language and gestures, Unilever Nigeria Plc fosters an environment where employees feel heard and understood, regardless of their cultural background.

As a large multinational corporation, Unilever Nigeria Plc requires a balance between centralisation and decentralisation in decision-making. The formal rules and regulations necessitated by its size are communicated effectively to maintain order and ensure the smooth functioning of the business (Unilever Nigeria, 2022). According to Hofstede's model, this approach is another factor influencing the success of adapting to Nigerian culture, characterised by a high level of uncertainty avoidance.

Despite having formal rules, Unilever Nigeria Plc demonstrates flexibility in its corporate culture. The company invests in ensuring that its culture remains adaptable to the specific requirements of different countries. This flexibility is particularly crucial when dealing with a culturally diverse population, as evidenced by Unilever's operations in Nigeria. The alignment of Unilever's core values with aspects of Nigerian culture has facilitated the creation of a positive and inclusive corporate culture (Unilever Nigeria, 2022).

Communication stands at the heart of Unilever Nigeria's organisational culture, serving as a powerful tool for integration, decision-making, and adaptation (Unilever Nigeria, 2022). By recognising and respecting the diverse communication styles and preferences within its workforce, Unilever Plc has successfully shaped a corporate culture that embraces the rich cultural tapestry of Nigeria. As the company continues to navigate the complexities of a globalised world, effective communication remains a linchpin for sustaining a positive and inclusive organisational culture.

Conclusion

Organisational culture is the cornerstone of a successful company, defining its values, beliefs, and norms while shaping how employees interact, make decisions, and work together, and communication is an essential part of constructing and maintaining this culture. This can be seen particularly well at Unilever Nigeria Plc, a multinational corporation operating in a diverse and dynamic Nigerian environment.

Despite the existence of formal rules and regulations at Unilever Plc, the company has made substantial investments to ensure its corporate culture remains adaptable to the specific requirements of employees in different countries.

However, conducting business with a culturally diverse population poses challenges for any company, as evidenced by Unilever's experiences. Operating in Nigeria, particularly for a Western organisation, is intricate, with the company facing various problems stemming from cultural differences among its employees. Nevertheless, some similarities across cultures have proven beneficial for Unilever and its employees, especially concerning the core values of Nigerian culture. This alignment has played a significant role in creating favourable working conditions and fostering a positive corporate culture throughout the company. A comparison of Unilever's corporate culture with Nigeria's business culture reveals that the company has embraced conditions conducive to its operations, minimising potential obstacles in line with Nigeria's business culture. The organisation's management found the Nigerian business culture relatively easy to comprehend, facilitating its transmission to employees, given Unilever's established culture that a culturally diverse workforce can readily adapt.

Unilever Nigeria Plc can serve as an exemplary model underscoring the paramount of communication in fostering a unique and harmonious organisational culture in a culturally diverse and dynamic environment. This company's commitment to embracing cultural diversity and understanding the implications of cultural differences on its organisational culture positions it for success.

Bibliography

Bakalarska, M., Nawrot, K.A., & Masłoń-Oracz, A. (2018). *Przewodnik po rynkach afrykańskich*. Warszawa: Bank BGŻ BNP Paribas.

Bartosik-Purgat, M. (2010). *Otoczenie kulturowe w biznesie międzynarodowym*. Warszawa: PWE Publications.

Brooks, I. (2006). *Organisational Behaviour: Individuals, Groups, and Organisation*. Northampton: Pearson Education.

Burns, A.C. (2008). *Business Research Methods and Statistics Using SPSS*. London: Sage Publications.

Cameron, K.S., & Quinn, R.E. (2011). *Diagnosing and Changing Organizational Culture: Based on the Competing Values Framework*. San Francisco: John Wiley & Sons.

Curado, C., Henriques, P.L., Jerónimo, H.M., & Azevedo, J. (2022). The contribution of communication to employee satisfaction in service firms: A causal configurational analysis. *Vision*. https://journals.sagepub.com/doi/10.1177/09722629221101157

Dai, Y., Li, H., Xie, W., & Deng, T. (2022). Power distance belief and workplace communication: The mediating role of fear of authority. *International Journal of Environmental Research and Public Health*, *19*(5), 2932.

Denison, D.R., & Mishra, A.K. (1995). Toward a theory of organizational culture and effectiveness. *Organization Science*, *6*(2), 204–223.

DeVito, J.A. (2008). *The Interpersonal Communication Book*. New York: Pearson.

Ejim, E. (2023). *What Is the Relationship between Organizational Culture and Communication?* www.smartcapitalmind.com/

Engel, J.F., Warschaw, M.R., & Kinnear, T.C. (1998). *Promotion Strategy*. Chicago: Irwin.

Giritli, H., Oney-Yazıc, E., Topcu-Oraz, G., & Acar, E. (2007). Organizational culture: The case of Turkish construction industry. *Engineering Construction & Architectural Management*, *14*(6), 519–531.

Golembiewski, R.T. (2000). *Handbook of Organizational Behavior, Revised and Expanded*. New York: Routledge.
Göker, S.D. (Ed.). (2020). *A Closer Look at Organizational Culture in Action*. Çanakkale: IntechOpen.
Griffin, E., Ledbetter, A., & Sparks, G. (2021). *A First Look at Communication: Theory*. New York: McGraw-Hill.
Hall, E.T. (1976). *Beyond Culture*. New York: Anchor Books.
Hofstede, G. (2001). *Culture's Consequences: Comparing Values, Behaviors, Institutions, and Organizations across Nations*. Thousand Oaks, CA: Sage Publications.
Hofstede, G. (2011). Dimensionalizing cultures: The Hofstede model in context. *Online Readings in Psychology and Culture*, *2*(1), 1–26.
Hofstede, G., Hofstede, G.J., & Minkov, M. (2010). *Cultures and Organizations: Software of the Mind*. New York: McGraw-Hill.
Hofstede Insights.com. (2023). *Country Comparison Tool*. www.hofstede-insights.com/country-comparison-tool?countries=nigeria
Jerab, D., & Mabrouk, T. (2023). The role of leadership in changing organizational culture. *SSRN Electronic Journal*. https://doi.org/10.2139/ssrn.4574324
Kaynak, E., Kara, A., & Maksüdünov, A. (2023). An empirical investigation of home buying behavior in a high-context culture: A strategic marketing-oriented approach. *International Journal of Housing Markets and Analysis*, *16*(6), 1145–1167. https://doi.org/10.1108/IJHMA-07-2022-0095
Ketprapakorn, N., & Kantabutra, S. (2022). Toward an organizational theory of sustainability culture. *Sustainable Production and Consumption*, *32*, 638–654.
Keyton, J. (2010). *Communication and Organizational Culture: A Key to Understanding Work Experience*. Thousand Oaks: Sage Publications, Inc.
Kotter, J.P., & Heskett, J.L. (2011). *Corporate Culture and Performance*. New York: Free Press.
Kozak, E. (2005). Komunikacja werbalna i niewerbalna w porozumiewaniu się międzykulturowym. *Kultura i Edukacja*, *4*, 52–58.
Lunenburg, F.C. (2010). Communication: The process, barriers, and improving effectiveness. *Schooling*, *1*(1), 1–11.
Maljers, F.A. (1997). Corporate strategy from a Unilever perspective. In F.A.J. Van Den Bosch & A.P. De Man (Eds.), *Perspectives on Strategy*. Boston, MA: Springer. https://doi.org/10.1007/978-1-4615-6179-8_5
Martin, J., & Meyerson, D. (1988). *Organizational Culture and the Denial, Channeling, and Acknowledgment of Ambiguity: Managing Ambiguity and Change*. New York: Wiley.
Mordi, F. (2017). My culture is better than yours: A Nigerian perspective on workplace diversity. *International Journal of Humanities and Cultural Studies*, *4*, 239–253.
Mruk, H. (Ed.). (2004). *Komunikowanie się w marketingu*. Warszawa: PWE Publications.
Murphy, D.F. (2009). *Study on the UNICEF-UNILEVER Partnership for Hygiene Promotion in Primary Schools in Nigeria: Final Report*. Abuja, Nigeria: UNICEF Nigeria.
Mwiinga, P. (2023). *Introduction to Information Communication Technology*. Zambia: Preston Mwiinga Enterprise.
O'Reilly, C.A., Chatman, J., & Caldwell, D.F. (1991). People and organizational culture: A profile comparison approach to assessing person-organization fit. *Academy of Management Journal*, *34*(3), 487–516.
Paleczny, T. (2008). Komunikacja międzykulturowa w globalizującym się świecie. *Państwo i Społeczeństwo*, *8*(1), 35–57.
Rita, A.S. (2022). Organizational culture: Conceptual discussion. *Scholars Journal of Research in Social Science*, *2*(1), 22–27.

Sahadevan, P., & Sumangala, M. (2021). Effective cross-cultural communication for international business. *Shanlax International Journal of Management*, *8*, 24–33.
Saputri, M., & Saraswati, G. (2017). High-low context communication in business communication of Indonesia. In Proceedings of the 3rd International Conference on Transformation in Communication. *Advances in Social Science, Education and Humanities Research, 150*, 228–293.
Schein, E.H. (2004). *Organizational Culture and Leadership* (3rd ed.). San Francisco: Jossey-Bass.
Schein, E.H. (2010). *Understanding Organizational Culture*. San Francisco: Jossey-Bass.
Sharma, R. (2017). Communication: The lifeline. *WWJMRD*, *3*(9), 259–262.
Shetty, D., Maddodi, C., Hameed, B., Shah, M., Ibrahim, S., Sharma, A., . . . & Somani, B. (2023). Leveraging Hofstede's cultural dimensions for devising COVID-19 control strategies. *Journal of Computers, Mechanical and Management*, *2*, 47–60.
Szczepańska, K., & Kosiorek, D. (2017). Factors influencing organizational culture. *Zeszyty naukowe Politechniki Śląskiej*, *100*, 457–468.
Tchindjang, M., Bopda, A., & Ngamgne, L. (2008). Languages and cultural identities in Africa. *Languages and Cultural Identities in Africa: Museum International*, *60*(3), 37–50.
Thomas, A., Thomas, A., Kinast, E., Schroll-Machl, S., & Weston-Horsmann, C. (2010). *Handbook of Intercultural Communication and Cooperation: Volume 1, Basics and Areas of Application*. Göttingen: Vandenhoeck & Ruprecht.
Trompenaars, F., & Hampden-Turner, C. (1997). *Riding the Waves of Culture: Understanding Diversity in Global Business*. London: Nicholas Brealey Publications.
Unilever. (2011). *Unilever Sustainable Living Plan*. www.unilever.com/files/origin/8d44b028edc3130ff3f735c640629db9eb0f3ec3.pdf/unilever-s-basis-of-preparation-2011-october-2012.pdf
Unilever. (2017). *Unilever Responsible Sourcing Policy*. www.unilever.com/files/92ui5egz/production/6fd19e491d1b12a1cf6d0e26b79703f31093ed6f.pdf
Unilever. (2023a). *Our Company*. www.unilever.com/our-company/
Unilever. (2023b). *Engaging with Stakeholders*. www.unilever.com/planet-and-society/responsible-business/engaging-with-stakeholders/
Unilever. (2023c). *Code of Business Principles and Code Policies*. www.unilever.com/files/92ui5egz/production/a7ad961ef886a578ab4dd316b4e5195cbc0965a0.pdf
Unilever. (2023d). *The Governance of Unilever*. www.unilever.com/files/a05bff1b-5b19-4c89-bf85-c085706e74f4/governance-of-unilever-accessible.pdf
Unilever Nigeria. (2017). *Unilever Nigeria Plc: Rights Circular*. www.unilever-ewa.com/files/origin/145938ef76df72a0a6469fdb56fed20e5d16ec8c.pdf/unilever-nigeria-plc-rights-circular_tcm1283-509709_en.pdf
Unilever Nigeria. (2022). *Unilever Nigeria Plc: Business and Purpose*. www.unilever-ewa.com/files/92ui5egz/production/1fb2192ba2968cd01cdb550c0a4ef1916208d886.pdf
Venaik, S. (2010). Avoiding uncertainty in Hofstede and GLOBE. *Journal of International Business Studies*, *41*(8), 1294–1315.
Vveinhardt, J. (2018). Introductory chapter: Organizational culture – How much underused potential does science have? *IntechOpen*. https://doi.org/10.5772/intechopen.81134

5 The importance of the nation brand and the effect of the country of origin on the internationalisation of enterprises

Joanna Bednarz and Aleksandra Myszk

Introduction

Countries have always competed for political, economic, and cultural influence. On the one hand, they try to "pull in: investors, tourists, business visitors, students, major events, researchers, travel writers, and talented entrepreneurs, and on the other push out products, services, policies, culture, and ideas" (Anholt, 2011, p. 8).

Developing a nation brand is associated with globalisation, which contributes to the unification of world markets (Anholt, 2011; Hakala et al., 2013). Countries try to build their position and image abroad. The strength of a nation brand may consist of many different elements like attractive products and services, activities of exporters, the government and its agencies, economic and cultural institutions, skilfully conducted promotion of the country abroad, and recognisable and essential people who are ambassadors of this country (Anholt, 2004; Dinnie, 2008; Fan, 2010; He et al., 2021; Zeybek & Gül Ünlü, 2016). Strong nation brands can create international credibility and attract foreign investors to distinguish a country as a good place to invest, giving them confidence (Dinnie, 2008; Stock, 2009). Well-known and appreciated brands promote the country and create its positive image (Hakala et al., 2013) and are attractive to tourists and organisers of cultural and sports events (Anholt, 2011). The vision of the nation brand is supported and strengthened by all communication activities between the country and the international environment (Anholt, 2005b). In this way, nation brands generate income for local communities (Anholt, 2005b; Hassan & Mahrous, 2019; Zeybek & Gül Ünlü, 2016).

Furthermore, entrepreneurs deciding to expand abroad should consider whether the image of the country of origin is recognisable and, if so, whether it will have a positive or negative impact. Strong nation brands strengthen national identity and facilitate the foreign expansion of domestic enterprises. This is because the reputation of the country of origin affects the company's brand image, the attitude of buyers, and, consequently, the sales of manufactured goods. Such products are well-perceived and considered more competitive than

DOI: 10.4324/9781032636962-7

competitors' products (Bednarz, 2006; Fan, 2010; Hakala et al., 2013; He et al., 2021; Kang & Yang, 2010). Simply, foreign consumers trust the country and the products and services produced there.

The aim of the chapter is threefold: to (1) present the concepts of a nation brand and the effect of country of origin, (2) show the areas in building a nation brand, and (3) evaluate examples of brands that benefit from the image of the home country, but at the same time contribute to building this image. Particular attention was paid to two chosen countries and cultures, Spain and Sweden, and to two domestic companies, Piel de Toro and IKEA.

Based on the literature review, two research questions were formulated:

RQ1: What are the sources of the image of Spain and Sweden?
RQ2: Which elements of the nation brand are highly prioritised in building the image of the Piel de Toro and IKEA brands?

To identify essential articles presenting content in the theoretical part, databases such as Web of Science, Scopus, EBSCOhost, Emerald, and Springer were applied. In turn, in the empirical part, the case study method was used to describe selected nation brands and company brands. The sources of information were scientific and popular science articles, websites of national institutions, and reports.

The structure of the chapter consists of seven sections. First, three theoretical issues were discussed: the essence of a nation brand, areas in which a nation brand can be built, and the concept of the effect of country of origin. Then, the nation brand of Spain and the company brand Piel de Toro were presented. The next section of the chapter concerns the brands of Sweden and the IKEA company. The chapter ends with conclusions regarding the importance of nation branding.

The nation brand concept

The concept was introduced by Anholt (2011) in 1996. Dinnie (2008) underlines that it is an exciting, complex, and controversial phenomenon. Scientists and practitioners find it a complicated nationwide, multidimensional, and context-dependent concept. It concerns the whole country's image and includes multiple levels and several components, such as politics, economy, society, environment, history, and culture (Dinnie, 2008; Fan, 2006; Fetscherin, 2010).

The nation brand is studied in marketing from two perspectives: macro, that is, broadly understood as a political and cultural identity, and micro, as the image of the country that can be associated with products (He et al., 2021). At the core of the nation brand concept are fields of marketing such as country of origin, destination brand, country image or country-product image, and country identity (Fan, 2006, 2010). However, two other areas of international relations and public diplomacy should also be added to this (Fetscherin, 2010; Kaneva, 2011). In the literature, the terms nation and country branding are used interchangeably. Nevertheless, it is worth clarifying that the term nation means a group of people, and the country refers to the area of land occupied by the nation (Fan, 2006; Papp-Váry, 2018).

Getting acquainted with the concept of a nation brand is difficult due to the variety of approaches of scientists, researchers, and practitioners. As a result of a systematic review of the literature for the years from 1998 to 2018, Hao et al. (2021) noted that in the area of the nation brand, there are four main research themes:

- nation branding and country image and reputation;
- nation branding and nation brand personality based on perceptions of and experiences with the country's government, companies, institutions, products, and people;
- nation brand strength;
- nation branding and integrated marketing communications.

Kaneva (2011) distinguishes three approaches to nation brand: technical-economic, political, and cultural. The technical-economic focus covers areas of management, marketing, and tourism studies. It is based on issues related to economic growth, profit maximisation, economic efficiency principles, specialisation, and capital accumulation. The nation brand is understood as a strategic tool to increase the country's competitive advantage in the global market. The political approach is related to the fields of international relations, public relations, and international communication. It focuses on the impact of the national image in a global system of international relations. Finally, the cultural approach includes media and cultural studies.

As noted earlier, the complexity of this concept and the lack of a clear distinction from other concepts have resulted in no single standard definition of a nation brand (Hao et al., 2021; Fetscherin, 2010). After reviewing the literature and considering the diversity of approaches, it is worth quoting some definitions. Fan (2006, p. 6) states that "nation branding concerns applying branding and marketing communications techniques to promote a nation's image". Fan (2010, p. 101) also clarifies that "nation branding is a process by which a nation's images can be created, monitored, evaluated and proactively managed to improve or enhance the country's reputation among a target international audience". Anholt (2005a, pp. 296–297) defines the nation brand as "the sum of people's perceptions of a country across the six areas of national competence: the cultural, political, commercial and human assets, investment potential, and tourist appeal". Kotler and Gertner (2002, p. 251) understand a nation brand as "the sum of beliefs and impressions people hold about places. Images simplify many associations and pieces of information connected with a place. They are a product of the mind trying to process and pick out essential information from huge amounts of data about a place". A detailed definition of a nation brand is provided by Hassan and Mahrous (2019, p. 148). According to them, a nation brand is "the total sum of all perceptions of a nation in the mind of international stakeholders that may contain some of the following elements: people, place, culture/language, history, food, fashion, famous faces (celebrities), global brands, etc.".

Areas of the nation brand

Zeybek and Gül Ünlü (2016) accurately state that country brand identity is a multidimensional and complicated concept. Even though many elements can potentially be used, in reality, a country's brand identity is built on a limited set of elements. All together, they must constitute the national identity as a whole.

Like Hassan and Mahrous (2019), other researchers also distinguish and describe the various elements of a nation brand. Fan (2006) lists several factors associated with a nation brand: place, natural resources, local products, people, history, culture, language, political and economic systems, social institutions, infrastructure, famous persons, and pictures or images. Torelli (2021) provides key factors impacting the dissemination of a nation's brand image: the political and economic power of a nation, the power of the language (the term lingua franca), and the attractiveness of a nation's cultural ideas (distribution of movies, music, and other mass-reaching cultural products).

However, when discussing the aspect of the areas of operation of the nation brand, two well-known approaches should be considered. Anholt (2005a, 2005b) developed the first approach, while the author of the second concept is Olins (2002). Both models differ not only in the number of areas but also in the approach perspective. Anholt's (2005a, 2005b) model presents the recipient's perspective and, thus, the channels of communication concerning the nation's brand. For this reason, this concept is used to estimate the value of nation brands. Olins (2002) developed a model that the sender of nation brand messages can use.

The model elaborated by Anholt (2005a) encompasses six elements and, because of this, is often called the hexagon of a nation brand. The distinguished areas are as follows:

- tourism shows the level of attractiveness and interest in visiting a given country;
- export concerns the image of products and services from a given country;
- investment and immigration reflect the interest and readiness of people to start living, working, studying, and doing business in a given country;
- culture and heritage concern the perception of the country through the prism of culture;
- governance reveals opinions about the government's competence;
- people are society's reputation for competence and such features as openness, kindness, and tolerance.

The second model of nation brand areas was developed by Olins (2002):

- tourism is perceived as an easy element to manage due to the high demand for tourist services and a wide range of potential recipients;
- public diplomacy, the aim of which is to raise the level of awareness, knowledge, and acceptance of a country abroad, build long-term relationships and ties, and convey a point of view of a given country;
- Foreign Direct Investment is based on the knowledge and experience of investors related to a given country that they consider important, has prospects and potential for business development;
- branded exports, whose task is to support the economic development of the country and the international competitiveness of domestic enterprises and products, and, consequently, to create lasting associations between the country's image and product categories that are ambassadors of this country.

Effect of country of origin

Image is a significant predictor of consumers' behaviour that influences their thoughts, feelings, and actions (Elliot & Papadopoulos, 2016). The image of products can be affected by the image of their country of origin (COO) (Fan, 2006). It is part of the product brand and associated with a specific product or product category. The COO or "made in" label influences people's minds and their purchasing decisions (Fan, 2006). The perception of the country's reputation is based on the personal experiences of buyers and the information they have (Kang & Yang, 2010), as well as stereotypical views (Hakala et al., 2013) with positive or negative associations (Bednarz, 2006). Stereotypes are heuristics used in consumer decision-making that can lead to specific choices (He et al., 2021). They can be a threat to building the image of the country because they simplify or even distort the image. Anholt (2011, p. 8) explains that "it's very hard for a country to persuade people to go beyond simple images and start to understand the rich complexity that lies behind them".

The COO effect affects not only the overall image of the country but also the perception of the category of products originating from that country. Examples include cosmetics, wine, and cheese from France, Swiss watches and chocolate, flamenco dancing and bull corrida from Spain, and modern interior design from the Scandinavian countries (Bednarz, 2014). Elliot and Papadopoulos (2016) confirmed that the image of a country affects consumers' beliefs and their openness to goods and travel to that country. Moreover, the knowledge and image of products from a given country influence the person's evaluation of product attributes and openness to travel to this country (Zeybek & Gül Ünlü, 2016).

The halo effect and the summary concept are two terms that describe the relationship between product and country. The halo effect occurs when consumers use information about a country to evaluate products they do not know. On the other hand, consumers use the summary concept when they know the products manufactured in a given country; on this basis, they shape opinions, associations, and beliefs about that country (Han, 1989; Kilduff & Tabales, 2017).

Widespread internationalisation of enterprises, numerous mergers and acquisitions, and offshoring strategies mean that the COO of the manufacturer and the country of origin of the brand may differ (Lin & Dong, 2021). Products can be made, designed, and assembled in various countries; these differences may hamper consumers' view of the product (Anholt, 2005b). Nevertheless, producers care about creating the best image of their products, and for this purpose, they often use the positive image of the country. An example of this can be two brands: Piel de Toro, which is associated with the values of Spain, and the Swedish brand IKEA.

Moda y fortuna, presto se muda – Spanish nation brand

There are stereotypes reproduced abroad that view Spain as an arrogant, haughty, inefficient, or simply badly governed, intolerant, and deeply religious country. There is also a prevailing image of Spain as an exotic or oriental country, still standing on the threshold of modernity, yet full of freedom-loving, passionate people who are, nevertheless, incapable of rational behaviour. All of this makes Spain sometimes perceived as non-European, or radically different from Europe (Diez Nicolás, 2003). A specific set of images associated with Spain is present in image campaigns: sun, sea, art and gastronomy, country life, and traditionalism (Soriano Procas & Terrón Barroso, 2021).

It is worth noting, however, that Spain's image on the international stage improved significantly after 1992, when Sevilla and Barcelona became hosts of the Olympic Games, causing Spain to finally rise to prominence as a country on the road to modernity. As Subirós (1998) suggests, Barcelona played a significant role in this success by implementing the so-called "Barcelona model" – a flagship example of an entrepreneurial city. These developments once and for all broke the post-transformation image of Spain as a grey and authoritarian country and guaranteed both the country and Barcelona a place on the world map.

The official implementation of the *Marca España* (Spanish Brand) project took place during the second mandate of the Workers' Party government in 2000. However, it was as early as 1999 that the FMRE (*Foro de Marcas Renombradas Españolas*, Forum of Leading Spanish Brands) took place, where 17 prestigious Spanish corporations discussed strengthening the competitiveness of domestic companies on the international stage. It is worth mentioning that the project, after being temporarily suspended, was restored in 2012 despite the ongoing economic crisis in the country. Since then, it has been the backbone of Spanish foreign policy (Diez Nicolás, 2003). As Diez Nicolás (2003) concludes, the project's main goal is to "convey a unified image of Spain, its political, social and cultural modernity, dynamic artistic creation and economic potential". He mentions that "this is a crucial objective since Spain's image remains largely unclear, subject to stereotypes, and does not offer satisfactory competitive strategies". To achieve this, the government has implemented the 3T strategy, proposed by Richard Florida, which consists of technology, talent, and tolerance.

First published in 2005 and still annually printed, the Anholt Nation Brands Index measures worldwide impressions of countries, using cultural dimensions, examining management style, population, exports, tourism investment, and immigration (Anholt, 2006). In this study, Spain ranked in the top 10 in issues examining culture, national heritage, and tourism but not in other categories (Anholt, 2009), prompting a flurry of comments suggesting that the endeavour promoting Spain abroad, *Marca España*, should be primarily identified with culture and the arts. Culture has indeed played a crucial role in creating a positive image of Spain and has provided the country with the much-needed confidence of its partners on the international stage. It can, therefore, be said that culture is an essential element of *Marca España*.

However, not only culture and tourism play a crucial part in promoting a positive image of Spain abroad. The beauty of Spanish has long been praised worldwide, hence the language's significant influence in showcasing *Reino de España* abroad. Spain's linguistic and cultural diversity was redefined in the 1978 Spanish Constitution. Spanish is the official language and is the country's main tongue, but Basque, Catalan, Galician, and Provençal are also in everyday use, constituting somewhat evidence of the incredibly rich linguistic heritage of Spain.

In conclusion, Spain is a country perceived as different from others, but with a well-developed tourist offer, it arouses fascination (Soriano Procas & Terrón Barroso, 2021). There is no project as innovative as *Marca España* in the whole of *Península Ibérica*, and there is no apparel brand in Spain that makes as much use of the country's image as Piel de Toro does.

Spanish brand Piel de Toro

The fashion brand Piel de Toro, founded in 1995 in the Andalusian city of Seville, sparked an avalanche of commentary in 2017 with its advertising campaign under the slogan: "*¿Una nación? España – ¿Una marca? Piel de Toro. Somos orgullosamente españoles*", "Nation? Spain. Brand? Piel de Toro. We are proud to be Spanish". The response might not have been so negative had it not been for the fact that the most widespread advertising campaign was carried out in Sevilla's neighbour Barcelona, the capital of Catalonia, which is battling now and then for independence and separation from Spain, specifically from the Spanish capital, Madrid, where every year, as *a comunidad autónoma*, it has to pay some of the highest taxes in the country (Blazquez, 6 March 2020).

Piel de Toro is a luxurious fashion brand based in Spain, famous for its products' top-notch quality and timelessness. The business started by producing surfing apparel and opened its first shops in 2010 in Sevilla and Madrid. Describing itself as a "heritage brand", Piel de Toro now operates in ten different countries and is planning to expand its influence to Africa (Diario ABC Sevilla, 14 September 2007). Today, there are 20 Piel de Toro shops in Spain; it is worth noting that the company is still owned by its founders, the Rodríguez Burgaz de Brioude family (Sobre Piel de Toro). It can therefore be mentioned that the brand, in addition to being a heritage brand, is also a family brand. The company proudly describes itself as *herencia del sur* (heritage of the South), emphasising its affiliation with heritage brands whose essence is "created from a mix of history, fashion, cultures, life and the places visited", and each product is "made from premium fabrics, with attention to every detail" (*Sobre Piel de Toro*). From the description provided by Piel de Toro on the company's website, it can be deduced that the brand owes its success to its attachment to its logo, which has grown over time to become a symbol of premium clothing. However, it is worth noting that the bull symbol used by the brand has adapted to trends and tendencies in the fashion industry, consolidating Piel de Toro's position in the market as a company that can draw on both Spanish traditions in a sophisticated way and take inspiration from the beach fashion present on the coast of the brand's home town, Seville.

As previously mentioned, the core value of every heritage brand is tradition, hence Piel de Toro's readiness to make the most of Spanish symbols and colours, hence red and yellow's frequent presence in the company's apparel. Furthermore, the brand's name, Piel de Toro, signifies "bull's skin". According to many Spaniards, the bull is said to be visible in the Iberian Peninsula's shape, making itself a prime symbol of the country worldwide. Nevertheless, according to conclusions drawn by *Observatorio de la Marca España* (2013), identifying the *Marca España* project with bullfighting results in a growing perception of the country as traditionalist, small-town, religious, and underdeveloped.

The company's target market is primarily consumers who "feel young", as the shop's success lies above all in skilfully mixing vibrant colours with modern designs and producing one-of-a-kind garments. An additional challenge to complete this aesthetic feast is the inclusion of the Spanish accent, the brand's symbol, in the clothing. It may come as a surprise that Piel de Toro products have become increasingly popular among foreigners, who consider the purchase of such clothing a must-do after a visit to Spain, making Piel de Toro products a kind of unusual souvenir.

As Piel de Toro points out, each of the company's collections is 100% designed and manufactured in Europe, which benefits the domestic market. This has to do with the brand's social responsibility, an arrangement that aims to promote social development through sponsorship and patronage activities, as well as maintain environmental sustainability while enabling the company's growth. Both objectives are made possible by the *Fundación Piel de Toro*, set up by the company. What is more, the brand promotes its image as a company that emphasises, above all, transparency and ethical, responsible production. This responsibility is reflected in the certifications obtained by Piel de Toro: the Clear To Wear certificate, which indicates that the material used to make the garment is skin-friendly, and the Safe To Wear certificate, which ensures that the garment does not pose a risk to the customer's health.

One of the pillars of a strong brand is its visibility in the business community. To achieve this, Piel de Toro has established numerous partnerships with businesses and organisations with which the brand shares similar values. Among them are Swarovski, the *Series Nacionales de Padel* (National Padel Games), the *Mutua Madrid Open*, which is part of the ATP (Association of Tennis Professionals), and the support of Spanish male and female athletes through the government project *España Compete*. It is worth mentioning that an element that significantly contributed to Piel de Toro's increased recognition in both the Spanish and foreign markets was the production of the official perfume for the Spanish national football team in 2014, during which the company conducted an extensive advertising campaign involving, among others, football players of the Spanish national team.

Moreover, heritage brands are primarily distinguished by taking from the traditions of either a country or a company. The uniqueness of heritage brands in the fashion industry is mainly based on the fact that what's characteristic of the apparel industry is its volatility. Fashion is subject to seasonality: what is new excites the industry. The newer a collection is, the more desirable it is. Then, however, there's the fact that everything has already appeared in fashion, and the latest trends are only a faint memory of what has long ago happened in the fashion industry. Heritage resists this tendency by relying on the tried-and-true. At the same time, these brands cannot be accused of repetition and banality; they have seasonal collections, but they base them on modular elements: white T-shirts or navy blue polo shirts. What is considered a shortcoming in the fast fashion industry, in the heritage industry, transforms into a brand's strength. Repetition is the advantage of heritage fashion brands, which, in addition to Piel de Toro, is also commonly implemented by some giants of the global fashion industry.

According to forecasts, the Piel de Toro brand is set to gain even more visibility in the global fashion market with the brand's expansion into the Latin American market and plans to open its first shop in South Africa (Molina, 21 December 2017). The company opened the first of its anticipated South American shops in 2017 in Buenos Aires, the capital of Argentina. A total of 50 new Piel de Toro shops are expected to open in Latin America by 2027, managed from an office in Montevideo, Uruguay (Molina, 2 May 2017). For the company, which has been part of Azbache since 2008, the future looks bright and vibrant, just like the colours on the Spanish flag.

For the wise rather than the wealthy – Swedish nation brand

Sweden, just like Spain, has implemented a broad strategy to shape its image abroad. Unlike Spain, however, it bases the strategy not on qualities such as vibrancy and one-of-a-kind temper but on constancy and implementing well-thought-out and modern solutions to contemporary problems. Opting for peace rather than disagreement, conflict-solving, and cooperation stands high on the Swedish hierarchy of values too. In Hofstede's (Hofstede Insights, n.d.) framework, Sweden scored high on a small distance of power and individualism. The aforementioned qualities stem partly from Nordic countries' "generous foreign aid policies, international solidarity, gender equality, penal humanitarianism, peace promotion, conflict mediation, social welfare and environmentalism" (Coetzee et al., 2023, pp. 4–5). Moreover, the aforementioned author advocates that "there is established literature that has identified common traits believed to represent so-called 'Swedishness' regarding a wide range of issues, among others, Sweden's willingness over the years to act as a mediator and bridge-builder during conflicts". All of those traits paint an interesting image of a country both industrious and prone to cooperation and growth, qualities that benefit business greatly.

Swedish governmental organisations responsible for nation branding are as follows:

1) The Swedish Institute (SI) was "established in 1945 to create a positive image of Sweden to build relations for international collaboration and exchange with other countries" (Svenska Institutet, n.d.). To create trust for Sweden overseas, the SI decided to focus on specific areas, such as

   - durability – concerning the environment, development, and balance;
   - new creativity – concerning the experience industry and popular culture;
   - openness – concerning freedom of speech and tolerance;
   - unlimited development – concerning technology, culture, and science.

   Many of the qualities listed earlier align with the image presented not only by Sweden but also by Swedish companies such as IKEA, "which reaches out to a lot of people around the world while showcasing the presence of Sweden and its culture" by giving Sweden "awareness, trust and goodwill abroad" (Nilsson Nyman & Rehn, 2008, p. 40). The SI has also launched films promoting Sweden's culture, among them are "Sweden – the Northern Attraction" and "Open Skies, Open Minds", strengthening the country's position as a place that is tolerant and innovative.
2) Visit Sweden, established in 1902, to promote the country's image abroad. The organisation's goals are "to argue the attraction for Sweden as a tourist destination, and also to maintain a long-term competitive advantage within the field of tourism to get a sustainable growth and employment" (Visit Sweden, n.d.).

Institutions responsible for branding Sweden are also ISA (Invest in Sweden Agency), MFA (Ministry of Foreign Affairs), and Export Council.

Swedish brand IKEA

There aren't many businesses in the furnishing industry as big as Sweden-based IKEA, a company that forecasts record-breaking profits for 2023, as it has just begun expanding in Spain. Present in foreign markets since 1973, IKEA is a home furnishing retailer that now operates in 37 countries globally. However, the company's beginnings have been named "humble", as mentioned on IKEA's official website (Inter IKEA Systems, n.d. c). The company "is named after the initials of founder Ingvar Kamprad, Elmtaryd, the farm on which he grew up, and Agunnaryd, the nearby village" (Inter IKEA Systems, n.d. c). Moreover, the founder himself is described as "just a regular, small-town boy from rural Sweden" whose "resourceful Småland upbringing, mixed with a good dose of stubbornness, defined his decades-long career at the helm of IKEA" (Inter IKEA Systems, n.d. c).

Based in a town that counts as many as ten thousand citizens, IKEA's beginnings were indeed modest. According to the company's official website, IKEA first marked its presence on the market thanks to articles such as pens, watches, and nylon stockings that the founder imported to Sweden. It is worth mentioning that Ingvar Kamprad, the founder, has first been distributing product samples to potential clients, only to later turn to both selling products directly to customers and using mail order business to help the company flourish. Such *modus operandi* wasn't at all known in Sweden in the '70s and '80s, hence the rapid success.

Registered as a trading company in 1943 in Älmhult in the South of the country, the company opened its first furniture store in 1953, only to evolve into the first IKEA department store five years later. However, Kamprad began selling furniture as soon as in 1948, after he "noticed that furniture was expensive in Sweden and decided to make stylish and affordable furniture available to everyone" (Vanathi & Raj, 2023, p. 1211). Furthermore, as stated by the authors, "the company quickly gained popularity for its flat-pack furniture, which allowed customers to assemble their own furniture at home using simple instructions and tools. This approach also enabled IKEA to save money on transportation and storage costs, allowing them to keep prices low" (Vanathi & Raj, 2023, p. 1211).

Moreover, it's worth highlighting IKEA's international presence, as it's now "a company that designs and markets ready-to-assemble kitchen appliances, home accessories, and furniture" and "currently one of the largest furniture retailers in the world, with more than 400 stores in over 50 countries" (Vanathi & Raj, 2023, p. 1211). The process described started in the 1960s in European countries and, later on, in the '80s, in North America.

Last but not least, one should bear in mind IKEA's streak for all that has to do with design and manufacturing that are both innovative and sustainable, initiatives such as the "Buy Back" programme that allows clients to sell their old IKEA furniture in exchange for store credit or investments in renewable energy over many years. The company also goes to the greatest lengths to reduce its carbon footprint, as it has set itself fairly ambitious ecological goals that have lots to do with running a climate-neutral business.

As for IKEA's target market, it's fairly varied. "The company targets young and middle-aged consumers who are looking for affordable yet functional furniture and home accessories. The company's products are designed to appeal to consumers who value simplicity, functionality, and affordability" (Vanathi & Raj, 2023, p. 1213). Furthermore, as the aforementioned authors state, IKEA's main target market are young professionals who are just starting out in their careers and may be living in smaller apartments and families, as they tend to have larger homes and need durable yet practical accessories, as well as students, DIY enthusiasts, and green consumers.

Such a tactic indeed paid off, as IKEA's retail sales reached EUR 44.6 billion for the financial year 2022 (FY22), opening 38 new IKEA sales locations, for example, in Chile, Spain, or South America, and providing jobs for as many as 231,000 workers. Moreover, IKEA's revenue has constantly been rising, as the revenue for FY22 grew 13% compared to FY21 (Inter IKEA Systems, n.d. a). According to IKEA's website, the company's revenue in FY22 was mainly based on products sold through stores (75%), but also on products sold online (22%) and services to customers (3%) (Inter IKEA Systems, n.d. b).

Gilmore (2002, p. 281) clearly states that "the core of a country's brand must capture the spirit of its people". Such a description of branding occurs in the case of IKEA, Sweden's flagship company, whose popularity surpasses even that of Ericsson, Volvo, or Electrolux. What makes it stand out isn't only the simple yet memorable logo that takes from the colours of the Swedish flag (blue and yellow) but also the company's *modus operandi* in foreign markets. IKEA has long been using "Swedish" symbols in promoting the company's presence in foreign markets. Such symbols are elks, used in Germany and Austria's marketing campaign, Vikings wearing traditional helmets in Canada, the US, and Japan, and bears used along with the concept of "cosiness" to highlight IKEA's presence on the Danish market.

Many times, traditional Scandinavian names of IKEA's products have confused consumers worldwide. Such a situation is not a result of coincidence. In fact, IKEA has long been using the quirkiness of Swedish and Norwegian words to gain publicity by confusing non-Swedish and non-Norwegian speakers. The perfect example of such is *Järvfjället*, a gaming chair named after a mountain in Swedish Lapland, or *Skärhamn*, a door handle that bears the name of a fishing village on Tjörn island of the Swedish West Coast (Inter IKEA Systems, n.d. e). The aforementioned is one of many marketing strategies that the company implements. Another strategy, not less important, is using traditional Scandinavian cuisine as a way of further highlighting IKEA's originality among other, unified woodwork companies. *Kanelbullar* (traditional Swedish sweet buns with cinnamon and cardamom) and *kötbullar* (fairly popular Swedish meatballs, usually served with lingonberry jam) are the most famous examples of the strategy that strengthens not only the global position of IKEA but the Swedish nation brand itself.

Tolerance and inclusivity are said to be other Swedish qualities that come in handy in the multicultural society of today's Sweden. These features are also commonly used in IKEA's marketing strategies, as the brand "focused campaigns on the ethnic diversity of the Swedish population by showing different ethnic groups as customers". Moreover, "one of the best known and longest running campaigns was *Not for the rich but for the wise* – implying that IKEA offered high quality for low prices and that clever customers realised this" (Burt et al., 2011, p. 187).

Why is IKEA so special, though? Good value for money and interesting design probably play a considerate part, as "twentieth-century Scandinavian design conceptualised design as simple and rational solutions to practical problems, where the intended use of a design would be obvious and its materials of enduring quality" (Teilmann-Lock, 2020, p. 4). Characterised by "the strive for unity and formal purity", according to Teilmann-Lock, Scandinavian design soon became widely known because of IKEA's foreign presence. "What was especially admired in Scandinavian design was its 'simplicity', 'honesty' and the way that each piece of furniture would contribute to the general functionality" (Teilmann-Lock, 2020, p. 9). There's no doubt that the aforementioned adjectives describe IKEA's products fairly well.

As for IKEA's approach itself, according to the company's statement, "at IKEA, our mission is to offer a wide range of well-designed, functional home furnishing products at prices so low that as many people as possible will be able to afford them" (Inter IKEA Systems, n.d. f). Inclusivity and pragmatism are, indeed, highly valued qualities in Swedish companies and the society itself.

However, the company's widely known catalogues constituted the primary tool used to mark IKEA's presence not only in domestic but foreign markets too. According to the IKEA Museum, "the catalogue had been by far the most important tool for positioning IKEA as a brand" and as for the statistics, "at most there were 220 million copies printed, in 69 different versions, 32 languages, and more than 50 markets", every catalogue being a sort of store's display window. All the same, with digitalisation advancing and the life tempo quickening, the company printed its last catalogue in 2021. At the end of the day, the paper passed into history (Inter IKEA Systems, n.d. d)

Conclusion

Nations should manage their image in such a way as to attract tourists, add value to products manufactured in the country, attract foreign investments and talented residents (Anholt, 2004; Stock, 2009), and promote the country, creating its positive image (Hakala et al., 2013). Spain and Sweden have implemented such activities with the help of national organisations. Spain bases the promotion of its image abroad mainly on tourism, while Sweden prefers to invest in exports. Tourism is one of the foundations of the success of Piel de Toro products, and the same can be said about the impact of exports on IKEA's global position. Both countries benefit from their rich culture and heritage. The elements of a national brand that have a high priority in building the image of the Piel de Toro and IKEA brands are the culture and heritage of the country of origin, tourism, and export. Piel de Toro and IKEA benefit from this, but also contribute to strengthening the country's image. They strengthen the company's international position, increase its revenues, and create an unbreakable bond between the company and its country.

Bibliography

Anholt, S. (2004). Nation brands and the value of provenance. In N. Mongan, A. Protchard & R. Prode (Eds.), *Destination Branding: Creating the Unique Destination Proposition* (2nd ed., pp. 26–39). London: Elsevier Butterworth-Heinemann.

Anholt, S. (2005a). Anholt nation brands index: How does the world see America? *Journal of Advertising Research*, *45*(3), 296–304. https://doi.org/10.1017/S0021849905050336

Anholt, S. (2005b). *Brand New Justice: How Branding Places and Products Can Help the Developing World.* London: Elsevier Butterworth-Heinemann.

Anholt, S. (2006). *Sprawiedliwość marek: jak branding miejsc i produktów może uczynić kraj bogatym, dumnym i pewnym siebie*. Warszawa: Instytut Marki Polskiej.

Anholt, S. (2009). *Places*. London: Palgrave Macmillan.

Anholt, S. (2011). Beyond the nation brand: The role of image and identity in international relations. *The Journal of Public Diplomacy*, *2*(1), Art. 1, 6–12. https://doi.org/10.4337/9780857930842

Barómetro de la Marca España. (2013). *Resulrados de marzo- abril de 2013, Observatorio de la Marca España*. Madrid: Real Instituto Elcano.

Bednarz, J. (2006). The role of national branding: Implications for Poland. *Viesasis Administravimas Public Administration*, *3–4*(11–12), 75–79.

Bednarz, J. (2014). Impact of the image of Poland on the international competitiveness of Polish enterprises. *International Business and Global Economy*, *33*, 470–481. https://doi.org/10.4467/23539496IB.13.034.2419

Blazquez, P. (2020, March 6). Catalunya, entre las comunidades con los impuestos más altos de España. *La Vanguardia*. www.lavanguardia.com/economia/20200306/473981050748/catalunya-entre-las-comunidades-con-los-impuestos-mas-altos-de-espana.html

Burt, S., Johansson, U., & Thelander, Å. (2011). Standardized marketing strategies in retailing? IKEA's marketing strategies in Sweden, the UK and China. *Journal of Retailing and Consumer Services, 18*(3), 183–193. https://doi.org/10.1016/j.jretconser.2010.09.007

Coetzee, W.S., Larsson, S., & Berndtsson, J. (2023). *Branding "Progressive" Security: The Case of Sweden*. Trollhattan: University West.

Cuesta Roca, C. (2011). Nation branding in Spain: A shining example of nation branding. In *Cultural Diplomacy Outlook Report 2011: Chapter 4 – Nation Branding: Country-Specific Evaluations* (pp. 1–44). Washington, DC: Institute for Cultural Diplomacy.

Diario ABC Sevilla. (2007, September 14). José Manuel Soto, imagen de la campaña más patriotica en Barcelona. *ABC de Sevilla*. https://sevilla.abc.es/economia/sevi-piel-toro-hace-soto-campana-mas-patriotica-barcelona-201709141721_noticia.html

Diez Nicolás, J. (2003). Informe Proyecto Marca España. *Juan Diez Nicolas*. https://juandieznicolas.es/phocadownload/2._OTRAS_PUBLICACIONES/otrpub._2003-03_Marca_Espana.pdf

Dinnie, K. (2008). *Nation Branding: Concepts, Issues, Practice* (1st ed.). London: Elsevier Butterworth-Heinemann.

Elliot, S., & Papadopoulos, N. (2016). Of products and tourism destinations: An integrative, cross-national study of place image. *Journal of Business Research*, *69*(3), 1157–1165. https://doi.org/10.1016/j.jbusres.2015.08.031

Fan, Y. (2006). Branding the nation: What is being branded? *Journal of Vacation Marketing*, *12*(1), 5–14. https://doi.org/10.1177/1356766706056633

Fan, Y. (2010). Branding the nation: Towards a better understanding. *Place Brand and Public Diplomacy*, *6*, 97–103. https://doi.org/10.1057/pb.2010.16

Fetscherin, M. (2010). The determinants and measurement of a country brand: The country brand strength index. *International Marketing Review*, *27*(4), 466–479. https://doi.org/10.1108/02651331011058617

Gilmore, F. (2002). A country – Can it be repositioned? Spain – The success story of country branding. *Journal of Brand Management*, *9*, 281–293. https://doi.org/10.1057/palgrave.bm.2540078

Hakala, U., Lemmetyinen, A., & Kantola, S. (2013). Country image as a nation-branding tool. *Marketing Intelligence & Planning*, *31*(5), 538–556. https://doi.org/10.1108/MIP-04-2013-0060

Han, C.M. (1989). Country image: Halo or summary construct? *Journal of Marketing Research*, *26*(2), 222–229. https://doi.org/10.2307/3172608

Hao, A.W., Paul, J., Trott, S., Guo, C., & Wu, H.-H. (2021). Two decades of research on nation branding: A review and future research agenda. *International Marketing Review*, *38*(1), 46–69. https://doi.org/10.1108/IMR-01-2019-0028

Hassan, S., & Mahrous, A.A. (2019). Nation branding: The strategic imperative for sustainable market competitiveness. *Journal of Humanities and Applied Social Sciences*, *1*(2), 146–158. https://doi.org/10.1108/JHASS-08-2019-0025

He, J., Wang, C.L., & Wu, Y. (2021). Building the connection between nation and commercial brand: An integrative review and future research directions. *International Marketing Review*, *38*(1), 19–35. https://doi.org/10.1108/IMR-11-2019-0268

Hofstede Insights. (n.d.). *Hofstede Insights*. www.hofstede-insights.com/

Inter IKEA Systems. (n.d. a). Financial reports. *IKEA*. www.inter.ikea.com/en/performance/download-financial-reports

Inter IKEA Systems. (n.d. b). How we work: A year in review. *IKEA*. www.ikea.com/global/en/our-business/how-we-work/year-in-review/

Inter IKEA Systems. (n.d. c). How we work: Story of IKEA. *IKEA*. www.ikea.com/global/en/our-business/how-we-work/story-of-ikea/

Inter IKEA Systems. (n.d. d). IKEA and advertising. *IKEA*. https://ikeamuseum.com/en/explore/the-story-of-ikea/ikea-and-advertising/

Inter IKEA Systems. (n.d. e). The story of IKEA: Why is it called that? *IKEA*. https://ikeamuseum.com/en/explore/the-story-of-ikea/why-is-it-called-that/

Inter IKEA Systems. (n.d. f). Vision, culture and values. *IKEA*. https://ikea.jobs.cz/en/vision-culture-and-values/

Kaneva, N. (2011). Nation branding: Toward an agenda for critical research. *International Journal of Communication*, *5*(1), 117–141. https://doi.org/1932-8036/20110117

Kang, M., & Yang, S.U. (2010). Comparing effects of country reputation and the overall corporate reputations of a country on international consumers' product attitudes and purchase intentions. *Corporate Reputation Review*, *13*(1), 52–62. https://doi.org/10.1057/crr.2010.1

Kilduff, K., & Tabales, J.M. (2017). Country branding and its effect on the consumer in the global market. *Cuadernos de Gestión*, *17*(1), 83–104. https://doi.org/10.5295/cdg.150543kk

Kotler, P., & Gertner, D. (2002). Country as brand, product, and beyond: A place marketing and brand management perspective. *Journal of Brand Management*, *9*(4–5), 249–261. https://doi.org/10.1057/palgrave.bm.2540076

Lin, C.-P., & Dong, T.-P. (2021). The antecedents and consequences of exporting cultural products. *International Marketing Review*, *38*(3), 487–513. https://doi.org/10.1108/IMR-11-2019-0262

Molina, L. (2017, May 2). Piel de Toro desembarca en Argentina y planea 50 aperturas en Latinoamérica hasta 2027. *Modaes*. www.modaes.com/empresa/piel-de-toro-desembarca-en-argentina-y-planea-50-aperturas-en-latinoamerica-hasta-2027
Molina, L. (2017, December 21). Piel de Toro se vuelca en África y desembarca en Argelia y Túnez. *Modaes*. www.modaes.com/empresa/piel-de-toro-se-vuelca-en-africa-y-desembarca-en-argelia-y-tunez
Morgan, N., & Pritchard, A. (2004). Meeting the destination branding challenge. In N. Morgan, A. Protchard, & R. Prode (Eds.), *Destination Branding: Creating the Unique Destination Proposition* (2nd ed., pp. 26–39). London: Elsevier Butterworth-Heinemann.
Nilsson Nyman, L., & Rehn, S. (2008). *Branding Sweden*. Lund University. https://lup.lub.lu.se/luur/download?func=downloadFile&recordOId=1339542&fileOId=2435170
Olins, W. (2002). Branding the nation – The historical context. *Journal of Brand Management*, *9*(4–5), 241–248. https://doi.org/10.1057/palgrave.bm.2540075
Papp-Váry, A.F. (2018). Country branding: What branding? Relevant terminologies and their possible interpretations in the case of countries. *Economic and Regional Studies*, *11*(4), 7–26. https://doi.org/10.2478/ers-2018-0032
Rojas-Méndez, J. (2013). The nation brand molecule. *Journal of Product & Brand Management*, *22*(7), 462–472. https://doi.org/10.1108/JPBM-09-2013-0385
Sobre Piel de Toro. (2023, November 3). https://shop.pieldetoro.com/es/content/23-marca
Soriano Procas, M., & Terrón Barroso, A. (2021). When national stereotypes become a brand: The case of Spain's destination marketing. *Cuadernos de Turismo*, *47*, 179–202. https://doi.org/10.6018/turismo.474071
Stock, F. (2009). Identity, image and brand: A conceptual framework. *Place Branding and Public Diplomacy*, *5*(2), 118–125. https://doi.org/10.1057/pb.2009.2
Subirós, J. (1998). *El vol de la fletxa. Barcelona '92: Crónica de la reinvenció de la ciutat*. Barcelona: Electa.
Svenska Institutet. (n.d.). *Om SI: var historia*. https://si.se/om-si/var-historia/
Teilmann-Lock, S. (2020, September 11). *History and Current Status of Design in Scandinavia*. Copenhagen Business School. https://doi.org/10.2139/ssrn.3691070
Torelli, C.J. (2021). Dissemination and consensual perceptions of nation brands: A framework for future research. *International Marketing Review*, *38*(1), 36–45. https://doi.org/10.1108/IMR-11-2019
Vanathi, A., & Raj, A. (2023). An analysis of IKEA's global positioning. *International Journal of Law Management and Humanities*, *6*(2), 1211–1219.
Visit Sweden. (n.d.). *Visit Sweden: Om Oss*. https://corporate.visitsweden.com/om-oss/
Zeybek, B., & Gül Ünlü, D. (2016). A view on countries' tourism logos, slogans, contents and figural characteristics within the concept of country identity. *Information & Media*, *76*, 26–44. https://doi.org/10.15388/Im.2016.76.10380

6 Cross-cultural adoption of augmented reality – theories and practices

Małgorzata Bartosik-Purgat and Tomasz Grzegorczyk

Acknowledgements

This research was funded in whole or in part by the National Science Centre (Poland), grant no. 2022/47/B/HS4/00448.

Introduction

The development of new technologies has been rapid in recent years and is unlikely to slow down in the near future (Jung et al., 2018). This is due to the ever-increasing use of novel instruments that are created through the application of modern technological solutions. One technology that is making inroads into various areas of our lives is augmented reality (AR), which involves combining virtual and real images (Bartosik-Purgat & Ratajczak-Mrozek, 2018). AR is currently used in entertainment, including games, education, tourism, healthcare, and various types of industries to shopping (e.g. Caboni & Hagberg, 2019; Jung et al., 2018; Khalil et al., 2023; Li & Fang, 2020; Rauschnabel et al., 2017; Yawised et al., 2023). AR applications are continually making significant strides in improving the user experience and expanding the possibilities for human–computer interaction. It is made possible by the use of AR glasses as well as smartphones and tablets (Jung et al., 2018). However, the frequency of use of AR tools is not only a matter of its application instruments but also customers' attitudes towards its use.

Research on consumer adoption of AR technologies can be categorised on the basis of the device. For example, AR can be integrated into a virtual mirror, in which a camera captures an image of the user and then superimposes a virtual layer over that image and the effect is shown on a screen reflecting the mirror (Javornik et al., 2017). Consumer attitudes to this technology have been the subject of research concerning the use of these technologies in in-store retailing (Caboni & Hagberg, 2019; Dacko, 2017), for example, for cosmetics (Berman, 2019) and clothing (Lee & Leonas, 2018), but also about education and culture, for example, virtual museum tours (Jung et al., 2016).

DOI: 10.4324/9781032636962-8

However, much of the research on consumer attitudes towards the use of AR technology relates to mobile applications, for example, smartphones or tablets. Mobile AR also includes mobile magic mirrors, which allow consumers to virtually try on, for example, clothes and choose the right colour or size (e.g. Baytar et al., 2020), eyeglasses (Boardman et al., 2020; Javornik et al., 2017), shoes (McLean & Wilson, 2019; Schapsis et al., 2021), watches (Song et al., 2019), jewellery (Shi et al., 2020), and furniture in their home (Ozturkcan, 2021). The technology helps consumers make informed decisions in online stores.

The adoption and the usage of AR technologies are often influenced by many diverse factors and have been presented by researchers with the use of the UTAUT2 model (Venkatesh et al., 2016). However, cultural traits as predictors of consumers' decisions on AR technologies are still underestimated and under-researched. Many factors concerning individual cultural traits affect the level of adoption (Lee et al., 2020). For example, Bagchi et al. (2003) contended that individuals' perceptions and subsequent technology usage can vary among countries with distinct national cultures due to differences in their environment, history, and developmental levels (Lee et al., 2020). While numerous applications of AR have gained extensive adoption, it is also acknowledged that cultural diversity plays an important role in shaping the adoption of technology in general, including AR specifically (Jung et al., 2018). Nonetheless, there is still a scarcity of research concerning the impact of cultural differences on AR. A few studies (e.g. Cardon & Marshall, 2008; Kim et al., 2011) have demonstrated that the manner in which behavioural intentions towards using technologies are formed varies across different cultures (Jung et al., 2018).

Why is it so crucial to identify the cultural factors impacting consumer decisions on the adoption of new technologies? The answer is that basic cultural factors such as values, attitudes, and beliefs can substantially impact consumers' behaviours and decisions (Bartosik-Purgat & Rakowska, 2023; Lee et al., 2020). That is why understanding how different cultures perceive and implement AR becomes crucial, especially from the perspective of companies or organisations utilising AR applications in commercial activities. To increase the likelihood of acceptance of new AR solutions among users (potential consumers), it becomes important to examine their cultural characteristics.

The main purpose of this chapter is to identify cultural traits that may affect the level of adoption of AR among individual users. The main research method used in the chapter is a narrative literature review. In this chapter, we used an inductive approach, which allows for identifying new factors and preparing a conceptual framework for further empirical research.

The chapter's structure is as follows. In the first part, we present the AR technology (features, implementation, and determinants of adoption by previous research). Secondly, we characterise the cultural factors that may impact the adoption of AR among consumers, and thirdly, we present the results of the study according to the narrative literature review, and finally, conclusions (including implications, limitations, and further research proposal) are implemented.

Augmented Reality (AR) technology

Concept and areas of implementation of augmented reality

AR enables the presentation of virtual information in various formats, such as text, graphics, images, 3D models, videos, or audio. This information is then overlaid onto the real-world image (Azuma, 1997) and presented (most often) on mobile devices such as smartphones or tablets. AR glasses are another device which can make even better use of this technology. While they have already been introduced to the market (Rauschnabel et al., 2018) by, for example, Google, Microsoft, or Lenovo, due to hardware and software limitations as well as the price, they have not succeeded in achieving mass popularity yet. Another type of AR device is called a "magic mirror" (Caboni & Hagberg, 2019), which is often used in-store, for example, for a swift try-on of clothing (Lee & Leonas, 2018).

AR can also facilitate observing, analysing, and executing complex tasks, proving its usefulness in medicine, education, and tourism. Grzegorczyk et al. (2019) found that consumers regard AR as most useful in those areas. This technology also enables the control of multiple factors in industries like aviation and automotive. It expedites decision-making processes in these and other domains such as medicine, architecture and education. AR serves as a source of entertainment and information in educational, leisure, and tourism applications. For example, AR has the potential to assist tourists through text translation by merely pointing their smartphone camera at the text. Allal-Chérif (2022) shows how cathedrals (e.g. Notre-Dame de Paris, France) can benefit from augmented and virtual reality to provide an intense cultural, historical, and religious experience for the visitors who can access them from the comfort of their homes.

As an interactive technology, AR facilitates "learning by doing" through interactions with virtual objects (Martinez et al., 2014). This includes manipulating 3D models, playing videos, and scaling objects. Baier et al. (2015) suggest that retailers can utilise AR to engage consumers through activities such as "virtual trial and product education" and employing gamification techniques. For example, studies focused on consumers virtually trying on products from the comfort of their homes, including clothes (Baytar et al., 2020), eyeglasses (Boardman et al., 2020; Javornik et al., 2017), shoes (McLean & Wilson, 2019; Schapsis et al., 2021), watches (Song et al., 2019), jewellery (Shi et al., 2020), and furniture (Grzegorczyk et al., 2019; Ozturkcan, 2021). This approach aims to enhance the overall customer experience and comfort. AR technology also enables the presentation of supplementary product information, potentially aiding consumers in making informed product decisions (Rese et al., 2017). The staggering success of the AR mobile game Pokemon GO has also been the subject of many studies (Alomar et al., 2019; Li & Fang, 2020; Rauschnabel et al., 2017).

Despite its significant potential, AR is still not popular among consumers who "vote" with their wallets, which is ultimately a better bellwether for assessing the technology's success. Consequently, researchers have been trying to identify the factors influencing consumers' acceptance and adoption of this technology. Acceptance is understood as consumers' willingness to use the technology, while adoption as the first act of using or buying it.

Consumer adoption of augmented reality

Originating from information systems research, the technology acceptance model (TAM) is a prevalent tool to explain and forecast the factors that influence organisations and consumers in adopting technologies (Kim & Forsythe, 2008; Rauschnabel et al., 2018). The initial TAM focuses on the perceived usefulness and perceived ease of use of a particular technology, which influences consumers' behavioural intention to use. The improved version of TAM (by Venkatesh et al., 2012, 2016), tailored to consumer use, is called the Unified theory of acceptance and use of technology (UTAUT2). According to this framework, technology acceptance hinges on several factors, such as performance expectancy, effort expectancy, social influence, facilitating conditions, hedonic motivation, price value, and habit, with age, gender, and experience serving as moderating factors. However, recent studies often do not solely rely on TAM or UTAUT2 to investigate the acceptance of specific technologies; instead, they combine these models with other theories and variables.

An example of this trend is Khalil et al.'s (2023) study of an immersive exhibition shown via AR at the Atelier des Lumieres in Paris. Consumer acceptance was found to be determined not only by usefulness and ease of use but also by user satisfaction and social mimicry (which is characterised by fear of missing out and social pressure). Similarly, Holdack et al. (2022) extended UTAUT2 with perceived informativeness as a predictor of acceptance of AR glasses. The findings suggest that perceived enjoyment plays a significant mediating role in how perceived informativeness and other variables impact attitude and usage intention.

Some studies focus on AR applications designed for a specific device. For instance, Oyman et al. (2022) studied the acceptance of an AR-supported mobile app which makes it possible to try cosmetic products virtually. The findings indicated that consumer novelty seeking had a positive and direct effect on perceived augmented reality (understood as the closeness of a visualised object to its real counterpart). Surprisingly, technology anxiety turned out not to harm this factor. When it comes to the intention to use AR glasses, the perceived threat to other people's privacy is also of importance (Rauschnabel et al., 2018).

Some researchers concentrate on a specific type of AR apps, such as games. For example, the consumer evaluation of the AR game experience depends on factors like locatability, navigability, and controllability, which are connected to its playfulness and feeling of challenge (Li & Fang, 2020). Others focus on a particular field, like education. Papakostas et al. (2023) showed that adopting mobile AR applications in education is influenced directly by quality output, perceived usefulness, and perceived ease of use and indirectly by playfulness.

Some authors suggest studying the value-based adoption of AR (Bartosik-Purgat et al., 2021), while others (Erdmann et al., 2021) have already undertaken such an approach. Erdmann et al. (2021) evaluated the effect of immersion (experiential dimension), technical complexity (technical dimension), and the significance of subjective norms (social dimension) on the online purchase intention through AR technology. Another study proposes a novel conceptual framework that validates the relationships between three benefits (usefulness, enjoyment, and presence), two sacrifices (technicality and perceived cost), perceived value, and use-diffusion regarding AR-based mobile applications (Yoon & Oh, 2022).

It is not just the first-time use of AR apps that has been studied but also the intention to reuse them. The connection between how consumers perceive augmentation and their behavioural intentions is strengthened by a mediation pattern involving three interconnected cognitive factors: a sense of immersion, product presence, and perceived realism (Daassi & Debbabi, 2021).

In conclusion, the adoption of AR-based mobile applications, as well as AR glasses and in-store devices, is dependent on both its hedonic and utilitarian traits (Grzegorczyk et al., 2019). While the great majority of studies confirm that usefulness, ease of use, and perceived use enjoyment (factors derived from the UTAUT2 model) are crucial for AR adoption, researchers also study factors specific to particular types of AR devices or applications, for example, technology anxiety or immersion.

Studies on AR adoption have been conducted in various countries, for instance in Pakistan (Saleem et al., 2022), Germany (Holdack et al., 2022), Poland (Grzegorczyk et al., 2019), Taiwan (Li & Fang, 2020), France (Khalil et al., 2023), Greece (Papakostas et al., 2023) and the Middle East countries (Alsharhan et al., 2021). However, little concern has been given to the relationship between the country of study participants and acceptance, and even less to the cultural factors that influence the adoption of AR – even though previous research confirms the significant impact of cultural differences on (especially high-) technology adoption (e.g. Ashraf et al., 2014; Baker et al., 2010; Phillips et al., 1994; Sun et al., 2020). However, some researchers do underline the need for incorporating cultural factors into AR adoption research (e.g. Li & Fang, 2020).

Cultural factors impacting the adoption of AR

Hofstede's cross-cultural dimensions

National culture is an area of life consisting of many elements, among which are values, norms, social customs and mores, religion, language, and modes of communication. These are factors, most of which are difficult to recognise at first glance but which significantly influence people's behaviour and their perception of the world and assessment of various situations. They are the deepest level in the onion model of national culture proposed by Hofstede et al. (2010), who placed values in the centre of the onion (the elements which do not move). Values can be interpreted as "how people believe things should be" (good vs. bad, dirty vs. clean, ugly vs. beautiful, unnatural vs. natural, abnormal vs. normal, paradoxical vs. logical, irrational vs. rational). This is an invisible level but impacts the three other outer layers: rituals, heroes (icons), and symbols. The next layer away from the "values" core is called "rituals", associated with the common rituals and traditions rooted in the society. Rituals are, for example, the ways people greet each other, practise their religion, eat meals, or even pay respect. The next layer is connected with the heroes or icons – persons who are admired by a particular society (they usually tend to represent many of the culture's values and beliefs). The final outer layer represents symbols such as artefacts, architecture, words, and traditional clothing, but also symbols such as national flags. The three layers – rituals, heroes, and symbols (without values) – can be learned and acquired through practice (Hofstede, 2001).

The rich amount of literature on different typologies of national cultures makes it impossible to point out which framework is the most robust and comprehensive. This part of the chapter presents classifications presented by Hofstede et al. (2010) as six cultural dimensions ("6D"). They indicated, based on certain schemes of values, attitudes, preferences, and behaviours evaluated by the respondents in the empirical research, the following cultural groups:

- individualism–collectivism;
- power distance (high and low);
- uncertainty avoidance (high and low);
- masculinity–femininity;
- time orientation (long and short);
- restraint–indulgence.

Examples of cultures highlighted in the Hofstede study relative to individual dimensions are shown in Table 6.1.

In *individualistic* cultures, the individual is perceived as a basic community element. In *collectivistic* cultures, people are part of a larger group (family, organisation, and nation). Their identity is gained through belonging to the group. Individualists attach importance to individual decisions, independence, and responsibility. Collectivists, on the other hand, subordinate their private life to the social good, friendships are extremely important, as are family ties and all relationships.

The *power distance* is defined as the degree to which "less influential members of society" recognise that power is not distributed equally. This dimension determines inequalities and distances between people. It is connected with the existence and acceptance of hierarchies in various areas and social situations. There is acceptance of inequalities and significant hierarchies between people in high power distance cultures. Moreover, they are even desirable: less powerful persons

Table 6.1 Hofstede's cultural dimensions – examples of countries

Cultural dimensions	*Examples of cultures with higher-intensity characteristics*	*Examples of cultures with lesser-intensity traits*
Individualism	The United States of America, Canada, Australia	Turkey, Japan, Brazil, Thailand
Power distance	Malesia, Guatemala, Panama, Philippines, Mexico	Austria, Denmark, Ireland, Sweden, Norway, Finland
Uncertainty avoidance	Greece, Portugal, Guatemala, Uruguay, Japan, Turkey	Dania, Sweden, the United States of America, Canada
Masculinity	Japan, Austria, Venezuela, Switzerland, Italy, Mexico	Sweden, Norway, The Netherlands, Denmark, Finland
Long-time orientation	China, Japan, Germany, Russia	Mexico, Argentina, Australia, the United States of America
Restraint	Egypt, Russia, China, Poland	Mexico, the United States of America, Argentina

Source: Hofstede et al. (2010)

feel safer when they have superiors (in the company) who are responsible and they can rely on. In turn, in cultures of low power distance, partnerships and egalitarianism dominate, and all interpersonal inequalities should be reduced. At the same time, power can be used where necessary. Regarding the management of particular groups (individualistic or collectivistic), it should be pointed out that there are significant differences between superiors and subordinates in organisations of high power distance in terms of responsibilities, delegating tasks, and amount of salary (Hofstede et al., 2010). However, such situations and relations are positively evaluated or interpreted among members of high power distance groups. On the contrary, they feel safe and confident that hierarchically superior people will provide them with appropriate working conditions and take responsibility for the effects of the task's realisation. By comparison, low power distance cultures are characterised by partnership and egalitarian relations between superiors and subordinates.

Uncertainty avoidance can be defined as the degree of threat felt by community members in the face of new, unknown, and uncertain situations. It is thus an indicator of public sensitivity to changes in new situations and is difficult to predict. In cultures of low uncertainty avoidance, each day brings joy, before which there are no fears and reasons to feel anxiety or stress. Great respect is given to what is different here. The members of these cultures usually show a greater tendency to take risks. For example, people with low uncertainty avoidance change their jobs more often than people from high uncertainty avoidance groups in search of better conditions. The second group perceives the future as unknown and difficult to predict and as such, they are less risk-taking and do not like changes and uncertain situations.

Cultures described as *masculine* are characterised by significant activity in goal achievement (even to an aggressive level). They like to compete and achieve success, signing up to the mantra "live in order to work". The prevailing view is that a man should care for the family's material well-being, and a woman should take care of and protect children. Materialism dominates over disinterestedness, and money is necessary because one should seek independence (including financial independence). By contrast, for *feminine* cultures, the quality of life is not measured in material terms. They claim that people should "work in order to live". In addition, the "exchange" of roles between the sexes is observed here. For example, in feminine cultures, a man can replace a woman in an educational role. Women will more often take managerial positions, as well as taking on political functions or holding high state positions.

The *dimension of long- and short-time orientation* refers to time perception and planning. Short-time orientation cultures do not tend to save and plan for the long term. In turn, the effects resulting from current activities count for more. As such, there is an attitude towards short-term goals and concentration on the present. At the other end of the dimension, long-time orientation cultures are eager to save money for the future (mainly investing). They work and invest their time today to achieve positive future effects. These cultures are characterised by great patience and consistency in achieving their goals and intentions.

Lastly, the *indulgence–restraint* dimension presents the degree to which people can control their desires and impulses. Indulgence shows granting permission to fulfil an individual's fundamental and innate aspirations associated with experiencing joy and engaging in pleasurable activities (Hofstede et al., 2010). These cultures are characterised by a positive attitude to life and deriving joy from it, optimism, and a desire to meet the present needs. Free time is also valued in these cultures. The restraint dimension refers to the belief that pursuing happiness should be overseen and closely governed by societal standards (Hofstede et al., 2010). These cultures indicate tendencies of criticism and pessimism and a lack of emphasis on the importance of free time and satisfying their desires. Representatives of restrained cultures claim that social (and legal) norms limit human activities.

AR and culture in scientific research

Research on the influence of cultural characteristics on the adoption of AR technology is still only infrequently conducted, and as a result, the literature on the topic is limited. Perhaps this is partly due to the fact that elements of national culture are difficult to operationalise and measure in scientific research (Hasan & Ditsa, 1999), because of which the study of cultural differences may be a challenge (sometimes even a barrier) for researchers.

An analysis of the literature regarding how to consider the influence of cultural factors on the adoption of AR technology among consumers (and other consumer behaviours about the development of new technologies) indicates different methods. Therefore, the papers available in the literature can largely be divided into two groups. The first group of papers deals with studies where the authors use available data in the form of various cultural typologies (e.g. Hofstede's) and compare them with results on AR adoption in culturally diverse groups of consumers surveyed (e.g. Jadil et al., 2022; Im et al., 2011; Jung et al., 2018; Lee et al., 2013). Such papers were identified in the largest number during the literature review. In the second group, researchers measure the adoption of AR technology in different countries and compare the results while trying to explain the differences (if identified) through the prism of cultural diversity (e.g. Castillo & Bigne, 2021; Lee et al., 2020).

In the first group of indicated research and papers, the authors usually use the cultural dimensions identified by Hofstede. Some researchers have recognised uncertainty avoidance (UA) as the primary cultural factor that significantly shapes the differences in technology acceptance across various cultures (e.g. Cardon & Marshall, 2008; Sundqvist et al., 2005). However, there is no consensus on this among the authors. For example, Png et al. (2001) identified that societies with high UA are less likely to adopt new technologies.

Jung et al. (2018, 2020) presented one of the broadest studies on this matter. The authors measured the dependence of mobile AR adoption in cultural heritage tourism (the effects of aesthetics and perceived attributes, including enjoyment, on behavioural intention to use AR) on the cultural traits of respondents (Jung et al., 2018). This research was conducted among Korean (South Korea) and Irish (Ireland) tourists using Hofstede's cultural dimensions. The general findings underlined the importance of cultural differences in AR technology adoption. Some results were surprising in the light of literature and specifics of particular elements. For example, in Ireland's more masculine culture, the influence of perceived usefulness was moderate, and the influence of perceived ease of use was moderate. By contrast, the correlation between perceived enjoyment and the intention to use AR was more robust in South Korea's culture, characterised by higher power distance traits. Concerning the impact of social influence on the intention to use AR, participants from South Korea, where collectivism, higher uncertainty avoidance, and a greater power distance prevail, exhibited a greater reliance on social influence (Jung et al., 2018). In terms of time orientation, Korean representatives (long-term orientation) indicated the importance of educational elements in the use of AR technology, whereas representatives of the Irish group (short-term orientation) emphasised escapist experiences made possible through the use of AR applications (Jung et al., 2020).

Im et al. (2011) achieved similar findings concerning Korean culture earlier. The authors studied the relationships between the elements of the UTAUT model and the cultural traits of participants from Korea and the U.S. concerning two technologies that are the MP3 player and Internet banking. Hofstede's cultural dimensions were also used in that study. When examining Korea and the United

States, it was observed that the influence of perceived ease of use on the intention to use and the impact of intention on actual usage behaviour were more pronounced in the American sample (Im et al., 2011).

In another study, Lee et al. (2013) examined the influence of cultural features (again using Hofstede's dimensions) on mobile phone adoption patterns in the U.S. and South Korea. These results suggest that within individualistic societies like the United States, participants tend to gather information from direct and official channels independently. Conversely, within collectivistic cultures like South Korea, people rely more on the personal assessments of innovation shared by peers who have already embraced the innovation (Lee et al., 2013).

The first group of papers can also include the study of Jadil et al. (2022), who studied the relationship between cultural factors and consumer intentions towards s-commerce (social commerce). Using the meta-analysis method, Jadil et al. (2022) investigated the drivers of individuals' intentions according to s-commerce, including the cultural dimensions presented in Hofstede's model. They generally concluded that Hofstede's cultural dimensions significantly influence the adoption of decisions according to s-commerce. Similarly, Hung and Chou (2014) identified the relationships between cultural dimensions from Hofstede's model and the adoption of mobile commerce (m-commerce) using the TAM model in Taiwan and Malaysia. Their findings show that cultural dimensions such as uncertainty avoidance, individualism, and long-term orientation have a meaningful and similar impact on the perceived usefulness and perceived ease of use concerning the adoption intentions of mobile commerce in both countries. The other dimensions, such as power distance and masculinity, have different effects in Taiwan and Malaysia (Hung & Chou, 2014).

In another project, Feng and Mueller (2019) studied advertisements developed using AR technology in individualistic and collectivistic countries (the dimension from Hofstede's cultural model). These cultural characteristics proved an important variable in differentiating AR advertising messages. The main results indicate that AR ads in individualistic country groups contain product information and allow the user to control the virtual AR content. In contrast, ads created in collectivist countries typically allow the viewer to become part of AR (Feng & Mueller, 2019).

In the second group of scientific papers, Han et al. (2009) studied attitudes and purchase intentions towards AR services of tutoring robots in Japan, Korea, and Spain. The study found differences between the cultures studied. Spanish parents appeared to have more negative attitudes towards purchasing tutoring robots than Korean and Japanese parents. On the other hand, Korean parents had higher expectations for the practical use of tutoring robots in augmented reality services than Japanese and Spanish parents. Japanese and Spanish parents were more conservative towards robotic tutors than Korean parents, whilst Korean parents are the most liberal towards educating their children with AR service robots (Han et al., 2009).

In another study, Lee et al. (2020) conducted a cross-cultural comparison to examine the different relationships between technology visibility, consumer perceptions, and adoption intentions between Chinese and Korean consumers regarding virtual fitting rooms. Their findings showed that the adoption intention of the Korean group was influenced by their emotions and desire for immersive experiences, while the Chinese group focused more on practicality (Lee et al., 2020).

Monteiro et al. (2022) identified the factors of adopting virtual reality for practical learning with the UTAUT model and a cross-cultural analysis (in division into developed and developing countries and regions). The findings showed the differences between developing and developed groups concerning the particular elements of the UTAUT model. The authors explain these differences in attitudes concerning the technology development level, underlining that culture significantly impacts the factors linked to the willingness to utilise virtual reality as an educational tool (Monteiro et al., 2022).

In a similar discussion, Castillo and Bigne (2021) conducted research among consumers in the United States and Nicaragua (culturally and developing diverse markets). In their research, they developed a model that extends the Technology Acceptance Model (TAM) through factors that influence consumer acceptance of self-service technologies (SSTs) based on augmented reality (AR) in the retail sector. Referring to the TAM model, the findings indicate that elements such as aesthetics and navigation (exploring the interactive environment in different ways to find product-related information) are significant predictors of perceived usability and ease of use. Moreover, perceived ease of use also depends on consumers' sense of self-efficacy. At the same time, the authors also found that technological readiness and the need for personal interaction were not influential factors of perceived usefulness and ease of use. Importantly, for the purpose of the discussion in this chapter, the cross-cultural comparison in the Castillo and Bigne (2021) study showed that both countries had similar overall attitudes towards AR-based SSTs.

Conclusion

An analysis of papers available in scientific databases such as Scopus and Emerald concerning the relationship between the influence of cultural traits on attitudes towards and adoption of AR technology revealed that there has been little research in this area to date. Out of the research that was identified, one of the most valuable projects for the topic discussed in this chapter was that conducted by Jung et al. (2018, 2020).

The literature finds more correlations between the influence of cultural factors and other consumer activities related to the use of new technologies, such as mobile banking (e.g. Im et al., 2011; Kumar et al., 2023; Wu & Liu, 2023), the use of robots (e.g. Castelo & Sarvary, 2022; Han et al., 2009), m- and s-commerce (e.g. Harris et al., 2005; Hung & Chou, 2014; Jadil et al., 2022), or general attitude and acceptance of new technology (Wu & Liu, 2023) compared to attitude and adoption of AR technology.

Cross-cultural studies more often use the cultural characteristics identified in Hofstede's model, which justify certain behaviours in the countries/cultures studied. A smaller number of studies can be identified as comparative articles, in which the authors compare the behaviour of individuals and attempt to assess it in the context of cultural variation. There appear to be no studies where researchers try to measure both the cultural traits of individuals and the level of new technology adoption (including AR) by the consumers surveyed. This is a very important area for cross-cultural research and consumer acceptance of new technologies. These findings are of great applied importance as diverse stakeholders can use the knowledge of the cultural factors that affect consumer adoption of AR in effectively promoting and designing AR products and services.

Bibliography

Allal-Chérif, O. (2022). Intelligent cathedrals: Using augmented reality, virtual reality, and artificial intelligence to provide an intense cultural, historical, and religious visitor experience. *Technological Forecasting and Social Change, 178*. https://doi.org/10.1016/j.techfore.2022.121604

Alomar, N., Alsaleh, M., & Alarifi, A. (2019). Behavioral consequences of Pokémon GO: The exaggerated picture. *Computers in Human Behavior, 90*, 223–245. https://doi.org/10.1016/j.chb.2018.08.040

Alsharhan, A., Salloum, S.A., & Aburayya, A. (2021). Technology acceptance drivers for smart glasses in the middle east: A quantitative study. *International Journal of Data and Network Science, 6*(1), 193–208. https://doi.org/10.5267/J.IJDNS.2021.9.008

Ashraf, A.R., Thongpapanl, N., & Auh, S. (2014). The application of the technology acceptance model under different cultural contexts: The case of online shopping adoption. *Journal of International Marketing, 22*(3), 68–93. www.jstor.org/stable/43966458

Azuma, R.T. (1997). *A Survey of Augmented Reality, 4*(August), 355–385.

Bagchi, K., Cerveny, R., Hart, P., & Peterson, M. (2003). The influence of national culture in information technology product adoption. *Proceedings of the 9th Americas Conference on Information Systems (AMCIS)*, Paper 119 (pp. 957–965). Tampa, FL.

Baier, D., Rese, A., & Schreiber, S. (2015). Analyzing online reviews to measure augmented reality acceptance at the point of sale: The case of IKEA. In E. Pantano (Ed.), *Successful Technological Integration for Competitive Advantage in Retail Settings* (pp. 168–189). Hershey, PA: Business Science Reference.

Baker, E.W., Al-Gahtani, S.S., & Hubona, G.S. (2010). Cultural impacts on acceptance and adoption of information technology in a developing country. *Journal of Global Information Management, 18*(3), 35–58. https://doi.org/10.4018/jgim.2010070102

Bartosik-Purgat, M., Grzegorczyk, T., & Rakowska, W. (2021). Consumer acceptance of AR technology in e-commerce in the light of the Covid-19 pandemic: A conceptual perspective. In E. Mińska-Struzik & B. Jankowska (Eds.), *Towards the "New Normal" After COVID-19 – A Post-Transition Economy Perspective* (pp. 186–195). Poznań: PUEB Publications.

Bartosik-Purgat, M., & Rakowska, W. (2023). Cross-cultural business-to-business communication – The experiences of Polish companies with the Chinese and Americans. *International Journal of Emerging Markets, ahead-of-print* (ahead-of-print). https://doi.org/10.1108/IJOEM-01-2022-0013

Bartosik-Purgat, M., & Ratajczak-Mrozek, M. (2018). Big data analysis as a source of companies' competitive advantage: A review. *Entrepreneurial Business and Economics Review, 6*(4), 197–215. https://doi.org/10.15678/EBER.2018.060411

Baytar, F., Chung, T., & Shin, E. (2020). Evaluating garments in augmented reality when shopping online. *Journal of Fashion Marketing and Management*, *24*(4), 667–683.

Berman, B. (2019). Flatlined: Combatting the death of retail stores. *Business Horizons*, *62*(1), 75–82.

Boardman, R., Henninger, C.E., & Zhu, A. (2020). Augmented reality and virtual reality: New drivers for fashion retail? In G. Vignali, L.F. Reid, D. Ryding & C.E. Henninger (Eds.), *Technology – Driven Sustainability: Innovation in the Fashion Supply Chain* (pp. 155–172). Cham: Palgrave Macmillan.

Caboni, F., & Hagberg, J. (2019). Augmented reality in retailing: A review of features, applications and value. *International Journal of Retail & Distribution Management*, *47*(11), 1125–1140. https://doi.org/10.1108/IJRDM-12-2018-0263

Cardon, P.W., & Marshall, B.A. (2008). National culture and technology acceptance: The impact of uncertainty avoidance. *Issues in Information Systems*, *9*(2), 103–110.

Castelo, N., & Sarvary, M. (2022). Cross-cultural differences in comfort with human-like robots. *International Journal of Social Robotics*, *14*, 1865–1873. https://doi.org/10.1007/s12369-022-00920-y

Castillo, S.M.J., & Bigne, E. (2021). A model of adoption of AR-based self-service technologies: A two country comparison. *International Journal of Retail & Distribution Management*, *49*(7), 875–898. https://doi.org/10.1108/IJRDM-09-2020-0380

Daassi, M., & Debbabi, S. (2021). Intention to reuse AR-based apps: The combined role of the sense of immersion, product presence and perceived realism. *Information and Management*, *58*(4), 103453. https://doi.org/10.1016/j.im.2021.103453

Dacko, S. (2017). Enabling smart retail settings via mobile augmented reality shopping apps. *Technical Forecasting & Social Change*, *124*, 243–256.

Erdmann, A., Mas, J.M., & Arilla, R. (2021, September). Value-based adoption of augmented reality: A study on the influence on online purchase intention in retail. *Journal of Consumer Behaviour*, 912–932. https://doi.org/10.1002/cb.1993

Feng, Y., & Mueller, B. (2019). The state of augmented reality advertising around the globe: A multi-cultural content analysis. *Journal of Promotion Management*, *25*(4), 453–475.

Grzegorczyk, T., Sliwinski, R., & Kaczmarek, J. (2019). Attractiveness of augmented reality to consumers. *Technology Analysis and Strategic Management*, *0*(0), 1–13. https://doi.org/10.1080/09537325.2019.1603368

Han, J., Hyun, E., Kim, M., Cho, H., Kanda, T., & Nomura, T. (2009). The cross-cultural acceptance of tutoring robots with augmented reality services. *International Journal of Digital Content Technology and its Application*, *3*(2), 95–102.

Harris, P., Rettie, R., & Cheng, C.K. (2005). Adoption and usage of m-commerce: A cross-cultural comparison of Hong Kong and the United Kingdom. *Journal of Electronic Commerce Research*, *6*(3), 210–224.

Hasan, H., & Ditsa, G. (1999). The impact of culture on the adoption of IT: An interpretive study. *Journal of Global Information Management*, *7*(1), 5–15.

Hofstede, G. (2001). *Culture's Consequences: Comparing Values, Behaviors, Institutions, and Organizations across Nations* (2nd ed.). Thousand Oaks, CA: Sage Publications.

Hofstede, G., Hofstede, G.J., & Minkov, M. (2010). *Cultures and Organizations; Software of the Mind* (3rd ed.). New York: McGraw-Hill.

Holdack, E., Lurie-Stoyanov, K., & Fromme, H.F. (2022). The role of perceived enjoyment and perceived informativeness in assessing the acceptance of AR wearables. *Journal of Retailing and Consumer Services*, *65*, 102259. https://doi.org/10.1016/j.jretconser.2020.102259

Hung, C.L., & Chou, J.C.L. (2014). Examining the cultural moderation on the acceptance of mobile commerce. *International Journal of Innovation and Technology Management*, *11*(2), 1450010.

Im, I., Hong, S., & Kang, M.S. (2011). An international comparison of technology adoption. *Information & Management*, *48*(1), 1–8. https://doi.org/10.1016/j.im.2010.09.001

Jadil, Y., Jeyaraj, A., Dwivedi, Y.K., Rana, N.P., & Sarker, P. (2022). A meta-analysis of the factors associated with s-commerce intention: Hofstede's cultural dimensions as moderators. *Internet Research*, *ahead-of-print* (ahead-of-print). https://doi.org/10.1108/INTR-10-2021-0768

Javornik, A., Rogers, Y., Gander, D., & Moutinho, A. (2017). MagicFace: Stepping into character through an augmented reality mirror. *Proceedings of the 2017 CHI Conference on Human Factors in Computing Systems* (pp. 4838–4849). New York: ACM.

Jung, T.H., Lee, H., Chung, N., & tom Dieck, M.C. (2018). Cross-cultural differences in adopting mobile augmented reality at cultural heritage tourism sites. *International Journal of Contemporary Hospitality Management*, *30*(3), 1621–1645. https://doi.org/10.1108/IJCHM-02-2017-0084

Jung, T., Tom Dieck, M.C., Lee, H., & Chung, N. (2016). Effects of virtual reality and augmented reality on visitor experiences in museum. In A. Inversini & R. Schegg (Eds.), *Information and Communication Technologies in Tourism* (pp. 621–635). Cham: Springer.

Jung, T., Tom Dieck, M.C., Lee, H., & Chung, N. (2020). Moderating role of long-term orientation on augmented reality adoption. *International Journal of Human-Computer Interaction*, *36*(3), 239–250.

Khalil, S., Kallmuenzer, A., & Kraus, S. (2023). Visiting museums via augmented reality: An experience fast-tracking the digital transformation of the tourism industry. *European Journal of Innovation Management*. https://doi.org/10.1108/EJIM-09-2022-0479

Kim, J., & Forsythe, S. (2008). Adoption of virtual try-on technology for online apparel shopping. *Journal of Interactive Marketing*, *22*(2), 45–59. https://doi.org/10.1002/dir.20113

Kim, Y., Sohn, D., & Choi, S.M. (2011). Cultural difference in motivations for using social network sites: A comparative study of American and Korean college students. *Computers in Human Behavior*, *27*(1), 365–372.

Kumar, P., Chauhan, S., Gupta, P., & Jaiswal, M.P. (2023). A meta-analysis of trust in mobile banking: The moderating role of cultural dimensions. *International Journal of Bank Marketing*. https://doi.org/10.1108/IJBM-02-2022-0075

Lee, H., & Leonas, K. (2018). Consumer experiences, the key to surviving in an omnichannel environment: Use of virtual technology. *Journal of Textile and Apparel Technology Management*, *10*(3), 1–23.

Lee, H., Xu, Y., & Li, A. (2020). Technology visibility and consumer adoption of Virtual Fitting Rooms (VFRs): A cross-cultural comparison of Chinese and Korean consumers. *Journal of Fashion Marketing and Management*, *24*(2), 175–194. https://doi.org/10.1108/JFMM-01-2019-0016

Lee, S.G., Trimi, S., & Kim, C. (2013). The impact of cultural differences on technology adoption. *Journal of World Business*, *48*(1), 20–29. https://doi.org/10.1016/j.jwb.2012.06.003

Li, C.Y., & Fang, Y.H. (2020). I searched, I collected, I experienced: Exploring how mobile augmented reality makes the players go. *Journal of Retailing and Consumer Services*, *54*(151), 102018. https://doi.org/10.1016/j.jretconser.2019.102018

Martínez, H., Skournetou, D., Hyppölä, J., Laukkanen, S., & Heikkilä, A. (2014). *Drivers and Bottlenecks in the Adoption of Augmented Reality Applications*, *1*. https://doi.org/10.11159/jmta.2014.004

McLean, G., & Wilson, A. (2019). Shopping in the digital world: Examining customer engagement through augmented reality mobile applications. *Computers in Human Behavior*, *101*, 210–224.

Monteiro, D., Ma, T., Li, Y., Pan, Z., & Liang, H.N. (2022). Cross-cultural factors influencing the adoption of virtual reality for practical learning. *Universal Access in the Information Society*. https://doi.org/10.1007/s10209-022-00947-y

Oyman, M., Bal, D., & Ozer, S. (2022). Computers in human behavior extending the technology acceptance model to explain how perceived augmented reality affects consumers' perceptions. *Computers in Human Behavior*, *128*(December 2021), 107127. https://doi.org/10.1016/j.chb.2021.107127

Ozturkcan, S. (2021). Service innovation: Using augmented reality in the IKEA place app. *Journal of Information Technology Teaching Cases*, *11*(1), 8–13.

Papakostas, C., Troussas, C., Krouska, A., & Sgouropoulou, C. (2023). Exploring users' behavioral intention to adopt mobile augmented reality in education through an extended technology acceptance model. *International Journal of Human-Computer Interaction*, *39*(6), 1294–1302. https://doi.org/10.1080/10447318.2022.2062551

Phillips, L., Calantone, R., & Lee, M.L. (1994). International technology adoption. *Journal of Business & Industrial Marketing*, *9*(2), 16–28.

Png, I.P.L., Tan, B.C.Y., & Wee, K.L. (2001). Dimensions of national culture and corporate adoption of IT infrastructure. *IEEE Transactions on Engineering Management*, *48*(1), 36–45.

Rauschnabel, P.A., He, J., & Ro, Y.K. (2018). Antecedents to the adoption of augmented reality smart glasses: A closer look at privacy risks. *Journal of Business Research*, *92*(November), 374–384. https://doi.org/10.1016/j.jbusres.2018.08.008

Rauschnabel, P.A., Rossmann, A., & Tom Dieck, M.C. (2017). An adoption framework for mobile augmented reality games: The case of Pokémon Go. *Computers in Human Behavior*, *76*(August), 276–286. https://doi.org/10.1016/j.chb.2017.07.030

Rese, A., Baier, D., Geyer-Schulz, A., & Schreiber, S. (2017). How augmented reality apps are accepted by consumers: A comparative analysis using scales and opinions. *Technological Forecasting and Social Change*, *124*, 306–319. https://doi.org/10.1016/j.techfore.2016.10.010

Saleem, M.F., Asim, M., & Chandio, J.A. (2022). Effect of augmented reality advertising on purchase intention. *Journal of Marketing Strategies*, *4*(1), 157–172. https://doi.org/10.52633/jms.v4i1.164

Saleem, M.F., Kamarudin, S., Shoaib, H.M., & Nasar, A. (2022). Retail consumers' behavioral intention to use augmented reality mobile apps in Pakistan. *Journal of Internet Commerce*, *21*(4), 497–525. https://doi.org/10.1080/15332861.2021.1975427

Schapsis, C., Chiagouris, L., & Pham, N.C. (2021). Are consumers ready for augmented reality? Factors influencing online footwear purchasing intentions using AR technology. *Journal of Marketing Development and Competitiveness*, *15*(2), 21–36. https://doi.org/10.33423/jmdc.v15i2.4331

Shi, M., Zhang, C., & Hu, J. (2020). An innovative marketing strategy: Adopting AR & VR in jewelry sales. *2020 2nd International Conference on Applied Machine Learning (ICAML)*, Changsha, China, (pp. 333–338). IEEE.

Song, H.K., Baek, E., & Choo, H.J. (2019). Try-on experience with augmented reality comforts your decision: Focusing on the roles of immersion and psychological ownership. *Information Technology & People*, *3*(4), 1214–1234.

Sun, S., Lee, P.C., Law, R., & Zhong, L. (2020). The impact of cultural values on the acceptance of hotel technology adoption from the perspective of hotel employees. *Journal of Hospitality and Tourism Management*, *44*(March), 61–69. https://doi.org/10.1016/j.jhtm.2020.04.012

Sundqvist, S., Frank, L., & Puumaliainen, K. (2005). The effects of country characteristics, cultural similarity and adoption timing on the diffusion of wireless communications. *Journal of Business Research*, *58*, 107–110.

Venkatesh, V., Thong, J.Y.L., & Xu, X. (2012). Consumer acceptance and use of information technology. *MIS Quarterly*, *36*(1), 157–178. http://papers.ssrn.com/sol3/papers.cfm?abstract_id=2002388

Venkatesh, V., Thong, J.Y.L., & Xu, X. (2016). Unified theory of acceptance and use of technology: A synthesis and the road ahead. *Journal of the Association for Information Systems*, *17*(5), 328–376.

Wu, Z., & Liu, Y. (2023). Exploring country differences in the adoption of mobile payment service: The surprising robustness of the UTAUT2 model. *International Journal of Bank Marketing*, *41*(2), 237–268.

Yawised, K., Apasrawirote, D., Chatrangsan, M., & Muneesawang, P. (2023). Travelling in the digital world: Exploring the adoption of Augmented Reality (AR) through mobile application in the hospitality business sector. *Journal of Advances in Management Research*, *ahead-of-print* (ahead-of-print). https://doi.org/10.1108/JAMR-01-2023-0023

Yoon, S., & Oh, J. (2022). A theory-based approach to the usability of augmented reality technology: A cost-benefit perspective. *Technology in Society*, *68*(December 2021), 101860. https://doi.org/10.1016/j.techsoc.2022.101860

Part II

Cultural aspects of international business

7 Internationalisation of the company

Amica's path to the culturally diverse markets

Małgorzata Bartosik-Purgat, Alina Jankowska-Brzóska, and Michał Staszków

Introduction

Internationalisation is one element of the strategy of companies which aim to expand into foreign markets. Companies wishing to offer products and services beyond their domestic market choose different ways and forms (Bolivar et al., 2023; Nisar et al., 2012; Ti et al., 2023). Such decisions are often dictated by various motives, such as increasing production and seeking new markets, increasing profits, and reducing labour costs.

An essential step before making a decision to enter a specific country and determining the approach is to conduct a study of the foreign environment. This involves assessing the conditions in the foreign market where the company aims to expand. Among the aspects of the environment, the most commonly examined ones include economic, infrastructural, political, technological, sociocultural, and climatic conditions (Bartosik-Purgat, 2019; Cuervo-Cazurra et al., 2015). The elements of the foreign environment that are sometimes wrongly assessed as unimportant in international business are the cultural factors of a country (Bartosik-Purgat & Rakowska, 2023). These are sometimes described as invisible barriers to international activities, which, as it often turns out, are of great importance in the internationalisation process.

The main purpose of this chapter is to identify strategic cultural elements that could serve as significant barriers to entering new markets. These aspects are illustrated through the example of Amica, the largest leading manufacturer of household appliances in Poland. While Amica has been operating in Poland for almost 80 years, it is expanding its activities into other European countries.

The research methods utilised in the chapter are twofold: first, the literature review concerning the theories and research in the context of internationalisation will be employed; second, qualitative methods such as IDIs and observation are applied in order to prepare the case study. The databases used in the research were Emerald, Elsevier, and Taylor and Francis. Results related to the described

DOI: 10.4324/9781032636962-10

topics (such as internationalisation and cultural differences) are published in the journals included in these databases. However, the Polish company Amica has been rarely addressed in academic literature. To complement the available literature, additional sources – including journals and materials pertinent to the presented topic, such as Amica's annual reports – were explored. Furthermore, a case study detailing Amica's expansion in a culturally diverse market was crafted on the basis of in-depth interviews with top management responsible for the company's internationalisation.

The chapter first presents the internationalisation issue, its motives and forms, then moves to the cultural diversification of markets, especially concerning Hall's cultural dimensions. The subsequent section delves into the case of Amica and its evolution in selected international markets and cultures. Ultimately, the chapter concludes by offering insights, encompassing business implications and projections for the future.

Internationalisation – purposes, motives, and forms

Internationalisation means increasing economic involvement in international markets. It may take place sequentially, in stages or steps, and even occur at the beginning of the entity's existence, bypassing the stage of developing operations on the domestic market. Internationalisation may be based on expanding the sales market, optimising operating costs, or obtaining (e.g. in the form of a capital takeover) access to the raw material base, local brands, or distribution networks. In recent decades, the topic of internationalisation has been analysed by scholars in the fields of organisation theory, marketing, and broadly understood international business (Ruzzier et al., 2006). This is because the internationalisation process is a complex phenomenon influenced by various aspects, including financial, geographical, and cultural ones.

Classic theories of international trade, such as A. Smith's theory on differences in absolute production costs between countries and the theory of comparative costs by R. Torrens and D. Ricardo, did not focus on the role of enterprises as participants in international exchange. These theories mainly analysed economic aspects and did not consider capital expansion. However, criticism of these theories prompted more detailed research on the international expansion of enterprises, which resulted in

- theory of international trade by E. Heckscher, B. Ohlin, and R.A. Samuelson (H-O-S) – exchange between countries as a result of uneven distribution of production factors on a global scale;
- neo-factor theories, enriching the H-O-S theory with additional production factors – the engine of exchange may be human capital or natural resources;
- M.V. Posner's technology gap theory – technological innovations stimulate foreign expansion;

- J. Dreeze and D.B. Keesing's theory – international exchange as a benefit from the scale of production and sales;
- S.B. Linder's theory of product differentiation – exchange as a stimulator and the effect of intra-industry specialisation;
- S.B. Linder's concept of a unified demand structure – explains trade between countries with similar structures and levels of development.

Increasing processes and forms of internationalisation (not only exports but also licences, franchises, foreign direct investments, alliances, and mergers and acquisitions) have given rise to the need of creating new theories that also explain the development of the internationalisation process and international capital expansion of enterprises. Reddy (2014) analysed 67 studies on methods of internationalisation, including mergers and acquisitions, in which he summarised 17 theories describing internationalisation models, including the theory of foreign direct investment, market imperfections theory, theory of transaction cost economics, internalisation theory, eclectic paradigm, Uppsala theory of internationalisation, resource-based-view theory, resource dependence theory, theory of competitiveness advantage, agency theory, institutional theory, liability of foreignness concept, and market efficiency theory (Reddy, 2014). The number of theories related to internationalisation highlights the complexity of this topic and how it has evolved over recent decades.

The internalisation theory, rooted in the theory of monopoly advantage and drawing from R.H. Coase's theory of transaction costs (Williamson, 1999), posits that resources and activities deemed valuable and essential for current and future operations by the market or the enterprise should be retained within the enterprise or brought under its control (e.g. through foreign operations). Advantages associated with information and knowledge hold paramount significance in this context.

Dunning's eclectic theory of international production (OLI paradigm) (Dunning, 2001) is a compilation and creative development of several theories mentioned earlier. According to the OLI theory, undertaking international capital expansion is determined by several types of advantages that a company has. These are ownership-specific advantage – Oh, Location-specific advantage – L, and internalisation-specific advantage – I.

One of the commonly known theories regarding internationalisation is the so-called Uppsala model. This model explains internationalisation as a gradual and step-by-step process resulting from a company's acquisition of knowledge and experience in international operations. The development of internationalisation is a result of the so-called cumulative cyclical processes, as described by Johanson and Vahlne (2006). The information gathered, and positive experiences from initial internationalisation attempts reduce uncertainty and encourage more advanced steps, in terms of both time and capital commitment. Still, accumulating knowledge about the foreign market requires overcoming resistance to new challenges.

Signals coming from abroad are often interrupted or distorted by factors such as geographical distance, language, and cultural differences. Expansion into a foreign market often becomes an option considered only after exhausting the possibilities in the domestic market. While there are studies that challenge the notion of gradual internationalisation, such as research on the "phenomenon of born global" (Sharma & Blomstermo, 2003), many companies persist in their international expansion efforts by adhering to the principles of the Uppsala model (Wach, 2012).

As in the case of numerous theories and research on the essence of internationalisation, there are many studies on the motives of internationalisation (e.g. Daszkiewicz, 2016; Benito, 2015; Cuervo-Cazurra et al., 2015; Reddy, 2014). One of the first classifications was proposed by Hollander (1970), who divided motives into commercial and non-commercial. Dunning (2001) listed four main motives for internationalising companies: searching for resources, searching for markets, increasing efficiency, and acquiring strategic assets. Yip and Hult (2011) also identify the following four elements: market factors, cost factors, government factors, and competitive factors. Cuervo-Cazurra et al. (2015) reviewed the motives for internationalisation and presented their classification based on behavioural economics:

- *sell more* – where the company leverages its current resources and security in more favourable conditions in the host country;
- *buy better* – where the company exploits its existing resources while steering clear of unfavourable conditions in its home country;
- *upgrade* – where the company searches for new resources and security in more favourable conditions in the host country;
- *escape* – where the company seeks new resources while avoiding unfavourable conditions in its home country.

One of the most important strategic decisions of a company is the form in which it will expand abroad. Wach (2012) divided the forms of internationalisation into three groups:

- export – indirect export, direct export, cooperative export;
- contractual – assembly transactions, management contracts, turnkey investments, sub-deliveries, licences, franchises;
- investment – foreign branch, joint venture, daughter company.

In a comprehensive review of the literature on internationalisation, Reddy (2014) defined *growth strategies*, which included, among others, joint ventures, strategic alliances, and mergers and acquisitions. In the case of Amica, foreign expansion often took the form of acquisition. In the theory of organisation and management, researchers indicate that one of the fundamental motives for using the form of acquisition is the desire to strengthen market shares and the effectiveness of the company's operation on the global market (Coeurdacier et al., 2009). The process of taking over a company in a foreign market involves not only legal but also cultural difficulties. Rottig (2017) indicates that some of these operations do not achieve their intended goals and show high failure rates. Despite the relatively low chances of success, acquisitions remain a crucial tool that multinational corporations use to expand their business. The number, size, and importance of such acquisitions are expected to continue to increase in the context of the progressing globalisation of world economies. Therefore, it becomes essential to better understand the factors that influence the success or failure of such acquisitions. When trying to identify factors that influence the success or failure of acquisitions, researchers pay particular attention to the challenges associated with integrating organisations with different cultures (Rottig, 2017). Rottig's research (Rottig et al., 2013; Rottig, 2017) delves into the impact of cultural differences on the effectiveness of the acquisition process, confirming the intricate nature of enterprise internationalisation.

Cross-cultural dimensions

The multifaceted nature and complexity of national culture and management at the intersection of different cultures have led researchers to distinguish models that take into account specific features of cultures. They are known in the literature as classifications or cultural dimensions and typically illustrate the two extreme sides of a specific feature among different nations or cultural groups, between which there are examples of lesser intensity. Identifying these cultural dimensions for a given cultural group enables an awareness of the potential behaviours of employees from that culture and facilitates the development of appropriate management activities.

This section of the chapter presents classifications selected on the basis of the degree of their implementation in cultural diversity management, as outlined by E.T. Hall (1989). The classifications include different types of communication (high-low context communication) and attitudes towards time (monochronic and polychronic time).

In the first division, the essential element is the degree of using context in establishing contact, communication, and maintaining partnership. In this respect, Hall (1989) has distinguished between *high- and low-context* cultures. According to his interpretation, in the first group (high-context), only a small part of the information falls within the directly encoded part of the message, most of the information is embedded in context. In low-context cultures, most of the information is in the direct code (Hall, 1989). Selected examples of cultures in Hall divisions are presented in Table 7.1.

High-context cultures rely on indirect communication, often using terms and expressions understood only by members of their cultural group. This communication style is not designed to pose challenges for individuals outside the cultural

Table 7.1 Hall's dimensions – examples of cultures

Criterion	*Cultural dimensions*	
Level of context	**High context**	**Low context**
	Japan, China, Thailand and other Asian cultures, France, Spain, Italy, East and West Africa, Saudi Arabia, Argentina, Brazil, Chile, Colombia, Greece	Australia, Austria, Canada, Denmark, Finland, Germany, Ireland, Great Britain, The Netherlands, Sweden, Switzerland, the United States
Attitude to time	**Monochronic**	**Polychronic**
	Germany, Sweden, Norway, Finland, Japan, the United States, Canada	Arab countries, Latin American countries, South and Southeast Asia

Source: Hall (1989)

context; instead, it represents a standard way of conveying information. High-context communication often involves understatement and silence, especially when expressing negation or disagreement, which those from different cultures may misinterpret. In high-context cultures, "yes" may not always signify agreement, and "no" may not always indicate refusal; sometimes, the true meaning must be inferred. Non-verbal cues, such as hand gestures and facial expressions, play a significant role because verbal communication is not always the primary channel (Verluyten, 2014).

In Eastern cultures, using the word "no" is very common. However, the situation is quite different in Asian countries. The Japanese, for instance, use the word *hai* ("yes") very often, but it does not mean that they agree with everything. Indeed, the word *hai* often expresses an understanding of what is being said rather than consent. When negotiating with Asians, it is essential to understand that "yes" is not always an affirmative response. Before taking "yes" for an answer, one must ascertain if it was merely a polite response that meant no. Asian businesspeople are not likely to say "no" directly to a proposal; instead, they reply in ways that are synonymous with "no."

Additionally, high-context cultures are groups focused on building long-term relationships with a desire to get to know the other person. In these cultures, understanding the other party and building trust take precedence over hastily completing a one-time transaction, which applies to all forms of cooperation. They place a strong emphasis on individuals for whom trust is the paramount factor in collaboration. For this reason, sometimes the oral form of a contract becomes the standard one, as it is concluded with people and not with companies. The oral form of contract is a manifestation of trust in cooperation. In high-context cultures (predominantly Asian), there is also the concept of face-saving. It refers to the image which a person achieves in the group (society, organisation, and family). The "loss of face" by an individual also compromises the group (a reference to collectivism), for it weakens the group. China represents a culture that is characterised by high-context features. Two Chinese cultural terms that are crucial for understanding business practices in this part of the world (and other parts of Asia) are *mianzi* and *guanxi*. *Mianzi* pertains to the concept of "face", representing the social status or image that an individual or an institution (including a company) holds in society or a particular group. *Mianzi* is acquired through the fulfilment of social roles recognised and highly valued by group members. It also involves adhering to group-established rules, building a societal reputation, and displaying hospitality.

As previously noted, high-context cultures significantly influence the development of long-term relationships, emphasising a preference for conducting business with individuals or entities they are familiar with. This is why they actively cultivate relationships with numerous individuals, other companies (such as suppliers and distributors), and other collaborating institutions (e.g. *guanxi* in China). *Guanxi* is a "complex cultural construct deeply rooted in China that centres around the exchange of favours to establish trust and strong connections" (Niedermeier et al., 2016, p. 36). The *guanxi* concept concerns not only the relationships between individuals (family members, friends, business partners, etc.) but also those between companies (suppliers, deliverers, government institutions, etc.), which are presented as connections, exchanging information and support among parties who belong to *guanxi* (Chang et al., 2017). The connections achieved by building *guanxi* create significant and strategic advantages for businesspersons. *Guanxi* is something more than interpersonal relationships because it refers to relations (very often informal relationships) that include obligations and trust. The basis for those social connections is mutual interests and benefits for both sides. The significance of *guanxi* lies in the fact that Chinese businesspeople typically avoid initiating relationships with individuals unknown to them. Having *guanxi* implies a mutual exchange of favours among people, whether they are occupied with business or work for public institutions.

By contrast, *low-context cultures* communicate directly, expressing their thoughts and views very clearly. Context is not essential for understanding the message. It is a literal situation – "yes" usually means "yes" and "no" means "no" (Verluyten, 2014). There are no allusions, symbols, indirect messages, or the importance of non-verbal language (verbal communication is more critical). The individuality of expressing traits is also observed in representatives of low-context groups, as they are generally individualists who rely on themselves. Information, facts, arguments and statistical data are also crucial for the representatives of these cultures (they believe in numbers more than intuition). The implications of this attitude and the nature of such communication are evident, for example, in presentations for various forums. These presentations are often rich in tables, charts, or quotes from industry experts. In low-context cultures, information, and data are deemed trustworthy when supported by empirical research. Additionally, a fast and efficient transaction is essential. While building relationships is significant, it may not be as crucial at the initial stages of cooperation. In low-context cultures, strict adherence to a contract is essential, and collaboration is often formalised through a written contract concluded between the companies represented by individuals.

Hall (1989) also emphasises the importance of participants' attitudes to time in cross-cultural communication. In a subsequent attempt at classification, Hall points to *monochronic cultures*. These cultures place great importance on punctuality and adhering to previously planned schedules, unlike *polychronic cultures*, which tend to treat time more flexibly.

Monochronic cultures count on punctuality, planning, development, and the implementation of schedules. Most activities are aimed at achieving effects (benefits) in the future. Representatives of monochronic cultures are accustomed to well-organised work and focus on one task at a time because scattering can destabilise actions and lead to delays in achieving goals. Working time is strictly separated from personal time.

In polychronic cultures, the attitude to time is more flexible than in the case of monochronic cultures. Schedules are essential in planning and organising tasks but can be changed if necessary. Breaks in the workday play an essential role, even at the expense of extended working hours, as they contribute to the establishment of relationships between employees. They have a more beneficial effect on cooperation. Compared to monochronic cultures, individuals in polychronic cultures often handle multiple tasks simultaneously, and the boundary between working time and personal time is less distinct. The collaboration between individuals with highly monochronic and polychronic tendencies may initially face challenges such as a lack of understanding, ambiguities, irritations, and conflicts. Successfully navigating these differences requires a high level of tolerance, awareness of the existing variations, and a mutual effort to understand each other among business partners or co-workers. Armed with this understanding, one can mitigate the adverse effects of diverse perceptions of time.

Amica Inc.

History, products, and international expansion

The history of Amica Inc. dates back to 1945 when the Metal Products Factory was established in Wronki near Poznań, Poland. In the early days, the company offered services related to overhauling tractors and agricultural machinery. It was not until 1957 that the company introduced coal and gas cookers under the Wromet brand as one of the first manufacturers on the Polish market. The next landmark year in the company's history was 1961, when the reconstruction of the plant and production of gas cookers was completed, increasing production capacity. This enabled the first steps in the company's foreign expansion. Due to Poland's political situation, companies operating in this country could export to the USSR. The company expanded its international experience in the 1980s under the name Wromet. During this period, it initiated the export of stoves to the German market, marking its initial venture into Western expansion ("Mediateka (AMICA)", n.d.).

In the initial years following the commencement of the transformation of the Polish economy in 1993, the company transformed into a state-owned entity known as Amica Holding Inc., and a year later, it underwent privatisation. The brand Amica was established in 1992. The company's listing on the Warsaw Stock Exchange in 1997 facilitated investment activities and the initiation of foreign expansion. The post-privatisation development strategy, with a focus on foreign expansion, has proven to be successful.

Nowadays, Amica Group stands as a prominent European home appliance manufacturer with nearly 80 years of industry experience. The company offers a comprehensive range of intelligent large and small household appliances, known for practical solutions, cutting-edge technology, and contemporary design. Amica Group's operations are categorised into commercial and manufacturing segments. Commercial activities involve outsourcing the production of appliances beyond the country (e.g. Asia) designed and manufactured under the special supervision of dedicated Amica teams and transporting them to target markets. Manufacturing activities revolve around the production of household appliances (e.g. ovens, floor-standing kitchens, and various types of cooktops) at the production plant located in Wronki. Additionally, a significant aspect of the company's business is providing maintenance services for electrical and gas appliances.

The Amica brand is one of the most recognisable brands in Poland, and thanks to its regional brands, its products are also known in other European countries. The group's portfolio includes brands: Amica (Central and Western Europe), Hansa (Eastern Europe), Gram (Scandinavia), CDA (the United Kingdom), and Fagor (Spain and France). It employs more than 3,000 people worldwide, thanks to which it delivers about 5 million appliances a year to customers in nearly 70 markets worldwide. Today, Amica Group is an international company – 70% of the company's revenues are generated outside Poland ("Amica: Raport Roczny 2021 (AMICA)", 2022). As a result of its trading activities in various countries, the Group also has offices in the UK, France, Spain, Germany, the Czech Republic, Denmark, Kazakhstan, and Ukraine.

The main steps in building Amica Group's foreign expansion were the following ("Amica: Raport Roczny 2021 (AMICA)", 2022; Borzęcki, 2023; "Mediateka (AMICA)", n.d.; "Nasze marki (AMICA)", n.d.; "Amica zwiększa obecność w Chinach (AutomatykaB2B)", 2019; "Grupa Amica rozwija swoją sprzedaż w Chinach (InfoWire.pl)", 2020; Supernak, 2021; Borzęcki, 2023):

- the 1990s – establishing by Amica, a company in Germany – the first subsidiary;
- 1997 acquisition of Hansa brand – Hansa is a brand that today is present in most markets in Eastern Europe (e.g. Ukraine, Lithuania, Latvia, Estonia, and

Moldova), parts of Southern Europe (e.g. Bulgaria, Hungary, Romania, Balkans countries, and Greece), as well as Central Asia. The Hansa brand offers innovative technology, modern design, and quality at an affordable price. Its product range includes freestanding kitchens, dishwashers, and built-in ovens, among others;

- 2000 – acquisition of the Danish traditional brand Gram, present in Denmark since 1899. It is distinguished primarily by its distinctive product design and high-quality workmanship. Gram has been present in the Amica portfolio since 2001. It offers products valued not only by Scandinavians but by customers and proponents of northern style and design. It is available in Denmark, Norway, Sweden, Finland, and Iceland;
- 2009 – Amica Group is developing its own sales channels in China with distribution points spread throughout the market. Amica brand products are perceived as prestigious by Chinese customers. For example, in Shanghai, the Group's business partner Qingdao Gram Appliances has opened a Gram showroom where customers can also see the company's other brands, namely Amica, CDA, Fagor, and Hansa;
- 2012 – the establishment of a subsidiary of Hansa Ukraine;
- 2015 – acquisition of the British brand CDA. CDA is a British brand of high-quality home appliances based in Nottinghamshire. The brand strives to make its products a practical and stylish part of many kitchens. CDA's products are available in the United Kingdom and Ireland;
- 2017 – acquisition of the French Sideme. This distributor of home appliances specialises in supplying a broad portfolio of products under distributors' trademarks and private labels: Curtiss, Le Chai, and Caviss. These brands are recognised primarily in France and the Benelux countries. Sideme has plans to distribute products under the Fagor brand in the French market;
- 2019 – long-term Fagor brand licence agreement in Spain. Fagor Electrodoméstico offers reliable household appliances equipped with the latest technology. Under the Fagor brand, Amica offers heating appliances, washing machines, refrigerators, dishwashers, hoods, and microwave ovens in Spain, France, and Portugal, with plans to relaunch the brand in other countries, where the Fagor brand is known;
- 2021 – establishing a company in Hansa Central Asia (Kazakhstan). The main task of this company is to develop sales of the Hansa brand throughout the Central Asian region.

Amica's international development is significant, primarily in European markets and, in recent years, also in Asia. In this expansion, Amica employs various processes and forms of internationalisation (e.g. acquisitions, and subsidiaries), as described in the theoretical part of this chapter. Each of these forms has its advantages and disadvantages. However, regardless of the form of internationalisation or the stage of development in a foreign market, Amica strives to operate according to the saying, "In business, we think globally, we act locally". For Amica's management, "locally" means considering the conditions of a given foreign market. The presence of Amica and its brands in diverse countries is a commitment for its employees and customers. Significant differences related to the conditions existing in individual markets often involve cultural challenges for Amica's managers and key decision-makers.

Cultural differences in the international expansion of Amica

The internationalisation of companies offers numerous benefits for their development, including gaining new markets for products, acquiring existing products and brands in foreign markets, and the opportunity to compete globally. However, these decisions often present challenges for managers entering culturally distant markets. In the case of Amica, cultural differences played a crucial role in acquisitions in markets such as the United Kingdom, France, and Spain. In Asia, cultural differences also presented significant challenges for Polish managers at Amica. To a lesser extent, these differences became a barrier to expanding into the German or Scandinavian markets, although some variations in management style and business operations were also noted in these regions. The following paragraphs outline the most significant cultural differences encountered during the internationalisation of Amica's operations in selected countries.

When preparing to acquire a company in a foreign market, Amica always conducts due diligence, which involves an examination of the general condition of the company. Due diligence covers various aspects of the company's functioning, including financial, legal, commercial, tax, and technological (Porsgaard et al., 2018). However, due diligence typically does not include an examination of the organisational culture of a particular company and the national culture of a given country, which significantly influences organisational behaviour.

Sometimes, the failure to recognise prevailing cultural differences in a given market is attributed to the acquiring company's mindset of understanding the market segment and industry. Companies acquiring foreign entities may assume that knowing everything about a particular industry segment in one country means they also understand the same business in other countries. Nonetheless, this approach is misleading because business processes, even within the same industry but in different markets, can differ. These differences encompass various aspects, including values, norms, customs, hierarchical systems, and many other elements that constitute national culture.

In the acquisition process, both parties should familiarise themselves with the applicable rules of business conduct and behaviour in the workplace. After the acquisition, efforts should be made by both parties to understand the differences arising from other cultural systems and tolerate them. Unfortunately, cultural differences are often ignored by acquirers, and they do not treat them as an essential element that needs to be considered during the preparations. Acquirers may try to adapt the acquired company to their own "rules of the game", which, in turn, can be met with resistance from the other side.

The United Kingdom

Amica entered the UK market through the acquisition of the UK company CDA. This form of internationalisation allows Amica to be present in the UK. During the acquisition process, the decision was made to create several specialists known as synergy managers to facilitate the acquisition process with minimal conflicts. Several individuals in these synergy manager positions were chosen to be sent from Poland to the acquired British company.

The idea of creating such a position was innovative, however, the lack of a detailed action plan related to this position hindered its initial success. Moreover, the British side was not adequately prepared to receive these specialists, and the goals and benefits for both parties were not effectively communicated. Consequently, the synergy managers were unsure about their tasks and acted chaotically. Additionally, employees of the British company did not perceive the benefits of these activities and began to downplay them. Communication was undoubtedly a significant barrier to introducing these specialists and their acceptance by the employees of the British company. Brits tend to be indirect in expressing themselves, stating what they think. Poles often tend to use direct communication, even with expressing negative opinions and critical remarks.

Stereotypical perceptions of one culture over another can also pose challenges in the British market. In the British market, Poles are often perceived as employees who are managed rather than as superiors or decision-makers. The difficulties in accepting different roles by employees of a British company, unfortunately, contribute to communication problems in the relationship between the subsidiary and the parent company. Representatives of the British company expect support from the parent company when problems arise, along with ongoing monitoring. Poles would like to have an ongoing influence on the UK business, while the company wants to operate independently, expecting support from the parent company only when problems arise.

The mentioned problems between representatives of both companies are indeed attributed to cultural differences related to communication, the importance and perception of hierarchy in the organisation, and stereotypes.

Denmark

The acquisition of the Danish brand Gram has enabled Amica to enter Scandinavian markets. Significant cultural differences in business and management styles have led the Danish company to seek a high degree of independence from the Polish company. The primary reason is the substantial difficulty in accepting the Polish management style, which is autocratic and relies on delegating decisions rather than working them out collaboratively. Scandinavian countries' culture emphasises the importance of the quality of life and the significance of achieving a work–life balance. These differences sometimes lead to uncomfortable situations in the cooperation between the investor (Amica) and the Danish subsidiary, especially when outsourcing additional tasks and arranging meetings. Examples include the late organisation of business meetings by the Polish company, while the Danes would also like to have time for themselves and their families during the working day.

France

Amica entered the French market by acquiring the French company, a distributor of home appliances. Initially, as an investor, Amica conducted due diligence on the acquired business. During due diligence, it became evident that there were unacceptable issues in the acquired company according to Amica's standards. The decision was made to investigate and address these issues in detail after the acquisition and the payment of some of the outstanding money. However, this approach proved to be less effective, as the motivation to resolve problems, especially on the French side, decreased after the takeover. Cultural differences in the approach to working with foreigners influenced the emergence of contentious situations during cooperation. For instance, the French have difficulty accepting decisions made for them (in this case, decisions by representatives of Amica as an investor). This behaviour sometimes leads them to downplay decisions made by Amica managers and make their own, which often differ significantly.

Furthermore, the polychronic nature of Amica's French business partners sometimes influences how work is organised. These characteristics of French business partners contribute to their perception by Polish managers that they (French) work chaotically, impacting situations where the French side encounters difficulties in meeting deadlines. Standards regarding schedules, the importance of deadlines, and work organisation differ between the acquired French company and the Polish investor's company. Communication problems also arise because the French representatives belong to a moderately contextual culture, while Polish managers communicate in a polite but direct manner. Additionally, depending on the region, communication issues may arise due to different levels of English proficiency. The ideal solution would involve Polish managers being proficient in French.

Spain

In Spain, Amica is present thanks to a long-term brand licence agreement with Fagor, the Spanish manufacturer of household appliances. Spain is a vast and culturally diverse market. The style of doing business, the organisation of the working day, communication methods, and the approach to time can vary significantly depending on whether the company is based in Malaga, Barcelona, Bilbao, or Madrid. Negotiations mainly took place in the Basque country. Contrary to stereotypical perceptions of Spaniards by Poles, negotiations at Fagor proceeded in a well-thought-out and organised manner, in a calm and collaborative atmosphere.

The experience of Polish managers working with Fagor representatives in Madrid reveals that Spaniards are diligent and dedicated to business development. They view cooperation with a Polish company as a project to be accomplished rather than a daily obligation tied to their work and the necessity of being present in the office for several hours. Their working hours differ from the Polish norm: they work four or five days a week, with work on Fridays concluding around 2.30 p.m. In the summer, the work schedule changes due to high temperatures, with work ending in the late afternoon. During the summer months, Spaniards generally work until 3 p.m. but commence work earlier.

The examples from Western European markets illustrate Amica's internationalisation path through acquisitions, as attempts to establish greenfield operations were unsuccessful, partly due to low brand recognition. The aforementioned cases highlight the contrasting management styles between the Polish company and firms in the mentioned markets. The Polish management style tends to be more autocratic, resembling styles observed in Eastern Europe. Conversely, the described markets favour a more partnership-oriented approach, with organisations preferring an independent model of thinking and action. These companies, in their relationship with the headquarters (Amica), prefer participation in decision-making, which is better received than accepting pre-made decisions at the headquarters level for implementation.

The challenges in communication and the perception of hierarchies may also be influenced by the characteristics of the generation occupying senior managerial positions in Polish companies. Currently, the majority of top managers in the Polish market belong to Generation X. Many Polish managers from Generation X are known for their intense work ethic, often at the expense of work–life balance, which may be incomprehensible to their counterparts in the same generation in Western European countries and younger generations. These differences in lifestyles and perceptions of the surrounding world likely impact business success as well.

Polish managers representing Amica describe the German business style as orderly and stable, characterised by clearly defined business processes. They observe similarities between the German and Polish business styles, including high punctuality, a formal way of communicating, and shared features in organisational culture. This commonality is also noted in the management of German companies, aligning with what has been indicated about the functioning of Polish companies and managers. Still, the formal communication tends to diminish in younger representatives and those working together for an extended period. Such a diverse situation is observed when considering Asian cultures.

China

Amica's managers emphasise that in the case of countries where the culture of doing business differs significantly from that of Europe (e.g. China), it is best to learn the basics of business savoir-vivre before the first meeting with representatives of that culture. In China, Amica set up a representative office to assist with supplier relations. This allowed the company's products to make their presence felt in East Asian markets. During the cooperation with Chinese partners, Amica's employees pointed out several very important aspects that differentiate their style of doing business from that of the Chinese market and neighbouring cultures.

According to Polish managers, one of the first tasks foreigners face is understanding and respecting *guanxi* and *mianzi*. This is an essential element of the Asian style of doing business of building long-term relationships and trust with the other party in the process of negotiation and getting to know each other. Next, negotiations should not be conducted aggressively, as in such a situation, one can often encounter a refusal to cooperate. Managers from Amica involved in Asian markets also stressed the importance of maintaining "face" (*mianzi*). They stress that negative expressions of opinion or unfavourable feedback given to a Chinese person in the presence of others can make him "lose face" (lose *mianzi*).

In negotiations and business interactions in China, Polish negotiators emphasised the significance of various elements of business protocol, which may be overlooked in Western European markets. For instance, the exchange of business cards follows a specific protocol in Chinese culture. It is customary to present the card with both hands, preferably with a slight bow, and using one hand is considered disrespectful. In Asian cultures, a business card holds significant importance and can serve as a representation of the individual in their absence.

Moreover, the behaviour during a business dinner in China has notable differences from European business protocols. The host leads the table and is usually the most critical person in the Chinese team, initiating the dinner and inviting others to start their meal. Chinese restaurants that host foreign guests often have round tables that can be rotated, allowing everyone to sample various dishes. Rice is served at the end of the meal, and it's considered a superstition to stick chopsticks into the rice (as it is believed to bring misfortune). Instead, chopsticks are placed aside. Chinese dinners usually commence and conclude early, with establishments closing around 10 p.m.

According to Amica managers involved in the company's development in China, local employees, especially those representing the Eastern part of the country, are very well prepared to cooperate with Europeans. Mostly, they are very familiar with English and European business savoir-vivre. In addition, many of them educate their children (often the successors of the companies) in European schools and thus are very familiar with European realities.

Describing the case of Amica's development in Eastern markets, one should also highlight the situation of women in business and the home appliance industry. It is puzzling that few women are in the presented industry, especially in sales positions and company management.

Conclusion

The foray of a company into a foreign market invariably entails risks and challenges stemming from variations in different facets of the environment. Among the foremost factors which influence the success of the internationalisation process are cultural disparities.

In the context of Amica, the Polish company's internationalisation encounters challenges primarily rooted in cultural dimensions, notably differentiating communication styles, time perceptions, hierarchical structures, and approaches to building relationships and trust. Consequently, Amica employs culturally tailored strategies to penetrate foreign markets. A fundamental principle contributing to success in these markets is the acknowledgement and respect for local values and customs in business dealings.

Amica has adopted various solutions, one being carefully delineating the general manager's role. Optimal results are often achieved by appointing a local manager who possesses familiarity with the market and its culture. However, this approach would involve additional time for the manager and Amica to define rules of cooperation. Another strategy involves appointing a Polish individual who knows very well the Polish management style and easily understands the needs of the mother company but, on the other hand, will need to adapt to the new cultural environment. Finally, the management skills and ability to adapt to new environments prevail in decisions about the general manager for foreign markets. Delegating an appropriate degree of autonomy in business decision-making to local managers, without undue daily oversight and imposition of Polish practices, also proves effective. This aligns with the ethos of "thinking globally in business but acting locally".

However, what remains paramount to success in the internationalisation process is the genuine eagerness to comprehend the values, customs, and behaviours of individuals from diverse cultures. Cultivating openness and tolerance towards new cultures undoubtedly plays a pivotal role in fostering success in international endeavours.

Bibliography

AMICA. (2022, March 31). *Amica: Raport Roczny 2021*. https://odpowiedzialnybiznes.pl/wp-content/uploads/2022/04/amica_2021_skonsolidowany_raport_roczny_final.pdf

AMICA. (n.d. a). *Mediateka*. https://press.amica.pl/mediateka

AMICA. (n.d. b). *Nasze Marki*. www.amica-hm.pl/pl/4/strona/2/nasze_marki

AutomatykaB2B. (2019, December 31). *Amica zwiększa obecność w Chinach*. https://automatykab2b.pl/gospodarka/52122-amica-zwieksza-obecnosc-w-chinach

Bartosik-Purgat, M. (2019). *New Media in the Marketing Communication of Enterprises in the International Market*. Warsaw: PWN Publications.

Bartosik-Purgat, M., & Rakowska, W. (2023). Cross-cultural business-to-business communication – The experiences of Polish companies with the Chinese and Americans.

International Journal of Emerging Markets, *ahead-of-print* (ahead-of-print). https://doi.org/10.1108/IJOEM-01-2022-0013

Benito, G.R. (2015). Why and how motives (still) matter. *The Multinational Business Review*, *23*(1), 15–24.

Bolivar, L.M., Casanueva, C., & Castro Abancéns, I. (2023). International alliance networks, expansion modes and coopetition. *Multinational Business Review*, *31*(2), 197–219. https://doi.org/10.1108/MBR-06-2022-0091

Borzęcki, A. (2023, June 23). *Czy gwiazda polskiego eksportu otrząśnie się z marazmu? Różnica między tempem rozwoju a wyceną jest zaskakująca! Analiza fundamentalna specjalnie dla FXMAG*. www.fxmag.pl/artykul/tylko-na-fxmag-analiza-fundamentalna-gwiazdy-polskiego-eksportu-zaskakujaca-roznica-miedzy-tempem-rozwoju-biznesu-a-wycena-gieldowa

Chang, E.C., Chou, T.J., Huang, C., & Wang, X. (2017). The categories, rules, and demonstrations of *Guanxi* in Chinese society. *Journal of Business-to-Business Marketing*, *23*(4), 311–325.

Coeurdacier, N., De Santis, R.A., & Aviat, A. (2009). *Cross-Border Mergers and Acquisitions: Financial and institutional forces*. www.ecb.europa.eu/pub/pdf/scpwps/ecbwp1018.pdf

Cuervo-Cazurra, A., Narula, R., & Un, C.A. (2015). Internationalization motives: Sell more, buy better, upgrade and escape. *Multinational Business Review*, *23*(1), 25–35. https://doi.org/10.1108/MBR-02-2015-0009

Daszkiewicz, N. (2016). *Internacjonalizacja przedsiębiorstw działających w branżach high-tech*. Warsaw: PWN Publications.

Dunning, J.H. (2001). The eclectic (OLI) paradigm of international production: Past, present and future. *International Journal of the Economics of Business*, *8*(2), 173–190.

Dunning, J.H., & Lundan, S.M. (2008). *Multinational Enterprises and the Global Economy*. London: Edward Elgar Publishing.

Hall, E.T. (1989). *Beyond Culture* (2nd ed.). New York: Anchor Books.

Hollander, S.C. (1970). *Multinational Retailing*. East Lansing: Michigan State University Press.

InfoWire.pl. (2020, December 20). *Grupa Amica rozwija swoją sprzedaż w Chinach*. https://infowire.pl/generic/release/477810/grupa-amica-rozwija-sprzedaz-w-chinach

Johanson, J., & Vahlne, J.E. (2006). Commitment and opportunity development in the internationalization process: A note on the Uppsala internationalization process model. *Management International Review*, *46*, 165–178.

Niedermeier, K.E., Wang, E., & Zhang, X. (2016). The use of social media among business-to-business sales professionals in China. *Journal of Research in Interactive Marketing*, *10*(1), 33–49.

Nisar, S., Boateng, A., Wu, J., & Leung, M. (2012). Understanding the motives for SMEs entry choice of international entry mode. *Marketing Intelligence and Planning*, *30*(7), 717–739.

Porsgaard, C.B., Haubjerg, M., & Hansen, Z.N.L. (2018). A framework for operational due diligence. *Production Engineering Research and Development*, *12*, 633–645. https://doi.org/10.1007/s11740-018-0842-z

Reddy, K.S. (2014). Extant reviews on entry-mode/internationalization, mergers & acquisitions, and diversification: Understanding theories and establishing interdisciplinary research. *Pacific Science Review*, *16*(4), 250–274.

Rottig, D. (2017). Meta-analyses of culture's consequences for acquisition performance: An examination of statistical artifacts, methodological moderators and the context of emerging markets. *International Journal of Emerging Markets*, *12*(1), 8–37.

Rottig, D., Reus, T.H., & Tarba, S.Y. (2013). The impact of culture on mergers and acquisitions: A third of a century of research. *Advances in Mergers and Acquisitions*, *12*, 135–172.

Ruzzier, M., Hisrich, R.D., & Antoncic, B. (2006). SME internationalization research: Past, present, and future. *Journal of Small Business and Enterprise Development*, *13*(4), 476–497.
Sharma, D.D., & Blomstermo, A. (2003). The internationalization process of born globals: A network view. *International Business Review*, *12*(6), 739–753.
Supernak, B. (2021, July 20). Grupa Amica założyła w Kazachstanie spółkę Hansa Central Asia. *Inwestycje.pl*. https://inwestycje.pl/biznes/grupa-amica-zalozyla-w-kazachstanie-spolke-hansa-central-asia/
Ti, L.L., Ng, B.K., & Rasiah, R. (2023). Motivations behind SME greenfield investment in emerging markets. *Management Decision*, *61*(6), 1656–1676. https://doi.org/10.1108/MD-04-2022-0482
Verluyten, S.P. (2014). *Intercultural Skills for International Business and International Relations: A Practical Introduction with Exercises*. Haag: Acco Publications.
Wach, K. (2012). *Europeizacja małych i średnich przedsiębiorstw: Rozwój przez umiędzynarodowienie*. Warszawa: Wydawnictwo Naukowe PWN.
Williamson, O.E. (1999). Strategy research: Governance and competence perspectives. *Strategic Management Journal*, *20*(12), 1087–1108.
Yip, G.S., & Hult, G.T.M. (2011). *Total Global Strategy*. Princeton, NJ: Prentice Hall.

8 Cultural barriers in Foreign Direct Investments

The case of Zanglory Investments Ltd. in Zanzibar

Wiktoria Rakowska, Łukasz Puślecki, and Dorota Malicka

Introduction

Foreign Direct Investments (FDIs) have become a highly dynamic force in international economic activities, alongside the trade in goods and services (Gomółka et al., 2020). FDI, often considered one of the most extensive forms of internationalisation, entails substantial financial commitments and a deep engagement with foreign markets (Götz, 2020). This strategic approach involves investing in and establishing operations in a foreign country, which sets it apart from other, less involved methods of international business expansion, such as exporting or licensing. FDI typically requires a long-term commitment and a significant capital investment, as companies aim to establish a physical presence and tap into new markets, sometimes even necessitating changes to their existing operational practices to cater to local market requirements.

Several variables significantly impact FDI location choice: economic, political, technological, and socio-demographic. Among the factors that can influence the internationalisation process as well are cultural differences (Bartosik-Purgat, 2019).

Over the past ten years, cultural factors as explanations for foreign investments have been increasingly recognised and acknowledged (Kapás & Czeglédi, 2020). However, the existing body of literature remains somewhat restricted, not just in the quantity of research conducted but, more crucially, in terms of the profound influence that culture wields on foreign investments (Bhardwaj et al., 2007; Kayalvizhi & Thenmozhi, 2018; Kristjánsdóttir et al., 2020). Indeed, when deciding to internationalise in the form of FDI, companies tend to select a country with a similar culture (Lucke & Eichler, 2016). However, many contradictions are also noted (Holmes et al., 2013), such as China's numerous FDIs in Africa (countries with a highly different cultural background).

Companies are increasingly drawn to culturally diverse countries in the contemporary global business arena, especially emerging markets (Beugelsdijk et al., 2018; UNCTAD, 2023). The appeal lies in the potential to access a broader customer base, develop cross-cultural expertise, and tap into substantial growth opportunities. However, this approach has its complexities. Firms must adeptly

DOI: 10.4324/9781032636962-11

navigate cultural differences and manage risks tied to regulations and infrastructure in these markets.

This study examined the cultural differences that emerged during Zanglory Investments Ltd.'s foreign direct investment (FDI) endeavours in the Zanzibar region. Zanglory Investments Ltd. is a Polish construction firm registered in Zanzibar, specialising in real estate construction and management on Pemba Island. The company has been operating in Zanzibar effectively since 2021, continuously grappling with challenges stemming from cultural differences.

To achieve its research objective, the study formulated two primary research questions:

RQ1: What were the primary cultural challenges for Zanglory Investments Ltd. in foreign direct investment in Zanzibar country?

RQ2: What activities can assist companies in effectively managing cultural differences during their expansion into new foreign markets?

A methodological approach was developed to address the research questions involving a narrative literature review and utilising qualitative techniques. This included a semi-structured interview with the Market Development Manager of Zanglory Investments LTD. and observational methods, all employed in the case study preparation. The study primarily sourced data from databases including Emerald, Elsevier, and Web of Science, as well as scientific reports and Zanglory Investments' website.

This chapter is structured as follows: it begins by delving into the body of literature on Foreign Direct Investment (FDI), encompassing its definition, various forms, and the driving motives behind it. Next, it explores the concept of cultural distance, defines it, and elaborates on how it can impact FDI. Subsequently, it offers a detailed case study focusing on the operations of Zanglory Investments in Zanzibar. To conclude, it aligns the findings with the broader academic conversation, ultimately shaping conclusions and providing actionable recommendations.

Foreign Direct Investment – definition, forms, and motives

Foreign Direct Investment (FDI) is defined as international capital flows to expand a company's operations beyond national borders. It embodies the notion of investments made by individuals, businesses, or governments from one country into an enterprise located in another. The hallmark of FDI is that it involves acquiring substantial control or influence over the foreign entity, typically by owning at least 10% of its shares (OECD, 1996). FDI is not merely a financial transaction; it represents a deep commitment to engage in, shape, and benefit from the global economy. Foreign Direct Investment is considered the most advanced mode of internationalisation, signifying a substantial resource commitment and greater risk when contrasted with other methods of entering foreign markets (Götz, 2020).

In the literature, several forms of Foreign Direct Investments are identified, each varying in the activity's degree of involvement and purpose. One option is horizontal expansion, which involves extending operations into fresh markets or geographic areas within the same industry. Alternatively, the company can pursue vertical growth by entering new domains of operation, such as taking on responsibilities for supply chain management or post-sales service (Bi et al., 2020).

FDI can also be divided by the degree of control and ownership the investing company seeks to exert over its foreign operations. In greenfield investment, a company establishes an entirely new business operation in another country. This typically involves building new facilities, factories, and offices and developing operations from scratch on undeveloped land (Emodi et al., 2022). Brownfield investments refer to investments made in existing industrial or commercial facilities, properties, or projects, typically involving the redevelopment, refurbishment, or expansion of these properties. We can distinguish (Chen et al., 2019):

- merger and acquisition (M&A): FDI through mergers or acquisitions entails acquiring an existing foreign company or merging it with one's operations. This can involve purchasing a controlling stake or the entire company;
- joint ventures: joint ventures represent a partnership between companies from different countries to jointly manage a new business or project. Each partner contributes and shares responsibilities and profits;
- cross-border mergers: cross-border mergers involve combining two or more companies from different countries to create a new entity, often headquartered in a different country.

Deciding on the most suitable method to expand into foreign markets is a multifaceted process that can significantly influence the success of a business. This process is not to be taken lightly, as it thoroughly evaluates various factors, including market conditions, competitive landscape, regulatory environments, and resource capabilities. The Ownership-Location-Internalization (OLI) framework, also known as the eclectic paradigm, developed by Dunning (1977) is a significant theoretical framework in international business and Foreign Direct Investment. It provides a comprehensive and systematic approach to understanding when firms engage in FDI. The OLI framework postulates that there are three key factors influencing a firm's decision to invest abroad: ownership, location, and internationalisation motives (Table 8.1).

Dunning's Eclectic Paradigm posits that a firm's foreign value-adding activities are contingent upon three critical conditions. First, firms should possess unique and sustainable Ownership Advantages (O) that set them apart from their competitors. Second, they must weigh the benefits of adding value to their

Table 8.1 Motives for Foreign Direct Investments

Motives	*Description*
Ownership advantage	Ownership advantages refer to a firm's unique benefits or assets, which can be in the form of proprietary technology, brand recognition, managerial skills, or other competitive strengths. Firms with distinctive ownership advantages are likelier to seek international expansion to leverage these assets in foreign markets.
Location advantage	The significance of the host country's characteristics. Location advantages include access to resources, a favourable business environment, market size, infrastructure, and other factors that make a particular country an attractive destination for FDI. Firms seek locations that offer complementary assets to enhance their competitiveness.
Internationalisation advantage	These advantages arise from the firm's desire to control its foreign operations and the transaction costs of utilising external markets or partners. Indicate when it is more favourable for an organisation to handle the production of a specific product internally, as opposed to outsourcing it to a third party.

Source: Own elaboration based on Dunning (1977)

Ownership Advantages internally rather than selling them to foreign firms, a concept referred to as Internalisation Advantages (I). Finally, the Location Advantages (L) of a foreign market play a crucial role in determining the extent to which companies are interested in creating, accessing, or leveraging their Ownership Advantages in that particular location (Batschauer da Cruz et al., 2022). In line with this model, to engage in FDI effectively, a company must possess all three groups of advantages (Pak & Park, 2005). Without any of these motives, the company should explore alternative approaches for entering the market or consider staying at the domestic one (Kimiagari et al., 2023).

When expanding their operations globally, companies encounter a range of pivotal choices, including determining the location and scale of investments, as well as structuring and managing foreign ventures to optimise gains while mitigating risks and setbacks. This process of internationalisation involves strategic decision-making (Beugelsdijk et al., 2018; Marano et al., 2016). Consequently, it becomes crucial to gain a comprehensive understanding of the factors that can either drive the success or hinder the progress of Foreign Direct Investment. In identifying these determinants, researchers emphasise the challenges associated with commencing business activities in culturally diverse environments (Kostova et al., 2018; Magnusson et al., 2008). Therefore, effectively managing these cultural divergences can exert substantial influence over a company's performance in foreign markets. This underscores the importance of cultural sensitivity and adaptability for enterprises venturing into international realms.

Cultural differences in Foreign Direct Investments

Despite the increased interconnectedness of countries facilitated by globalisation, cultural differences persist as a significant influence on international business, drawing the interest of scholars (Bartosik-Purgat & Rakowska, 2023; Leung et al., 2005; Srivastava et al., 2020). Cultural distance becomes particularly relevant in understanding how these differences shape the dynamics of cross-border interactions and business operations (Könning et al., 2021; Orsini & Magnier-Watanabe, 2023).

Cultural distance is defined as the differences between the national cultural characteristics of home and host countries (Hofstede, 2001). This concept, first introduced by Kogut and Singh (1988), pertains to the disparities in cultural norms, practices, religions, and values between nations, which can profoundly impact the success of FDI ventures. In the literature, the concept of cultural distance has been examined in various ways, with one of the most commonly used methods being the application of Hofstede's cultural dimensions (Bhardwaj et al., 2007; Kayalvizhi & Thenmozhi, 2018; Kristjánsdóttir et al., 2020; Yayla et al., 2023). This approach involves authors comparing the specific levels of each of these dimensions between the host country and the home country of the multinational corporation. Hofstede's cultural dimensions (2001) emphasise six primary cultural factors that can shed light on cultural differences (Table 8.2).

In addition to Hofstede's dimensions, cultural differences can also become evident in communication (Bartosik-Purgat & Rakowska, 2023). In the domains of communication and business, the studies carried out by Hall (1976) and Gesteland (2003) hold a prominent and pervasive position. Hall classified cultures into low-context (e.g. Scandinavian countries, Germany, and Switzerland) and high-context (e.g. Japan, China, Arabian, and Latin American countries) based on their communication style. Low-context cultures favour direct, precise, and open communication. High-context cultures employ indirect, ambiguous, and reserved communication with many metaphors and gestures, often leading to misunderstandings (Chen et al., 2020). Trust, relationships, and the concept of "face" hold importance in high-context cultures.

Effective communication in international business hinges significantly on the objectives of the participants, whether it is establishing long-term cooperation or conducting single, transactional interactions. Central to this process is the role of relationships. Gesteland's framework (2003), which categorises cultures into relationship-focused and deal-focused, sheds light on this dichotomy. Relationship-focused cultures prioritise building trust and interpersonal connections as the foundation for successful communication. This approach often requires

Table 8.2 Hofstede's cultural dimensions

Cultural dimensions	*Description*
Power distance	This dimension reflects the extent to which a society accepts and expects an unequal distribution of power and authority within organisations and institutions.
Individualism vs. Collectivism	It measures the balance between individual and collective interests in a given culture. Individualistic cultures prioritise personal goals, while collectivist cultures emphasise group cohesion and interdependence.
Masculinity vs. Femininity	Masculine cultures emphasise assertiveness, competition, and achievement, while feminine cultures focus on cooperation, nurturing, and quality of life.
Uncertainty avoidance	It assesses a culture's tolerance for ambiguity and propensity to rely on rules, regulations, and structured systems to reduce uncertainty.
Long-term orientation vs. Short-term orientation	This dimension examines a society's orientation towards future rewards and planning. Long-term-oriented cultures emphasise persistence, thrift, and adaptability, while short-term-oriented cultures prioritise immediate gratification.
Indulgence vs. Restraint	It focuses on a culture's approach to enjoying life and having fun. Indulgent cultures are more permissive and value personal happiness, while restrained cultures emphasise controlling desires and impulses.

Source: Own elaboration based on Hofstede (2001)

more time and patience in negotiations and collaboration (Thanetsunthorn & Wuthisatian, 2019). In contrast, deal-focused cultures emphasise professional, task-oriented relationships and efficient transactions, often displaying readiness to engage with unfamiliar partners. Recognising and adapting to these cultural differences in the significance of relationships is paramount in building successful international business relationships (Bartosik-Purgat & Rakowska, 2023).

In cultural distance, time-related aspects also hold significant importance, influencing the dynamics of cross-cultural interactions. This is particularly evident in the contrast between polychronic and monochronic time orientations (Hall, 1976; Gesteland, 2003). Polychronic time cultures, often found in regions like the Middle East and Latin America, emphasise the fluid and simultaneous handling of multiple tasks and prioritise interpersonal relationships over punctuality. In these cultures, time is considered more elastic, and flexibility in scheduling is common. On the other hand, monochronic time cultures, prevalent in Western societies, prioritise sequential, precise scheduling and punctuality. Time is often viewed as a finite and linear resource (Dathe et al., 2023). Significant cultural differences between countries in areas such as time perception, communication styles, trust-building, religion, and other facets are indicative of a high cultural distance.

Studies examining the influence of cultural differences on Foreign Direct Investment (FDI) reveal that culture significantly impacts choices related to market entry strategies (Ha et al., 2020; Yiu & Makino, 2002), FDI location decisions (Siegel et al., 2012), and effective management (Alofan et al., 2020). According to the cultural familiarity theory, firms are less inclined to invest in countries with substantial cultural divergence, and their performance tends to be less favourable when they do so (Du et al., 2012). Similarly, Bhardwaj et al. (2007) delved into the impact of two cultural factors, namely, uncertainty avoidance (Hofstede, 2001) and trust from the World Values Survey (WVS), along with their combined effects on FDI. Their findings substantiated their hypotheses: higher uncertainty avoidance correlates with reduced inward FDI, while greater trust is associated with increased inward FDI.

Siegel et al. (2012) obtained similar outcomes, however, using a different approach to the culture measurement. Instead of using Hofstede's cultural dimensions, they examined cultural aspects using Schwarz's cultural dimensions, emphasising egalitarianism. The key findings of their research revealed that cultural disparities, in a broad sense, impact decisions regarding the location of Foreign Direct Investment (FDI). Notably, the study highlighted that a higher degree of disparity in egalitarianism had an adverse effect on FDI inflows.

Nevertheless, some contradictions arise, and companies increasingly opt for investments in culturally distant countries (UNCTAD, 2023). Western businesses, driven by intensifying global competition, are pursuing internationalisation strategies on an unprecedented scale, often venturing into relatively "distant" realms encompassing developing and emerging host countries. Concurrently, emerging market enterprises vigorously expand their presence in distant Western territories (Gubbi et al., 2010; UNCTAD, 2023). In light of this context, it may be essential to re-evaluate the traditional belief that cultural differences pose obstacles to international expansion. Instead, strategies should be more emphasised for effectively managing these differences (Beugelsdijk et al., 2018). Understanding and managing cultural distance are paramount for companies engaging in international expansion, as it can either facilitate or hinder the achievement of their strategic objectives in foreign markets.

As an example of a company that ventured into investment in a distant and relatively unfamiliar African country like Tanzania, Zanglory Investments serves as a prime illustration. A case study has been designed on the basis of the company's experiences in foreign direct investment. Within this analysis, the principal cultural challenges faced by the company are elucidated, alongside the effective strategies deployed to address these obstacles.

Zanglory Investments Company Limited in Zanzibar

Zanzibar – general characteristics

Situated along the East African coast, Zanzibar is a dynamic archipelago characterised by its two main islands, with Unguja being the more celebrated of the two, complemented by the still developing Pemba Island. The archipelago boasts a rich and diverse cultural tapestry, as this island paradise has long been a melting pot of various influences, including African, Arab, Indian, and European. This unique blend of traditions, customs, and practices defines the cultural richness of Zanzibar. One of the most striking facets of Zanzibar's culture is its strong Swahili influence, with Swahili being the primary language spoken on the islands. The local population takes immense pride in their Swahili heritage (Maoulidi, 2011).

In contrast to the rest of Tanzania, Zanzibar is predominantly Muslim, with Islam playing a central role in daily life (GOV, 2023). Islamic principles often guide their daily routines and interactions, and this influence extends to their dress code. Modesty in clothing is commonly observed, with many women wearing hijabs and men donning traditional Islamic attire. The cultural and religious values deeply embedded in the society impact not only the attire but also the general conduct and practices of the island's residents.

Zanglory Investments Company Limited – history

Zanglory Investments Company Limited was established in 2021. It is notable for its unique structure, as it is funded by a private investor from Poland but registered in Zanzibar, granting it local status. The company's origins can be attributed to two main driving forces. Firstly, Zanglory Investments leverages over two decades of experience in the Polish land development sector. This extensive history has endowed the company with an in-depth understanding of the complexities and opportunities within the real estate industry.

The second driving force behind the creation of Zanglory Investments is rooted in thorough research conducted on Pemba and Unguja. These picturesque islands inspired the company's founder. During their time on these islands, Investor encountered numerous international visitors who expressed a common desire: to invest in the captivating coastal regions or own property along the Indian Ocean shoreline. However, the intricacies of such investments often remained challenging due to their obligations in their home countries, which limited their ability to navigate the process effectively. Recognising the increasing market demand and comprehending the obstacles faced by individual investors, the management of Zanglory Investments identified a prime opportunity for Foreign Direct Investment in Zanzibar.

Acknowledging the specific needs of individual investors, the company uncovered an overlooked market with a strong demand for suitable housing and investment opportunities, especially in Pemba, where tourism is still in its developmental stages. Given Pemba's less advanced development compared to Unguja, the main island of Zanzibar, it presents significant untapped potential for expansion. Consequently, the management of Zanglory Investments decided to construct a residential development on Pemba that would meet these needs while providing attractive and competitive solutions in the real estate market.

Cocco Lagoon: a haven on Pemba Island

Cocco Lagoon stands as the first 5-star condominium resort on Pemba Island. Managed by Zanglory Investments (SMC-Private) Company Limited, this project encompasses an area of 4 hectares, offering an oasis of luxury with its opulent villas and apartments. The project's primary objective is to introduce a diverse range of accommodations, comprising two villas, one bungalow type, and three distinct apartment buildings, totalling around 250 units. This venture attracts a dual clientele: those who desire to purchase beachfront villas and apartments for personal use and investors seeking opportunities for generating passive income.

Cocco Lagoon not only provides residents with ownership of these properties but also paves the way for investors. The compound is thoughtfully designed to transform into a fully operational hotel complex, ensuring income generation even when property owners opt not to reside on the island. The property management, hotel services, concierge assistance, and a spectrum of amenities, including a lagoon-sized swimming pool, beachfront bar, spa, water sports, and recreational facilities, are meticulously orchestrated by Zanglory Investments Ltd. Cocco Lagoon endeavours to harmoniously blend the allure of a tropical paradise with the practicality of a sound investment, making it an alluring destination for both residents and investors alike.

Exploring land acquisition challenges on Pemba Island

In January 2021, before the establishment of Zanglory Investments, one of the project managers embarked on a journey to Pemba Island in the Indian Ocean. The primary mission was to immerse in the local culture, understand the community, and grasp the region's intricacies, anticipating smoother future operations. However, the outset was far from easy.

Communication emerged as one of the initial hurdles on Pemba Island. It quickly became evident that the local population needed to improve their English proficiency. While a few government offices know English, most interactions require an assistant to bridge the gap between Swahili, the local language, and English. This challenge underscored the significance of effective cross-cultural communication.

The journey into property acquisition on Pemba Island unveiled a distinctive process entirely dissimilar to conventional land acquisition in places like Poland. Here, foreign investors could only purchase land if they registered a project in the Zanzibar Investment Promotion Authority (ZIPA) or were clients under a previously registered project. This regulation aimed to safeguard the island against indiscriminate land purchases by foreigners, preventing the lands from falling into disuse and later being sold.

Delving into the island's land ownership structure, it became apparent that it was far from straightforward. Most land parcels lacked official surveys, and extended families typically owned them for generations. Verifying ownership required onsite visits by judges, gathering witness testimonies, and obtaining permission letters from local Sheha (village representatives). Negotiating financial terms with numerous family members, often numbering, posed its own set of challenges.

During the first meetings, the price of land was prohibitively high, making negotiations particularly challenging, given the difficulty in conveying the limitations of the available budget. The Project Manager had the onerous task of elucidating the project's objectives and ensuring that the venture would create employment opportunities, primarily focusing on hiring individuals from the local community to convince them to sell the land and accept the foreign investor.

The local community's substantial demands for land acquisition necessitated a delicate balance between budget constraints and their expectations. Communicating effectively and building mutual understanding was essential to align these expectations with the project's scope. In addition to clarifying the project's intentions and the promise of job creation, the Project Manager had to underscore the significance of prioritising local employment. This was an essential commitment, considering the island's substantial unemployment rate.

Navigating these negotiations and demonstrating the project's commitment to the local community required patience, cultural sensitivity, and a deep appreciation of the island's socio-economic context. The willingness to engage in these discussions and the firm commitment to fulfilling promises proved instrumental in overcoming the initial land acquisition hurdles. These early experiences underscore the significance of effective communication, cultural awareness, and the commitment to local empowerment.

Religion

In the context of implementing the project in Zanzibar, religion emerged as a significant factor influencing various aspects of the operation. Given the prominent role of Islam in the region, the first consideration was adhering to appropriate dress codes. It was not uncommon for local administrative personnel to express concerns or even refuse service if they found the attire of Zanglory Investments' representatives to be inappropriate. A conservative and respectful dress code was adopted to navigate this challenge, emphasising the importance of respecting the local culture.

Furthermore, the practice of Islam had a noticeable impact on daily activities. Local workers would pause their daily tasks to participate in prayer sessions. This routine interruption was a cultural norm deeply ingrained in the workday, and foreign investors had to adapt and accommodate these religious practices in their project planning and scheduling. To further accommodate the employees' religious needs, particular prayer areas were established in the workplace. These designated areas allowed workers to perform their daily prayers, highlighting the commitment to respecting and facilitating their religious practices. This thoughtful gesture reinforced the importance of harmonious coexistence and cultural sensitivity in the project's execution.

Time management

Cultural diversity plays a pivotal role in shaping the dynamics of international business operations. Companies venturing into foreign markets often confront myriad cultural distinctions that influence their day-to-day operations. The case of Zanglory Investments, a Polish company investing in Zanzibar, serves as an excellent illustration of how understanding and adapting to cultural subtleties are essential for successful business endeavours.

One of the fundamental cultural differences that international companies must grapple with in Zanzibar is the perception of time. Being late for meetings and consultations is not considered a sign of disrespect; it is a common occurrence, often stemming from unforeseen circumstances. Understanding the local perspective is crucial in doing business in Zanzibar because punctuality is rarely observed as a virtue. As a result, foreign investors must be prepared to demonstrate patience and flexibility, recognising that waiting is often an integral part of the process. The Swahili saying "POLE POLE", meaning "slowly, slowly", reflects the local approach, emphasising the importance of taking one step at a time. In this context, attempting to expedite matters can be met with bewilderment.

In the context of the Cocco Lagoon project, the risk analysis identified several key challenges, one of the most significant being the potential for project delays. These delays could arise from many factors, including bureaucratic processes, cultural nuances, and regulatory hurdles. The project's success hinged on the team's ability to navigate these challenges effectively.

A prominent example of this challenge manifested during the application process for construction permits. The initial assumption was that all permitting proceedings could be streamlined through the One Stop Center, represented by ZIPA on Zanzibar Island, despite the project's location on Pemba Island. However, in practice, this centralised approach encountered resistance from local officials and stakeholders who felt marginalised in the application process.

Recognising the importance of local relationships and respect for all stakeholders, the team swiftly adapted its approach. It was essential to demonstrate the commitment to fostering positive relations with the local community and officials. Consequently, the company began liaising with both ZIPA PEMBA on Pemba Island and the central ZIPA office on Zanzibar Island, ensuring that all stakeholders were involved in the permitting process. The bureaucracy involved in obtaining construction permits was far from straightforward. While the theoretical timeline for processing permits was approximately two weeks from the submission of complete documentation, the practical reality was often far more complex. Frequent follow-ups were essential to ensure that all required documents were in place and that the documents had transitioned from the intake desk to the department responsible for issuing construction permits.

The meticulous oversight of these processes was crucial to maintaining efficiency; only after an official site visit, which often involved not only government officials but also engagement with the local community adjacent to the project site, was the construction permit granted. This site visit underlined the importance of direct relationships and the pivotal role of personal interactions in securing approvals.

Building relationships

In building a business, particularly in the context of Zanzibar, the dynamics can often defy conventional expectations. While Polish business ventures may hinge on meticulous documentation, on the Zanzibar archipelago, the foundation of business and relationships lies in a more unconventional tool: WhatsApp. This stark contrast was a revelation to the initial employees of the Cocco Lagoon project, who embarked on the pre-development phase on the island. Here, it is not uncommon for most officials and politicians to readily exchange their private phone numbers, and even during office visits, requests for official documentation are often routed through WhatsApp, as it is deemed faster and more convenient.

The Zanzibari business culture places a profound emphasis on personal relationships and face-to-face interactions. While business communication predominantly occurs in Poland via emails and phone calls, in Zanzibar, the norm is personal meetings. Establishing bonds with local stakeholders, delving into their family lives, and displaying a genuine interest in their daily affairs are integral to conducting business. Notably, it is commonplace for individuals working in government offices, and even politicians, to readily share their private phone numbers, engage in discussions about personal matters, and extend invitations to foreign business partners for casual coffee sessions. These interactions are regarded as gestures of friendship and mutual trust, and the act of a personal visit is a profound sign of respect. A practical illustration of this cultural norm can be witnessed in the operations of Zanglory Investments, which is actively involved in investments in the Wambaa area. Before initiating any business activities, the company took meticulous steps to secure the local community's investment consent. The "Sheha", a local community representative, was consistently informed about significant events, permissions, and reports as a mark of respect. Cultivating a close relationship with the local community was deemed crucial to ensure that Zanglory's operations harmonised with the local culture and that the company was perceived as a respected and welcoming presence.

Furthermore, observing and acknowledging all national and religious holidays are imperative. Sending well wishes on these occasions is considered a courteous gesture, and the same applies to birthdays and other significant life events. In Zanzibar, these cultural nuances underscore the essence of genuine human connection in business operations and serve as a testament to the significance of embracing local customs and practices in pursuing successful business ventures.

Communication

Effective communication has been a persistent challenge for businesses operating in Zanzibar's culturally vibrant yet distinctive environment. Zanzibaris often uphold a cultural ethos that extols possibility and positivity, readily affirming that anything can be accomplished, even in situations where practicality may dictate otherwise. The inherent cultural aversion to refusal is noteworthy, and it frequently results in officials granting preliminary approvals and accepting document submissions for procedures, only to later encounter insurmountable hurdles. In challenging situations, the local community would often draw upon the reassuring mantra "HAMNA SHIDA", which means "Don't worry", emphasising that there are solutions to every problem and encouraging a positive outlook. This discrepancy can lead to significant time losses, as during follow-ups, affirmation is maintained that everything remains possible and is currently in the procedural pipeline, only to culminate in an ultimate rejection. This challenge has been a significant facet of the business landscape, characterised by a cultural optimism that contrasts with the need for clear, forthright procedural guidance.

The high-context communication prevalent among the residents of Zanzibar posed a considerable challenge for Polish representatives of the company. They grappled with the nuances of this cultural communication style, often needing clarification to discern which statements should be taken seriously. The intricate dance of understanding and acceptance proved to be a perplexing experience, as the cultural context embedded in Zanzibari interactions required heightened sensitivity. Navigating this high-context communication landscape was paramount for the Polish representatives, as it dictated the success of their business endeavours in this culturally rich yet distinct environment.

Conclusions

Cultural differences can lead to misunderstandings, conflicts, and even failed business initiatives if improperly managed. Therefore, companies engaging in FDI must navigate these cultural gaps by adapting their strategies, products, and services to align with the local culture. This may involve customising marketing approaches, tailoring management practices, and ensuring sensitivity to local customs and values. Cultural distance is about acknowledging differences and leveraging them as opportunities. Companies that embrace and adapt to cultural diversity are often better positioned to thrive in foreign markets. By appreciating and respecting local cultures, multinational corporations can build trust, foster positive relationships, and enhance the overall success of their FDI ventures.

It should be considered that doing business in a new and challenging environment involves a high degree of risk. To mitigate the risks, it is necessary to adequately prepare the entire investment process, taking into account all the aspects related to cultural differences discussed in the chapter, such as religion, culture, language, communication, and relationships. What became evident through the case study of Cocco Lagoon investment is that proper preparation in understanding and respecting the local culture, appreciating the significance of personal relationships, and displaying a willingness to adapt to the cultural and bureaucratic intricacies were paramount to the project's success. The proactive measures taken to address the risk of delays contributed to the project's smooth progress and, ultimately, its success, highlighting the importance of cultural adaptability and local engagement in international business operations.

In the vibrant business landscape of Zanzibar, navigating cultural nuances is paramount for successful entrepreneurship. Managing a business on this island requires a delicate balance of cultural awareness and practical strategies to bridge gaps. One key aspect is understanding the local perception of time, where punctuality may hold a different weight than in Western cultures. Flexibility and patience become invaluable assets during meetings and negotiations. Building meaningful relationships takes centre stage in Zanzibari business culture, emphasising personal connections and face-to-face interactions. To mitigate the risk of doing business, it is also worth using intermediaries – representatives of the local community who are well acquainted with the conditions in a given country, the language, the legal regulations, and who have developed relationships that the investor can also use. Hiring local people fosters a deeper understanding of the cultural landscape and establishes a connection with the community, fostering a sense of inclusivity. Leveraging communication tools like WhatsApp, rather than relying solely on formal emails, aligns with local preferences. Of note is the company's extensive team, which also includes native islanders, as well as the opening of an office on the second island of Unguja, which is used to present the offer to tourists now arriving on the more famous island of Zanzibar. Considering the negotiation aspects, it is essential to remember that a mutually satisfactory agreement is sought in a negotiation – an outcome referred to as a "win-win". It is worth being prepared to make certain concessions to achieve the desired outcome and to use local intermediaries (if necessary) in this regard (Schroeder, 2018).

Additionally, demonstrating respect for national and religious holidays and engaging in casual social interactions contribute to building trust. Overcoming language barriers by incorporating bilingual staff fluent in Swahili and English enhances communication channels. It is also worth showing a genuine interest in local culture and not comparing its culture with your own. Successfully running a business in Zanzibar necessitates not only embracing these cultural subtleties but also viewing them as opportunities for connection and collaboration.

The case study presented in this chapter can be used by other companies interested in setting up operations in Tanzania, including Pemba Island in particular. The recommendations presented can be helpful, especially in the initial phase of investment activities, where the investor faces the most problems due to a lack of adequate knowledge of the existing conditions of doing business in emerging markets.

Bibliography

Alofan, F., Chen, S., & Tan, H. (2020). National cultural distance, organizational culture, and adaptation of management innovations in foreign subsidiaries: A fuzzy set analysis of TQM implementation in Saudi Arabia. *Journal of Business Research*, *109*, 184–199. https://doi.org/10.1016/j.jbusres.2019.11.037

Bartosik-Purgat, M. (2019). *New Media in the Marketing Communication of Enterprises in the International Market*. Warsaw: PWN Publications.

Bartosik-Purgat, M., & Rakowska, W. (2023). Cross-cultural business-to-business communication – The experiences of Polish companies with the Chinese and Americans. *International Journal of Emerging Markets*, *ahead-of-print* (ahead-of-print). https://doi.org/10.1108/IJOEM-01-2022-0013

Batschauer da Cruz, C.B., Eliete Floriani, D., & Amal, M. (2022). The OLI Paradigm as a comprehensive model of FDI determinants: A sub-national approach. *International Journal of Emerging Markets*, *17*(1), 145–176. https://doi.org/10.1108/IJOEM-07-2019-0517

Beugelsdijk, S., Kostova, T., Kunst, V.E., Spadafora, E., & van Essen, M. (2018). Cultural distance and firm internationalization: A meta-analytical review and theoretical implications. *Journal of Management*, *44*(1), 89–130. https://doi.org/10.1177/0149206317729027

Bhardwaj, A., Dietz, J., & Beamish, P.W. (2007). Host country cultural influences on foreign direct investment. *Management International Review*, *47*(1), 29–50. https://doi.org/10.1007/s11575-0070003-7

Bi, Y., Ren, Z., & Bao, K. (2020). Does distance matter in foreign direct investment sub-national location choice? Evidence from China. *Frontiers of Business Research in China*, *14*(1), 1–19. https://doi.org/10.1186/s11782-020-00080-8

Chen, I.C., Chuo, Y.Y., & Ma, H.W. (2019). Uncertainty analysis of remediation cost and damaged land value for brownfield investment. *Chemosphere*, *220*, 371–380. https://doi.org/10.1016/j.chemosphere.2018.12.116

Chen, L., Zhang, X., & Li, Z. (2020). Understanding the Chinese information culture and its impact on IT perceptions. *Information Technology & People*, *33*(1), 56–82. https://doi.org/10.1108/ITP-03-2018-0128

Dathe, T., Müller, V., & Helmold, M. (2023). Understanding the Chinese culture. In *Business Opportunities and Risks in China: Strategies and Recommendations from a European Perspective* (pp. 109–123). Cham: Springer International Publishing.

Du, J., Lu, Y., & Tao, Z. (2012). Institutions and FDI location choice: The role of cultural distances. *Journal of Asian Economics*, *23*(3), 210–223. https://doi.org/10.1016/j.asieco.2010.11.008

Dunning, J.H. (1977). Trade, location of economic activity and the MNE: A search for an eclectic approach. In B. Ohlin, P.O. Hesselborn & P.M. Wijkman (Eds.), *The International Allocation of Economic Activity* (pp. 395–418). London: Palgrave Macmillan.

Dunning, J.H. (2002). *Global Capitalism, FDI and Competitiveness*. London: Edward Elgar Publications.

Emodi, N.V., Wade, B., Rekker, S., & Greig, C. (2022). A systematic review of barriers to greenfield investment in decarbonisation solutions. *Renewable and Sustainable Energy Reviews*, *165*, 112586. https://doi.org/10.1016/j.rser.2022.112586

Gesteland, R.R. (2003). *Cross-Cultural Business Behavior: Marketing, Negotiating, and Managing across Cultures*. Copenhagen: Copenhagen Business School Publications.

Gomółka, K., Kacperska, E., Kraciuk, J., & Wojtaszek, M. (2020). *Bezpośrednie inwestycje zagraniczne Świat-Europa-Kaukaz-Polska*. Warszawa: Szkoła Główna Gospodarstwa Wiejskiego.

Götz, M. (2020). Primer on the cluster impact on internationalisation in the form of FDI in the time of industry 4.0. *European Spatial Research and Policy*, *27*(1), 195–220.

GOV. (2023). *Polska w Tanzanii*. www.gov.pl/web/tanzania/ie

Gubbi, S.R., Aulakh, P.S., Ray, S., Sarkar, M.B., & Chittoor, R. (2010). Do international acquisitions by emerging-economy firms create shareholder value? The case of Indian firms. *Journal of International Business Studies*, *41*, 397–418. https://doi.org/10.1057/jibs.2009.47

Ha, N.M., Binh, Q.M.Q., & Dang, P.P. (2020). Cultural distance and entry modes in emerging markets: Empirical evidence in Vietnam. *Journal of Risk and Financial Management*, *13*(1), 14. https://doi.org/10.3390/jrfm13010014

Hall, E.T. (1976). *Beyond Culture*. Garden City: Anchor Books Publications.

Hofstede, G. (2001). *Culture's Consequences: Comparing Values, Behaviors, Institutions and Organizations across Nations*. Beverly Hills, CA: Sage Publications.

Holmes, R.M., Miller, T., Hitt, M.A., & Salmador, M.P. (2013). The interrelationships among informal institutions, formal institutions, and inward foreign direct investment. *Journal of Management*, *39*, 531–566. https://doi.org/10.1177/0149206310393503

Kapás, J., & Czeglédi, P. (2020). The impact of culture on FDI disentangled: Separating the "level" and the "distance" effects. *Economia Politica*, *37*(1), 223–250. https://doi.org/10.1007/s40888-020-00175-8

Kayalvizhi, P.N., & Thenmozhi, M. (2018). Does the quality of innovation, culture and governance drive FDI?: Evidence from emerging markets. *Emerging Markets Review*, *34*, 175–191. https://doi.org/10.1016/j.ememar.2017.11.007

Kimiagari, S., Mahbobi, M., & Toolsee, T. (2023). Attracting and retaining FDI: Africa gas and oil sector. *Resources Policy*, *80*, 103219. https://doi.org/10.1016/j.resourpol.2022.103219

Kogut, B., & Singh, H. (1988). The effect of national culture on the choice of entry mode. *Journal of International Business Studies*, *19*, 411–432. https://doi.org/10.1057/palgrave.jibs.8490394

Könning, M., Strahringer, S., & Westner, M. (2021). Unravelling the impact of cultural distance on IT outsourcing success – Insights from three major sourcing reconfigurations. *Journal of Enterprise Information Management*, *34*(3), 811–837. https://doi.org/10.1108/JEIM-06-2019-0151

Kostova, T., Nell, P.C., & Hoenen, A.K. (2018). Understanding agency problems in headquarters-subsidiary relationships in multinational corporations: A contextualized model. *Journal of Management*, *44*(7), 2611–2637. https://doi.org/10.1177/0149206316648383

Kristjánsdóttir, H., Guðlaugsson, Þ.Ö., Guðmundsdóttir, S., & Aðalsteinsson, G.D. (2020). Cultural and geographical distance: Effects on UK exports. *Applied Economics Letters*, *27*(4), 275–279. https://doi.org/10.1080/13504851.2019.1613495

Leung, K., Bhagat, R.S., Buchan, N.R., Erez, M., & Gibson, C.B. (2005). Culture and international business: Recent advances and their implications for future research. *Journal of International Business Studies*, *36*, 357–378. https://doi.org/10.1057/palgrave.jibs.8400150

Lucke, N., & Eichler, S. (2016). Foreign direct investment: The role of institutional and cultural determinants. *Applied Economics*, *48*(11), 935–956. https://doi.org/10.1080/00036846.2015.1090551

Magnusson, P., Baack, D.W., Zdravkovic, S., Staub, K.M., & Amine, L.S. (2008). Meta-analysis of cultural differences: Another slice at the apple. *International Business Review*, *17*(5), 520–532. https://doi.org/10.1016/j.ibusrev.2008.04.003

Maoulidi, S. (2011). Between law and culture: Contemplating rights for women in Zanzibar. In D. Hodgson (Ed.), *Gender and Culture at the Limit of Rights* (pp. 32–54). University of Pennsylvania Press. https://doi.org/10.9783/9780812204612.32

Marano, V., Arregle, J.L., Hitt, M.A., Spadafora, E., & van Essen, M. (2016). Home country institutions and the internationalization-performance relationship: A meta-analytic review. *Journal of Management*, *42*(5), 1075–1110. https://doi.org/10.1177/01492063156249

OECD. (1996). *Benchmark Definition of Foreign Direct Investments*. Paris: OECD Publishing.

Orsini, P., & Magnier-Watanabe, R. (2023). Foreign coworker nationality, cultural distance, and perception of cultural diversity in the workplace. *Journal of Asia Business Studies*, *17*(2), 256–278. https://doi.org/10.1108/JABS-10-2021-0413

Pak, Y.S., & Park, Y.R. (2005). Characteristics of Japanese FDI in the East and the West: Understanding the strategic motives of Japanese investment. *Journal of World Business*, *40*(3), 254–266. https://doi.org/10.1016/j.jwb.2005.05.003

Pananond, P. (2015). Motives for foreign direct investment: A view from emerging market multinationals. *The Multinational Business Review*, *23*(1), 77–86. https://doi.org/10.1108/MBR-02-2015-0008

Schroeder, J. (2018). *Etykieta biznesu w kontaktach międzynarodowych. Przewodnik po krajach świata*. Polska Izba Gospodarcza Importerów, Eksporterów i Kooperacji, Poznań: Wydawnictwo WENA.

Siegel, J.I., Licht, A.N., & Schwartz, S.H. (2012). Egalitarianism, cultural distance, and foreign direct investment: A new approach. *Organization Science*, *24*(4), 1174–1194. https://doi.org/10.1287/orsc.1120.0776

Srivastava, S., Singh, S., & Dhir, S. (2020). Culture and international business research: A review and research agenda. *International Business Review*, *29*(4), 101709. https://doi.org/10.1016/j.ibusrev.2020.101709

Thanetsunthorn, N., & Wuthisatian, R. (2019). Understanding trust across cultures: An empirical investigation. *Review of International Business and Strategy*, *29*(4), 286–314. https://doi.org/10.1108/RIBS-12-2018-0103

UNCTAD. (2023). *World Investment Report*. https://unctad.org/system/files/official-document/wir2023_en.pdf

Yayla, S., Kutlubay, O.C., Cicek, M., & Yeniyurt, S. (2023). Once upon a time in a foreign market: The role of cultural distance in the economic performance of multilateral non-equity partnerships. *International Business Review*, *32*(4), 102139. https://doi.org/10.1016/j.ibusrev.2023.102139

Yiu, D., & Makino, S. (2002). The choice between a joint venture and wholly owned subsidiary: An institutional perspective. *Organization Science*, *13*, 667–683. https://doi.org/10.1287/orsc.13.6.667.494

9 Danish values in the structures of the Polish subsidiary of VELUX

Magdalena Steier

Introduction

Increasing processes of globalisation and integration mean that there is now much more intense intercultural interaction and exchange. This provides new opportunities for organisational development but also causes challenges in the shaping of organisational cultures. Numerous studies confirm that national culture significantly determines how each organisation operates (Gerhard, 2008). Some theories argue whether globalisation and integration can lead to developing one common culture (Eriksen, 2020) and how this might impact organisational convergence (Lee et al., 2010). Thus, a question arises as to whether it is worth considering how national culture affects the functioning of the organisation or putting it into a more practical framework: Is it possible to transfer national values, norms, and behavioural patterns from the origin country to another one where a subsidiary entity operates? To what extent are misunderstandings affected by cultural differences? And are these misunderstandings likely to be minimised or even resolved?

The first section of the chapter provides readers with the definitions of national culture and organisational culture. It also verifies what both definitions have in common, and how the differences can influence each other. The section is based primarily on a substantial literature review and personal observations about Danish and Polish cultures. After this, the similarities and differences in management styles, communication, and employee engagement are presented. In the following section, a case study based on the example of the Danish company VELUX and its integration in the Polish context is presented, outlining the company's history and the challenges related to the Polish employees' understanding of Danish culture.

National culture and organisational culture

Values are the fundamental element of company culture but are also a crucial part of almost every definition of national culture (Gerhard, 2008). In international

DOI: 10.4324/9781032636962-12

companies, shared values may govern management systems (Wolf, 2006), so it is valuable to inquire how the values of the parent company influence its operations across various international contexts and what the challenges of implementing them in the local environment are.

The etymology of the word "culture" comes from the Latin "culture agri", which means farming. It was primarily introduced by the ancient Romanal orator Cicero, who presented the concept of "cultura animi", using an agricultural metaphor for developing a philosophical soul, understood teleologically as the highest possible ideal for human growth (Kahler, 1961). Over the centuries, the term "culture" has increasingly been used by philosophers and later by social science researchers (Ansah & Louw, 2019). In this chapter, there is a focus on two aspects of culture: national and organisational culture.

According to Kluckhohn (1951), culture consists of patterns of thoughts, feelings and behaviours acquired and transmitted primarily through symbols that represent the distinctive achievements of particular groups of people; the essence of culture consists of traditional ideas and the associated values of behaviours (Kluckhohn, 1951). This is one of the definitions, but in the literature, many cultural models allow researchers to identify cultural similarities and differences based on established criteria. Some of the most essential culture models have been introduced by Hofstede et al. (2010), Hall (1989), Trompenaars and Hampden-Turner (1997) and The Global Leadership and Organisational Behaviour Effectiveness (Dorfman et al., 2012).

Hofstede et al. (2010) defined culture as a collective, programmed mindset that distinguishes representatives of one society from another (Hofstede et al., 2010). National culture is the term used to describe a group of people who have grown up within the same country and share similar values (Hofstede et al., 2010); according to Hofstede et al. (2010), national culture consists of four layers: symbols, heroes, rituals, and values (Hassan & Hassan, 2020).

The dimensions of national culture are reflected in social life, whilst manifestations of certain behaviours characteristic of a specific culture can be observed even in the first years of a person's life. Initially, norms and values are passed on in the family and at school (Meca et al., 2023). This has constructed a specific, shaped world view that is passed on to subsequent generations and determines employee behaviour. All the dimensions are briefly characterised in the next parts of the chapter, after which the dimensions for Poland and Denmark are described in detail.

In the late 1960s and 1970s, Hofstede et al. (2010) conducted research among IBM employees in 72 countries, collecting approximately 116,000 surveys across various organisational positions (Shi & Wang, 2011). The studies aimed to identify criteria for describing and comparing cultures between countries. An essential outcome of Hofstede's research was the distinction of four basic cultural dimensions: *Power Distance*, *Individualism–Collectivism*, *Masculinity–Femininity*, and *Uncertainty Avoidance* (Sent & Kroese, 2022). In the late 1980s, this concept was enriched with a fifth dimension, long- and short-term orientation (Gaspay & Legorreta, 2007). In 2007 Minkov (2007) introduced a new cultural factor: indulgence versus restraint, which became the sixth dimension of Hofstede's et al. (2010) framework (Heydari et al., 2021).

The power distance dimension refers to the degree to which individuals accept the unequal power distribution. In high power distance cultures, there is wide acceptance of imbalances in power between subordinates and their superiors, and there is a strong tendency towards power centralisation. Conversely, in low power distance cultures, there is a desire to reduce inequalities among people, and subordinates perceive each other as equal partners. In this context, hierarchy pertains to different roles and positions and much less power imbalance (Gerlach & Eriksson, 2021).

The individualism–collectivism dimension characterises the positioning of an individual against a group and measures the degree of prioritising self-interest over the group's interest. Individualism refers to societies in which individuals are independent and everyone focuses on themselves and their families. By contrast, collectivism represents societies in which people belong to cohesive groups from the moment of birth (Hofstede et al., 2010).

Masculinity–femininity indicates the differences in the gender roles. Masculinity cultures represent characteristics such as activity, aggressiveness, competitiveness, rivalry, and achievement, whilst in feminine cultures, gentleness, caring, and cooperation are preferred (Gerlach & Eriksson, 2021).

Uncertainty avoidance is the degree of threat perceived by members of a particular community in the face of new, unknown, and uncertain circumstances. It also determines the degree to which societies are willing to accept the unpredictability and uncertainty of the future (Sent & Kroese, 2022).

Long-term versus short-term orientation determines the time horizon of a particular society and the importance placed on the past, present, and future (Sent & Kroese, 2022). Short-term orientation is associated with a focus on immediate results, seeking fast achievements and choosing short-term goals, whereas long-term orientation, on the other hand, is linked to foresight, perseverance, humility, patience, and long-term objectives (Venaik et al., 2013).

The indulgence versus restraint dimension describes the degree to which individuals prioritise the importance of their desires and impulses for happiness and pleasure. A low score indicates indulgence, meaning that people seek leisure and entertainment, whereas a high score indicates restraint and control of needs (Heydari et al., 2021; Prim et al., 2017).

The cultural dimensions proposed by Hofstede et al. (2010) are supported by comprehensive international studies, enabling cultural comparison between countries. However, it should be noted that one person cannot be perceived as a token of a whole culture, and the same is also true of the reverse: a culture does not characterise all individuals (Bennett, 1998). However, people from one community are more likely to act in a similar way that applies to that culture, especially when they are together.

As described earlier, there is significant research on national cultural differences. The following section focuses on organisational culture. In the literature, there are different approaches and understandings on this topic (Ostroff et al., 2013).

The most well-known model defining organisational culture and structuring its elements was presented by Schein (2004), who defined organisational culture as a typical pattern and integration of shared norms, thoughts, and beliefs that result from common experiences and learnings. Schein (2004) distinguished three levels of organisational culture: artefacts, values, and assumptions.

Hofstede et al. (2010) describe organisational culture as "the collective programming of the mind that distinguishes the members of one organisation from another" (Hofstede et al., 2010, p. 520). Measuring organisational culture is typically more straightforward and precise than evaluating national culture. Differences between national cultures are most visible in the values, while differences among organisations operating within the same nation are primarily reflected in their practices (Hofstede et al., 2010). In fact, organisational culture, in contrast to national culture, can be modified by these practices. Organisational culture is a crucial factor that significantly influences business performance. The right culture can be the driving force behind the success of an organisational strategy, whereas an inappropriate culture can result in weak performance or even failure (Krupskyi & Kuzmytska, 2020).

Understanding organisational culture requires knowing the various factors that influence its formation. One of these factors is elements of national culture. An organisational culture that is aligned with the national culture is more likely accepted by employees because it partially reflects their norms and values. However, challenges may arise when a company spreads its operations and expands abroad (Khan & Panarina, 2017). In such cases, the shaping of organisational culture can be influenced by both the national culture of the origin company's country through the impact of the headquarters and by the national culture of the host country, affecting the organisation through employees and indirectly through the institutional environment. In particular, it is essential to recognise the influence of the origin country's culture because an excessive influence can lead to conflicts between the beliefs and norms of the organisation and of the employees based in subsidiaries (Adler & Zeynep, 2018).

Polish and Danish national culture in light of Hofstede's dimensions

Analysing the influence of Danish culture on shaping a company's organisational culture in Poland, it is worth evaluating the research results of Hofstede et al. (2010) in relation to those two countries. Table 9.1 presents the characteristics of the individual dimensions for Poland and Denmark.

Power distance. With a score of 18 points, Denmark has a very low level of this dimension compared to Poland (Hofstede et al., 2010). The Danish leadership

Table 9.1 Cultural dimensions of Denmark and Poland

Dimension	*Denmark*	*Poland*
Power distance	18	68
Individualism–Collectivism	74	60
Masculinity–Femininity	16	64
Uncertainty avoidance	23	93
Long-term vs. Short-term orientation	35	38
Indulgence vs. Restraint	70	29

Source: Hofstede et al. (2010)

style is characterised by coaching, with a strong emphasis on employee autonomy. The Danes have a highly democratic mindset, and subordinates expect to be consulted. They believe in independence and equality and prefer accessible supervisors and a management approach focusing on facilitation and empowerment (Andrijauskienė & Dumčiuvienė, 2017). Power is more decentralised, as a hierarchy indicates social inequality, which is unacceptable. For this reason, in Denmark, superiors and subordinates are perceived as equal. Organisations have a flat organisational structure, whilst managers rely on the expertise of their team members and they manage by objectives. By contrast, Poland, with a result of 68, is considered a hierarchical culture (Hofstede et al., 2010). This means that society accepts inequalities and hierarchical structures. In Poland, a high power distance culture, the superior expects obedience from the employees, and the superior and subordinate do not consider themselves equal. Power is centralised, and employees expect to get clear directives regarding what to do (Daniels & Greguras, 2014).

Individualism–Collectivism. Both countries (Denmark = 74, Poland = 60) are perceived as individualistic societies (Hofstede et al., 2010), and the scores show that in both, there is a high preference that individuals focus on themselves and their close families (Mihet, 2012). In Denmark, small talk is kept to a minimum, and they do not need to make relationships in the workplace. However, Polish culture is characterised by a unique combination of high rates of power distance and individualism. This means that despite being highly individualistic, Poles still value hierarchy. Combining these two dimensions creates a specific "pressure" within this culture, making relationships sensitive ("International Cultural Environment And SMEs' Report Summary (Eurokey)", n.d.).

Masculinity–Femininity. Denmark has a score of 16 for this dimension and is therefore considered a feminine society (Hofstede et al., 2010). In countries characterised as feminine, it is essential to balance professional work and family life, and people work to live. In these cultures, managers support their teams and are involved in decision-making. In feminine countries, equality and solidarity are valuable. Poland, with a score of 64, is described as a masculine society (Hofstede et al., 2010). In such countries, people live to work, and the ability to earn high incomes is essential. For Poles, professional work is important, and success is achieved through competition and rivalry. Employees seek challenges – an ambitious job provides a sense of satisfaction. Moreover, in masculine countries, an autocratic management style dominates. Managers are perceived as powerful and assertive; the emphasis is on justice, and rivalry and conflict are usually resolved by battling them out (Matuska & Grubicka, 2014).

Uncertainty avoidance. With a mark of 23, Denmark scores low on this dimension (Hofstede et al., 2010). This means that Danes do not need predictability in their work life. They accept that plans change quickly and new things come up and perceive this as a natural part of their work life. Additionally, curiosity is natural for Danes (Andrijauskienė & Dumčiuvienė, 2017). This mixture of a highly individualistic style and curiosity means that Danes display a high acceptance of innovative actions and ideas. By contrast, Poland, with a score of 93 for this dimension, has a very high preference for avoiding uncertainty (Hofstede et al., 2010). Countries with high uncertainty avoidance follow strict codes of belief, and they might be intolerant of unconventional behaviour or ideas. They might also be resistant to implementing innovative solutions. Thus, in Poland, there is a strong need for rules (even if the rules do not work). In cultures with high uncertainty avoidance, people are less likely to take risk because they fear lack of success and the consequences of failure (Mihet, 2012).

Long-term versus Short-term orientation. Both countries scored low for this dimension (Denmark = 35, Poland = 38), which indicates that those cultures are normative (Hofstede et al., 2010). People in these societies have a vital concern for seeking the ultimate Truth, and they tend to have normative thinking patterns, displaying respect for traditions. Such societies also focus on achieving quick results (Andrijauskienė & Dumčiuvienė, 2017).

Restrained versus Indulgence. Denmark, with a high rate of 70 for this dimension, is classified as an indulgent country (Hofstede et al., 2010). In indulgent cultures, people are willing to realise their needs and desires towards enjoying life and happiness. Leisure time is essential to them, and they feel comfortable spending money as they wish. They are optimistic and represent a positive attitude. By contrast, with a score of 29, Poland represents a restrained culture (Hofstede et al., 2010) and has a tendency for cynicism and pessimism. These societies do not prioritise leisure time and keep their desires under control. Poles have a perception that social norms restrain their actions and that indulging one's self is not acceptable (Chudnovskaya & O'Hara, 2022).

A comparative assessment of Polish and Danish culture thus indicates that they have similarities in areas such as individualism and long-term orientation. That said, the cultural differences between Poland and Denmark highlighted in Table 9.1 suggest differences in mentality, and these cultural differences can also be observed in personal contact between employees from both cultures while cooperating.

In Poland, a country with high power distance, hierarchy and authority play a more significant role than in Denmark. In Polish culture, superiors and subordinates often consider themselves unequal, and the superior's authority is emphasised through visible signs of respect. The management style tends to be official, and the manager is the one who has the ultimate right and makes decisions independently (Daniels & Greguras, 2014; Bulawka et al., 2023). In Denmark, however, flat structures are established, along with a less formal style of communication, which means, for example, that everyone addresses each other by their first name, regardless of their position within the organisation. In Denmark, anyone can go and knock on their superior's door, express their dissatisfaction, or suggest a better idea or solution (Daniels & Greguras, 2014).

As a result, in Denmark, a consultative management style is broadly used. When a manager needs to decide, they talk to their colleagues and ask for their opinion. Even though the manager makes the decision, every employee can express their view (Daniels & Greguras, 2014). This way of working together may cause confusion for Poles, not because they are not creative and do not want to take responsibility, but because it is accepted that the superior makes decisions and does not always have to ask subordinates for their opinion. Indeed, Poland has a hierarchical management style, meaning employees expect to be told what they should do at work (Matuska & Grubicka, 2014). In comparison, in Danish culture, an employee's opinion is important because everyone is perceived as an equal individual, which indicates the importance of mutual respect. Poles are reluctant to express their opinion in public and may thus be confused that everyone is expected to share their point of view on a topic (Bulawka et al., 2023).

In Denmark, communication tends to be low-context (Hall, 1989). Danes are more direct when it comes to stating their thoughts and opinions, but they nevertheless still value being polite. Denmark is a cooperative rather than competitive society, and discussions should, therefore, be pleasant and emphasise common ground. At the same time, they are straightforward, open, and honest and go straight to the point (Bulawka et al., 2023). In Danish companies, problems are solved through open discussions leading to compromises (Head et al., 1993). For this reason, in Danish communication, criticism is framed as a constructive suggestion for improvement and is directed at processes rather than at individual persons (Daniels & Greguras, 2014). This is important in the manager–employee relationship. If employees disagree with managers on how they have organised the work, the employees may criticise it. Polish people tend to be also direct in their communication style (Hall, 1989).

Poles value friendly contacts at work and need to get to know the person they will be working with. On the basis of this, they build trust (Bulawka et al., 2023). However, this is not necessary in Denmark. In Denmark, people might seem to be closed because they do not need to build close relationships with co-workers. This is one of the essential aspects of cooperation between Poles and Danes. Poland is a rather relationship-focused culture. In such cultures, people need to build a relationship to trust co-workers. For Danes, not building professional trust may generate challenges for others (Bartosik-Purgat & Rakowska, 2023). For example, due to a lack of trust, Poles do not admit that they do not know something, and they do not ask questions. For Poles, lack of knowledge or not having the right answer is a sign of failure (Bulawka et al., 2023). On the other hand, in Denmark, it is very important to ask questions if people are in doubt, and this helps avoid mistakes resulting from ignorance. Subsequently, this difference in cultures can have a considerable impact on cooperation in a culturally mixed team.

Trust is a foundation of significant social interactions within business and government. When Danish people think about trust, they think of "general societal trust", which is proven in their approach that they have the ability to trust others even if they have not met them before. Trust is visible both in daily private life and in the workplace, and business relations are built on integrity, reliability, and transparency ("Trust. A cornerstone of Danish culture (Ministry of Foreign Affairs of Denmark)", 2023). For more than 30 years, Denmark has been at the very top of trust distribution rankings in different global values surveys (Sønderskov & Dinesen, 2014), and other research shows that an employee in a trusting workplace feels safe and positive, which subsequently leads to higher job satisfaction (Knoll & Gill, 2011).

When describing Danish values, the concern for social responsibility and customer centricity cannot be overlooked. Sustainability is an essential part of life for Danes. The official statement of the Ministry of Foreign Affairs of Denmark says, "For hundreds of years, Denmark was a society based on agriculture and fishing, and Danes still feel closely tied to the land and the water around them. This respect for nature is why Denmark is a pioneer in promoting sustainability" ("Trust. A cornerstone of Danish culture (Ministry of Foreign Affairs of Denmark)", 2023). Sustainability has a different meaning to people. "To the Danes, sustainability is a holistic approach that includes renewable energy, water management, waste recycling, and green transportation, including the bicycling culture" ("Trust. A cornerstone of Danish culture (Ministry of Foreign Affairs of Denmark)", 2023). The Danish Government has launched the Global Climate Action Strategy: "A Green and Sustainable World", which expounds on the goal of emissions reductions of 70% by 2030 and achieving climate neutrality by 2050 ("New Climate Action Strategy (Ministry of Foreign Affairs of Denmark)", 2023).

When working in an international environment, behaviour is often evaluated according to the norms and stereotypes established in the native culture. Any deviation from behavioural patterns may be seen as incomprehensible, inappropriate, and sometimes impolite. Therefore, being aware of the cultural differences is essential (Chudnovskaya & O'Hara, 2022).

The VELUX Group

VELUX Group is a manufacturing and sales company of roof windows, sunlight, skylights, sun tunnels, and related accessories. It is a Danish company that belongs to VKR Holding A/S. For more than 80 years, the mission of VELUX

Group has been to create better indoor environments by bringing daylight and fresh air into homes and other buildings worldwide. Today, it is one of the most well-known and largest companies specialising in the production and sale of roof windows. The company is present in 35 countries, with 16 production sites in 9 countries and sales companies in 35 countries ("About us (VELUX)", n.d.).

In 1941, an engineer, Villum Kann Rasmussen, founded a company specialising in glass roof structures. His first order was to supply roof windows to several school buildings in which loft space was converted into classrooms. His idea was to convert the dark roof space into bright living spaces – full of daylight and fresh air ("About us (VELUX)", n.d.). On the invoice, he wrote VELUX – "VE" from the words "ventilation" and "LUX" from the Latin word for "light". Villum patented his first roof window in 1942 ("History (VELUX)", n.d.). Over the years, the company has developed and expanded. According to the founder, the key factors to achieve success were his strong commitment to fair dealings, high-quality standards, and drive for technical innovations. In 1965, Villum Kann Rasmussen formulated the Model Company Objective, which still guides the way of doing business in the VELUX Group to this day. As Villum Kann Rasmussen committed: "A model company works with products useful to society and treats its customers, suppliers, employees of all categories and shareholders better than most other companies. A model company makes a profit which can finance growth and maintain financial independence" ("Corporate Social Responsibility (VKR Holding A/S)", n.d.). In 1975, the VELUX Group set up a sales company and subsequently established their own production facility in the United States and Canada. The founder died in 1993 at the age of 84. He left behind rapidly expanding companies and two non-profit foundations that continue their operations successfully to this day. One year before his father's death, Lars Kann-Rasmussen, the founder's son, took responsibility for the VELUX Group. In 2005, the company launched a vision: "To lead the development of better living environments with daylight and fresh air through the roof" ("History (VELUX)", n.d.). This statement represented the understanding of the significance of natural daylight and ventilation, the relationship between these elements, and the quality of people's lives.

Since being established, the VELUX Group has taken responsibility for environmental protection and sustainability. In 2009, the VELUX Group initiated a "Model Home 2020" project. The company showed that building sustainable buildings for the future is possible. In 2020, the Velux Group presented its Sustainability Strategy 2030, in which the company strived to pioneer climate and nature action, innovate sustainable products, and secure a responsible business. This includes taking responsibility for both past and future carbon emissions. The VELUX Group also began a 20-year partnership with the World Wide Fund for Nature (WWF) ("History (VELUX)", n.d.).

In 2021, the VELUX Group marked its 80th anniversary. Throughout this time, VELUX Group has been the market leader in residential roof windows.

VELUX values

The VELUX values were launched in 1997, and in 2022, the values were revised to reflect better changes within the VELUX Group and the current world. The updated VELUX Values are as follows ("VELUX Values (VELUX)", n.d.):

- commitment – we are passionate about what we do and go the extra mile to pursue our shared goals;
- mutual respect – we respect and care for one another and treat others as they would like to be treated;
- customer centricity – we put the people who live, work, and play under the roof at the centre of everything we do;
- social responsibility – we act as a Model Company, driven by our Purpose to create well-being for people and the planet;
- courage – we have the courage to be ambitious and try things we have never done before;
- agility – we constantly look for new opportunities and move quickly to explore and realise them.

These values guide daily work life and support the Model Company Objective and corporate strategy.

VELUX Group in Poland

The VELUX Group and its sister companies in Poland belong to the Danish holding VKR. They are the largest producer and exporter of roof windows in Poland (Scandinavian-Polish Chamber of Commerce, n.d.). They employ 4,790 people ("VELUX: Raport zrównoważonego rozwoju 2020–2021. W drodze do ambitnego celu (VELUX)", 2022), p. 14), with the majority working in four plants located in Gniezno (two), Namyslow (one), and Wedkowy (one). The VELUX Group in Poland consists of a trading company in Warsaw named VELUX Polska and factories in Gniezno and Namyslow.

The company is constantly growing and investing in new technologies while ensuring the highest quality standards, workplace safety, and environmental protection. Their product range includes a wide variety of attic and flat roof windows, as well as various types of blinds, roller shutters, insulation kits, and remote control options. These products help create a healthy indoor climate for work, study, play, and relaxation.

VELUX Polska, the trading company, was founded in 1990 in Warsaw. The company sells VELUX roof windows to a network of wholesalers throughout Poland. It also operates in the e-commerce segment, offering a wide range of roller shutters and accessories to individual customers through its online store, veluxshop.pl. Within the company's structure, there is also a Shared Services

Center that provides support for many other European markets ("About us (VELUX)", n.d.).

In Gniezno, there are two factories – one for wooden windows and another for metal and plastic components used in VELUX roof windows. The VELUX Group is the largest employer in the city, employing over 800 people. The VELUX Group actively participates in local community life and, for many years, has been supporting various local events and initiatives, including the city's major sports events.

In Namyslow, there is an aluminium window and flashing factory which employs approximately 800 people. The plant in Namyslow is a highly valued workplace as the factory received the award of "leading company in implementing continuous improvement processes" during the International Gemba Kaizen Congress. In Namyslow, there is also a VELUX Group distribution centre that serves the Polish and European markets.

Since the beginning of the VELUX Group's presence in Poland, the company has been actively participating in the country's economic and social life, including the life of local communities. In Poland, there are VELUX Foundations that, as of 2021, had donated approximately 172 million PLN to institutions and social organisations working on projects related to science, environmental protection, social development, and culture and preventing the social exclusion of children and youth, as well as initiatives aimed at vocational education development. The VELUX Group also has an Employee Foundation that supports employees and their families, as well as local entities such as schools, hospitals, and municipal cultural centres.

Thus, social responsibility is a concept that forms the basis of VELUX's business activities. The VELUX Group companies' activities in Poland related to sustainability development were published in a report titled "On the Way to an Ambitious Goal", which covers 2020–2021 ("VELUX: Raport zrównoważonego rozwoju 2020–2021. W drodze do ambitnego celu (VELUX)", 2022). The VELUX Sustainability Report highlights four areas of the company's impact on the external environment: environment, workplace, contributions to the economy, and social engagement.

1. Environment – By the year 2030, the company aims to achieve carbon neutrality, reduce emissions within its value chain by 50%, and decrease the carbon footprint of its products. The company is working towards using 100% renewable energy for its factory electricity consumption and maximising resource efficiency, following the zero-waste principle.
2. Workplace – Ensuring the safety, health, development, and well-being of all employees in the VELUX Group is a top priority for the company. The company promotes a diverse and inclusive workplace, appreciates employee commitment, and supports them in challenging life situations through the VKR Employee Foundation.

3. Society – The company creates high-quality, innovative products that are useful for society. Through its activities in various regions and the support of the VELUX Foundation and the Employee Foundation, the company contributes to developing local communities. VELUX also aims to raise awareness among Poles regarding sustainable construction and the impact of buildings on the health of current and future generations.
4. Economy – For over 30 years, the company has been influencing the Polish economy as a large and stable employer, a leading producer and exporter of windows, and an investor cooperating with Polish suppliers. It aims to create as much value in production and exports as possible, with the profits returning significantly to the state budget and local communities.

VELUX organisational culture

VELUX's social responsibility concept is based on the principles of the Model Company Objective formulated by the company's founder in 1965. The basis of VELUX's corporate culture is the Model Company concept, understood as a socially responsible company model that not only provides products that are useful for the environment but also treats its customers, suppliers, employees, and shareholders with the highest respect and responsibility ("VELUX Values (VELUX)", n.d.). The company builds relationships with its employees based on six fundamental values: commitment, mutual respect, customer centricity, social responsibility, courage understood as ambition and taking new initiatives, and agility, which means seeking new solutions and opportunities.

The company pays particular attention to values-based management. It creates a friendly atmosphere inspired by Danish models of work culture and corporate social responsibility. Encoded Danish values can be observed in the organisational culture of VELUX, such as low hierarchy, flat structures and informal communication style, where employees and superiors are considered equal. The company strongly emphasises promoting a management culture based on dialogue with employees, mutual respect, and trust. There is a focus on ensuring employees have the space to express their thoughts. Employees are encouraged to share their insights and ask direct questions openly. An "open-door" policy is also practised, which means that the manager is accessible to their employees and the communication barriers are eliminated.

Managers use a coaching management style. Trust and employee engagement are crucial, as well as providing employees with developmental opportunities through task delegation that enhances their skills. Giving feedback works in both directions, which means that it is not only the supervisor who can share their insights regarding an employee's work but the employee can also provide feedback to the supervisor. An employee may also disagree with the superior's opinion, and the management team does not perceive such behaviour negatively.

In VELUX, the communication style is direct – all employees address each other by their first name, including supervisors, which does not diminish the role of a leader in any way but, at the same time, dramatically enhances team integration. The informal way of communication is sometimes misunderstood among production workers, where the supervisor is the person to be addressed by the job title. In VELUX, mutual respect is essential, which means that employees care for each other and treat others as they would like to be treated. The company also provides space for diversity and inclusivity.

VELUX is also characterised by its high level of openness in communication, focus on continuous information exchange, and the use of consultative decision-making style. Important decisions are discussed and made collectively by the group. This style is sometimes frustrating for newly employed people because Poles are used to making decisions quickly or discussing them in a small group. However, over time, employees come to appreciate this form of cooperation because their opinions are valued, and they have a sense of influence on what happens in the organisation.

In VELUX, both mutual respect and employee–supervisor relationships are essential. A sense of belonging, stability, and security are crucial. Employees work based on employment contracts. They can participate in pension programmes financed by the employer and receive medical care. The administrative employees have the possibility of hybrid work. The company provides employees with access to sports and cultural events, organises company picnics for employees and their families, and conducts well-being training. Work flexibility and work–life balance are also significant. Creating a friendly workplace atmosphere, reasonable workspace organisation, and healthy and safe working conditions are essential for the company. To this end, the management team ensures that workplaces in administrative and production departments are ergonomic. If the risk of a potential accident is identified in production, a team is established to take preventive actions. Within the team, an awareness that everyone is part of a team is embedded, where employees are also responsible for their colleagues and seek improvements even in positions they don't personally work in.

Another element transferred to the Polish context from Danish culture is the acceptance of innovative ideas, openness to experimentation, and the courage to try things the company has not done before. At VELUX, employees gain freedom in carrying out their tasks, which is associated with greater responsibility but is also highly motivating. This results from the high social trust that characterises the Danes and influences their working style. In short, at VELUX, people and their ideas get the opportunity for development.

The company promotes a Kaizen culture, where there is a space for releasing good ideas that can improve work or be transformed into products and solutions for customers. Each employee can submit an idea for process improvement or enhancements in ergonomics and safety at work. In this way, solutions that affect the company's and employees' development are created. The best and most universal improvements are implemented worldwide in all of the Group's production plants. In 2020–2021, 4,000 ideas proposed by employees were implemented in VELUX factories in Gniezno and Namysłów ("History (VELUX)", n.d.).

VELUX is one of the examples of a global market leader company that makes buildings efficient. Sustainability is an essential part of the business in Poland. In 2020, VELUX launched the Sustainability Strategy 2030, titled "It is our nature" ("Sustainability Strategy 2030 (VELUX)", n.d.), comprising 15 targets. In this transformational journey, VELUX initiates climate and nature actions, innovates sustainable products, and secures a responsible business. For the VELUX Group, their Sustainability Strategy is visible in actual actions. Since the announcement of the strategy, the company has increased its share of renewable energy in electricity consumption in factories up to 78%, over 90% of roof windows are packaged without the use of plastic, 98% of waste is reused, and 100% of the wood obtained by the VELUX Group in Poland comes from certified FSC or PEFC plantations. In addition, the company has established a long-term partnership with WWF, under which it carries out forest protection and planting projects, helping to combat climate change, preserve biodiversity, and improve the quality of life of local communities.

In the opinion of Danes, Poles are enterprising, creative, and committed. Work is an essential part of life for Poles, so they put much effort into it. Danish culture, on the other hand, creates favourable conditions for reinforcing the already existing strengths of Poles, providing employees with the opportunity to unleash their creativity, innovation, and commitment. As a result, based on the above-detailed case study, the combination of Danish and Polish culture can contribute to achieving good results.

Conclusion

Working in an international environment means the appearance of intercultural differences and challenges. This applies to both national culture and organisational culture. Several factors influence the relationship between the parent company and the host country, with the result that some will have a friendly and bonding nature. In contrast, others may lead to conflicts and organisational rifts. Therefore, in international organisations, there should be the common sense of a shared foundation of corporate culture at a global level.

VELUX is an example of a company where national culture plays a significant role in shaping organisational culture in its subsidiary and where the influence of the headquarters' main values on the local corporate culture is observed. The research introduced in this chapter confirms a contrast in communication style, management style, and employee engagement focus between Polish and Danish business cultures. VELUX operates internationally, but in the Polish subsidiary, it represents and promotes Danish values such as trust in employees, social responsibility, and mutual respect. Those cultural differences might cause challenges, for example, in how employees communicate with managers or in decision-making. However, it is possible to transfer national values, norms, and behaviours from the origin country to subsidiary entities by implementing these elements into the daily duties, being transparent and understanding employees' fears surrounding such changes.

Successful management of such an organisation is only possible when there are commonalities in thinking and shared values. These efforts create a sense of unity, positively impacting employees' performances, and, at the same time, reducing the risk of potential conflicts. Moreover, both sides must benefit as this ensures long-lasting, harmonious cooperation. Misunderstandings and conflicts arise primarily when there is a lack of mutual understanding between representatives of different cultures and where there is a desire to unconditionally impose one culture as dominant, leading, and perceived as better or more developed (Adler & Zeynep, 2018).

Bibliography

Adler, N., & Zeynep, A. (2018). Cross-cultural interaction: What we know and what we need to know. *Annual Review of Organizational Psychology and Organizational Behavior*, *5*(1), 307–333. https://doi.org/10.1146/annurev-orgpsych-032117-104528

Andrijauskienė, M., & Dumčiuvienė, D. (2017). Hofstede's cultural dimensions and national innovation level. *DIEM: Dubrovnik International Economic Meeting*, *3*(1), 189–205.

Ansah, M.O., & Louw, L. (2019). The influence of national culture on organizational culture of multinational companies. *Cogent Social Sciences*, *5*(1), 1–15. https://doi.org/10.1080/23311886.2019.1623648

Bartosik-Purgat, M., & Rakowska, W. (2023). Cross-cultural business-to-business communication – The experiences of polish companies with the Chinese and Americans. *International Journal of Emerging Markets*, *ahead-of-print* (ahead-of-print). https://doi.org/10.1108/IJOEM-01-2022-0013

Bennett, M. (1998). *Intercultural Communication: A Current Perspective: Basic Concepts of Intercultural Communication: Selected Readings*. Yarmouth, ME: Intercultural Press.

Bulawka, H., Molek, J., & Wozniak, J. (2023). When east meets west: Polish business communication from a cross-cultural perspective. *Journal of Intercultural Communication*, *23*(2), 97–108. https://doi.org/10.36923/jicc.v23i2.188

Chudnovskaya, E., & O'Hara, L. (2022). Indulgence versus restraint: Exploration of a new cultural dimension in context. *Journal of Intercultural Communication*, *22*(2), 41–52. https://doi.org/10.36923/jicc.v22i2.54

Daniels, M., & Greguras, G. (2014). Exploring the nature of power distance. *Journal of Management*, *40*(5), 1202–1229. https://doi.org/10.1177/0149206314527l3

Dorfman, P., Javidan, M., Hanges, P., Dastmalchian, A., & House, R. (2012). GLOBE: A twenty year journey into the intriguing world of culture and leadership. *Journal of World Business*, *47*(4), 504–518. https://doi.org/10.1016/j.jwb.2012.01.004

Eriksen, T.H. (2020). *Globalization: The Key Concepts*. London: Routledge Publications.

Eurokey. (n.d.). *International Cultural Environment and SMEs' Report Summary*. https://ec.europa.eu/programmes/erasmus-plus/project-result-content/31af73d2-2adb-4060-8700-5604dfef307b/OUTPUT1.pdf

Gaspay, A., & Legorreta, L. (2007). *Cultural Effects on Distance Learning Applications: A Comparison of Long Term Oriented and Short Term Oriented Cultures*. http://aisel.aisnet.org/mcis2007/3

Gerhard, B. (2008). How much does national culture constrain organizational culture? *Management and Organization Review*, *5*(2), 241–259. https://doi.org/10.1111/j.1740-8784.2008.00117.x

Gerlach, P., & Eriksson, K. (2021). Measuring cultural dimensions: External validity and internal consistency of Hofstede's VSM 2013 scales. *Frontiers in Psychology*, *12*(1), 1–9. https://doi.org/10.3389/fpsyg.2021.662604

Hall, E.T. (1989). *Beyond Culture*. New York: Anchor Books.

Hassan, E.M., & Hassan, E.M. Jnr. (2020). The connection between national culture and organizational culture: A literature review. *Britain International of Humanities and Social Sciences (BIoHS) Journal*, *2*(1), 179–189. https://doi.org/10.33258/biohs.v2i1.168

Head, T.C., Larsen, H.H., Nielsen, P.L., & Sorensen, Jr., P.F. (1993). The impact of national culture on organizational change: A Danish case study. *International Journal of Public Administration*, *16*(11), 1793–1814.

Heydari, A., Laroche, M., Paulin, M., & Richard, M-O. (2021). Hofstede's individual-level indulgence dimension: Scale development and validation. *Journal of Retailing and Consumer Services*, *62*.

Hofstede, G., Hofstede, G.J., & Minkov, M. (2010). *Cultures and Organizations: Software of the Mind: Intercultural Cooperation and Its Importance for Survival*. London: McGraw-Hill.

Kahler, E. (1961). Culture and evolution. *The Centennial Review*, *5*(3), 239–259.

Khan, M., & Panarina, E. (2017). The role of national cultures in shaping the corporate management cultures: A four countries theoretical analysis. *Journal of Eastern European and Central Asian Research (JEECAR)*, *4*(1), 1–25. https://doi.org/10.15549/jeecar.v4i1.152

Kluckhohn, C. (1951). The study of culture. In D. Lerner & H.D. Lasswell (Eds.), *The Policy Sciences* (pp. 86–101). Stanford, CA: Stanford University Press.

Knoll, D.L., & Gill, H. (2011). Antecedents of trust in supervisors, subordinates, and peers. *Journal of Managerial Psychology*, *26*(4), 313–330. https://doi.org/10.1108/02683941111124845

Krupskyi, O.P., & Kuzmytska, Y. (2020). Organizational culture and business strategy: Connection and role for a company survival. *Central European Business Review*, *9*(4), 1–26. https://doi.org/10.18267/j.cebr.241

Lee, S.M., Olson, D.L., & Trimi, S. (2010). The impact of convergence on organizational innovation. *Organizational Dynamics*, *39*(3), 218–225.

Matuska, E., & Grubicka, J. (2014). Diffusion of the national business culture? -The example of Swedish impacts in Poland. *Andragogika, Zlin – Czech Rep., Special Issue*, *48*(1), 2–13.

Meca, A., Allison, K., Ayers, K.L., & Cruz, B. (2023). The role of family cultural values in adolescent health and psychosocial functioning. *Encyclopedia of Child and Adolescent Health*, *2*(1), 660–669. https://doi.org/10.1016/B978-0-12-818872-9.00068-6

Mihet, R. (2012). Effects of culture on firm risk-taking: A cross-country and cross-industry analysis. *Journal of Cultural Economics*, *37*(1), 109–151. https://doi.org/10.1007/s10824-012-9186-2

Ministry of Foreign Affairs of Denmark. (2023, April 4). *Trust: A Cornerstone of Danish Culture*. https://denmark.dk/people-and-culture/trust

Ministry of Foreign Affairs of Denmark. (n.d. a). *New Climate Action Strategy*. https://um.dk/en/foreign-policy/new-climate-action-strategy

Ministry of Foreign Affairs of Denmark. (n.d. b). *Sustainability*. https://denmark.dk/innovation-and-design/sustainability

Minkov, M. (2007). *What Makes Us Different and Similar: A New Interpretation of the World Values Survey and Other Cross-Cultural Data?* Sofia: Klasika i Stil.
Ostroff, C., Kinicki, A.J., & Muhammad, R.S. (2013). Organizational culture and climate. In I.B. Weiner, N.W. Chmitt & S. Highhouse (Eds.), *Handbook of Psychology* (p. 12), *Industrial and Organizational Psychology* (pp. 643–676). Hoboken, NJ: John Wiley & Sons. https://doi.org/10.1002/9781118133880.hop212024
Prim, A., Filho, L.Z., Zamur, G., & Di Serio, L.C. (2017). The relationship between national culture dimensions and degree of innovation. *International Journal of Innovation Management*, *21*(1). https://doi.org/10.1142/S136391961730001X
Scandinavian-Polish Chamber of Commerce. (n.d.). https://www.spcc.pl/en/firma/profil/17307
Schein, E. (2004). *Organizational Culture and Leadership* (4th ed.). San Francisco, CA: Jossey-Bass.
Sent, E.M., & Kroese, A. (2022). Commemorating Geert Hofstede, a pioneer in the study of culture and institutions. *Journal of Institutional Economics*, *18*(1), 15–27. https://doi.org/10.1017/S174413742000051X
Shi, X., & Wang, J. (2011). Cultural distance between China and US across GLOBE model and Hofstede model. *International Business and Management*, *2*(1), 11–17. http://doi.org/10.3968/j.ibm.1923842820110201.004
Sønderskov, K., & Dinesen, P. (2014). Danish exceptionalism: Explaining the unique increase in social trust over the past 30 years. *European Sociological Review*, *30*(6), 782–795. https://doi.org/10.1093/esr/jcu073
Spencer-Oatey, H. (2012). What is culture? A compilation of quotations. *GlobalPAD Core Concepts*. Available at GlobalPAD Open House: www.warwick.ac.uk/globalpadintercultural
Trompenaars, F., & Hampden-Turner, C. (1997). *Riding the Waves of Culture: Understanding Cultural Diversity in Business*. London: Nicholas Brealey.
VELUX. (2022). *VELUX: Raport zrównoważonego rozwoju 2020–2021. W drodze do ambitnego celu*. https://velcdn.azureedge.net/-/media/marketing/pl/pdf/velux-raport-zrowowazony-rozwoj.pdf
VELUX. (n.d. a). *About Us*. www.velux.com/who-we-are/about-us
VELUX. (n.d. b). *History*. www.velux.com/who-we-are/history
VELUX. (n.d. c). *Sustainability Strategy 2030*. www.velux.com/what-we-do/sustainability/sustainability-strategy
VELUX. (n.d. d). *VELUX Values*. www.velux.com/who-we-are/values
Venaik, S., Zhu, Y., & Brewer, P. (2013). Looking into the future: Hofstede long term orientation versus GLOBE future orientation. *Cross Cultural Management: An International Journal*, *20*(1), 361–385. https://doi.org/10.1108/CCM-02-2012-0014
VKR Holding A/S. (n.d.). *Corporate Social Responsibility*. https://vkr-holding.com/vkr/csr/?lang=en
Wolf, T. (2006). Culture, leadership, and organizations: The GLOBE study of 62 societies [review]/House, R. J., Hanges, P.J., & Javidan, M., Eds. *Journal of Applied Christian Leadership*, *1*(1), 55–71.

10 Challenges in managing a Polish-Ukrainian team

Exploring intercultural, international, and interlingual differences

Klaudia Bączyk-Lesiuk, Aleksandra Cybulska, and Monika Guzek

Introduction

Navigating the intricate landscape of managing a Polish-Ukrainian team requires a deep understanding of intercultural, international, and interlingual differences. The amplifying trends of globalisation and workforce mobility accentuate the urgency to strengthen the competencies of managers in international companies. Within this context, managers in organisations play a pivotal role in identifying and leveraging opportunities, as well as discerning risks inherent in the complex international environment (Yalcinyigit & Aktas, 2023).

Managerial performance is significantly shaped by acquired knowledge and experience, predominantly influenced by personality attributes and managerial competencies. These create a unique quality of intellectual capital. Employees' skills, knowledge, and abilities form the foundation upon which the organisation develops its capabilities. It's through the collective expertise and talents of the workforce that the company can enhance its overall abilities and effectively use its capacity by hiring intercultural human resources. Recognising and utilising the diverse skills of employees is crucial for promoting innovation, productivity, and sustained success within the organisation (Piwowar-Sulej, 2021). Nowadays, companies focus a significant part of their activities on operating in an international environment. This phenomenon is related not only to the desire to scale business and presence in foreign markets but also to the global political and social situation and employee mobility. This involves hiring individuals from diverse cultures who are responsible for daily cooperation and communication. While being fluent in the host country's language contributes to effective cooperation, essential qualities include a willingness to communicate, openness, a curiosity to understand others' perspectives, and respect for diversity. Consequently, there is a growing demand in the labour market for individuals possessing well-developed intercultural competencies (Ahmad & Saidalavi, 2019).

Therefore, in the specialised domain of international human resources management (IHRM), a pronounced role emerges in recruiting managers attuned

DOI: 10.4324/9781032636962-13

to the dynamic intricacies of the global market, particularly within the unique context of a Polish-Ukrainian team. The importance of this subject has significantly intensified in the context of the augmented representation of Ukrainians in Polish organisations. This increase has been particularly notable since February 2022, following the heightened hostilities in Ukraine, which precipitated a sudden influx of individuals of Ukrainian origin into organisations in Poland. This surge has introduced a heightened level of complexity to managing multicultural teams, necessitating a more comprehensive understanding of the cultural, linguistic, and international intricacies involved (JCD Research, n.d.).

This chapter aims to identify the challenges inherent in managing a Polish-Ukrainian team, specifically examining intercultural, international, and interlingual differences. The study employs a theoretical framework, extensively exploring existing literature and recent research findings that delve into the intricacies of managing teams of composed Polish and Ukrainian members. The resulting insights from this analysis are intended to provide an understanding of the challenges which are faced within such teams and identify factors that foster improved cooperation and communication. This exploration shows the complexities tied to managing a Polish-Ukrainian team, providing valuable solutions and directions for managers navigating similar multicultural contexts.

The role of intercultural competencies

The human relations trend that emerged in the theory and practice of management science in the 1950s influenced the interest in cross-cultural competencies. It developed "across a range of concepts within the social systems school such as interactionism, the organisation as an intentional, decision-making and structural-functional system" (Mazur, 2012, p. 182). In contrast, in the last 25 years of the twentieth century, organisations were predominantly approached from two perspectives: situational-personalist and cultural-communicative. During this period, competencies began to be interpreted as the specialised training, knowledge, aptitude, experience, and skills required to hold a particular position (Mazur, 2012). Competence is a broad concept that expresses the ability to transfer skills and knowledge to new situations within a professional context. It also includes organisation and planning of work, readiness to innovate, and the ability to cope with unusual tasks. The term encompasses the personality traits necessary to work effectively with colleagues, managers, and customers (Enehaug et al., 2022).

The growth of companies and their international operations has contributed to an increasing highlight of the importance of developing intercultural competencies among managers. These are defined as the capacity to shape the process or influence the dynamics of multicultural interaction to prevent misunderstandings and create opportunities for solutions to shared challenges in a way acceptable to all stakeholders (Menlimuratova, 2023).

Intercultural competence primarily manifests itself through the ability to accept, respect, and make effective use of the judgements, tasks, and actions of other individuals in order to create the right conditions to adapt and develop cooperation and arrive at effective solutions for integrating and shaping a shared world (Iwaniuk, 2014). Moreover, competence researchers also point out that intercultural competence is attributed to a specific person, and each person is characterised by reflexivity, rationality, and linguistic ability to communicate. Thus, it can be deduced that each individual has access to his or her competence based on an action's effectiveness and reflection on that action. Intercultural competence is fundamentally influenced by the individual oneself (Fink & Mayrhofer, 2009).

The aforementioned definitions aim to underscore the significance of cross-cultural competence, highlighting its desirability and utility for individuals. Being inherently flexible, individuals possess the capacity to adapt their behaviour based on the situation and cultural context. A conceptualisation of cross-cultural competence, defined as "a set of skills essential for effective and appropriate interaction with individuals who exhibit linguistic and cultural diversity", has been expounded by Fantini and Tirmizi (2006, p. 12). He identified several components of intercultural competence, encompassing factors such as level of personal development, proficiency in the official language of the country, communication skills, cooperation, ability to create interpersonal relationships, adopted attitudes, and awareness of ongoing phenomena. Meanwhile, in their contemplations, Fink and Mayrhofer (2009) underscore the paramount importance of personality predispositions, highlighting their inherent connection with social mechanisms. These mechanisms, such as stereotyping, stigmatisation, and us-them categorisation, are focal points of scrutiny within the realms of social psychology and sociology. These aspects, identified as potent barriers to intercultural interaction, are frequently noticed through participants' experiences in intercultural communication training, seminars, and courses. Acknowledging these intricacies underscores the intricate interplay between individual personality traits and broader societal influences in shaping the landscape of intercultural dynamics.

McCrae and Costa (2005) identify five factors that influence the personality model that characterises the international manager who is capable of working in a diverse environment: extraversion, neuroticism, openness to new experience, agreeableness, and conscientiousness. Each factor is characterised by a variable level of susceptibility, that is, experiencing positive and negative emotions, ease of expressing own opinions, and establishing interpersonal contacts. Taking into consideration the character differences of the individuals employed, it is important to acknowledge that each person has different capabilities to develop their competencies, including intercultural skills. Emphasising the quantitative aspect of communication, which focuses on explicit and short-term benefits, requires fundamental intercultural skills. However, if the interaction is to be sustained over the long term, an emotional or motivational element (qualitative aspect) should be involved, resulting in empathy, a positive attitude towards otherness, imagination, and creativity (Fink & Mayrhofer, 2009).

Undoubtedly intercultural competencies have emerged as a pivotal focal point within the realm of international leadership management. This heightened recognition has spurred a surge in interest from both researchers and business practitioners, signifying the growing importance and relevance of this topic. The dynamic landscape of global business operations demands a nuanced understanding of intercultural competencies as an essential facet for effective leadership in diverse and cross-cultural contexts. This surge in attention underscores the pivotal role that mastering intercultural competencies plays in the contemporary discourse of international management.

Intercultural competence and the effectiveness of an international manager in the Polish-Ukrainian context

At present, human capital is recognised as one of the most important resources of a company's competitive advantage. Therefore, there is increased interest in the effective performance management of international managers.

In the literature, labour effectiveness is understood as the ratio of labour outcomes, in the sense of outputs, to the broader labour input (Enehaug et al., 2022). Two main dimensions of measuring work effectiveness are mentioned, that is, the quantitative and qualitative dimensions. In the quantitative dimension, the employee is considered as a tool for achieving the company's business goals by influencing the company's performance through specific, parameterised methods that are expected to deliver possibly reliable results. In contrast, in the qualitative dimension, work effectiveness is measured by considering soft employee attributes such as loyalty, job satisfaction, or ethics (Fink & Mayrhofer, 2009).

In managing a Polish-Ukrainian team, the effectiveness of international human resource management is related to the employee's performance and the ability to cope with work in a culturally different environment. From the company's perspective, managers' goal is to generate profits and create an environment that prevents employee turnover. However, for employees, the purpose of their work is not only to perform tasks and earn money. In the context of the current situation regarding the war in Ukraine, the atmosphere in the workplace and building a psychologically safe place that is focused not only on achieving results but also on assisting (including psychological support) its employees are very important. The quality of interpersonal contacts is currently a tool for building psychological safety in Polish-Ukrainian teams (JCD Research, n.d.).

The effectiveness of international managerial personnel is thus first and foremost linked to the employee's deliverables and the ability to cope with working in a culturally different environment. From the company's perspective, managers' goal is to generate profits. However, for employees, their work's purpose is not only to perform tasks and earn money. Significant influences on their performance include the atmosphere in the workplace, opportunities for professional development, and the quality of interpersonal contacts. Measuring work performance is also a target of human resources departments to find out which factors motivate employees to work more effectively and whether the specific objectives set for them are properly chosen. In practice, performance appraisal considers several aspects, including the complexity of the tasks assigned and the experience of their execution, as well as the level of influence of the assessed person on the outcome.

Employee performance can be measured through a variety of methods and tools. To assess performance, it is necessary to define a set of desirable skills for a particular position, create a specific competency model, and then assess the individuals assessed in terms of the most relevant skills. Conducting such research makes it possible to determine an individual's behavioural traits, the individual's style of thinking, and also makes it possible to predict the ability to develop a person's competencies and thus be more effective (learning rate and development potential rate) (Olszak, 2015).

Numerous studies have been conducted worldwide on the qualifications of international managers that determine success in a culturally diverse environment. Arthur and Bennet, based on a survey of 338 managers, identified the five most important factors that have a high impact on the effectiveness of working in an international environment. These included management knowledge, work experience, motivation, flexibility, and, above all, adaptability. They also emphasised openness to other cultures and settled family situations. Conversely, Fish and Wood state that the effectiveness of working internationally is determined by an aptitude for intercultural communication, people management skills, transformational skills, and foreign internships (Sihad, 2016).

On the basis of his many years of research and experience in recruiting and training international managers, Marx (1999) argues that an individual's success and effectiveness are determined by one's ability to cope with culture shock in international business. Nowadays, it is already embedded in occupational risk. Only quite a few managers can cope with it; others, on the contrary, feel disoriented and are unable to achieve high performance at work. Marx's research shows that among British managers, one in seven works ineffectively in cross-cultural teams, whereas in the United States, the percentage is assumed to be between 25% and 40% (Marx, 1999). Contrary to that, research conducted among managers working in subsidiaries of multinational corporations in Poland shows that intercultural interactions positively influence the development of employees and largely contribute to their effectiveness (Rozkwitalska et al., 2014).

In the specific case of managing a Polish-Ukrainian team, the ability to navigate and mitigate culture shock becomes even more critical for international managers. Understanding the positive impact of intercultural interactions on employee development highlights the potential for effective management in this unique cultural context (JCD Research, n.d.).

Hay Group's periodic employee opinion surveys indicate that there are also other factors influencing employee engagement and effectiveness in most companies, regardless of the industry or country in which they operate. Determinants influencing employee effectiveness may include trust and cooperation between employees, clear and engaging organisational direction, and opportunities for development within the company (Wójcik, 2016).

In the Polish-Ukrainian team scenario, building trust and fostering cooperation between team members from different cultural backgrounds is paramount for overall team effectiveness. Providing a clear and engaging organisational direction that accommodates the cultural diversity within the team is essential. Opportunities for professional development must be tailored to cater to the multicultural nature of the team, contributing to enhancing overall effectiveness.

The most important fact is repeatedly emphasised by researchers and business practitioners: an effective international manager is not something that one is born with; it is a skill that is acquired, meaning that an individual has to continuously develop their competencies. One can become internationally effective only when one works on one's feelings, mindset, or social skills, which are components of intercultural competence.

In the context of managing a Polish-Ukrainian team, continuous development of intercultural competence is imperative for international managers. The emphasis on working on personal attributes, mindset, and social skills underscores the dynamic nature of intercultural effectiveness, especially in a diverse team setting.

Comparative analysis of Polish and Ukrainian cultures: differences and similarities

(Un)known culture

The outbreak of war in Ukraine proved to be a great challenge for everyone, including Poles, who until then knew relatively little about their neighbours. This unforeseen circumstance not only brought attention to geopolitical realities but also intensified the need for effective intercultural understanding, particularly in contexts like managing Polish-Ukrainian teams. The shared challenges stemming from the conflict underscored the importance of fostering a deeper appreciation for the cultural nuances and experiences of team members, creating momentum for enhanced intercultural competence among managers in these diverse settings. Surveys conducted until then on the relationship between Poles and Ukrainians were often linked to the historical aspect (e.g. referring to the events in Volhynia in 1943), current events in Ukraine (often of a political nature, such as the presidential election), or treated collectively, along with a description of Poland's other neighbours. The growing sense of threat and interest in the situation in Ukraine, noticeable since 2014 (CBOS, 2014), has shown how important the situation in the East is to Poles. Even then, the majority of Polish citizens were sceptical about the potential encroachment of foreign troops on Polish territory, seeing the threat primarily in economic and energy security. The start of the war in 2022 only intensified the threat, confronting both Poles and Ukrainians with a new challenge – living in a cross-cultural environment (in both the private and professional aspects, which is the subject of this chapter's research – note the authors). A sense of cultural proximity was also one, but not the only, of the reasons why Poles assisted refugees from Ukraine: "we are very close culturally and the society we have is very similar to Ukraine. If it was a completely different cultural-religious society, the situation would be completely different (Warsaw, younger); Also, a lot of Ukrainians were already in Poland before and Polish society got used to the Ukrainian language, and simply accepted this culture (Warsaw, younger); Culturally they are very similar, so that here there was no between us . . . . unless one goes back into the history, Volhynia and so on, but without that, we are the brothers (Warsaw, older)" (CBOS, 2023, p. 5).

In the area of Polish-Ukrainian cooperation, especially in the early stages, a language barrier might be visible. Both Ukrainian and Polish belong to the Slavic language groups. However, Ukrainian represents the East Slavic group and Polish represents the West Slavic group, which makes them share many features. This apparent similarity is particularly evident in the phenomenon called interlingual homonymy. According to the definition presented in the Great Dictionary of Correct Polish Language edited by Markowski (2006, p. 1708), homonymy is "the phenomenon of the sameness of sound (homophony), and often the sameness of writing (homography) of two or more linguistic elements – words or their forms – which do not share common meaning elements". The emergence of Polish-Ukrainian pairs of interlingual homonyms can have many, various reasons. Most often, however, it is because the lexical units of both languages have (or may have) a common Pto-Indo-European or Pto-Slavic origin. In the process of development, these words retained their similar sound but diverged in lexical meaning. In addition, some pairs of interlingual homonyms arose from divergence in words borrowed from other languages under the influence of intralinguistic processes. Interlingual homonyms can also arise as a result of the process of transition of words from Polish to Ukrainian and vice versa. Sometimes interlingual homonyms (but also paronyms) can be formed as a result of accidental coincidence in the sound of words of two languages: match – меч, kit – кіт. From a historical perspective, as emphasised by Stanishevska (2019), they often stem from interlingual influences, which can sometimes result in phonetic or graphical similarities in vocabulary, especially in the case of linguistically closely related languages. In the context of cross-linguistic homonymy, these barriers are primarily due to etymological and historical links between the Polish and Ukrainian languages. When analysing this phenomenon, both common Pto-Indo-European or Pto-Slavic roots and external influences, such as the processes of borrowing words from other languages, are taken into account. There is also the possibility that interlingual homonyms arise as a result of accidental phonetic or graphic convergence of the words of the two languages. This is especially true for languages with close genetic affinities. The homonymic relations discussed, although mysterious at first glance, are commonly present in language, both in intra-linguistic, interlinguistic, and universal contexts. They represent subtle linguistic pitfalls that require attention and understanding for both effective communication and the study of linguistic structure.

Interestingly, in other surveys where the relationship between refugee assistance and nationality was asked, the majority, 62%, said that it has no effect (Polityka Insight, 2022). Today, almost two years after the outbreak of the war, Poles continue to support the struggle of Ukrainians, however, a certain apprehension can be seen in the public mood linked, among other things, to the fact that many Ukrainian citizens have found their way very well into the Polish labour market, thus representing educated and experienced people. Surprise at this fact and the political and economic conflicts stimulated by the media (such as the use of the grain scandal in the election campaign) have caused Polish-Ukrainian teams to face further calls, not only cultural but also those driven by politicians and media figures. A new phenomenon has also been observed in the community, called Positive Attitude Dissonance (PAD), which shows its essence lies in the dissonance (contradiction) of perception about this community (Staniszewski, 2023).

Importance of cultural dimensions in team management

Knowledge of cultural dimensions, aside from their generalising nature, is one of the most important theoretical aspects that facilitate cooperation between representatives of given cultures. Studies are still being conducted around the world to isolate the dimensions that differentiate countries. Among the best-known typologies are those conducted by Hofstede (2001), Trompenaars and Hampden-Turner (1997), Gesteland (2003), Lewis (2005), and House et al. (2004). Although each contains elements relevant when working in a multicultural team, the authors will limit themselves to presenting only a few selected ones to understand the different cultural patterns of Poles and Ukrainians.

A starting point for discussing differences and similarities between cultures can be the concept proposed by Hofstede (2001). Using specific dimensions (Power Distance, Individualism/Collectivism, Motivation towards Achievement and Success, Uncertainty Avoidance, Long-Term Orientation, and Indulgence), he facilitated a detailed comparison of many countries, creating a new paradigm for considering cultural elements in international economics, communication, and cooperation (Hofstede & Hofstede, 2005). One dimension of culture that carries over to the business context, among others, is Power Distance. When analysing this dimension, it becomes crucial to seek answers to questions such as How much respect or obedience is shown to an authority figure? Or how godlike is the superior? Poland (68) and Ukraine (92) show differences in this dimension. Although both countries accept social hierarchy and employees are accustomed to clear instructions from superiors, Ukraine, with a particularly high score, manifests a deep social hierarchy. Ukrainians attach great importance to status symbols, emphasising differences between social positions. This is also confirmed by a 2016 study, which indicated that Polish managers tend to favour a more egalitarian approach to management compared to their Ukrainian counterparts (Małota, 2017).

When considering the individualism/collectivism dimension, it should be noted that Poland scores 47 on this dimension, suggesting no clear preference for either individualism or collectivism. Polish society exhibits a loose social framework in which individuals care mainly for themselves and their families. Ukraine, on the other hand, scores 55, indicating greater independence of individuals. However, this is not reflected in the study conducted by Małota (2017), which indicates that both Polish and Ukrainian societies exhibit collectivist traits, with the latter being more pronounced.

The dimension that differentiates both countries is also Motivation towards Achievement and Success. Poles (64) are considered a Decisive society, indicating that work is highly important for them, with an emphasis on justice, competition, and results. Ukraine, with a low score (25), requires a modest approach to oneself, expecting individuals in similar positions not to boast, but rather downplay their achievements.

Hall (1989), an American anthropologist and ethnologist, introduced an important division of culture into two opposing contexts: low context and high context. The concept of context refers to surrounding events, verbal and non-verbal communication, as well as accepted norms of behaviour in a given culture. Analysing this issue in the context of the cultures of Poland and Ukraine, there are slight differences, as an average level of this indicator characterises both cultures. The level of contextualisation of both countries is on the borderline that separates high contextualisation culture from low contextualisation culture. This manifests itself, for example, in the approach to verbal messages and the focus on clear, direct communication, where information transmission is understood without considering deeper contexts or nuances. Often, a natural feature of communication between the two cultures is the use of direct refusal and the expression of negative positions with the word "no". In both countries, the younger generation shows greater independence, valuing egalitarian principles of social order in contrast to their older fellow citizens. At the same time, young citizens show less inclination towards conservatism, far more preferring a force and energy approach to solving complex problems (Prokopenko & Kryvoruchko, 2017).

Meyer (2015), in her best-selling book "The Culture Map", devotes a lot of space to task-based and relationship-based approaches. Cultures with a clear task-oriented focus tend to segregate affective and cognitive trust, particularly emphasising cognitive trust in the context of professional relationships. On the other hand, cultures with a clear relationship-oriented focus rely on both aspects of trust, both cognitive and affective, even in the workplace environment. Poland is in the middle position in this comparison, heading towards task-based. For Ukrainians, on the other hand, relationships and getting to know co-workers thoroughly are very important. Relationship building is done by eating meals together, going out for drinks, or meeting at the coffee machine. Relationships are built gradually, but they have a lot of impact at work. In Poland, there is an increasing separation of professional and private life, and teamwork is not necessarily linked to mutual affection. Nevertheless, being at the centre of the scale makes it easier for Poles to adapt to the expectations of representatives of other cultures, who need to create a bond to work well. Awareness of different team-building approaches seems to be very important when multicultural groups are formed.

All of the above cultural dimensions and the analyses carried out in their context serve to identify the differences and similarities that determine the characteristic features of a given society. Compared to other cultures, these characteristics manifest themselves, among other things, through a different system of capturing social roles, evaluating the behaviour of individuals, attachment to conventions, or planning for the future. Recognising these aspects is an important resource for better understanding and effective management of Polish-Ukrainian teams. However, it is worth emphasising that each individual is unique, so individual differences should be kept in mind and taken into account in the context of cross-cultural cooperation.

Challenges of working in a Polish-Ukrainian team: implications and recommendations

Recommendations for managers managing Polish-Ukrainian teams operating in Poland can cover many aspects. Based on a review of scientific literature and reports, a few are listed to facilitate cooperation in a multicultural environment:

1. inclusive team approach – the diversity of the team means that traditional management approaches can not only fail to facilitate collaboration but also hinder it. That's why it's so important to understand "inclusive leadership", which, according to Bourke (2016), involves: treating people and groups fairly – tasks are based on their unique characteristics, rather than on stereotypes, personalising individuals – it involves understanding and valuing the uniqueness of diverse others while also accepting them as members of the group, leveraging the thinking of diverse groups for smarter ideation and decision-making that reduces the risk of being blindsided (Gibson, 2022). It seems important in this context, therefore, to create an open, democratic culture that guarantees respect for each member. Only by ensuring, and more importantly, understanding inclusive leadership, will it help prevent potential conflicts and create a favourable working environment (Abarovskyi, 2023);

2. adaptation of management strategy to cultural dimensions – this point would include understanding and taking into account cultural differences between Poland and Ukraine in the management of the organisation, both onsite and online (Abarovskyi, 2023). It would be important not only to become familiar with the theory of each criterion but also to learn how to learn from it and put in place viable solutions to prevent the deepening of differences. The most important issue still seems to be to make team members aware and create a space of mutual understanding and respect for differences. In addition, important elements at this point would be to adapt communication strategies and motivational activities to the specifics of the two cultures;
3. emphasise the individualism of the individual – although knowledge of the dimensions of cultures can facilitate the understanding of certain classic behaviours, it is nevertheless based on a kind of generalisation. Team building, therefore, must not be based on fostering divisions and thus often upholding stereotypes (which, as studies among Poles and Ukrainians have shown, are less positive than autostereotypes) (Levus & Maksymych, 2023), but on creating conditions for the development of individual skills and talents, operating across cultural or national divides;
4. psychological support – due to the difficult migration situation following the outbreak of war, many migrants are in crisis. Providing psychological support, but also organising training on how to cope with stress and adapt to the new environment can contribute to faster acculturation and finding their way in the new situation;
5. media monitoring and conflict management – it seems natural that a person cannot function without other people; even if he declares that he tries to function away from social media and television, he can't avoid discussions with cross-cultural overtones in his environment. Awareness of the media's influence on the perception of intercultural conflicts can significantly prevent and anticipate conflicts that may arise in the Polish-Ukrainian team. Therefore, it is worthwhile to focus on reliable information and develop the ability to analyse media content without giving in to catchy slogans and driven conflicts. Understanding and being willing to discuss difficult issues is a key leadership task. Keeping in mind Ukraine's high power distance and collectivist attitude, it is important to realise that employees are more likely (due to habit) to look up to those in a higher position. A leader should skilfully manage conflict by helping the team find a solution;
6. conflict prevention – it is also worthwhile to establish a system of effective conflict resolution in the team. Everyone must know the methods of dealing with them, and often systemic solutions are introduced in such situations. Educating staff on how to consciously avoid escalating conflicts, if only through training in this area, can result in fewer conflicts and greater tolerance among team members. At the same time, it is worth noting that conflicts can contribute to improved work outcomes when properly managed. Gibson

(2022) confirms this by listing five essentially possible approaches: avoidance, accommodation, forcing, compromising, and win-win (Gibson, 2022);

7. team building through common goals – this is a universal principle that can help unite a team, regardless of background. Emphasising common values and organisational goals can result in a cohesive team that focuses more on action and common elements than on differentiating ones;
8. creation of integration programmes – serves primarily to create, often on an intuitive basis, a cohesive team, aware of the potential of individual members. Integration events and programmes support the building of relationships between employees, not only based on formal methods. It is important to make team members aware of the importance of informal methods of getting to know each other and encourage them to participate in cultural and social events.

The recommendations listed are only an outline, and the effectiveness of managerial actions largely depends on the specific contexts of the group, the individual needs of employees, and other factors requiring a flexible approach.

Conclusion

The above considerations clearly show the significant impact of possessing and developing intercultural competencies on the effectiveness of managing Polish-Ukrainian teams. The assumed similarity between employees from both countries due to geographical proximity can create many challenges and conflicts within the organisation. Given the historical and geopolitical context, the need for nuanced intercultural understanding is paramount, especially in light of recent events such as the war in Ukraine.

In recent years, the increased mobility of employees from Ukraine and the war in Ukraine have changed the situation for many HR teams, but also for many managers. Until now, the issue of managing cultural diversity has been an important, but not a primary challenge in many organisations. The influx of Ukrainian employees and the complex historical backdrop underscore the urgency of addressing cultural diversity as a central concern for HR teams and managers alike.

The spectre of the great resignation, the necessity for employers to adapt to the labour market situation, as well as the care of the existing team further demonstrate that the topic of cultural diversity cannot remain just a slogan. In navigating the challenges posed by the great resignation and evolving labour market dynamics, acknowledging and actively managing cultural diversity becomes integral for organisational resilience.

To be able to perform their duties and managerial functions effectively, the modern manager must possess the relevant knowledge, experience, or the desired set of personality traits and managerial skills and demonstrate well-developed intercultural competencies. In management, intercultural competence is seen as the ability to work effectively across cultural differences. They not only facilitate dealing with the new and unusual. They are a pool of knowledge and practical skills that influence appropriate communication decisions about subjects representing a foreign cultural background and also allow overcoming the effects of culture shock. The evolving labour situation demands modern managers to not only hone traditional skills but also acquire and demonstrate heightened intercultural competencies, especially when managing diverse Polish-Ukrainian teams. The impacts of culture shock, heightened by events from last years, necessitate a proactive approach to fostering cross-cultural understanding.

The literature describes the many benefits of consciously using cultural diversity and the benefits it brings to employees and organisations. Firstly, it allows relative control over multicultural processes within an organisation to be maintained. It supports the creation of a coherent system of values, formed through negotiation, a well-considered vision, and objectives for the tasks to be performed. Secondly, it provides an opportunity to bring together different points of view and ways of thinking which develops the creativity and innovation of employees. It enables dialogue to develop shared values and attitudes and becomes the foundation for a strong group identity among members, as well as an awareness of interdependence and co-responsibility. Thirdly, familiarising oneself with other cultures and being with their representatives minimises the natural fear of strangeness, so the quality of cooperation increases and a synergistic effect emerges. It allows other employees and their cultures to be recognised as capital, being a factor in creating a friendly working environment where the employee feels his or her contribution to the company is valued. In the unique context of Polish-Ukrainian collaboration, these benefits take on added significance. Effective management ensures control over multicultural processes, fosters innovation through diverse perspectives, and creates a cohesive environment amidst cultural differences, all contributing to a resilient and inclusive workplace.

It should be remembered, however, that the effectiveness of work in Polish-Ukrainian teams is not only manifested in the quality of the work performed. Managers and employees by their attitude directly impact the implementation of the strategy and the creation of a safe and inclusive workplace. Developing cultural intelligence at all levels of the company's organisational hierarchy has an impact on creating and implementing a strategy that responds to the challenges of multiculturalism. Beyond task-oriented effectiveness, the attitudes and cultural intelligence of managers and employees play a pivotal role in implementing strategies for an inclusive and safe workplace, vital in the context of multicultural challenges posed by Polish-Ukrainian collaboration.

Bibliography

Abarovskyi, S.S. (2023). Doslidzhennia vplyvu riznykh metodiv upravlinnia komandoiu na rezultatyvnist ta zadovolenist robotoiu v multykulturnykh virtualnykh komandakh. *Suchasnyi menedzhment*, 19–23.

Ahmad, S., & Saidalavi, K. (2019). Cultural intelligence and leadership effectiveness in global workplaces. *International Journal on Leadership*, *7*(1), 1–7.
Bourke, B. (2016). Meaning and implications of being labelled a predominantly white institution. *College and University; Washington, 91*(3), 12–18, 20–21.
CBOS. (2014). Zainteresowanie sytuacją na Ukrainie i poczucie zagrożenia w październiku. *Komunikat z badań*. https://cbos.pl/spiskom.pol/2014/k_144_14.pdf
CBOS. (2023). *Polacy o Ukraińcach. Komunikat z badań*. www.cbos.pl/PL/publikacje/fokusy/pliki/2023/fk_005_2023.pdf
Enehaug, H., Spjelkavik, Ø., Falkum, E., & Frøyland, K. (2022). Workplace inclusion competence and employer engagement. *Nordic Journal of Working Life Studies*, *12*(1). https://doi.org/10.18291/njwls.128260
Fantini, A., & Tirmizi, A. (2006). Exploring and assessing intercultural competence. *World Learning Publications*. Paper 1. http://digitalcollections.sit.edu/worldlearning_publications/1
Fink, G., & Mayrhofer, W. (2009). Cross-cultural competence and management – Setting the stage. *European Journal of Cross-Cultural Competence and Management*, *1*, 42–65. https://doi.org/10.1504/ejccm.2009.026733
Gesteland, R.R. (2003). *Cross-Cultural Business Behavior: Marketing, Negotiating, and Managing across Cultures*. Copenhagen: Copenhagen Business School Publications.
Gibson, R. (2022). *Bridge the Culture Gaps: A Toolkit for Effective Collaboration in the Diverse, Global Workplace*. London: Nicholas Brealey Publications.
Hall, E.T. (1989). *Beyond Culture* (2nd ed.). New York: Anchor Books.
Hofstede, G. (2001). *Culture's Consequences: Comparing Values, Behaviors, Institutions, and Organizations across Nations* (2nd ed.). Thousand Oaks, CA: Sage Publications.
Hofstede, G., & Hofstede, G.J. (2005). *Cultures and Organizations: Software of the Mind, Revised and Expanded* (2nd ed.). New York: McGraw-Hill.
House, R., Hanges, P.J., & Javidan, B. (2004). *Culture, Leadership, and Organizations: The GLOBE Study of 62 Societies*. Thousand Oaks, CA: Sage Publications.
Iwaniuk, I. (2014). Kompetencja wielokulturowa – różnorodność podejść do definicji tego pojęcia we współczesnej myśli pedagogicznej. *Języki Obce w Szkole*, No. 4. https://lib.iitta.gov.ua/7656/1/iwaniuk.pdf
JCD Research. (n.d.). *Polska – Ukraina. O komunikacji w zespołach międzykulturowych: szanse, wyzwania, dobre praktyki*. https://research.jcd.pl/komunikacja-miedzykulturowa.pdf
Karaszczuk, H., & Pryjmaczok, O. (2006). Homonimia międzyjęzykowa (ukraińsko-polska). *Annales Universitatis Mariae Curie-Skłodowska Lublin-Polonia*, *24*, 157–173.
Levus, N.I., & Maksymych, O.M. (2023). Uiavlennia Ukraintsiv pro sebe ta pro Poliakiv: porivnialnyi analiz etnichnykh stereotypiv. *Vcheni zapysky TNU imeni V.I. Vernadskoho. Seriia: Psykholohiia*, *34*(4), 44–49. https://doi.org/10.32782/2709-3093/2023.4/08
Lewis, R.D. (2005). *When Cultures Collide: Managing Successfully across Cultures*. Boston: Nicholas Brealey Publishing.
Malota, W. (2017). Poland and Ukraine in cross-cultural management: Ukrainian and polish culture of management and work – Similarities and differences. *Perspektywy Kultury*, *17*(2), 17–29.
Markowski, A. (Ed.). (2006). *Wielki słownik poprawnej polszczyzny*. Warszawa: PWN Publications.
Marx, E. (1999). *Breaking Through Culture Shock*. London: Nicholas Brealey Publishing.
Mazur, B. (2012). Kompetencje międzykulturowe w opinii podlaski menedżerów. *Współczesne Zarządzanie*, *1*, 182–191.
McCrae, R.R., Costa, P.T. (2005). *Osobowość dorosłego człowieka: perspektywa teorii pięcioczynnikowej*, Kraków: WAM.

Menlimuratova, E. (2023). Main characteristics of intercultural competence. *Middle European Scientific Bulletin, 41*, 41–46.
Meyer, E. (2015). *The Culture Map*. New York: Public Affairs.
Olszak, C.M. (2015). Business Intelligence and Analytics in Organizations. In: Mach-Król, M., M. Olszak, C., Pełech-Pilichowski, T. (eds) *Advances in ICT for Business, Industry and Public Sector. Studies in Computational Intelligence*, vol 579. Springer, Cham. https://doi.org/10.1007/978-3-319-11328-9_6
Piwowar-Sulej, K. (2021, January 1). Human resources development as an element of sustainable HRM – With a focus on production engineers. *Journal of Cleaner Production*. https://doi.org/10.1016/j.jclepro.2020.124008
Prokopenko, O., & Kryvoruchko, L. (2017). Podobieństwa i różnice kulturowe jako podstawa rozwoju wzajemnie korzystnych stosunków między Polską a Ukrainą. *Perspektywy Kultury, 17*(2), 7–16.
Polityka Insight. (2022). *Polacy wobec Ukraińców. Analiza postaw społecznych*. www.politykainsight.pl/_resource/multimedium/20314977
Rozkwitalska, M., Chmielecki, M., & Przytuła, S. (2014). The positives of cross-cultural interactions in MNCs. *Actual Problems of Economy, 157*(7), 382–392.
Sihad, K. (2016). *Ewolucja podejścia do kwalifikacji menedżera międzynarodowego w przedsiębiorstwach międzynarodowych*. In: Glinkowska B. (eds) Uwarunkowania – procesy – wyniki badań, Łódź: Wydawnictwo Uniwersytetu Łódzkiego.
Stanishevska, O. (2019). *Źródła polsko-ukraińskich homonimów i paronimów*. https://conf.ztu.edu.ua/wp-content/uploads/2019/06/309.pdf
Staniszewski, R. (2023). *Społeczna percepcja uchodźców z Ukrainy, migrantów oraz działań podejmowanych przez polskie państwo. Raport porównawczy z badań opinii publicznej, które zostały przeprowadzone na próbach ogólnopolskich osób w wieku 16–65 lat oraz próbie regionalnej w latach 2022–2023*. https://dev-spolecznapercepcjamigrantow2.ckc.uw.edu.pl/wp-content/uploads/sites/147/2023/05/Raport-2023-dr-Robert-Staniszewski-Broszura.pptx.pdf http://dx.doi.org/10.13140/RG.2.2.11000.93444
Trompenaars, F., & Hampden-Turner, C. (1997). *Riding the Waves of Culture: Understanding Diversity in Global Business*. London: Nicholas Brealey Publications.
Wójcik, E. (2016). *Kitas interkulturell gedacht*. Wiesbaden: Springer VS.
Yalcinyigit, S., & Aktas, H. (2023). A research on the relationship of social intelligence and cultural intelligence with leadership styles. *Istanbul Business Research, 52*(1), 107–132. http://doi.org/10.26650/ibr.2023.52.947907

11 How international FMCG companies maximise employees' intrinsic motivation by adapting to cultural differences in expression of basic psychological needs

Marek G. Tomalak

DISCLAIMER: Opinions presented in this chapter are personal views of the author, based on almost 15 years of international experience in regional and local managerial roles in Switzerland, Russia, Ukraine, and Ireland with globally leading FMCG companies. These opinions may be different from the position of the PepsiCo Company.

Introduction

In today's increasingly complex and multicultural business landscape, international companies navigate a dynamic global economy with growth opportunities and market talent scarcity. In this environment, it becomes paramount to seize these growth opportunities and elevate employees' motivation and performance by addressing the basic psychological needs for autonomy, competency, and relatedness.

Companies employ diverse human resources tools and strategies to operate effectively in this diverse landscape. They accommodate cultural differences in expressing basic psychological needs while fostering a unifying corporate culture that serves as the bedrock for collaboration and group identification.

The author embarks on a comprehensive exploration of this intricate dynamic in this chapter. The first part presents the theory of basic psychological needs, the pivotal frameworks of cultural differences, and the various leadership styles that arise from these intersections. Next, a detailed case study of PepsiCo Europe, with a focus on the company's efforts across the entire spectrum of HR practices, is scrutinised. Finally, through recruitment, development, evaluation, feedback, career planning, and team management, the way PepsiCo navigates the terrain of cultural differences while fostering a cohesive corporate culture is described.

Ethical consideration

Speaking of cultural differences may raise a concern of stereotyping and bring questions if – instead of talking about culture – people should not be judged as individuals, not just as a product of their environment.

DOI: 10.4324/9781032636962-14

Erin Meyer, INSEAD professor and expert in cultural differences, addressed this question in the introduction to her bestselling book "The Culture Map" (Meyer, 2014): "If you go into every interaction assuming that culture doesn't matter, your default mechanism will be to view others through your own cultural lens and to judge or misjudge them accordingly. . . . Yes, every individual is different. And yes, . . . you shouldn't make assumptions about individual traits based on where a person comes from. But this doesn't mean learning about cultural contexts is unnecessary. . . . you need to have an appreciation for cultural differences as well as respect for individual differences. Both are essential. . . . Cultural patterns of behaviour and belief frequently impact our perceptions (what we see), cognitions (what we think), and actions (what do). The goal . . . is to help you improve your ability to decode these three facets of culture and to enhance your effectiveness in dealing with them" (pp. 12–14).

It is worth underlining that individuals' needs and motivations are influenced by myriad factors, with culture being only one of them and of varying magnitude. The author strongly advocates against stereotyping and favours leveraging cultural knowledge to enhance our world view while respecting individual differences.

Theoretical background

Intrinsic motivation and self-determination theory

Intrinsic motivation and Self-Determination Theory (SDT) are essential psychological concepts that shed light on human motivation and behaviour. **Intrinsic motivation** refers to the inherent desire and satisfaction derived from engaging in an activity for its own sake rather than for external rewards or incentives. This type of motivation is driven by internal factors such as curiosity, interest, and a sense of accomplishment, leading to higher enjoyment and engagement in the task (Deci & Ryan, 2017).

Self-determination theory, developed by Deci and Ryan in the 1980s, explores the three basic psychological needs that underlie intrinsic motivation (Deci & Ryan, 1985, 2000):

- Autonomy: The need to feel in control of one's actions and choices, to have a sense of agency and independence in decision-making;
- Competence: The desire to feel capable and effective in achieving goals, mastering skills, and overcoming challenges;
- Relatedness: The need to connect and establish meaningful relationships with others, experiencing a sense of belonging and support.

Impact of basic psychological needs on employees' intrinsic motivation

When basic psychological needs, as defined by SDT, are satisfied, employees are more likely to experience higher levels of intrinsic motivation, leading to improved performance and overall job satisfaction.

Autonomy in the workplace gives employees a sense of control over their work, the freedom to make decisions, and the opportunity to engage in tasks aligned with their interests and values. When employees feel autonomous, they are more intrinsically motivated to take ownership of their work, leading to increased creativity, innovation, and initiative (Deci & Ryan, 2000, 2017; Gagné & Deci, 2005).

The need for **competence** at work refers to employees' desire to feel capable and effective in performing their tasks as well as expanding their skills, gaining valuable experience, and building their expertise. When employers provide opportunities for skill development, offer constructive feedback, and recognise achievements, employees are more likely to feel capable, valued, and motivated to excel in their roles (Deci & Ryan, 2000, 2017; Gagné & Deci, 2005).

Relatedness is critical for fostering a positive work environment. When employees feel connected to their colleagues and supervisors, experience a sense of camaraderie, and receive social support, they are more motivated to contribute to the team's success, leading to improved collaboration and teamwork (Deci & Ryan, 2000, 2017; Gagné & Deci, 2005).

Several research studies support the link between basic psychological needs, intrinsic motivation, and employee performance. For instance, Gagné and Deci (2005) conducted a meta-analysis demonstrating how satisfying psychological needs positively influenced intrinsic motivation and performance in various organisational settings.

Cultural differences in manifestations of needs for autonomy, competence, and relatedness

Employees from Eastern and Western cultures seem to exhibit some cultural differences in their manifestations of needs for autonomy, competence, and relatedness in the workplace, shaped by historical, social, and economic context, while the underlying needs are largely universal (Chirkov et al., 2003).

In Western cultures, there is a greater emphasis on individualism and personal autonomy. Employees may value the freedom to make independent decisions and have more control over their work schedules and tasks. They also expect to be consulted and proactively voice their opinions explicitly. By contrast, employees from Eastern cultures may emphasise collective decision-making more. They may prefer a structured hierarchical approach to work, where superiors significantly direct tasks and activities. They may easily accept facts that not everybody needs to be consulted on every topic and may not always share their opinions unless asked explicitly (Meyer, 2014).

Competence. In Western cultures, employees often seek continuous formal development and opportunities to acquire new skills. They may prioritise self-improvement and actively seek training programmes to enhance their competence. In Eastern cultures, employees might value experience and practical expertise gained through years of work in a particular field, emphasising practical knowledge over formal training and certifications (Deci & Ryan, 2017; Meyer, 2014, 2015, 2017).

Relatedness. In Eastern cultures, the sense of community and group cohesion is generally strong. Employees may place a high value on harmonious relationships within the workplace, and camaraderie among colleagues is essential. In Western cultures, while interpersonal relationships are valued, there might be a greater focus on task-oriented communication and efficiency (Hofstede, 1984; Meyer, 2014, 2015, 2017).

An example of these differences can be observed in team dynamics. In Western cultures, teams might be more fluid and flexible, allowing members to work autonomously. In contrast, in Eastern cultures, teams tend to have a more hierarchical structure with a stronger role of the leaders and sharply defined responsibilities (Triandis, & Gelfand, 2012; Meyer, 2014, 2015, 2017).

It is important to note that cultural differences are complex and can vary within regions and individuals. Sharp differences appear among generations and industries, often overshadowing cultural differences (e.g. Gen Z representatives may be more similar to each other across East and West than to Gen X within the same region) (Meyer, 2014, 2015, 2017).

Understanding cultural differences and their influence on employees' intrinsic motivation and performance is crucial for effective leadership in a diverse workplace. However, an organisation's success depends not only on recognising cultural nuances but also on how managers adapt their leadership styles to accommodate these differences. Effective leadership that acknowledges and embraces cultural diversity can foster a more inclusive and motivating work environment, ensuring that employees from various backgrounds feel valued and empowered (Meyer, 2014, 2015, 2017). The following section will explore the significance of adopting leadership styles that align with cultural variations and how this approach can enhance employee engagement, productivity, and overall organisational success.

Leadership styles (task vs. people orientation) in the context of cultural differences

One of the most popular frameworks for understanding leadership styles is based on two task versus people orientation dimensions. This model identifies four primary leadership styles: autocratic, democratic, withdrawn, and transformational. Each style reflects varying degrees of focus on tasks and people, influencing how leaders interact with their teams and drive organisational success (Bass, 1985; Hersey & Blanchard, 1988; Northouse, 2019; Yukl, 2013):

- autocratic leaders are highly task-oriented and tend to make decisions independently, with little input from their team members. They exercise authority

and control over their subordinates, setting strict guidelines and expecting compliance. While this style can be effective in certain situations, such as crisis management or when quick decisions are required, it may decrease employees' motivation and creativity due to limited autonomy and involvement;
- democratic leaders prioritise people orientation, encourage employees' participation in decision-making, and value their input. This leadership style fosters open communication, collaboration, and a sense of empowerment among team members. By involving employees in the decision-making process, democratic leaders can enhance job satisfaction and create a positive work environment that promotes innovation and problem-solving;
- withdrawn leaders are low on both task and people orientation. They tend to be hands-off, allowing employees a high degree of autonomy and freedom in their roles. While this style can be effective when managing a team of skilled and self-motivated individuals, it can lead to inefficiencies and a lack of direction if employees require more guidance and structure;
- transformational leaders excel in both task and people orientation. They inspire and motivate their teams to achieve extraordinary results by fostering a strong sense of purpose and vision. Transformational leaders actively engage with their employees, offering support, guidance, and developmental opportunities. This style empowers employees, encouraging them to grow both personally and professionally, and has been associated with higher levels of employee satisfaction and organisational performance.

By understanding and employing the appropriate leadership style of "task versus people" orientation – relevant to employees' culture and exhibited needs for autonomy, competence, and relatedness – leaders can effectively guide their teams to achieve success (Gagné & Deci, 2005; Deci & Ryan, 2017).

When considering cultural differences, certain leadership styles may be better suited to meet the needs of employees from Eastern and Western cultures.

Autonomy. Employees in both Eastern and Western cultures may need autonomy, but the level of emphasis and preferred leadership style may vary. In Western cultures, where individualism is more prominent, a democratic leadership style encouraging employee participation in decision-making can be beneficial. This approach allows employees to have a say in their work processes, fostering a sense of autonomy and empowerment. On the other hand, in Eastern cultures, where collectivism is more pronounced, a leadership style that balances some autonomy with guidance and direction might be preferred. Here, a transformational leadership style can be effective, as it allows leaders to inspire employees with a shared vision while also valuing their contributions and individual strengths (Gagné & Deci, 2005; Deci & Ryan, 2017).

Competence. Employees in both regions need to feel competent and effective in their work. In Western cultures, where continuous formal development is often valued, a transformational leadership style can support this need by providing employees with opportunities for skill enhancement, training, and mentoring. By recognising and fostering their competencies, transformational leaders can empower employees to excel in their roles. In Eastern cultures, where practical experience is highly valued, a mix of transformational and autocratic leadership may be more suitable. When used judiciously, authoritarian leadership can provide clear guidance and structure, ensuring that employees feel competent in performing their tasks (Deci & Ryan, 2000, 2017).

Relatedness. Both regions share a common need for relatedness and meaning in their work. Transformational leadership, which emphasises a compelling vision and a sense of purpose, can resonate with employees in both Eastern and Western cultures. By aligning employees' work with a broader purpose and demonstrating how their contributions make a meaningful impact, transformational leaders can enhance employees' intrinsic motivation and job satisfaction (Bass, 1985; Deci & Ryan, 2017).

It is important to note that individual and inter-industry differences within each region significantly affect how leadership styles are perceived and received. Leaders should be culturally sensitive and adopt a flexible approach, considering employees' unique needs and preferences (Northouse, 2019; Yukl, 2013).

Attitude towards decision-making and authority

Meyer (2014) presents an alternative way to look at leadership challenges in various cultures, focusing on two main aspects: how people make decisions and how they see authority. Authority is about how much respect and importance people attribute to someone's position or rank. People can have different attitudes towards authority, ranging from strongly believing in hierarchies to believing in equality (egalitarianism). Decision-making is about who makes the decision and how they do it – whether the leader decides alone or the team makes a decision together. Some cultures tend to have a top-down approach, while others prefer group agreement (consensus).

According to Meyer's research (Meyer, 2014), in cultures with top-down decision-making (like Russia), decisions are made quickly but can be changed if new information or arguments arise. When people from these cultures have made a decision, it is often more like a temporary arrangement that can be adjusted later (a small "d" decision). In cultures that favour consensus-based decision-making (common in much of the West), many people are usually involved in making decisions. This can take more time as they negotiate and agree as a group. However, once a decision is reached, it's implemented quickly because, while building consensus, they already worked out the details and got key people on board. In these consensus cultures, the term "Decision" is like having a capital "D", indicating a commitment that is significant and not easily changed (Meyer, 2014).

Meyers' (2014) cultures and leadership styles taxonomy links neatly with culture-specific manifestations for autonomy, competence, and relatedness – both among leaders and their followers. Adapting leadership style to those needs makes a difference in individuals' motivation, performance, group coherence, and productivity.

Having explored the importance of leadership styles and attitudes in addressing the needs of employees from different cultures, it becomes evident that effective Human Resources (HR) practices are essential in creating an inclusive and motivating work environment. HR practices, such as recruitment, development and training, performance review and feedback, career planning, and others, should be tailored to accommodate employees' diverse cultural needs and preferences. At the same time, they should serve the creation of a shared corporate culture, enabling seamless collaboration and group identification. In the following section, using the example of PepsiCo Europe, one of the leading global FMCG companies, we will delve into these HR practices, highlighting how cultural differences influence their design and implementation to foster employees' engagement, motivation, and overall organisational success.

PepsiCo Company's bio

PepsiCo is a global food and beverage company with a rich history dating back to its founding in 1965 through the merger of Pepsi-Cola and Frito-Lay. Headquartered in Purchase, New York, PepsiCo has grown to become one of the world's leading consumer goods companies. Its mission is to *create more smiles with every sip and every bite* for its consumers, customers, associates, communities, planet, and shareholders. For associates in particular, PepsiCo aims to create more smiles by creating meaningful opportunities to work, gain new skills, build successful careers, and maintain a diverse and inclusive workplace – as articulated in the Company mission statement (PepsiCo, 2023g).

On a global scale, PepsiCo operates in more than 200 countries and territories, producing a diverse portfolio of well-known brands across beverages, snacks, and nutrition, including Pepsi, Lay's, Gatorade, Tropicana, and Quaker Oats, among many others. The company's commitment to innovation, quality, and sustainability has made it a household name worldwide (PepsiCo, 2023g).

As a regional division, PepsiCo Europe oversees the company's operations in Europe, encompassing a vast and culturally diverse market – from Turkey, Israel, Kazakhstan, and Russia in the East through the entire European Union to the UK in the West. PepsiCo Europe has a presence (local offices) in numerous countries, with regional headquarters in Geneva, Switzerland. It continuously innovates and tailors its offerings to cater to European consumers' unique tastes and preferences while striving to minimise its environmental footprint. Through its local partnerships, manufacturing facilities, and distribution networks, PepsiCo Europe plays a significant role in shaping the food and beverage landscape across the continent (PepsiCo, 2023g).

Business challenge

Operating across a wide range of markets and cultures, PepsiCo Europe had to balance adapting to the cultural differences of its employees and building a unifying corporate culture to facilitate collaboration across borders and help group identification. While doing that, PepsiCo Europe also strived to increase employee motivation and job satisfaction. In the following sections, the author will review PepsiCo's approach to critical steps in the employee journey – from articulating and promoting desired behaviours through recruitment, development, goal setting, evaluation, feedback, and career planning to team management – and how PepsiCo caters for cultural differences, satisfying basic psychological needs while building unifying corporate culture.

Corporate culture versus cultural differences

PepsiCo lists seven corporate behaviours (known as The PepsiCo Way; see Figure 11.1) constituting its corporate culture. These include *"Raising the bar on talent and diversity", "Acting with Integrity", "Being consumer-centric", "Acting as owners", "Focusing and getting things done", "Voicing opinions fearlessly",* and *"Celebrating success"*. These behaviours sit in the centre of individual and team objectives, get into annual work plans, and are measured through formal Organizational Health Survey (OHS) and individual 360 Feedback. They affect all aspects of employees' experience (PepsiCo, 2023b).

While specific, they do support the basic psychological needs, as defined by SDT, in particular **autonomy** (*"act as owners", "voice opinions fearlessly"*), **competence** (*"be consumer-centric", "focus and get things done"*), and **relatedness** (*"celebrate success"*). While local expressions of those needs, driven by employees' cultures of origin, might be different, common corporate norms nudge employees to behave more consistently, in line with desired standards. Sharp articulation of those behaviours provides employees with mental tools enabling more automated responses (deference to authority). One may hear phrases like *"In the spirit of voicing opinion fearlessly*

The PepsiCo Way	raise the bar on talent & diversity	act with integrity	be consumer centric
act as owners	focus & get things done fast	voice opinions fearlessly	celebrate success

Figure 11.1 The PepsiCo Way – PepsiCo corporate behaviours (PepsiCo, 2023b)

I want to say that . . . " creating a safety zone for otherwise uncomfortable, culture-opposite behaviours.

PepsiCo employees, while bringing their own individual style to work, are also encouraged to embrace the corporate norms defined by The PepsiCo Way to build better rapport and more effective collaboration with their team members and partners (PepsiCo, 2023b). Companies like PepsiCo enable employees to embrace corporate behaviours across all stages of the employee journey – through recruitment, onboarding and training, feedback, goal setting, evaluation, and career planning. The topic will be tackled separately in the following subsections concluding with team management practices.

Recruitment

Besides competencies and critical experiences, selecting individuals with profiles compatible with the corporate culture or flexible enough to adapt to corporate norms is an important element of multinational companies' hiring model (PepsiCo, 2023a). Large multinational corporations often recruit young graduates into entry positions early in their careers to develop their operating style and avoid maladaptive habits. At a later stage, one of the main sources of talent became peer companies – multinationals of similar culture and values (PepsiCo, P&G, Mars, Unilever, and similar).

It is obviously not to say that all new hires are identical. On the contrary, diversity of background and thinking patterns is highly desired and valued to enrich company competitiveness – yet basic norms and behaviours like honesty (integrity), inclusiveness (diversity and talent), or leadership (getting things done) are critical in every hiring process (PepsiCo, 2023a).

Candidates are assessed through recruitment tools, including standardised competency tests (measuring cognitive and interpersonal potential) and assessment centres (measuring interpersonal skills), followed by interviews where hiring managers look for examples of past behaviours to assess competencies, experience, and motivations. Hiring manager would often prompt for cases of leadership (*"how did you lead a project from idea to execution"*), collaboration (*"how did you engage diverse partners to achieve a common goal"*), conflict management (*"how did you handle an opposing important stakeholder"*), and similar. The recruiter would assess the difficulty of the context, sophistication and adequacy of actions taken, and scale of results achieved, including what measures the candidate identified as important.

While all stages of the recruitment process assess candidates' potential across ***GREAT 5*** *(Growth, Relationship, Thinking, Agility, and Execution)*, the interview stage allows for the most in-depth exploration. It helps to resolve any doubts stemming from the earlier stages of the process and uncover more subtle cultural indicators (PepsiCo, 2023a, 2023e).

A natural problem at the interview stage is the level of subjectivity and cultural biases of the recruiter. It is resolved by post-interview calibration among several recruiters (typically three) of different backgrounds (nationalities, functions, and seniority). Most recruitments for managerial positions in PepsiCo are made with an outlook of candidates reaching higher ranks and progressing careers internationally (or at least interacting actively with international partners); therefore, effort in identifying candidates with the right profiles is intentional and considered an important investment.

The recruitment process would be identical for employees of East and West while visible stylistic differences appear among candidates' self-presentation (e.g. preference for "We" vs. "I" in the East – suggesting more collectivism) and selection of facts (e.g. focus on formal education, credentials, and awards – more prominent in the West). Experienced recruiter easily filters through those to uncover underlying objective facts and capabilities.

More fundamental differences may appear in attitude towards authority (hierarchical vs. egalitarian) and decision-making (top-down vs. collective), visible in past experiences or even direct interaction with the interviewer (e.g. Western candidates tend to be less intimidated by the interviewing situation). These may be a function of culture but also individual personality and must be assessed carefully.

Finally, the recruitment process also considers employees' basic psychological needs. In the increasingly talent-scarce market, companies like PepsiCo treat each interaction as an element of corporate image building. Recognising candidates' needs for autonomy, competency, and relatedness, companies will encourage them to autonomously ask questions of their interest, demonstrate additional competencies, and build informal connections with the interviewer and the working environment (e.g. the candidate would be often walked around the office to get the feel of the place and team). The interviewer would also explain the autonomy granted to potential new hires, how her or his competencies will be built, and how relations are nurtured in the company. The interview is a good opportunity for the candidate to calibrate her or his expectations and understand if the match is correct and if both parties find themselves compatible (PepsiCo, 2023a, 2023e).

Onboarding and training

Onboarding, on-the-job training, and formal development programmes – besides skills development – serve to unify culture by connecting employees of diverse backgrounds. They introduce standardised language and formal or informal processes to establish common communication platforms and behavioural norms, influencing and modulating cultural differences (PepsiCo, 2023d, 2023g).

Training programmes and collaboration at PepsiCo are often structured to include representatives of diverse cultures, carried out in business English, including the use of unifying, corporate-specific idioms, terms, and abbreviations, with common evaluation standards and often in international locations.

Many corporate values, like an egalitarian attitude to authority or a collective process of decision consultation, are being reinforced through formal or informal processes and ways of working (e.g. open office setting, addressing by first name, projects signed off by representatives of all functions involved, all-teams town hall meetings and newsletters) (PepsiCo, 2023d, 2023e).

In a corporate world like PepsiCo, peer group learning is a powerful form of development. Individuals and groups are frequently invited to share their ***"best practices"*** – holistic case studies of strategies, tactics, capabilities, and behaviours which brought positive outcomes. Other participants are invited to question and occasionally challenge those in public, provoking discussions and crystallising a consensus approach. Corporate values underlie both – the business case and the debate itself – making participants gradually gravitate towards a common ground.

A specific form of mandatory training is the so-called ***Code of Conduct training*** – a dedicated annual training reminding employees of the set of values which PepsiCo expects them to hold. This training is often accompanied by other "hard values" training like Anti-Bribery or Anti-Violence – which promote non-negotiable values and behaviours, their interpretations in the corporate world (often much stricter than defined by the rule of law, and consistent across the globe regardless of the local legal system), means of dealing with potential issues, and formal certification of acknowledgement signed by the employees at the end of the course. Again, this training provides a powerful common set of rules and language that superimpose on local cultural differences and enable closer integration through unifying corporate culture. As an example, the approach towards nepotism (hiring or managing family members) or bribery would be equally strict across Ukraine, Switzerland, Russia, or Ireland. In fact, it would be more stringent than most countries' cultural norms, bringing it to a common highest denominator and providing employees with clear red lines and specific guidelines for behaviour. Considering global reputation and legal risks, corporate culture cannot allow exceptions in these areas, regardless of local cultural norms (PepsiCo, 2023f).

Employees' differences in expression of autonomy, competence, and relatedness are respected in how training is organised. Typically, an employee would enjoy a certain level of autonomy in how he or she plans his or her development, including aligning the developmental plan with the manager, pursuing voluntary online courses, and choosing when (within the time limit) to complete the mandatory ones. Building competence comes through the very nature of training programmes but is often reinforced further by the exclusive nature of some of them (only for High Potential talents), facilitation and evaluation by authority figures (senior executives or recognised educational institutions), and formal acknowledgements (certifications). Finally, relatedness is typically supported by the collective experience of the training, including co-creation, debate, and informal exchanges among participants and trainers during training and accompanying leisure activities – building a sense of belonging, camaraderie, and collective identity (PepsiCo, 2023d).

There is much space for companies and training facilitators to customise the format to respect local cultural differences, yet generally, training and development programmes bring to life unifying corporate culture above local cultural differences.

Feedback

Feedback is probably the most direct tool for building awareness of cultural differences and unifying corporate culture. Taking the form of informal ad hoc interactions or formal, standardised 360 assessments between individuals, groups, or superiors and subordinates (both ways), feedback is a powerful tool to adjust behaviours (PepsiCo, 2023c).

Feedback in companies like PepsiCo tends to be structured around corporate norms (PepsiCo, 2023b) but also around five leadership principles called the **GREAT 5**:

1. **Growth:** curiosity and ability to learn from novel situations by constantly pushing outside their comfort zone and helping others to learn and develop.
2. **Relationships:** building and maintaining trusting relationships across organisational boundaries by modelling integrity, transparency, and authenticity, and being respectful and inclusive of others.
3. **Execution:** the energy, enthusiasm, and inspiration an individual brings to motivate others to action and to accomplish ambitious goals, simplifying complexity to drive quality results.
4. **Agility:** adapting a person's style and approach to an ever-changing business environment, managing pressure, and embracing and championing change to drive transformation.
5. **Thinking:** how an employee brings in and uses external insights (business, customer or consumer, industry, and global), thinks creatively, and takes a long-term and holistic perspective to make informed decisions.

The **GREAT5** applies to all employees regardless of their position (PepsiCo, 2023a).

Feedback (scaled from 1– serious *improvement needed* to 5 – *exceptional*) is collected from managers, peers, and subordinates, compared against global norms and enhanced with optional verbatims. As an outcome, the employee receives a formal report highlighting overall scores and critical areas of focus (top strengths and weaknesses). The 360 feedback highly depends on the subjective expectations of the assessment's individuals. For example, on the dimension of *"Creating an inclusive culture where every voice is being heard"*, the same person can be judged differently by a Westerner, used to express her or his opinions proactively versus an Easterner who may expect to be asked explicitly for his or her view. Consecutive rounds of providing and receiving feedback, combined with in-depth follow-up analysis, open discussions, and action planning are intended to calibrate and rebalance the behaviours.

The culture of giving feedback is continuously refined and ranges from straightforward forms, either institutionalised or spontaneous (e.g. on-the-spot feedback from peers in multifunctional teams) to more subtle, high-context one-on-one feedback wrapped in a set of positive messages. In any case, the culture of feedback is considered a critical enabler of the growth and agility of the company while also helping to build a unifying corporate culture (PepsiCo, 2023c).

In the author's opinion, autonomy, competency, and relatedness may be at stake when giving or receiving feedback, and their culture-specific expressions may dictate different actions-reactions. It seems, for instance, that in Western cultures, even direct feedback is not seen as undermining the individual sense of autonomy, competency, and relatedness. On the contrary, it tends to be viewed as an enabler of autonomous improvement and competency building, if it allows for sufficient space for autonomous actions, learning, and practising new behaviours. It tends to be independent of a relationship, focusing on facts and behaviours and not requiring prior deep trust. On the other hand, feedback in Eastern cultures tends to be treated with a bit of reservation, potentially questioning individual autonomy, competency, and even relatedness. Employees may see it sometimes as a way of controlling or manipulating one's behaviour rather than improving one's capabilities. Feedback in the East also appears more effective when built on strong, trusting relations or hierarchy, otherwise, it may get invalidated and rejected.

In summary, expressions of basic psychological needs about feedback differ among individuals, even if some cultural patterns may exist. Adjusting the form of feedback delivery and the mindset when receiving it may help equalise the cultural differences and improve the satisfaction of basic psychological needs, overall engagement, and team performance.

Goal setting and evaluation

The change of approach to "management by objectives" had been a critical transformation in the corporate world, allowing more efficient expansion of complex international operations without the need for hands-on supervision, thus amplifying employees' intrinsic motivation through autonomy, competency, and relatedness. In management by objectives, individuals are given a set of clear goals and measures at the outset of a period (typically, the new year) and granted considerable freedom in deciding how and with whom to pursue them (Drucker, 1954).

PepsiCo would set new objectives annually at the top of the organisation, framing them in three areas: *Faster* (related to business growth), *Stronger* (related to building talents, capabilities, and systems), and *Better* (related to sustainability of operations and impact on the planet and societies). Each of those objectives would have specific measures attributed (*KPI – Key Performance Indicators*), allowing for objective performance assessment in the middle and at the end of the year (Mid-Year and End-Year Review). These objectives would then be cascaded to lower levels, detailed and enriched to deliver corporate ambition collectively. Finally, those objectives would be linked to employees' individual evaluations and compensation schemes, allowing them to rate employees on a scale from 1 (*missed all critical goals*) to 5 (*exceeded all critical goals*) and attribute specific salary increases and bonus payouts.

While higher-level objectives and measures, such as Revenue, Share of Market, Profit, and Cash Flow, are consistent and comparable across all markets and cultures, there may be some level of difference in how specific goals and tactics are detailed out while cascading down the organisation. This allows to accommodate specific cultural differences by markets and cultures. In the author's experience, objectives cascaded in the Eastern cultures seem to be more direct, concise, and specific, while goals cascaded in the Western cultures appear a bit broader and ambiguous – accommodating for low versus high context communication and collective and egalitarian versus directive and hierarchical approach to authority and decision-making. NOTE: These differences, however, also depend on the individual approach of the manager, the nature of the function, and the specific business context; thus, culture plays some but is not an exclusive role here.

At PepsiCo, all objectives and performance results are recorded formally in the PDR – Performance and Development Review system. At the end of the year, the employee and manager would also describe in the PDR "how" the goals have been achieved, considering the GREAT 5 (*Growth, Relationship, Thinking, Agility, and Execution*) (PepsiCo, 2023a), leading to an assessment of results and competencies displayed by the individual. In the author's experience, managers from Western cultures tend to attribute a bit more weight to the people-oriented aspects, while managers from Eastern cultures seem to focus a bit more on pragmatic, task-related achievements.

In summary, the "management by objectives" approach directly builds on the basic psychological needs for autonomy (co-deciding on "what" and "how"), competency (building the skill set needed to achieve the goal), and relatedness (instilling a sense of trust and shared goals between employees and supervisors). Cultural differences in expressing those needs may influence the way objectives are cascaded, interpreted by employees, and assessed by managers. Remaining sensitive to cultural differences from both sides improves intrinsic motivation and the organisation's overall performance.

Career planning

Another unique characteristic of the people management process at international companies, like PepsiCo, is frequent and intentional **assignment changes**. Individuals are expected to change roles every two to four years, through either promotions or lateral moves across teams or functions (PepsiCo, 2023d). Typically, the high-potential talents would move faster and more frequently, but all individuals would be expected to change within five years except for narrowly defined groups of experts and very senior roles.

Regular role changes offer several intuitive benefits to the individuals (autonomy of exploration, new competencies development, and new relationships) as well as to the organisation (applying new thinking and challenging prior approaches without personal attachment or biases) (PepsiCo, 2023d).

Regular role changes also play the role of culture modulator. Like rocks rubbing against one another, individuals become more rounded when exposed to multiple role models and team compositions, gaining a more universal understanding of corporate culture and norms. Role changes also require a positive match between hiring managers and employees. Such a match starts from a strong competency fit (experience, ratings, and unique capabilities) but also a personal match (often taking into account the culture of the receiving team). Matchmaking happens through a formal "People Planning Process" followed by direct internal interviews and references. Such a process again incentivises behaviours corresponding with the company's accepted cultural norms as more broadly compatible and effective.

International assignments are a subset of regular assignment changes when an employee is encouraged and supported to take a role in overseas subsidiaries or headquarters of the company (PepsiCo, 2023d). More than any, such roles accelerate the process of cultural adaptation, as the employee gets disconnected from home culture and exposed to a variety of cultures simultaneously: host country culture, corporate culture, and (often) multiple cultures of new colleagues. In such cases, the corporate culture becomes a connecting factor and the most familiar experience, thus reinforcing even stronger employee behaviour and norms.

At PepsiCo, all assignment changes are part of the bigger, intentional process of people and career planning, happening at employee–manager and functional levels (PepsiCo, 2023d).

At the employee–manager level, besides regular (formal and informal) performance reviews and feedback sessions, there are also dedicated formal sessions – the so-called *Candid Career Conversations* – to discuss employees' career aspirations, realistic chances, and actions required to progress. The employee is asked to fill out a template called ACE (for *Aspirations, Competencies, Engagement*) outlining her or his ambitions, advantages, and motivators, which can be calibrated versus the manager's perception and broader organisational context. Specifically, the employee is asked to indicate the next mid- and long-term role he or she wants to pursue, and the discussion tends to focus on critical actions required to reach those destinations.

At the functional level, the people planning process takes the form of a more strategic, long-term resource planning, identifying capability gaps to be closed versus forecasted business needs. It also includes succession planning for each team leader ranging from "*emergency backfill*" through "*ready immediately*" up to a horizon of "*ready in 3–5 years*". Quality and robustness of such a bench guarantee stability of business operations while potential gaps trigger specific actions, for example, capability building, creation of intermediary developmental roles, or external talent search.

Companies like PepsiCo intentionally leverage career planning and assignment changes to satisfy employees' basic psychological needs for autonomy, competency, and relatedness. Employee involvement in career planning – setting up destinations, actively discussing required actions, and calibrating with the manager – significantly boosts employee's sense of autonomy. When a new role opportunity emerges, the employee also has full autonomy to accept or reject it considering its fit to career vision and formal aspects like location, scope, and financial terms. While there may be consequences to later career progression, an employee's autonomy in this decision is critical for commitment and performance. Frequent assignment changes significantly boost the sense of competence and relatedness as they practically expose employees to a variety of learning opportunities and build a sense of belonging to new teams through shared goals, collaboration, and personal interactions (PepsiCo, 2023d).

Cultural differences in expressing basic psychological needs affect career planning and assignment changes. While generally, all employees want to progress in some way, their engagement in the planning process (autonomy), openness to learning and development, especially outside of their comfort zone (competency), and importance of stability and belonging (relatedness) can be very different across Eastern and Western cultures. Accommodating those differentiated needs while planning individual careers is critical to ensure optimal engagement and motivation.

Managing cross-cultural teams

The ultimate proficiency over cultures is the ability to create one. When managing individuals from different nationalities and backgrounds in one team, the role of a team leader is to create a common identity around shared values and behaviours (i.e. team culture), driving effectiveness and efficiency in achieving shared goals.

Creating a new culture requires understanding of values held by individual team members, identifying commonalities and tensions, and shaping the new culture intentionally on that basis. Global corporate culture typically serves as the bedrock and common denominator for further team culture enhancement as team members customise it to fit their individual and business needs.

Probably the most critical cultural difference visible in team management is the value of individualism versus collectivism. Teams originating from individualistic cultures may still be able to work well together, but the sense of individual autonomy and competency will be more important than relatedness or joint progress. On the other hand, teams created with representatives of collective cultures may value more the sense of relatedness, team autonomy, and joint competency versus individual progress or disruptions. Effective leaders will be able to satisfy the relevant needs and articulate the team culture around them (Meyer, 2014).

For example, the dominating cultural value of the leadership team in Russia back in 2018 has been "achievement". All individuals shared an intrinsic drive to perform competitively and win. While collaborating effectively and sharing common goals, each individual was ultimately interested in their own advancement (via promotions, growing scope of responsibility, etc.). Experienced team leaders leveraged those individual values, corporate culture, and business needs of a highly competitive business environment to forge a shared sense of pride, motivation, and collaboration, institutionalising certain behaviours, like challenging each other in public, celebrating competitive gains, enabling and celebrating promotions and individual growth of talents.

Differently, the dominating cultural value of the leadership team in Ukraine in 2019 has been joint development and improvement. Ukrainian team members valued the process of learning, solutions refinement, and progress towards perfection. While achieving a lot through those, team members valued the sense of camaraderie and belonging over individual progress. The role of the team leader (the author) was to enable team belonging and joint improvement through sufficient inclusion and process of consultations, as well as shaping the vision of continuous improvement as opposed to short-term, individual wins.

In the author's experience, cultural differences within teams become a complex interplay of individual differences as they translate across all dimensions of leadership and employee experience, including attitudes to authority, decision-making, communication, feedback, and trust building. In culturally homogenous teams, the prevailing cultural values tend to be amplified through interpersonal reinforcements like peer pressure and managerial role modelling. In heterogeneous teams, differences may be equalised or marginalised but may also explode to serious tensions in unfavourable circumstances (e.g. crisis situation). Unifying corporate culture can help modulate team behaviours and manage maladaptive tensions in both cases. Thanks to corporate culture, team members gain language, framework, and higher-level mandate to self-regulate and maintain a productive, motivating, and inclusive work environment.

Promoting basic psychological needs for autonomy, competency, and relatedness in managing teams of different cultures will almost always help increase intrinsic motivation and job satisfaction, yet should be done mindfully, concerning the unique composition and norms of the team members.

Conclusion

Despite progressing globalisation, cultural differences remain visible and continue playing a role across the corporate world. They may affect individual and team engagement, intrinsic motivation, and performance by satisfying basic psychological needs for autonomy, competency, and relatedness. Cultural differences can be observed on multiple dimensions, including attitude to decision-making and authority.

International companies, like PepsiCo, build their own corporate culture, aiming to create a common space (language, behaviours, and norms) for all its employees. Corporate culture forges unique team identity and promotes desired behaviours, thus creating a sense of belonging and competitive advantage in the marketplace.

While corporations tend to be very sensitive and respectful to individual and cultural differences, the corporate culture influences selected employees' behaviours, allowing them to interact with each other with less friction and more efficiently.

Corporate culture in companies like PepsiCo tends to represent the strictest interpretation of existing norms (e.g. anti-bribery and anti-violence), embedding ethical behaviour, safeguarding PepsiCo's reputation and protecting employees' safety.

Corporate culture is being established through all stages of employee engagement – from hiring through development, goal setting, evaluation and feedback, career planning and assignment changes, and team management.

Within a global corporate culture, there is space to adjust to individual and cultural differences in basic psychological needs for autonomy, competency, and relatedness. Satisfying those needs leads to increased engagement, motivation, job satisfaction, and overall well-being of employees, which leads to improved efficiency and effectiveness of business operations – creating value for the company, its associates, and all other stakeholders.

Bibliography

Bass, B.M. (1985). *Leadership and Performance Beyond Expectations*. New York: Free Press.

Chirkov, V., Ryan, R.M., Kim, Y., & Kaplan, U. (2003). Differentiating autonomy from individualism and independence: A self-determination theory perspective on internalization of cultural orientations and well-being. *Journal of Personality and Social Psychology*, *84*(1), 97–110.

Deci, E.L., & Ryan, R.M. (1985). *Intrinsic Motivation and Self-Determination in Human Behavior*. New York: Springer Science & Business Media.

Deci, E.L., & Ryan, R.M. (2000). The "what" and "why" of goal pursuits: Human needs and the self-determination of behavior. *Psychological Inquiry*, *11*(4), 227–268.

Deci, E.L., & Ryan, R.M. (2017). *Self-Determination Theory: Basic Psychological Needs in Motivation, Development, and Wellness*. New York, NY: The Guilford Press.

Drucker, P.F. (1954, reissue 2006). *The Practice of Management*. New York, NY: Harper & Brothers (reissue Harper Business).

Gagné, M., & Deci, E.L. (2005). Self-determination theory and work motivation. *Journal of Organizational Behavior*, *26*(4), 331–362. https://doi.org/10.1002/job.322

Hersey, P., & Blanchard, K.H. (1988). *Management of Organizational Behavior: Utilizing Human Resources*. Englewood Cliffs: Prentice-Hall.

Hofstede, G. (1984). *Culture's Consequences: International Differences in Work-Related Values*. Beverly Hills, CA: Sage Publications.
Meyer, E. (2014). *The Culture Map: Breaking Through the Invisible Boundaries of Global Business*. New York: Public Affairs.
Meyer, E. (2015). Globalization: When culture doesn't translate. *Harvard Business Review Magazine*, October Issue.
Meyer, E. (2017). Cross-cultural management: Being the boss in Brussels, Boston, and Beijing. *Harvard Business Review Magazine*, July-August Issue.
Northouse, P.G. (2019). *Leadership: Theory and Practice* (8th ed.). New York: Sage Publications.
PepsiCo. (2023a). *Applicant Help/Interview Tips*. www.pepsicojobs.com/applicant-help
PepsiCo. (2023b). *Celebrating the PepsiCo Way*. https://stories.pepsicojobs.com/blog/2020/07/01/celebrating-pepsico-culture/?locale=en_us
PepsiCo. (2023c). *Employee Engagement*. www.pepsico.com/our-impact/esg-topics-a-z/employee-engagement
PepsiCo. (2023d). *Employee Learning and Development*. www.pepsico.com/our-impact/esg-topics-a-z/employee-learning-and-development
PepsiCo. (2023e). *How Does PepsiCo Hire and Develop Talent?* https://contact.pepsico.com/pepsico/article/how-does-pepsico-hire-and-develop-talent
PepsiCo. (2023f). *Who We Are: Acting With Integrity is the Right Thing to do, and Only Makes Our Business Stronger*. www.pepsico.com/who-we-are/our-commitments/global-code-of-conduct
PepsiCo. (2023g). *Who We Are: Mission and Vision*. www.pepsico.com/who-we-are/mission-and-vision
Triandis, H.C., & Gelfand, M.J. (2012). Converging measurement of horizontal and vertical individualism and collectivism. *Journal of Personality and Social Psychology*, *102*(4), 818–835. https://doi.org/10.1037/a0027247
Yukl, G.A. (2013). *Leadership in Organizations* (8th ed.). Boston: Pearson Education.

12 Remote work in culturally diverse business

A case of Duracell North Central Europe organisation's experience

Paweł Nowakowski

Introduction

The COVID-19 pandemic is often described as a grand experiment in working remotely. Indeed, millions of people worldwide were compelled to stay at home and perform their duties outside of the office (Chamakiotis et al., 2021). Consequently, the pandemic accelerated the development of remote working by transforming it from an experimental practice available to only a few into a widely prevalent phenomenon known as the "new normal". The pandemic and the ensuing lockdowns significantly affected most people's personal and professional lives worldwide. Undoubtedly, this phenomenon's unprecedented scale has also significantly impacted most industries and businesses.

While most of us can intuitively define what working from home is and how it operates, it is worth quoting one definition that has emerged in recent years. This would help organise further discussion. Work from home, also known as telework, telecommuting, anywhere work, distributed work, and virtual work, is work completed outside the employee's physical office within the organisation. It involves using various technologies to communicate with colleagues and customers (Collins et al., 2016).

Although the percentage of people working remotely has significantly increased, we can still not assess its long-term consequences in social and economic realms. At this point, we observe primarily short-term effects. We can empirically evaluate its impact on a company's productivity, employees' satisfaction, sense of security, and development prospects. There are numerous publications on this subject. The aim of this chapter, however, is to assess the cultural and national aspects that may play a role in remote work within organisations that apply this model of work. To achieve this, it is crucial to identify and understand the advantages and disadvantages of remote working while acknowledging that their direction and strength may depend on various factors, such as culture, nationality, or individual circumstances.

DOI: 10.4324/9781032636962-15

Benefits of remote work

Productivity and Satisfaction: A factor frequently invoked as a benefit associated with remote work is the noticeable increase in employee productivity (Kähkönen, 2023). Several factors can contribute to this, with a notable emphasis on the increase in employee satisfaction and motivation. It is also related to the noticeable improvement in the quality of life, including a better work–life balance and reduced distractions (such as interactions with co-workers or noise in the office), leading to enhanced focus (Dolot, 2020). Increased productivity can also be linked to the psychological contract theory between the employer and employee (Rosseau, 1995), which informally defines the mutual obligations of both parties based on the principle of social exchange. In this case, the benefits of remote working as a form approved by the employer may create a sense of reciprocity in the employee working harder or longer.

Time Savings and Cost Reduction: This is one of the most frequently mentioned benefits of remote working. In many cases, especially in larger cities, commuting to work significantly extends the time spent away from home, limiting the opportunities for fulfilling family commitments. Furthermore, reducing commutes is associated with cost savings, such as fuel expenses, vehicle maintenance, public transportation costs, and parking fees (Dolot, 2020). On the employer's side, we discuss savings related to office rental or office operating expenses.

Flexibility in Task Execution: Working from home has required each of us to change how we manage our responsibilities, primarily demanding greater self-discipline while also providing significantly more flexibility in our work hours. In the case of more autonomous job positions, whether a particular report or project will be completed in the evening or early morning hours lies entirely with the employee, who is bound by the delivery deadline alone. This brings with it a host of benefits, including the freedom to manage work hours with greater flexibility (Chamakiotis et al., 2021), which can positively impact other aspects of our lives.

Remote work limitations

Work Intensification: Recently, many employees have experienced a phenomenon known as "online presenteeism" (Adisa et al., 2021). This entails the constant need for digital availability, driven by many seemingly endless meetings and an unspoken requirement for continuous confirmation and diligent task execution. It is a common perception that while working from home, the boundary between private life and the start and end of the workday may have blurred, adding an extra layer of stress and often contributing to increased family conflicts (Cooper & Kurland, 2002).

Limited Informal Communication: Remote work offers employees flexibility, autonomy, and time and cost savings, ultimately contributing to a better work–life balance (Koch et al., 2022; Dannhauser, 1999; Gajendran et al., 2015).

However, it also leads to a significant decrease in informal interpersonal relationships. This, in turn, may result in feelings of isolation and, from the company's perspective, a potential decline in the quality of information flow (Koch et al., 2022; Gajendran et al., 2015). Informal communication – although not part of formal organisational processes by its very nature – plays a critical role in shaping the internal communication of the company (Johnson et al., 1994; Koch et al., 2022), serving a variety of useful functions (Koch et al., 2022; Koch & Denner, 2022). Its primary functions include helping integrate employees and shaping organisational culture (Koch et al., 2022; Morrison, 2004); providing opportunities for social interaction with colleagues; serving as a pretext for breaks; reducing stress; and allowing for recuperation (Koch et al., 2022; Lilius, 2012). Informal communication also helps to vent frustration, increasing a sense of belonging (Koch et al., 2022; Fay & Kline, 2012). Finally, as a genuine compliment to formal communication, it enhances the quality and quickness of decision-making (Koch et al., 2022; Burke & Wise, 2003), thereby improving organisational efficiency. In remote working conditions, these functions are partially disrupted because informal communication is inherently spontaneous, and virtual coffee meetings, often initiated by superiors, may not adequately replace them.

Relationship with Superiors: like informal communication, remote working poses several challenges when building relationships with superiors. For natural reasons, communication within remote work is constrained regarding time and physical presence, resulting in significantly less time spent with colleagues (Cooper & Kurland, 2002). These contacts constitute one of the critical factors influencing professional success, impacting the development of our competencies, managing frustration or stress, and, perhaps most importantly, setting the direction for future actions. In remote working conditions, providing feedback tends to be more formal and requires scheduling meetings, often following formal management rules. What may be lacking in this arrangement is spontaneity and real-time feedback, which is significantly easier in office settings.

Career Development: The pace of professional competency development is directly proportional to the number of attended training sessions and gained project experiences and the quality of relationships with colleagues. While the first two areas in remote work are relatively easy to address, the third point brings about a set of challenges. Indeed, professional development primarily occurs through learning from colleagues, observation, and the exchange of ideas. Working from home limits these interactions. This can significantly prolong many processes, including onboarding new employees – not merely by slowing down knowledge acquisition but by undermining the motivation of newly hired staff as a result. Another aspect to consider, apart from the development of purely technical competencies, is an employee's development within the organisational structures. Employee promotions depend on various factors, with assessments of job performance quality being a crucial element. In an office-based work setting, the evaluation of job performance – not only the results but also the so-called soft skills, such as engagement, teamwork contributions, and relationship-building abilities – is more straightforward and happens more naturally. In the case of remote work, individuals who willingly share their insights and actively communicate with superiors may have more opportunities to be noticed and, consequently, to be promoted.

Sense of Security: The limitations of remote work and its impact on the efficiency of the company's internal communication, the quality of relationships with superiors, and, ultimately, professional development opportunities within the organisation can affect the level of stress and the sense of security among employees. This, in turn, influences their engagement, productivity, and their willingness to stay with the company (Cooper & Kurland, 2002). Therefore, organisations must be highly attentive and implement solutions and tools to address these challenges within the new work model effectively.

As mentioned at the beginning of this chapter, it is challenging to assess the long-term impact of remote work on the organisation's performance, employees' well-being, and motivation. The implementation of such work arrangements occurred amidst the shock caused by the pandemic, which is why the evaluation could have been significantly distorted by the exaggerated perception of the most critical benefit at that time, that is, the sense of safety derived from limited contact with other people. Moreover, assessing the benefits and drawbacks of remote work can vary significantly among individuals, as it heavily depends on the context in which we find ourselves – whether it is a familial, organisational, or cultural context.

Cultural dimensions of G. Hofstede's research

A crucial factor that can significantly influence an employee's ability to adjust to remote working and may amplify its benefits or drawbacks is the employee's cultural background. According to G. Hofstede (Hofstede et al., 2010), culture is the collective programming of the mind that distinguishes members of one group from another. His theory is based on the idea that individuals acquire specific behavioural patterns, perceptions of reality, and communication styles from their upbringing environment. It is essential to differentiate this unique programming from human nature – which has a more universal character – and, even more importantly, from individual personality traits. Differences between cultures are manifested in various ways, using symbols, heroes, rituals, or professed values, and interestingly, these elements do not always have to function in harmony (Hofstede et al., 2010, p. 6).

During his research conducted in 1980 and 1984 among IBM employees from 50 different countries, Hofstede surveyed 100,000 people. As a result, he defined initially five and later six dimensions, which make it possible to describe a culture and compare it with another. The six dimensions are the following: Individualism/Collectivism, Power Distance, Uncertainty Avoidance, Masculinity/Femininity, Long-/Short-Term Orientation, and Indulgence/Restraint. Each of them should be seen as a continuum, with extreme values appearing at opposite ends (Stor, 2011, p. 192).

Power Distance (PDI) dimension describes how a culture accepts that people are not always equal. This can relate to the power one holds, their position in an organisation or society, and their wealth. It may manifest in the relationship with a supervisor and the decision-making within an organisation. In cultures with a low PDI, employees are more independent, while supervisors tend to be less paternalistic and authoritarian. Decisions are often reached through deliberations and consultations (Hofstede et al., 2010, p. 61). In cultures with a high PDI, there is more widespread fear of superiors, and employees expect a more directive command style. This is also reflected in the organisational structure, which aligns with this management approach.

Individualism/Collectivism (IDV) dimension primarily concerns the degree of interdependence among individual members of society. It reflects how people define themselves, whether as "I" or "we". In individualistic societies, people prioritise themselves and their immediate families over larger social groups. Conversely, in collectivist societies, people belong to groups that take care of them in exchange for loyalty (Hofstede et al., 2010). As famously highlighted by E.T. Hall, there is a compelling correlation between a culture's level of individualism and the communication patterns of its members. Hall delineated two communication types: low-context and high-context cultures (Hall, 1959; Hofstede et al., 2010, p. 109). High-context communication does not require many words as much information is known to those engaged in the conversation and is context-dependent. This type of communication is common in collectivist cultures, where relationships are closer, and people share many common experiences. In contrast, low-context communication is more prevalent in highly individualised societies, where information is conveyed directly and explicitly. Many things that everyone in collectivist cultures understands may require more explanation in individualistic cultures (Hofstede et al., 2010, p. 109).

How does it translate into work relationships? In collectivist cultures, the employee–employer relationship often has a more profound (i.e. moral) dimension. Conversely, in individualistic cultures, it is viewed as a business transaction in which the employee receives compensation in exchange for their work rather than a moral or emotional connection. Notably, most staff management techniques, motivational strategies, and training programmes originate from individualistic cultures, where the employer typically seeks the employee's engagement. Indeed, in collectivist cultures, it is the other way around.

Masculinity/Femininity (MAS) dimension primarily concerns the social attitude towards gender roles and how they impact a given population. A society categorised as masculine is one in which gender roles are clearly defined. Men are assertive, challenging, and focused on material success, while women are modest, sensitive, and focused on the quality of life. A high index in this dimension suggests that society will prioritise competition, achievements, and success, with the latter defined as being the best in one's field of expertise. A low index, in turn, indicates that the prevailing values in society are care for others and the quality of life. In this case, the crucial question pertains to what drives individuals: pursuing excellence or pleasure derived from what they do. In essence, it is about whether our lives revolve around ego or relationships with others (Hofstede et al., 2010, p. 140). Naturally, this dimension significantly influences many aspects of our lives, starting from early childhood and later leaving its mark in the professional realm as well. In masculine cultures, meetings are an opportunity to present oneself in the best possible light, while in feminine cultures, meetings are an opportunity to find compromises, with consensus playing a pivotal role in determining the success and outcome of the meeting.

Uncertainty Avoidance (UAI) dimension of uncertainty avoidance relates to how a society, a given culture, deals with the fact that the future is inherently uncertain. It is related to the fundamental question: should we try to control the future or simply let it unfold? This ambiguity brings about anxiety, and various cultures have developed different ways to cope with it, in particular through the development of such fields as law, engineering, or – perhaps most importantly – religion. An integral part of this dimension is the level of experienced anxiety (Hofstede et al., 2010, p. 191).

In their attempts to alleviate the anxiety stemming from an unpredictable future, societies with a high UAI develop legal systems and institutions and formalise relationships between individuals to a greater extent. These cultures can be summed up in one sentence: the unknown is dangerous. Conversely, there are cultures with low UAI levels at the opposite end of the spectrum. People in these cultures embrace the notion that the unknown is interesting or intriguing (Hofstede et al., 2010, p. 201).

The dimension of uncertainty avoidance has a significant impact on the professional realm. Cultures with a high UAI tend to change jobs less frequently, look at their employers with a longer time horizon, and dedicate a substantial part of their lives to work, making it challenging to maintain a work–life balance. These societies also expect most organisational processes to be formalised, with order often valued more than creativity. This implies that innovation does not necessarily align with a high UAI. According to Hofstede, while this last statement may be true, cultures with a low UAI, despite being more innovative, might face challenges in transforming an idea into a final product or service due to their inherent limitations (Hofstede et al., 2010, p. 213).

Short- and Long-Term Orientation (LTO) dimension describes how a society maintains its connections with the past, copes with current challenges, and prepares for the future. Normative societies that score low on this dimension prefer to uphold time-honoured traditions and norms while viewing changes with suspicion. In turn, cultures that score high on this dimension adopt a more pragmatic approach, encouraging savings and investing in modern education to prepare oneself for the future (Hofstede et al., 2010).

High LTO societies also aim for social and economic equality. Conversely, meritocracy is common: social and economic status depends on individual achievements. A notable example of the differences between these two extremes is the approach to investing. In cultures with low LTO, people are more inclined to put their money into investment funds, which offer higher returns but have more significant risks. Conversely, in high LTO societies, investing in real estate is more common. While it may not provide quick returns, it is considered more secure and predictable in the long run (De Mooij & Hofstede, 2011, p. 266).

Indulgence/Restraint (IVR) dimension is defined as the degree to which people attempt to control their desires and impulses, often based on how they were raised. Relatively weak control is called "indulgence". In cultures with low IVR, giving in to pleasures to enhance personal happiness is not seen as negative. People can freely spend money and pursue their dreams without being subject to judgement. In turn, relatively strong control is called "restraint". Here, our reactions and aspirations are constrained by social norms and prohibitions, and the pursuit of happiness and immediate gratification may be perceived as something negative. Societies with high IVR levels tend to be more relaxed, valuing leisure time and well-being (Hofstede et al., 2010).

Duracell North Central Europe

Duracell North Central Europe (NCE) is part of Duracell Inc., a global leader in the disposable batteries category. NCE was established in 2019 through the merger of two previously existing organisational segments, namely North Europe – based in Frankfurt, responsible for markets such as Germany, Austria, Switzerland, and previously, Nordic markets – and Central Europe, with an office in Warsaw, managing sales across most markets in this part of the continent, that is, Central and Eastern Europe. This change was part of a consolidation project within larger organisational sectors of Duracell Holding, specifically Europe and Africa. The project aimed to optimise management processes, reduce costs, and enhance the company's regional competitiveness. As a result of merging the two entities, the North Central Europe segment was created, overseeing markets such as Germany, Poland, Austria, Switzerland, Ukraine, and Hungary. These markets differ in many respects, including product assortment, brand positioning, and market entry models. While cooperation with such clients as retail and wholesale in larger countries – for example, Germany, Poland, and Austria – is direct, smaller markets like Switzerland, Ukraine, and Hungary collaborate through national distributors, which serve as official brand representatives in their respective regions. The establishment of the new organisational segment, NCE, brought forth various challenges from the differences in the diverse markets comprising the new structure. It also stemmed from the necessity to unite teams that had never collaborated before and were operating from different locations in Europe, resulting in cultural differences. Table 12.1 illustrates the organisation's evolution concerning the proportion of employee's nationalities.

Table 12.1 Duracell North Central Europe, nationality structure (2019–2023)

Year	*Germany*	*Poland*	*Austria*	*Ukraine*	*Switzerland*
2019	52.1%	41.7%	2.1%	4.2%	0.0%
2020	45.8%	41.7%	2.1%	4.2%	2.1%
2021	60.4%	39.6%	4.2%	4.2%	2.1%
2022	47.9%	47.9%	4.2%	4.2%	2.1%
2023	39.6%	50.0%	4.2%	4.2%	2.1%

Source: Author's elaboration based on Duracell's internal data

Today, 50% of employees declare their nationality Polish, while 40% consider themselves German, Austrian, and Ukrainian nationals, each accounting for 4%. Changes in the number of employees in the discussed years resulted from a deliberate need to develop the Polish branch of the company and the continuation of the integration process between the two organisations. This involved combining functions and hiring individuals who, while formally belonging to the Polish company, work for the needs of the Europe and Africa sector, which is the parent sector of the NCE. The process of integrating the two organisations began in 2019 and is effectively ongoing to this day. Its crucial phase coincided with the onset of the COVID-19 pandemic, which, as a global phenomenon, not only impacted numerous processes across the entire company but also, as an additional stress factor, could have hampered the merger of the two entities, particularly in terms of sharing a common vision of development and organisational culture.

Before 2020, Duracell was a heavily office-based organisation accepting remote work in exceptional cases. Nonetheless, with the outbreak of COVID-19, the company underwent a significant cultural transformation. The pandemic led to an almost immediate shift to remote work for employees, and for those people whose roles required in-office presence, precise regulations and pandemic situation monitoring were implemented. The crisis management during this period did not deviate from the contemporary market standard. However, in contrast to most other companies, Duracell quickly adopted the perspective that the temporary rules followed during the crisis could be successfully applied even during the post-crisis period.

In the case of the NCE segment, in addition to the rules implemented at the global level (Duracell E&A) at the beginning of the pandemic and those required by local regulations, several solutions were applied to address the unique needs of the organisation, which was still in an advanced stage of integration. The primary focus was on ensuring transparent and open communication about the situation within the company. To achieve this, the so-called "organisational town hall" virtual meetings were introduced in the daily cycle shortly after the first lockdowns and the shift to remote work. During these meetings, managers informed employees about the situation at the NCE and global levels, and employees had the opportunity to share their experiences regarding the situation in their respective countries, in terms of both social and business aspects. Besides their informative purpose, these meetings aimed to alleviate tension and stress by providing a platform for exchanging experiences and mutual support, ultimately fostering unity and integration within the group.

Additionally, regular virtual team meetings were organised within individual departments, serving a similar purpose but at a smaller organisational unit level. In the initial months of the pandemic, working from the office was virtually impossible: only those individuals for whom office presence was critical for their duties had access to the buildings. Over time, as regulations were gradually relaxed, a "50% maximum occupancy rule" was established, along with a reorganisation of office space. To come to the office, employees were required to report their arrival through the HR system and undergo virus testing. Coming to the office was possible but subject to stringent conditions. As safety and office attendance regulations were relaxed, the communication approach also changed. Daily "town hall" meetings gradually decreased in frequency, taking on a more business-oriented character. By the same token, meetings of functional groups underwent a transformation driven by the managers' needs, taking on a more managerial focus.

The annual employee survey highly rated the organisation's efforts to ensure safety and support employees. In 2020, 33 out of 42 eligible employees participated in it, with over 82% of responses being positive (Glint Survey, 2020).

As it was mentioned earlier, Duracell relatively quickly decided that the rules established and further developed during the pandemic would become the new organisational standard. The rationale for such an approach was supported by both financial and market results and employee surveys, which were unequivocally positive in this area. A new set of rules regarding the new "way of work" model was introduced in 2022. It included the following:

- Employees have the option of working from home and are not obligated to come to the office on a daily basis;
- The frequency of coming to the office will be determined by the individual needs of each functional unit and agreements between employees and their managers;
- The office will primarily have a social and integration role, serving for hosting team meetings and facilitating interactions with organisational partners;
- Contracts between employees and the company will govern remote work arrangements;
- Employees will receive reimbursement for energy and Internet access costs, with rates adjusted to local conditions.

The above-listed rules can be seen as an official recognition of the practices that were already at work during the COVID-19 pandemic. Throughout that period, the organisation had the chance to adjust to the new reality, encompassing both formal and cultural aspects. The process of formalising these rules was notably flexible.

Cultural diversity in Duracell NCE

Nearly 90% of the NCE organisation comprises two nationalities: Polish and German. The other primary cultures present in the company include Ukrainians, Austrians, and individuals from South Africa and Canada. Figure 12.1 presents a comparison of the main mentioned nationalities based on Hofstede's 6 Dimensions model.

The further east NCE is located for the PDI dimension, the stronger the power distance becomes. In the case of Ukraine, the score is one of the highest in Europe, while Austria is at the opposite end of the spectrum, indicating significantly lower acceptance of differences in power. The implications for remote working can be substantial. Austrians, in principle, may exhibit greater independence, and the lack of contact with a supervisor might not be a problem. Still, this arrangement should be more formalised for Poles or Ukrainians, and regular meetings to confirm priorities and actions might be more applicable.

In the case of IDV, German, Austrian, and Polish cultures are more individualistic, while Ukraine exhibits a strongly collectivist character. There can be many significant implications for remote work. In collectivist cultures, this model may pose more challenges as individuals may expect more intensive contact with the entire group, a focus on building a sense of belonging, sharing a common vision, etc.

In the case of MAS, Austrian, German, and Polish cultures score significantly higher than the Ukrainian culture. This means that career development, building equity, and visibility within the organisation are much more important for these cultures. This can have several implications for remote work. Remote work, in most cases, extends the working hours. While this might not be a problem for societies with high MAS scores that strongly link life success to a professional career, it can be more challenging for societies with lower scores in this dimension. Building equity in the case of remote work also seems somewhat more

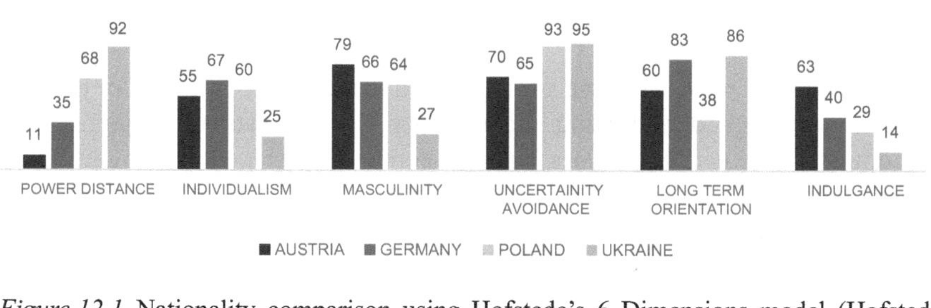

Figure 12.1 Nationality comparison using Hofstede's 6 Dimensions model (Hofstede Insights.com, 2023)

challenging due to significant limitations in interpersonal interactions. For societies driven by competition, where a career signifies life success, this could pose specific organisational challenges.

For the UAI dimension, all the cultures within NCE rank relatively high on the scale, with Poland and Ukraine achieving the highest scores. Nonetheless, Austria and Germany also belong to societies where the uncertainty about the future tends to be relatively strong. In the case of remote working – where, due to natural reasons, the flow of information, both through formal and informal channels, is not as effective as in an office setting – the level of uncertainty can be compounded. Thus, the organisation's key task will be to ensure that communication channels in the remote work model are clear and unobstructed.

Among all four cultures, Poland ranks the lowest on the LTO scale, making it a more normative society rather than a pragmatic one, potentially facing more significant challenges in adapting to a changing reality. In this context, remote working, which brings several new and previously unknown challenges, especially in human relationships, can be more difficult for low LTO societies, which may naturally adapt to change more slowly than cultures with a higher LTO index.

The last Hofstede dimension that defines culture is IVR. In this case, three of the four cultures examined in the NCE segment are characterised as "restrained", including Poland, Germany, and Ukraine. Austria, in turn, can be defined as a society with a relatively high IVR score. A widespread need to balance professional life with personal life remains characteristic of societies like the Austrian. It manifests primarily as a desire for more leisure time, relaxation, and continuous well-being improvement. Remote working – which, according to most available research, extends working hours and increases employee availability to the organisation – may pose more significant challenges for such cultures than for cultures defined as "restrained".

In summary, the Duracell NCE organisation is culturally diverse. For most of Hofstede's dimensions, the level and direction of change vary as you move from West to East. While it may be possible to categorise employees into two groups – western and eastern – within each of these groups, significant differences exist. This makes it challenging to implement a uniform management system, particularly regarding the tools used for remote work. The diversity of characteristics within a single culture also makes it difficult to determine definitively whether a particular society is more predisposed to work remotely than others. Austria, for instance, is a culture with high IVR scores, which may make it better suited to coping with the limited collectivism associated with working outside of the office. However, its high IVR also results in increased pressure for work–life balance, potentially posing a barrier to adapting to remote work.

Employee assessment of remote work at Duracell NCE in the light of primary research

This section is based on two short primary research: an interview with a group of 4 managers working with culturally diverse teams and an online survey completed by 33 individuals working for the NCE segment. In this last group, 18 respondents declared their Polish origin, 11 were of German origin, and 4 identified as other.

The survey, conducted from 22 September to 2 October 2023, consisted of 17 questions. Aside from basic demographic inquiries, respondents were asked to indicate the extent to which they agreed with statements on a 4-point scale: strongly agree, agree, disagree, strongly disagree. Three questions were of an open-ended nature. They are concerned with the most optimal frequency for coming to work and identifying the benefits and challenges associated with remote work. Regarding nationality, participants could choose only Polish or German, categorising others as "other" to ensure survey anonymity. In the context of the entire organisation, remote work had a generally positive reception. Most of the respondents (90.9%) saw more benefits in working from home compared to the office. An equal percentage perceived a positive impact on their family life, and 72.7% reported feeling happier. Notably, 97% confirmed having all the necessary tools for effective remote work, with only 12.1% expressing a willingness to return to the office. This inclination was mainly observed among Polish respondents and those of other nationalities.

Consistent with most remote work studies, this survey found that 93.9% of the overall sample reported increased productivity compared to working from the office. However, 69.7% believed that remote work led to longer working hours. In this aspect, German respondents (81.8%) and those of other nationalities exceeded the responses of Polish participants (69.7%).

When asked about their relationships with colleagues and the organisation, most respondents perceived a negative impact of remote work in these areas. For instance, 33.3% of respondents agreed that remote work, with the help of IT solutions, provides equal opportunities for building relationships. Notably, Polish respondents were more likely to hold this view (44.4%) than Germans (18.2%). A total of 69.7% indicated missing direct contact with others, with 81.8% of Germans expressing this sentiment in contrast to 61.1% of Poles.

Around 33.3% of total responses assessed the impact of remote working on team productivity as unfavourable – a score primarily influenced by a high percentage of German respondents (54.5%) compared to Poles (11.1%). Despite differences between both groups, there is a distinction in evaluating the effect of remote work on individual productivity, which had a positive connotation, and its impact on team productivity, which was predominantly seen as unfavourable.

The final two statements covered the employees' relationships with direct supervisors and the organisation. Regarding the former, 24.2% of the responses confirmed that remote work hurt relations with supervisors, with only 11.1%

of Poles stating that these relations improved when working in the office. This contrasted with 36.4% of Germans and half of those from other nationalities who believed the same. Regarding their bond with the organisation, 69.7% of respondents felt that their connections with it remained unchanged. Poles appeared more positive in this dimension, with 83.3% confirming that remote work had no impact on their relationship with their employer, compared to the 45.5% who assessed this impact negatively.

When it comes to the question regarding the benefits of remote work, the most commonly mentioned responses include flexibility, time savings, increased productivity, and well-being. On the downside, the most frequent concerns revolve around interpersonal relationships, such as the lack of personal contact and connections with others, the inability to spontaneous information sharing, and issues related to extended working hours, prolonged meetings, and limited line of sight into the overall functioning of the entire organisation.

To sum up, the survey conducted among NCE employees provides a generally positive assessment of remote work in terms of individual needs and its impact on the organisation's overall productivity. Still, it shows a significant insight into relationships within teams, including between co-workers and supervisors and subordinates. This should prompt organisations to pay close attention to this area.

The attempt to investigate the influence of culture and nationality on the perception and evaluation of remote work does not provide definitive answers. On the basis of the gathered information, one might be tempted to conclude that Poles assess remote work more positively than individuals of other nationalities within NCE. However, drawing such a conclusion would be overly ambitious due to the sample size, the specific organisational culture of NCE, and the historical factors that have shaped its teams and management practices. It is also interesting to note that – despite the generally more positive evaluation of remote work among Polish employees – there were unequivocally negative assessments within this group, favouring office work as more effective and satisfying. Therefore, evaluating the relationship between nationality and culture based on the surveyed sample appears inconclusive. Instead, one could hypothesise that this evaluation depends significantly on individual preferences and the employee's situation.

The insights from interviews with managers shed light on the challenges they face in their daily work when remotely managing culturally diverse teams. Both the survey and interviews confirm the observed increase in employee productivity, which may result from the reduction of distracting elements and enhanced focus. Nonetheless, this productivity may be disrupted by the number of meetings, which frequently take precedence in remote work. According to the opinions expressed in the interviews, productivity depends on individual predispositions and family situations. As one of the respondents mentioned, "I think that it very much depends on the individual, and we have had some instances where productivity dropped dramatically because some individuals need to be in a group to remain productive".

Another topic discussed in the interviews was the impact of remote work on job satisfaction. Almost all of the interviewees confirmed increased job satisfaction within the teams. However, doubts about the stability of these feelings also emerged, which could be related to the long-term and persisting limitations of personal interactions with others: "I certainly see this as a long-term risk, that sense of off-connection".

Furthermore, there is a risk that the benefits of remote work, and consequently, satisfaction in performing it, may become the norm over time, something very accessible, while the negative factors associated with it will gain strength: "I think that this is just like your salary increase. You get used to it and then keep forgetting when there's something else, more important, coming up".

Similarly to productivity, the level of satisfaction is also highly dependent on individual predispositions: "If you have individuals, who are not so sure about where they stand, they need some kind of emotional support or help to build their brand and equity in the company. Then being remote actually is kind of a mood buster".

Conflict management emerged as a significant concern among the challenges mentioned during the interviews related to remote work. Significantly, during difficult conversations, the inability to precisely observe the other person's reactions and body language can hinder the interpretation of messages and, as a result, lead to misunderstandings. In fact, this problem extends to the communication of feedback, which is a crucial aspect of team management and employee development. Remote work often takes on a more formal character: "It's different because you cannot see the body language, you cannot have a coffee together".

Another element mentioned as negative was the risk of feeling isolated and the frustration associated with it. This may particularly affect individuals who feel uncomfortable or are new in their roles. The lack of visible reference points provided by co-workers in similar positions can increase stress and uncertainty. One interesting observation from the interviews, pertaining to the nature of remote work, is the difficulty in sustaining concentration during meetings, potentially affecting their overall quality: "It's much easier when you're working remotely not to be 100% present because you've got another screen open, and you've got your phone next to you. If I'm sitting with you face-to-face in a meeting, there's no way I'm going to have my phone out".

Regarding questions related to the cultural factor, numerous doubts emerged regarding whether this element significantly influences how we adapt to working in a remote set-up. These doubts are supported by the survey results, which do not provide a definitive basis for drawing conclusions about the cultural impact on the employee's adaptation. Based on the conducted interviews, it can be inferred that individual predispositions have a more substantial influence on our remote work than one's culture or nationality of origin: "So I think that there are some differences in culture, but they're not as big as the differences between personality and style".

Undoubtedly, the language we use is an essential cultural factor that affects how effective we are when working from home within an international organisation. The everyday language employed for communication within the NCE's structures among individuals of different nationalities is English, which is not the native tongue of most employees: "I think the biggest difference is always that we're not communicating in our mother language".

Indeed, remote work comes with a set of challenges related to communication. This is due to the lack of physical contact, which makes it difficult to accurately observe the other person's reactions. To exacerbate the situation, communication in a foreign language, which naturally limits our ability to precisely convey and receive information, results in the effect of two overlapping barriers that can ultimately significantly impact the quality of the organisation's functioning.

In summary, remote work in international teams presents several challenges that do not differ significantly from those in nationally homogeneous organisations. The example of Duracell NCE did not reveal any differences between Poles and Germans in evaluating remote work. How it is perceived depends on individual preferences, life situations, family status, age, or professional experience. Indeed, the study conducted on Duracell NCE employees cannot be considered representative due to the sample size, low cultural diversity based on Hofstede's dimensions, and the influence of the organisational culture on the results.

Conclusion

Certainly, one of the critical elements is the necessity of creating a cohesive organisational culture that goes beyond cultural influences. A crucial factor to begin with is defining a shared vision for the organisation that is accessible and understandable to all employees. A shared sense of purpose and value-sharing is vital for building unity within the organisation. In the case of Duracell NCE, this has taken the form of "NCE philosophy" workshops where teams of individuals from various nationalities and functions collaborate to develop practical solutions to reinforce the values previously defined as crucial for the organisation.

Another significant aspect of ensuring effective organisational performance in remote work is technical support and tools that facilitate efficient communication. Many publications on remote working have identified this element as a factor that can increase stress or decrease employee efficiency. In this case, Duracell has developed a range of solutions to assist in this regard, including support in the form of financial assistance for home office equipment and compensations for electricity and Internet expenses.

Highlighting effective communication within the team, at both the organisational and the functional levels, is another crucial aspect. Communication is typically a developmental barrier and becomes even more important for culturally diverse teams, where language barriers, lack of physical contact, and potential differences in the perception of relationships with the organisation or superiors can hinder efficiency. In this case, ensuring continuous communication between employees and the organisation is essential at both the structural and functional levels. For Duracell, this is achieved through weekly town hall meetings, team-specific meetings, and a culture of regular employee–manager meetings, which serve as platforms for providing feedback in both directions.

Naturally, it is equally important to structure HR processes across the entire organisation, including the available tools, time requirements, and manager guidelines. The final element – which is one of the key factors contributing to the smooth operation of the remote work model within a multinational company like Duracell – is ensuring regular physical contact between employees. Within teams, this is a highly individual matter, dependent on their needs and the management style of the respective manager. At the organisational level, it is realised through joint training and team-building trips, whose primary goals, apart from discussing business matters, are integration and building bonds among individuals. While we cannot verify the real impact of these meetings on the effectiveness of Duracell NCE, based on the employees' statements, one could hypothesise that the role of direct meetings remains significant in ensuring the smooth functioning of the organisation in a remote work model.

Bibliography

Adisa, T., Ogbonnaya, C., & Adekoya, O.D. (2021). Remote working and employee engagement: A qualitative study of British workers during the pandemic. *Information Technology and People*, *36*(5), 1835–1850.

Burke, L.A., & Wise, J.M. (2003). The effective care, handling, and pruning of the office grapevine. *Business Horizons*, *46*(3), 71–76.

Chamakiotis, P., Panteli, N., & Davison, R.M. (2021). Reimagining e-leadership for reconfigured virtual teams due to Covid-19. *International Journal of Information Management*, *60*, 102381.

Collins, A.M., Hislop, D., & Cartwright, S. (2016). Social support in the workplace between teleworkers, office-based colleagues, and supervisors. *New Technology, Work and Employment*, *31*(2), 161–175.

Cooper, C., & Kurland, N. (2002). Telecommuting, professional isolation, and employee development in public and private organizations. *Journal of Organizational Behavior*, *23*(4), 511–532.

Dannhauser, C.L. (1999). Who's in the home office? *American Demographics*, *21*(6), 50–56.

De Mooij, M., & Hofstede, G. (2011). Cross-cultural consumer behavior: A review of research findings. *Journal of International Consumer Marketing*, *23*(3–4), 181–192.

Dolot, A. (2020). Wpływ pandemii COVID-19 na pracę zdalną – perspektywa pracownika [The impact of the COVID-19 pandemic on remote work – Employee perspective]. *E-Mentor*, *1*(83), 35–43.

Fay, M.J., & Kline, S.L. (2012). The influence of informal communication on organizational identification and commitment in the context of high-intensity telecommuting. *Southern Communication Journal*, *77*(1), 61–76.

Gajendran, R.S., Harrison, D.A., & Delaney-Klinger, K. (2015). Are telecommuters remotely good citizens? Unpacking telecommuting's effects on performance via i-deals and job resources. *Personnel Psychology*, *68*, 353–393.

Glint Survey. (2020). *Annual Duracell Employee Survey 'Glint Survey'*, November 2020.

Hall, E.T. (1959). *The Silent Language*. New York: Doubleday.

Hofstede, G., Hofstede, G.J., & Minkov, M. (2010). *Cultures and Organizations: Software of the Mind*. Revised and expanded 3rd Edition. New York: McGraw-Hill USA.

Hofstede Insights.com. (2023). *Country Comparison Tool*. www.hofstede-insights.com/country-comparison-tool?

Johnson, J.D., Donohue, W.A., Atkin, C.K., & Johnson, S. (1994). Differences between formal and informal communication channels. *The Journal of Business Communication, 31*(2), 111–122.

Kähkönen, T. (2023). Remote work during the COVID-19 pandemic: Identification of working life impacts, employees' data protection abilities and trust outcomes. *Journal of Organizational Change Management, 36*(3), 472–492.

Koch, T., & Denner, N. (2022). Informal communication in organizations: Work time wasted at the water-cooler or crucial exchange among co-workers? *Corporate Communications: An International Journal, 27*(3), 494–508.

Koch, T., Viererbl, B., & Denner, N. (2022). You don't meet anybody when walking from the living room to the kitchen: Informal communication during remote work. *The Journal of Communication Management, 26*(3), 331–348.

Lilius, J.M. (2012). Recovery at work: Understanding the restorative side of "depleting" client interactions. *Academy of Management Review, 37*(4), 569–588.

Morrison, R. (2004). Informal relationships in the workplace: Associations with job satisfaction, organisational commitment and turnover intentions. *New Zealand Journal of Psychology, 33*(3), 114–128.

Rosseau, D.M. (1995). *Psychological Contracts in Organisations, Understanding the Written and Unwritten Agreements*. London: Sage Publications.

Stor, M. (2011). *Strategiczne międzynarodowe zarządzanie zasobami ludzkimi*. Katowice: Wydawnictwo WUE.

13 The adoption of ESG practices in corporate strategies – does cultural background matter?

Barbara Jankowska and Maria Kubala

Introduction

While an increasing body of literature explores the significance of Environmental, Social, and Governance (ESG) practices, there is still a substantial knowledge gap concerning the role cultural dimensions play in the diffusion of ESG practices across different markets. Hence, a comprehensive analysis of how national culture influences the dissemination of ESG concepts within their respective markets is vital.

Traditionally, the analysis of ESG initiatives has focused on macroeconomic or microeconomic factors. The former includes economists advocating for ideas related to the economics of moderation (Kołodko, 2008), environmental economics, ecological economics (Poskrobko, 2011), or sustainable development economics (Rogall, 2010). Additionally, laws and regulations established by governments or international institutions also significantly impact ESG practices. This is particularly evident in the European Union, where there is a mandatory requirement for companies listed on stock exchanges to report non-financial risks in their annual reports (Directive EU, 2022). Companies themselves, along with their employees and customers, often serve as influencers for ESG practices. For instance, Generation Y (Millennials) and Generation Z want to identify with companies that positively impact society (Borucki, 2021). What is crucial to notice is that cultural differences can influence factors such as supporting regulations and the behaviour of employees or management. Therefore, a country's culture can contribute to shaping the strategies businesses adopt in response to the pervasive issue of sustainable development. When embracing ESG practices, cultural attributes can influence their incorporation into corporate strategies or their impact on the surrounding environment. Addressing how cultural backgrounds influence integrating ESG practices into corporate strategies becomes crucial.

Hence, this chapter begins by explaining the background and definition of the ESG concept, highlighting its business applications. Subsequently, definitions of national culture and its dimensions according to Hofstede are provided, along with their translation into the corporate context. After presenting these

DOI: 10.4324/9781032636962-16

definitions, the authors attempt to synthesise and illustrate the influence of Hofstede's cultural dimensions on ESG principles. In the second part of the chapter, an attempt is made to illustrate the research problem through a case study. Companies from different cultural backgrounds were selected, varying in their effectiveness in implementing ecological and societal practices. However, companies from the same industry with similar revenues, internationalisation strategies, stock market listings, and ESG concepts were chosen for comparative purposes. The analysis results may serve as a general basis for further quantitative research on the impact of cultural aspects on ESG practices.

Literature background

The definition of ESG

ESG, which stands for Environmental, Social, and Governance, encompasses all activities related to these areas. The concept of ESG was first introduced in 2004 in the UN report titled "Who Cares Wins", released by The Global Compact, with support from major financial institutions such as Deutsche Bank, Goldman Sachs, BNP Paribas, and the World Bank Group. This report led to developing recommendations for various stakeholder groups, including analysts, financial institutions, companies, and investors. These groups were expected to endorse, implement, and uphold principles related to the ESG concept within their respective domains of operation. The overarching goals of this support infrastructure were "to create stronger and more resilient financial markets, contribute to sustainable development, foster awareness and mutual understanding among stakeholders, and enhance trust in financial institutions" (The Global Compact, 2004, pp. ii–v).

Consequently, sustainability in business became a crucial factor for many funds, serving as both a guiding principle and a competitive advantage. Therefore, the Environmental, Social, and Governance (ESG) is perceived as an investing strategy that has gained significant traction, becoming the most popular approach and surpassing others in terms of assets. According to the Global Sustainable Investing Alliance, out of the global total of $35.3 trillion in sustainably managed assets, over 70%, equivalent to $25.2 trillion, is managed through ESG integration (Adams & Swedroe, 2022, pp. 12–14, 49).

To determine the affordability of an investment, it is crucial to assess all potential financial and non-financial risks that mutually influence one another. Non-financial-specific risks can be evaluated within the framework of ESG factors. Examples of ESG risks include waste generation and disposal (considered within environmental risks), employee retention and motivation (part of the social sphere), and violations of market rules in transactions with external entities (falling under governance issues) (Mikołajewicz & Nowicki, 2021, pp. 300–302). That is why Bradley (2021, pp. 9, 289–290) indicates that ESG is not only "a stand-alone investment strategy" but it is also a "risk management framework".

The ability to verify allows for identifying non-financial risks, their analysis, and implementing mitigative measures or exploring new opportunities. At the end of this process, it becomes possible to determine the company's value during the investment evaluation. Based on these steps, ESG results become apparent in the financial sphere of companies. Therefore, it is evident that "non-financial risks can have a material impact on risk-adjusted returns and long-term value" (Tulder & Mil, 2023, p. 730). This is why ESG risk management is crucial – it can maximise the company's resilience in the long term, consequently enhancing profitability.

In the ESG approach, attracting and retaining capital is a desirable outcome. However, its scope is much broader. Essentially, adopting ESG principles is a matter of doing what is ethically correct. Donors, employees, and other stakeholders also consider ESG factors when deciding whether to work for a specific organisation or engage with it (Brown & Brown, 2021, pp. 5–6). The choice of investor's strategy may depend on various factors, including individual preferences, regulations, available funds, and government policies. It is increasingly evident that cultural differences also play a significant role in shaping investors' attitudes towards ESG issues in their portfolios.

Cultural factors around firms

The national culture

The definition of culture is broad and may encompass the entire nation. Tylor (1889, p. 1) stated that culture is "the complex whole which includes knowledge, belief, art, law, morals, custom, and any other capabilities acquired by man as a member of society". Hall (1984, p. 82) added that culture also involves "words, actions, poses, gestures, tone and timbre of voice, facial expression, manner of treatment of time, space and material objects, the way a person works, plays, loves, and defends himself". Culture encompasses everything that can describe a person. According to Hofstede et al. (2010, p. 6), "culture is ultimately the collective programming of the mind that distinguishes members of one group of people from others". Considering this, when people have a mindset that is programmed in a specific way, it influences how they perceive the world around them, their values, and what is important to them. The phrase "programming of the mindset" implies that something causes us to behave in a certain way. People can be aware of this programming, but sometimes, it might be less obvious why they behave in a certain way. In order to correctly understand the person, it might be essential to understand the context of culture. That is why Hall (1984, p. 186) said that "culture is communication, and communication is culture". Understanding why a person behaves in a certain way enables deciphering the code and context in the channel between the message's sender and receiver.

Cultural dimensions

Cultural dimensions can describe specific features attributed to a particular culture. These dimensions are accurately described by scholars such as Hall, Lewis or Trompenaars, and Hampden-Turner. However, the most well-known and appreciated version of the cultural dimensions was developed by Hofstede and Hofstede (2007, pp. 51–248). He distinguished the following sections: power distance, individualism versus collectivism, uncertainty avoidance, masculinity versus femininity, and long-term orientation versus short-term normative orientation.

Power distance refers to "the range of expectations and acceptance for an unequal distribution of power, as expressed by less influential (subordinate) members of an institution or organisation" (Hofstede & Hofstede, 2007, p. 59). Low power distance is characterised by flatter hierarchies within organisations and decentralisation of control (Hofstede & Hofstede, 2007, p. 58). In such societies, there is less visible inequality between individuals, a narrower salary gap among employees, and a recognition that the experiences and opinions of everyone are equally important. On the other hand, high power distance exhibits the opposite characteristics to low power distance (Hofstede & Hofstede, 2007, pp. 67, 70).

Individualism means that the "well-being of the individual is prioritised over the good of the group, even if they constitute a minority". In contrast, collectivism is where "the well-being of the group takes precedence, placed above the good of the individual" (Hofstede & Hofstede, 2007, pp. 87–88). In the individualistic approach, it is believed that rules and regulations should be equal for everybody. Additionally, "individualism has been one of the factors contributing to deregulation and the reduction of social spending", leading to a limited role of the state in the economy (Hofstede & Hofstede, 2007, pp. 116, 120). Individualistic societies have higher rates of respect for human rights, and personal freedom is considered more important than addressing inequalities. In a more collective approach, "people are part of extended families or other internal groups that provide them protection and a sense of security in exchange for loyalty" (Hofstede & Hofstede, 2007, pp. 104, 108).

Uncertainty avoidance refers to the degree to which a society is comfortable with increasing or decreasing levels of safety. Cultures with high uncertainty avoidance require clear structures to interpret events (Hofstede & Hofstede, 2007, p. 185) accurately. In such cultures, the inherent uncertainty in life is perceived as a constant threat that must be countered (Hofstede & Hofstede, 2007, p. 189). One way to combat uncertainty is through regulation, driven by a strong emotional need to fit everything into a structured framework (Hofstede & Hofstede, 2007, p. 195). Conversely, low uncertainty means adopting a positive attitude towards chaos, lack of strict regulations, liberalism, higher tolerance, acceptance of protests, and increased voluntary work (Hofstede & Hofstede, 2007, p. 206).

"Masculinity is a characteristic of societies in which gender-related social roles are clearly defined. Men are expected to be assertive, tough, and focused on material success, while women are expected to be modest, tender, and concerned about the quality of life" (Hofstede & Hofstede, 2007, p. 133). In contrast, "femininity characterises societies where the social roles of both sexes are intertwined; both men and women are expected to be modest, tender, and concerned about the quality of life" (Hofstede & Hofstede, 2007, p. 133). The masculine approach assumes that people should prioritise work over leisure. Instant economic growth is deemed crucial, which often leads to adopting a more aggressive yet effective management style. In this perspective, equality is not a priority, and salaries don't have to be equal for everyone (Hofstede & Hofstede, 2007, p. 168). On the other hand, the femininity approach starkly contrasts this mindset.

"Long-term orientation entails developing virtues that yield benefits in the future, particularly persistence and frugality. The opposing end of this spectrum is short-term orientation, involving virtues tied to the past and present, such as 'respect for tradition,' 'saving face,' and fulfilling social obligations" (Hofstede & Hofstede, 2007, pp. 222–223). The long-term perspective is characterised by systematic efforts to gradually achieve results, often through prudent economic resource management and adaptability to changing circumstances (Hofstede & Hofstede, 2007, p. 224). Conversely, the short-term perspective prioritises rapid results, emphasising meeting deadlines and the importance of work–life balance, individualism, and freedom.

All cultural dimensions might reflect a specific behaviour of a person not only in private but also at work. That is why individuals may diffuse the national culture into, for instance, business organisations.

The organisational culture

The mentioned programming mindset and cultural dimensions consider entrenched beliefs or thoughts that might be challenging to change, regardless of the time and space in which people find themselves. This consideration also extends to the impact of culture at the microeconomic level within a company or organisation. As stated by Bartosik-Purgat (2020, p. 131), "when people find themselves in a specific organisational environment, they do not leave their values or beliefs outside its framework but carry them inside, creating a more intricate realm subject to decisions and actions aimed at achieving positive effects in the organisation". This underscores the notion that nations and the companies within them follow similar values and social and cultural norms favoured by management and employees, as well as their attitudes and how they shape organisational behaviour (Bartosik-Purgat, 2020, p. 131). Organisational culture is intricately connected with national culture, and the relationship between the two is reciprocal. National culture profoundly influences enterprises, steering the course of strategies, behaviours, performance, and various other activities. For instance, emotionally expressive countries experience constant fluctuations between high aspirations and negative expectations about the future. In such societies, individuals often seek immediate and maximal gains for themselves (Banaszyk et al., 2022). This example vividly demonstrates the impact of culture on the business environment.

Cultural dimensions and ESG

In light of the growing interest in managing non-financial ESG risks, it is worth considering whether values and beliefs that differ due to national cultural differences promote or hinder the integration of ESG practices into corporate strategies. ESG, which pertains to environmental, social, and corporate governance issues, can be particularly affected by extreme opinions regarding the practices and strategies employed, as they often involve matters related to values and beliefs that can stem from varying perceptions of ethics and morality. These values and beliefs can differ on the basis of cultural dimensions in various parts of the world. Consequently, the approach to ESG practices can vary and result from cultural differences, being one of the factors shaping the understanding of the described concept. For instance, the approach to equalising or not equalising wage levels among employees could result from the "programming of our minds" by a specific cultural dimension. In order to analyse potential supporting or hindering factors influenced by the culture, selected characteristics of cultural dimensions proposed by Hofstede and Hofstede (2007, pp. 54–248) were examined by the Authors. Based on them, five research propositions were developed.

RP1: Low power distance supports the development of ESG.

Low power distance supports the idea that inequalities between people should be reduced and social relationships should be the subject of particular concern. There is more room for decentralisation of management, which supports the development and appreciation of every employee. Law principles form the basis for system evolution, and diversity is promoted through multi-government elections.

RP2: Some features of both collectivism and individualism support the development of ESG.

In the second dimension, both selected features of individualism and collectivism can support ESG practices. It is challenging to determine which characteristics are more essential. On the one hand, ESG signifies expressing people's values and freedom, advocating for the limited role of the state in a free economy for development, promoting higher human rights standards, and considering individual interests. On the other hand, collectivism represents a more equality-oriented approach, emphasising harmony between groups, recognising group interests, valuing social relationships, and acknowledging the state's role through qualitative regulations.

RP3: Some features of both high and low uncertainty avoidance support the development of ESG.

Regarding the third dimension, high and low uncertainty avoidance features may support ESG practices. On the one hand, high uncertainty avoidance means being focused and prepared for any risk or threat. That is why people may quickly react and take control of the circumstances. Next, in a culture of high uncertainty avoidance, some rules and regulations might be helpful to some extent to create a reality where people can control the negative external results of their business behaviour or ensure they have some fundamental rights in society. On the other hand, due to lower uncertainty avoidance, more flexible and creative solutions may be made. People are perceived as more liberal and tolerant, which might be reflected in choosing riskier investments and creating more significant profits.

RP4: Femininity supports the development of ESG.

Next, a more feminine point of view may support ESG practices. This cultural dimension emphasises building relationships, gender equality, resolving conflicts through negotiation, humanising work, and supporting the weaker members of society. This perspective also places greater importance on environmental protection than masculinity's emphasis on continuous economic growth.

RP5: Long-term orientation supports the development of ESG.

When considering the last dimension, a longer-term perspective may support ESG practices. This cultural dimension emphasises systematic efforts to achieve gradual results, the ability to face unexpected circumstances with resilience and adaptability, lower social and economic differences, and substantial funds for investing. In contrast, a short-term orientation promotes less mathematical solutions and encourages creative propositions or judgements based on the reward system at work, focusing on skills.

Characteristics such as low power distance, femininity, or long-term orientation indicate their potential association with promoting ESG practices. Conversely, traits like collectivism, individualism, and high and low uncertainty avoidance appear to possess mixed attributes that might facilitate the adoption of ESG practices in specific markets. The concept of ESG is intriguing and unconventional as it seeks to bridge diverse domains, such as environmental, social, and financial spheres, where interests might seem conflicting. Therefore, specific cultural dimensions may not definitively indicate whether their application could support or hinder the described concept.

In conclusion, comprehending these cultural dimensions provides valuable insights into how different societies may embrace ESG principles, laying the groundwork for targeted strategies and initiatives. Consequently, it is worth investigating specific countries, focusing on their unique cultural characteristics, to discern visible trends related to ESG practices and investor behaviour in those nations.

Methodology

This chapter aims to investigate whether and how specific values and beliefs can either facilitate or hinder the incorporation of ESG practices into corporate strategies. In our research, we combine critical literature study and case study methods that allow us to move from data to theory and to look for the answers to the questions: "how" and "why". The research questions formulated determined the applied methods and techniques (Collis & Hussey, 2009). Case studies describe reality, test theories, and often create theories based on quantitative and qualitative information. Applying the case study method, the authors combine previous research results with new empirical insights (Andriopoulos & Slater, 2013).

Applying case studies is not easy since particular cases must be selected, and the selection criteria must be defined. The case study method, being the qualitative research method, often faces much criticism, especially from those who prefer the pure deductive approach and quantitative method (Milliken, 2001; Patton & Appelbaum, 2003). Some authors point to qualitative research's lack of intellectual credibility (Marshall, 1996, p. 522). While selecting cases, different approaches can be applied. Sometimes, the selection of study cases is subordinated to the search for cases that provide the broadest possible range of information so that the phenomenon under study can be best understood (Siggelkow, 2007).

For the research, we used the company websites and different reports on the Internet. The study's goal determined the selection of cases for our study. Purposive sampling was necessary since adopting ESG practices differs among companies representing different business sectors and operating within different cultural contexts. The location of headquarters in countries that differ in terms of their cultural factors seems to be an essential factor in explaining a company's greater or lesser involvement in ESG practices and sustainability.

Results of the research

Sustainability in Sweden and India

When examining the approach to sustainability, a stark contrast emerges between Sweden and India. The Global Sustainable Competitiveness Index 2022 underscores this disparity, ranking Sweden at the top with a score of 60.7 points, while India languishes at the 120th position with a score of 39.3 points (SolAbility, 2022, pp. 15–18, 24). Sweden, along with other Scandinavian nations, excels in this arena, and a key contributing factor seems to be the comprehensive integration of women into all spheres of life. With a remarkable female labour participation rate of 90% in 2017, Sweden demonstrates a commitment to gender equality that positively impacts its sustainability efforts. Another significant factor is Sweden's unwavering investment in education, with state spending constituting 8% of the GDP, well above the global average of 4.5%. Additionally, Sweden boasts relatively small income disparities, fostering a more equitable society, and further bolstering its sustainability achievements.

In stark contrast, India's performance in the report (SolAbility, 2022, p. 12) is characterised as average in resource efficiency and governance but significantly lacking in natural capital, social capital, and intellectual capital, leading to its low global ranking. However, there is a glimmer of hope as over 70% of intellectual capital indicators are positive, suggesting that India could enhance its global standing through education improvements. This disparity underscores the critical need for India to address its challenges comprehensively and invest substantially in areas like education and natural resource management to improve its sustainability outlook.

That is why, a clear contrast can be observed between Sweden and India in terms of sustainability outcomes. Sweden demonstrates significantly better results in a given area compared to India. Characteristics that distinguish Sweden, such as a high percentage of women in the workforce and minimal wage disparities, will directly or indirectly manifest in business practices concerning ESG concepts. Consequently, companies operating in Sweden may achieve superior outcomes in ESG practices compared to their Indian counterparts. The mentioned attributes impacting a nation's approach to sustainable initiatives are somewhat linked to their respective cultures, which notably differ between Sweden and India.

Cultural differences in Sweden and India by Hofstede

According to Hofstede's cultural dimensions in The Country Comparison Tool, Sweden and India exhibit significant differences in several aspects ("Country comparison tool (Hofstede Insights Oy)", 2023). In terms of power distance, Sweden stands out with significantly lower levels. This is due to the Swedes valuing power decentralisation, a consultative style, and appreciating each team member. In contrast, India adheres to a hierarchical culture where the boss holds absolute power, and employees are obliged to follow their directives. Next, Swedes are individualists, focusing on individual interests and immediate surroundings. In India, both individualistic and collectivist attitudes can be observed. The individualistic approach might stem from Hinduism, prevalent in India, which emphasises individual actions. On the other hand, collectivism is visible in family, neighbourhood, and caste dynamics, built on loyalty and mutual trust. Additionally, Sweden has significantly lower uncertainty avoidance compared to India. Swedes have a more relaxed approach to strictly defined rules, relying on experiences, which is related to the power distance dimension. In contrast, Indians tend to have a slightly higher uncertainty avoidance. Sweden predominantly exhibits femininity, emphasising work–life balance, equality, negotiations, and consensus. India, on the other hand, exemplifies masculinity, focusing on achieving success and following directives and prohibitions. Lastly, Sweden and India are positioned in the middle of the scale regarding their long-term orientation. This dimension is evaluated at approximately 50 out of 100 points for both countries. Consequently, it is challenging to categorise these nations as having a short-term or long-term perspective ("Country comparison tool (Hofstede Insights Oy)", 2023).

For this reason, as indicated earlier, the cultural dimensions observed more within the Swedish population could be the next factor contributing to success in the realm of sustainability and the associated ESG practices. The factor indicating lower power distance among Swedes is associated with reduced inequality, nurturing interpersonal relationships, and decentralisation. Furthermore, Sweden's high femininity index may promote compromise, negotiation tendencies, and increased participation of women in the workplace. These factors are linked to ESG practices and, as beliefs and values, can facilitate incorporating ESG practices into corporate strategies. On the other hand, characteristics from the collectivism versus individualism dimension and high and low uncertainty avoidance can either support or hinder ESG practices. For example, a collectivist inclination to care for everyone can support the idea of sustainability, which is based on the intention to care for oneself and future generations. Conversely, an individualistic approach to expressing one's opinion can support ESG practices, which promote workplace diversity. Moreover, lower uncertainty avoidance (Sweden) may facilitate the creation of a more flexible and liberal approach, which is crucial in the ESG approach, ensuring compliance with reporting guidelines and verifying data procedures to minimise non-financial risks. On the other hand, higher uncertainty avoidance (India) supports creating rules and regulations, ensuring compliance with reporting guidelines and verifying data procedures. Last but not least, the long-term approach directly relates to the essence of managing ESG risks based on creating a resilient business. The mentioned hypotheses, attempting to link cultural dimensions and their reflection in promoting or hindering the implementation of ESG practices, can be illustrated through examples from companies from Sweden and India.

Volvo Cars and Tata Motors

BIO of both companies

Volvo Cars, established in 1972 in Sweden, is a prominent player in the automotive industry. The headquarters is currently located in Sweden, but the company conducts research, development, and design activities in Scandinavia, Shanghai (China), and Camarillo (USA). In 2010, Volvo Cars was acquired by the Chinese conglomerate Geely, but it remains publicly listed on the Nasdaq Stockholm stock exchange. The company's primary strategy revolves around rapid growth through electrification, exemplified by introducing its first all-electric SUV, the Volvo XC40 Recharge P8, in 2019. Volvo also emphasises direct consumer relationships through its monthly subscription service, Care by Volvo, as well as leadership in new technologies, particularly in the realms of safety and autonomous driving. Volvo Cars currently positions itself as a premium brand, focusing on producing pure electric, fully electric, and plug-in hybrid vehicles. Looking ahead, the company plans to offer fully electric cars after 2030 exclusively. Operating in 100 countries globally, Volvo employs an independent dealer sales model, which, according to the company, reduces operational risks and environmental impact. This approach enables Volvo to establish long-term, personalised relationships with its customers. The company's mission is rooted in the vision of making life easier, better, and safer for everyone, aligning with its commitment to sustainable development. Volvo aims to disrupt the auto industry by leading in safety, sustainability, online business, and setting new global standards. Their ambitions for the mid-decade period guide them as they address both their own challenges and those faced by society at large ("About Volvo (Volvo Car Corporation)", n.d.).

On the other hand, Tata Motors Limited, established in 1945 in India, is a renowned automotive company that has expanded its operations globally. Besides India, it operates in the United Kingdom, South Korea, Thailand, South Africa, and Indonesia. The company's primary markets for vehicle sales are in Africa, the Middle East, Latin America, and Southeast Asia. Tata Motors is publicly listed on the New York Stock Exchange. The company's core strategy revolves around meeting future transportation needs while prioritising quality, safety, sustainability, and strategic partnerships. Tata Motors is a leader in India's commercial vehicle market, offering a diverse portfolio that includes sports utility vehicles, trucks, buses, and defence vehicles. Notably, Tata Motors is at the forefront of India's electric vehicle industry. Tata Motors operates through 88 consolidated subsidiaries, 2 joint operations, 3 joint ventures, and numerous equity-accounted associates, over which the company exerts significant influence. The company's mission, "to innovate mobility solutions with passion to enhance the quality of life", guides its vision. This vision emphasises delivering financial returns alongside sustainable solutions that align with customer expectations and a highly engaged workforce ("Company Profile (Tata Motors)", 2023).

ESG performance

Volvo Cars and Tata Motors implement sustainable strategies and annually disclose their ESG practices in their Annual Reports. For example, Volvo Cars has adopted practices focusing on "Climate and Environment", "Employee Development", "Human Rights", "Supply Partners", and "Business Ethics and Compliance" ("Geared for Growth. Volvo Group. Annual Report 2022. (Volvo Group)", 2022). Similarly, Tata Motors demonstrates its commitment to ESG performance by evaluating its efforts in the realms of "Environment" and "Society" ("77th Integrated Annual Report 2021–2022 (Tata Motors)", 2022).

Analysing the non-financial reports of both companies, many sustainable practices are highlighted, emphasising positive externalities. However, the reports differ in their structure. Prominent institutions creating frameworks for sustainable reporting include the Global Reporting Initiative (GRI), The United Nations Guiding Principles, and the Carbon Disclosure Project (CDP) (Hill, 2020, p. 169). That is why there is no universally accepted set of indicators precisely defining what constitutes a “good performance” in ESG (Bradley, 2021, p. 10). Consequently, the disparity in these frameworks poses a challenge for stakeholders to compare the mentioned documents and assess their actions accurately.

As a result, a company’s competitive position concerning its ESG practices is often determined by external institutions, expressing their evaluation through ratings. One of the most renowned rating agencies is MSCI. ESG Ratings, according to MSCI, range from leader (AAA, AA), average (A, BBB, BB) to laggard (B, CCC) (MSCI ESG Research LLC, 2023).

Volvo Cars has been evaluated among 70 companies in the automobile industry with an average rating (BBB). Among the best-rated aspects was “Corporate Behaviour”, which encompasses executive misconduct, corrupt practices, money laundering, and antitrust violations. Categories such as “Corporate Governance”, “Product Carbon Footprint”, “Labor Management”, and “Opportunities in Clean Tech” received average ratings. The lowest rated was “Product Safety and Quality” focusing on product safety, supply chain integrity, quality management, and responsible marketing practices (MSCI ESG Research LLC, 2023a).

Tata Motors, on the other hand, was rated among the same 70 companies in the automobile industry as a laggard (B), which is two grades lower than Volvo Cars. Among the highest-rated aspects was “Corporate Governance”, encompassing the influence of companies’ ownership, boards, and compensation practices on investors. The “Corporate Behaviour” and “Product Safety and Quality” categories received average ratings. Three categories, namely “Product Carbon Footprint”, “Labor Management”, and “Opportunities in Clean Tech”, received the lowest ratings (MSCI ESG Research LLC, 2023b).

The above ratings are based on the following results. Both companies have a decarbonisation goal; however, Volvo Cars has a comprehensiveness of 100% in covering the company’s entire footprint with the target, whereas Tata has only 0.22% comprehensiveness. “Comprehensiveness” refers to whether a target includes all scopes and geographic sources of the company’s total emissions. Furthermore, Volvo Cars’ Implied Temperature Rise is 1.5°C, demonstrating the company’s alignment with global temperature goals. In contrast, Tata Cars has an Implied Temperature Rise of above 3.2°C, indicating a strong misalignment with global objectives despite their commitment to a sustainable strategy. Additionally, Tata Motors is involved in controversies at a moderate to severe level in the Social and Governance categories, whereas Volvo Cars does not indicate any major controversies. Lastly, MSCI has noted that Volvo Cars references more UN 17 Sustainable Development Goals than Tata Motors.

Volvo Cars contributes to various goals such as "Gender Equality", "Affordable and Clean Energy", "Decent Work and Economic Growth", "Reduced Inequalities", "Responsible Consumption and Production", and "Climate Action". In contrast, Tata Motors is aligned with only two SDGs: "Gender Equality" and "Responsible Consumption and Production" (MSCI ESG Research LLC, 2023a, 2023b). The analysis above indicates that Volvo Cars has a stronger competitive position compared to Tata Motors regarding the implementation of ESG practices.

Corporate ESG strategies related to cultural dimensions

One of the reasons for Volvo's better performance in ESG could be the cultural dimensions it embodies. According to the research propositions (especially RP1 and RP4), these dimensions might contribute more positively to facilitating sustainable practices.

To answer whether values and beliefs may facilitate or hinder the incorporation of ESG practices into corporate strategies, the recent annual reports of Volvo Group and Tata Motors were analysed ("Geared for Growth. Volvo Group. Annual Report 2022. (Volvo Group)", 2022; "77th Integrated Annual Report 2021–2022 (Tata Motors)", 2022). Both reports contain financial and non-financial indicators as well as information regarding ESG efforts and sustainable development. Based on these reports, Table 13.1 was created to illustrate the cultural dimensions characteristic of Sweden and India, with sample practices attributed to them, as reported by the companies.

The first dimension analysed in Table 13.1 concerns power distance. Swedish Volvo Cars has practices that align with low power distance by promoting dialogue with all employees, utilising tools such as annual Pulse surveys, organising Volvo Global Dialogue between employees and management, and selecting employee representatives for the Board of Directors ("Geared for Growth. Volvo Group. Annual Report 2022. (Volvo Group)", 2022, p. 164). On the other hand, Tata Motors emphasises hierarchy within the company by defining pillars and key leadership behaviours, illustrating the culture through five levels of employee hierarchy, centralised and rigid communication methods, or management delegating and making decisions without the consent of other organisation members ("77th Integrated Annual Report 2021–2022 (Tata Motors)", 2022, pp. 92, 2018–2019, 460).

The individual employee development programme "Click and learn" ("Geared for Growth. Volvo Group. Annual Report 2022. (Volvo Group)", 2022, p. 165), exhibited by the Swedish corporation, may suggest focusing on an individual unit. Tata Group also provides development programmes and training initiatives not only for employees but also for students who cannot afford education ("77th Integrated Annual Report 2021–2022 (Tata Motors)", 2022, p. 95). That is why a more collectivist view is visible here, which also demonstrates the Common

Table 13.1 Corporate ESG practices related to cultural dimensions

Research propositions	*Cultural dimension Sweden*	*Volvo Cars practices*	*Cultural dimension India*	*Tata Motors practices*
RP1: Low power distance supports the development of ESG.	Lower power distance	The Pulse survey and regular department meetings conduct a dialogue with all employees (Volvo Group, p. 164). The yearly Volvo Global Dialogue gathers 50 employee representatives from over 20 countries and Volvo Group Management members (Volvo Group, p. 164). Three ordinary and two deputy members appointed by employee organisations are part of the AB Volvo Board of Directors (Volvo Group, p. 164).	Higher power distance	A refreshment of organisational culture defines the pillars and key leadership behaviours via five levels in the hierarchy of employees ("77th Integrated Annual Report 2021–2022 (Tata Motors)", 2022, p. 92). Means of communication: "The Quarterly, Half Yearly and Annual Results", "Calls or meetings with institutional investors on request", "The Company's website", "Annual Report", "Electronic Communication", "Centralised database of all complaints" ("77th Integrated Annual Report 2021–2022 (Tata Motors)", 2022, pp. 218–219). The Board of Directors authorises performing all such acts as may be necessary, to make all decisions pursuant to the powers granted herein, and to delegate all or any of its powers without further approval of the members ("77th Integrated Annual Report 2021–2022 (Tata Motors)", 2022, p. 460).

(Continued)

Table 13.1 (Continued)

Research propositions	*Cultural dimension Sweden*	*Volvo Cars practices*	*Cultural dimension India*	*Tata Motors practices*
RP2: Some features of both collectivism and individualism support the development of ESG.	Individualism	The "Click'n'Learn" concept gives employees access to various digital training opportunities. This approach provides a basis for individual development (Volvo Group, p. 165).	Individualism and Collectivism	Earn & Learn Diploma in Engineering program is indicated for students ("77th Integrated Annual Report 2021–2022 (Tata Motors)", 2022, p. 95). The Common Minimum Program (CMP) harmonises CSR across India ("77th Integrated Annual Report 2021–2022 (Tata Motors)", 2022, p. 103). The Arogya initiative focuses on malnutrition among children aged 0–6 ("77th Integrated Annual Report 2021–2022 (Tata Motors)", 2022, p. 103). To create an e-mobility ecosystem "Tata UniEVerse" ("77th Integrated Annual Report 2021–2022 (Tata Motors)", 2022, p. 144).
RP3: Some features of both high and low uncertainty avoidance support the development of ESG.	High uncertainty avoidance	Volvo Group Internal Control (Volvo Group, p. 202). The Group Executive Board and Group Management assess financial reporting risks (Volvo Group, p. 202). Environmental, health and safety laws affect operations, facilities, products, and services in each of the jurisdictions in which the Volvo Group operates (Volvo Group, p. 69).	High uncertainty avoidance	Risk Management Committee and Risk Management Program ("77th Integrated Annual Report 2021–2022 (Tata Motors)", 2022, p. 112).

RP4: Femininity supports the development of ESG.	Femininity	Currently, 28% of employees are women. The Volvo Group has set a goal of achieving at least 35% of women among employees, both overall and in management positions, by 2030 (Volvo Group, p. 164).	Masculinity	Currently, there are 6.5% of female employees in total workforce and 6.7% of women in all management positions. Tata Motors has set a goal of achieving at least 30% of women among employees by 2026 ("77th Integrated Annual Report 2021–2022 (Tata Motors)", 2022, p. 94).
RP5: Long-term orientation supports the development of ESG.	Short- and long-term orientation	Continuous learning, long-term employment, and engagement have been a priority for Volvo Group (Volvo Group, p. 165).	Short- and long-term orientation	The Integrated Annual Report provides a view on creating long-term value through a value-creation model, strategy, and environmental, social, and governance (ESG) focus ("77th Integrated Annual Report 2021–2022 (Tata Motors)", 2022, p. 2).

Source: Own compilation based on "Geared for Growth. Volvo Group. Annual Report 2022. (Volvo Group)", 2022 and "77th Integrated Annual Report 2021–2022 (Tata Motors)", 2022

Minimum Program promoting CSR activities across India and collaborations with e-mobility companies. Both of these dimensions can positively impact ESG practices, albeit affecting different entities.

The annual evaluation of Volvo Group's internal control over financial reporting, risk management, and compliance with rules and regulations ("Geared for Growth. Volvo Group. Annual Report 2022. (Volvo Group)", 2022, pp. 69, 202) can serve as an example of higher uncertainty avoidance in this case. Tata Motors also outlines its risk management programme and the committee responsible for controlling these risks ("77th Integrated Annual Report 2021–2022 (Tata Motors)", 2022, p. 112). Therefore, both companies have implemented ESG-specific approaches to risk control.

The Swedish company aims to increase its female workforce from 28% to 35% by 2030 ("Geared for Growth. Volvo Group. Annual Report 2022. (Volvo Group)", 2022, p. 164). In contrast, Tata Motors currently employs 6.5% women in its total workforce and 6.7% in management positions, aiming to reach 30% female representation among employees by 2026 ("77th Integrated Annual Report 2021–2022 (Tata Motors)", 2022, p. 64). Consequently, Volvo appears to adopt a more feminist approach compared to Tata Group. This implies a commitment to gender equality and justice, aligning with the social aspect of the ESG approach.

Furthermore, both companies have outlined long-term goals that promote sustainable and resilient business strategies, fostering the company's and its employees' growth. Such an approach has become a crucial element in the balanced development strategy of corporations ("77th Integrated Annual Report 2021–2022 (Tata Motors)", 2022, p. 2; "Geared for Growth. Volvo Group. Annual Report 2022. (Volvo Group)", 2022, p. 167).

In conclusion, the Volvo Group and Tata Motors analysis reveals distinctive approaches to some ESG practices via power distance or femininity versus masculinity approach. Moreover, both companies share common ground in their focus on sustainable development, risk management, and fostering resilient business strategies. These diverse strategies underline corporate approaches' complex and multifaceted nature to ESG practices, reflecting the evolving landscape of responsible business conduct.

Conclusion

The conducted analysis grounded in the literature allows for formulating several conclusions. Firstly, the comparative analysis of distinctive cultural dimensions and familiarity with the principles of sustainable development, along with the practical concept of ESG, reveal correlations between them. On the basis of this foundation, the authors have derived five research propositions, which try to respond to the main goal of this chapter – if and how values and beliefs may facilitate or hinder the incorporation of ESG practices into corporate strategies.

These propositions suggest that low power distance, femininity, and a long-term perspective in national culture support outcomes in the realm of ESG. Additionally, it has been observed that specific characteristics stemming from the collectivism versus individualism approach and high and low uncertainty avoidance either facilitate or hinder activities related to sustainable business. Drawing on the case studies of Swedish Volvo Cars and Indian Tata Motors, the translation of these cultural dimensions into the companies' business strategies becomes apparent. The annual reports of both companies extensively present their non-financial business practices. However, it is worth mentioning that due to the lack of a uniform reporting scheme, the documents present diverse practices, leading to difficulties in comparison and making direct comparisons challenging. Therefore, in the future, interviews with representatives of the companies broadening the understanding of the issues highlighted in the research propositions would be necessary. A structured questionnaire with questions about the impact of cultural differences on the non-financial practices of both companies could be directed to a more significant number of employees of both companies to contribute to more qualitative research. Furthermore, not all actions described in the reports unequivocally indicate the advantage of a specific cultural dimension, making the case study susceptible to error.

Bibliography

Adams, S.C., & Swedroe, L.E. (2022). *Your Essential Guide to Sustainable Investing: How to Live Your Values and Achieve Your Financial Goals with ESG, Sri, and Impact Investing*. Petersfield: Harriman House Ltd.

Andriopoulos, C., & Slater, S. (2013). Exploring the landscape of qualitative research in international marketing: Two decades of IMR. *International Marketing Review*, *30*(4), 384–412. https://doi.org/10.1108/IMR-03-2012-0061

Banaszyk, P., Gorynia, M., & Polowczyk, J. (2022). Jak emocje wpływają na inwestycje? *Rzeczpospolita*. www.rp.pl/opinie-ekonomiczne/art36763861-jak-emocje-wplywaja-na-inwestycje

Bartosik-Purgat, M. (2020). Zarządzanie różnorodnością kulturową w przedsiębiorstwach międzynarodowych. In R. Śliwiński (Ed.), *Strategiczne zarządzanie przedsiębiorstwem międzynarodowym*. Warszawa: Difin.

Borucki, B. (2021). ESG compliance – czym jest i jak wpływa na zarządzanie biznesem? *Puls Biznesu*. www.pb.pl/esg-compliance-czym-jest-i-jak-wplywa-nazarzadzanie-biznesem-1129208

Bradley, B. (2021). *ESG Investing For Dummies*. New Jersey: John Wiley & Sons.

Brown, D.L., & Brown, D.A.H. (2021). *ESG Matters: How to Save the Planet, Empower People, and Outperform the Competition*. Powell: Ethos Collective.

Collis, J., & Hussey, R. (2009). *A Practical Guide for Undergraduate and Postgraduate Students*. New York: Palgrave Macmillan.

Directive (EU) 2022/2464 of the European Parliament and of the Council of 14 December 2022 amending Regulation (EU) No 537/2014, Directive 2004/109/EC, Directive 2006/43/EC and Directive 2013/34/EU, as regards corporate sustainability reporting (Text with EEA relevance). http://data.europa.eu/eli/dir/2022/2464/oj

Hall, E. (1984). *Poza kulturą*. Warszawa: WN PWN Publications.

Hill, J. (2020). *Environmental, Social, and Governance (ESG) Investing: A Balanced Analysis of the Theory and Practice of Sustainable Portfolio*. London: Academic Press.
Hofstede, G., & Hofstede, G.J. (2007). *Kultury i organizacje*. Warszawa: PWE Publications.
Hofstede, G., Hofstede, G.J., & Minkov, M. (2010). *Cultures and Organizations Software of the Mind: International Cooperation and Its Importance for Survival*. New York: McGraw-Hill.
Hofstede Insights Oy. (2023, October 16). *Country Comparison Tool*. www.hofstede-insights.com/country-comparison-tool?countries=india%2Cpoland%2Csweden
Kołodko, G. (2008). *Wędrujący świat*. Warszawa: Prószyński i S-ka.
Marshall, M.N. (1996). Sampling for qualitative research. *Family Practice*, *13*(6), 522–526.
Mikołajewicz, G., & Nowicki, J. (2021). *Analiza finansowa przedsiębiorstwa z aspektami zrównoważonego rozwoju*. Poznań: Wydawnictwo Uniwersytetu Ekonomicznego w Poznaniu.
Milliken, J. (2001). Qualitative research and marketing management. *Management Decision*, *39*(1), 71–77.
MSCI ESG Research LLC. (2023). *ESG Ratings*. www.msci.com/our-solutions/esg-investing/esg-ratings
MSCI ESG Research LLC. (2023a). ESG ratings & climate search tool. *Volvo Car AB*. www.msci.com/our-solutions/esg-investing/esg-ratings-climate-search-tool/issuer/volvo-car-ab/IID000000002753308
MSCI ESG Research LLC. (2023b). ESG ratings & climate search tool. *Tata Motors Limited*. www.msci.com/our-solutions/esg-investing/esg-ratings-climate-search-tool/issuer/tata-motors-limited/IID000000002145995
Patton, E., & Appelbaum, S.H. (2003). The case for case studies in management research. *Management Research News*, *26*(5), 60–71.
Poskrobko, B. (2011). Od ekorozwoju do ekonomii zrównoważonego rozwoju. *Ekonomia i Środowisko*, *2*(40), 240–267.
Rogall, H. (2010). *Ekonomia zrównoważonego rozwoju*. Poznań: Zysk i S-ka Wydawnictwo Środowisko.
Siggelkow, N. (2007). Persuasion with case studies. *Academy of Management Journal*, *50*(1).
SolAbility. (2022). *The Sustainable Competitiveness Report* (11th ed.). Zurich: SolAbility Sustainable Intelligence.
Tata Motors. (2022). *77th Integrated Annual Report 2021–2022*. https://investors.tatamotors.com/financials/77-ar-html/pdf/Tata_Motors_IR_2021_2022.pdf
Tata Motors. (2023). *Company Profile*. www.tatamotors.com/about-us/company-profile/
The Global Compact. (2004). Who cares wins: Connecting the financial markets to a changing world. *United Nations Compact*. www.unpri.org/reporting-and-assessment/investorreporting-framework/5373.article
Tulder, R. van, & Mil, E. van. (2023). *Principles of Sustainable Business*. New York: Routledge.
Tylor, E.B. (1889). *Primitive Culture: Researches into the Development of Mythology, Philosophy, Religion, Language, Art and Custom*. New York: Henry Holt and Company. https://doi.org/10.1037/12987-000
Volvo Car Corporation. (n.d.). *About Volvo*. www.media.volvocars.com/global/en-gb/corporate/this-is-volvo
Volvo Group. (2022, February 28). *Geared for Growth: Volvo Group. Annual Report 2022*. www.volvogroup.com/en/news-and-media/events/2023/feb/annual-and-sustainability-report-2022.html

14 Women on board in the Volkswagen Group

Women in society, religion, and traditional beliefs

Alicja Hadryś and Patrycja Kasprzyk

Introduction

The gender gap in leadership is a global phenomenon rooted in cultural role expectations of men, women, and leaders. Although these expectations vary across cultures, women consistently face barriers from laws, socialisation, formal organisational policies, and informal organisational practices that limit their opportunities to become leaders and inhibit their ability to be effective when they do obtain such positions. Our world is globalised and interdependent economically, socially, technologically, and politically (Northouse, 2016). In recent years, women's representation in top management positions has become more visible and has received growing interest among researchers, businesses, and politicians. Although societies, especially in the Western world, move towards gender equality and diversity in top management positions, cultural and traditional "barriers" still seem to limit this trend. In many areas, progress has been too slow. At the current rate, it will take an estimated 300 years to end child marriage, 286 years to close gaps in legal protection and remove discriminatory laws, 140 years for women to be represented equally in positions of power and leadership in the workplace, and 47 years to achieve equal representation in national parliaments (United Nations, 2023). Leadership is always situational, evaluated in a particular political setting or cultural environment and through the lens of gender power relations. On the basis of the literature review, we assume that culture can be understood as a key influencing factor in supporting or limiting women as leaders. The culture of a respective country shapes the women's role within the society and, herewith the occupation of leadership roles within companies (Carrasco et al., 2015). Research shows that companies with women well-represented in executive roles are more likely to outperform their male peers and have been shown to achieve greater effectiveness, employee retention, and client satisfaction. Female leadership tends to be inclusive, open, transparent, empathetic, and vulnerable. For the first time, more than 10% of *Fortune 500* companies are run by women – although just 1% of the total are women of colour. And the number of women at the C-suite level has increased

DOI: 10.4324/9781032636962-17

by nearly 7% in the past five years (Gonzales, 2023). Women entrepreneurship is also growing worldwide, but obstacles remain, and men still outnumber women three-one when it comes to business ownership. Research also shows that, for example, women make up more than 70% of the healthcare workforce but hold just 25 % of leadership positions in the healthcare industry.

This chapter aims to contribute to a more profound knowledge about women's opportunities in management and the relationship between women in executive positions and culture-based factors in the Volkswagen Group (VW). We aim to find specific relationships between women in managerial positions and culture as an influencing factor. The main research methods used in this chapter are a literature analysis and a case study. A specific case of dependency study is the search for relationships and regularities that allow us to explain the examined reality to a greater extent than the previously used scientific theories and assumptions made on this basis. For this purpose, qualitative research (qualitative methods) plays a unique role. They are used when the researcher is interested in more profound knowledge on a given topic and getting to the heart of the problem when the representativeness of the results is less important than knowing the phenomenon's essence. Qualitative methods also allow for observing the reality of a given entity and capturing the context in which the examined relationships occur, which allows for a multidimensional and multi-threaded analysis of the collected information (Mielcarek, 2014).

The case study method involves analysing and discussing real situations. The advantages of the case study method as a tool that can be used in developing scientific theory include the ability to collect a large amount of detailed information on complex relationships, which allows one to understand, describe, and explain hitherto unknown problems (Palka, 2006). The external sources used for the study were information from papers obtained from scientific databases Web of Science, Scopus as well as Emerald Insight. The research objective is to analyse the influence of culture on women's access to executive positions. Sources of information also included materials available on the VW's international website and internal documents of the VW Group. The applied research methods answer the main research question:

RQ: Which aspects shaping culture influence women's access to management positions in VW?

The chapter consists of four parts. The introduction presents a general overview, primary goal, research method, and research question. The second part will focus on a general overview of women in managerial positions. In the third part, we will present the research findings of the content analysis concerning culture's influence on women's presence in executive positions. In the fourth part, we will present the case of VW concerning the identified dimensions of culture that influence the career possibilities women face in upper management positions.

Finally, the last section will summarise and discuss the results' implications and directions for possible future research.

Women in managerial positions

Nowadays, women in leading managerial positions are often discussed and very relevant when we talk about companies' development and the national and global economy. Although developing slowly worldwide, there is a tendency for an increasing participation of women in leading positions (Eagly & Carli, 2007; Evans, 2010; Northouse, 2018). However, the phenomenon of women in managerial positions can still be considered a rarity in the business world, much of which is due to specific barriers – subtle or obvious – women face (Eagly & Carli, 2007). The persistent gender imbalance among crucial decision-makers in large corporations and financial institutions remains a cause for concern. EU institutions recently agreed on a directive to increase the number of women on corporate boards by requiring Member States to ensure that companies listed on stock exchanges have at least 40 % of the under-represented gender among non-executive directors or 33 % among all directors. The European Institute for Gender Equality (EIGE) monitors the situation biannually for the largest listed companies in the Member States and annually for central banks and EU financial institutions. In October 2022, the share of women on the boards of the largest publicly listed companies registered in the Member States reached a new high of 32.2 %. Nevertheless, two out of every three board members remain men (European Institute for Gender Equality, 2019). Progress towards better representation of women on boards was plodding between 2003 and 2010 (0.5 percentage points (pp/year)) but accelerated between 2010 and 2015 (2.1 pp/year), mainly as a result of rapid improvements in Germany, France, and Italy following the introduction of legislative quotas. Despite progress among non-executives, women still account for only a fifth (21.1 %) of senior executive positions. Legislative quotas typically only apply to the top-level board or non-executive seats, leaving the executive positions little affected by legislation. The situation is very similar in the U.S., where approximately half of the U.S. workforce is female, and even more than 60% of master's degrees in the United States are achieved by women while their representation in upper management positions is just a fraction out of this (Eagly & Carli, 2007; Northouse, 2018; U.S. National Center for Education Statistics, 2016). This is supported by the fact that just 33 managers listed on the Fortune 500 list of 2019 are women, accounting for just 6.6% (Catalyst, 2019). However, this number marks a new all-time high in female CEOs of listed firms (Catalyst, 2020). At this point, it seems essential to mention that most of the advancement of women in leadership positions took place at lower levels of management rather than at these top positions within enterprises (Eagly & Carli, 2007; Eagly & Sczesny, 2009). While there have been improvements at the board level, women's underrepresentation in top positions endures. Less than 1 in 10 of the largest listed companies in Member States has a female chair (8.8%)

or a female chief executive officer (8.4%). Still, the disturbing fact is that the percentage of women in senior leadership roles in businesses has remained relatively steady. To sum up, gender equality varies from country to country due to different cultural understandings regarding the roles of men and women and the respective gender expectations (Eden & Forquer Gupta, 2017; United Nations, 2023).

Relationship between women in executive positions and culture

The gender gap in leadership positions is a global phenomenon rooted in cultural role expectations of men, women, and leaders. Although these expectations vary across cultures, women consistently face barriers from laws, socialisation, formal organisational policies, and informal organisational practices that limit their opportunities to become top managerial positions and inhibit their ability to be effective when they do obtain such positions. Culture might explain differences in women's presence in executive positions across societies and in the success or failure of business activities. Many barriers and obstacles women experience are gender-specific and stem from cultural values, norms, and customs (Anambane & Adom, 2018; Baughn et al., 2006). The role of women within society, religion's impact, and traditional beliefs within the culture are under-researched cultural factors influencing women's presence in executive positions (Bullough & de Luque, 2015; Hechavarría & Ingram, 2019; Manolova et al., 2020). Social customs and expectations are firmly embedded in any culture. Traditionally defined gender roles within the home put household and family responsibilities mainly on women, while men provide economically for the family by working outside (Milkie & Peltola, 1999).

Difficulties with objective classification and comparison of cultures result from the cultural conditions of researchers: differences in attribution, different understanding of the same concepts, different ways of asking research questions and solving scientific problems, etc. (Hofstede, 2001, 1998; House et al., 2014). In some research, authors mentioned that the perception of the role of women within society, religion, and traditional beliefs have the most significant impact on women's opportunities in the labour market (Chao, 2011; Cho & McLean, 2018; Ghosh & McLean, 2018; Heller & Gabaldon, 2018; Lyness & Grotto, 2018; Sidani et al., 2015; Van Emmerik et al., 2010).

The role of women within society and women in executive positions

In the literature, we can find evidence that the role of women within society influences female presence in executive positions. Regarding gender roles, individuals tend to behave according to societal and cultural expectations (Van Emmerik et al., 2010). This means that the role of women assigned by the culture impacts their opportunities in professional life (von Alberti-Alhtaybat & Aazam, 2018).

Cultures that strongly rely on traditional values tend to assign women the "guardian of the hearth" (Sidani et al., 2015; Alhadhrami et al., 2018; Cho & McLean, 2018; Chao, 2011). Cultural values and ideologies define women's career growth (Manzoor, 2015). There are countries (e.g. Saudi Arabia) with a robust male dominance which restricts women's possibility to make their own decisions due to their role within the society, as women's career growth is restricted by cultural barriers (Hodges, 2017; Manzoor, 2015; Samo et al., 2019; Sidani et al., 2015). Women in traditional settings face a lot of negative stereotypes in leadership as the expectations of successful leaders are contradictory to women's traditional role within the family (Cho & McLean, 2018; Lyness & Grotto, 2018; Quader & Oplatka, 2008; Sidani et al., 2015). Therefore, women are perceived as ineffective and unprofessional (Samo et al., 2019; Sidani et al., 2015; Quader & Oplatka, 2008). On the other hand, in developed countries, where the awareness of gender equality is higher and the perception of diversity in top management positions increases, there will be more progress towards women in top management positions in the coming years (Evans, 2010). This also positively influences women's access to education (Ghosh & McLean, 2018).

Religion and traditional beliefs and women in executive positions

Religion is another factor established by researchers to explain culture's influence on women in executive positions. Some say that religion is the most critical factor impacting women's status within the society (Hodges, 2017; Von Alberti-Alhtaybat & Aazam, 2018). The main reason is that religion is deeply rooted in societal expectations and significantly influences culture (Hodges, 2017). For example, countries with Islam as the dominant religion showed more patriarchal structures (Alhadhrami et al., 2018; Quader & Oplatka, 2008; Samo et al., 2019; Sidani et al., 2015; von Alberti-Alhtaybat & Aazam, 2018). In an Islamic context, women take part to a lesser degree in managerial positions and have limited freedoms in their everyday lives (Alhadhrami et al., 2018; Hodges, 2017; Manzoor, 2015; Samo et al., 2019; Sidani et al., 2015; Von Alberti-Alhtaybat & Aazam, 2018). Hence, female participation in the workforce is meagre (Sidani et al., 2015), especially in top management positions (Alhadhrami et al., 2018; Ghosh & McLean, 2018; Hodges, 2017; Manzoor, 2015). In patriarchal societies, women face barriers to obtaining top managerial positions (Sidani et al., 2015). Opposite, in a culture shaped by Christianity where women's presence in executive positions is on the rise and will get even more apparent in the future (Evans, 2010; Lyness & Grotto, 2018).

Researchers have identified traditional beliefs and values as another category influencing women's presence in managerial positions. This category shapes culture fundamentally. Beliefs and values are present in cultures even nowadays. Often, traditional views establish approaches to the presence of women in the business world (Hodges, 2017; Quader & Oplatka, 2008). When gender has traditionally assigned roles within society, it is more difficult for women to take management positions (Hodges, 2017). In conservative mentality cultures and countries, there is the belief that women should not be supported in their professional careers as they have to fulfil their duties at home (Hodges, 2017; Ghosh & McLean, 2018). Otherwise, they are perceived not to be a good family member (von Alberti-Ahtaybat & Aazam, 2018). The result is that women do not pursue managerial positions (von Alberti-Alhtaybat & Aazam, 2018; Chao, 2011). Additionally, women are perceived to act according to traditional and strict gender relations. Otherwise, their career advancement is hindered (Quader & Oplatka, 2008).

The Volkswagen Group worldwide and the percentage of women in management positions in the company (Volkswagen Group, n.d. a)

Headquartered in Wolfsburg, the Volkswagen Group is one of the world's leading car manufacturers and the largest car manufacturer in Europe. The Group comprises ten brands from seven European countries: Volkswagen Passenger Cars, Volkswagen Commercial Vehicles, ŠKODA, SEAT, CUPRA, Audi, Lamborghini, Bentley, Porsche, and Ducati. The passenger car range includes both compact and luxury cars. Ducati offers motorbikes. The Group has a wide range of commercial vehicle and truck products, from pickups to buses to large trucks. With a portfolio of strong global brands, through the use of leading technologies and innovative ideas, and the commitment of all employees, the Volkswagen Group is actively shaping the future of mobility by investing in electric and autonomous vehicles, digitalisation, and sustainability. The Volkswagen Group is one of the largest private employers in the world. As of 31 December 2022, the Group employed 675.805 people, 0.4% more than at the end of 2021. The Group operates globally with 115 production sites in 19 European countries and 10 in the Americas, Asia, and Africa. The Group's vehicles are sold in more than 150 countries.

A human resources policy that promotes work–life balance is a crucial feature of the Volkswagen Group's attractiveness as an employer. In particular, it helps to achieve greater gender equality. The Group is constantly working to develop family-friendly working time models and to bring more women into management positions. The percentage of women in management positions covers executive circles, senior management, and top management (including members of the Group Executive Boards) and stood at 17.2 percentage points in 2022. By 2025, the Group wants to increase the proportion of women in management positions to 20.2%. By 2025, it also wants to increase the degree of internationalisation of top management to 25.0%. In the past financial year, this was 23.4% (20.3%). The values for the proportion of women in management and internationalisation in top management were included in the Diversity Index, set at 100 in 2016. For 2022, the index was to increase to 136. This target was exceeded with a score of 140 (Volkswagen Group, n.d. a).

Volkswagen Poznań – a high proportion of women in management and an all-female management board (Volkswagen Group, n.d. a)

One of the companies of the Volkswagen Group is Volkswagen Poznań (VWP), belonging to the Brand Volkswagen Commercial Vehicles. The company, operating since 1993, currently has four production plants (Poznań-Antoninek plant, Białężyce plant near Września, Swarzędz plant, and Poznań Foundry Plant) employing a total of 9,500 people. Volkswagen Poznań is the largest manufacturer of cars and components in Poland and the largest employer in Wielkopolska. The Poznań plant is the only factory in the world where the Volkswagen Caddy is manufactured. Also, the plant in Białężyce is the only place of production of the Volkswagen Crafter and MAN TGE model. The Volkswagen Poznań foundry manufactures subassemblies for the critical models of the Group, such as the Volkswagen Golf or the Volkswagen ID. Buzz.

Volkswagen Poznań's human resources policy promoting gender equality enables the company to achieve high rates of hiring and promoting women to management positions. At the end of 2022, the ratio of women in senior and middle management positions at Volkswagen Poznań far exceeded the Volkswagen Group's targets (20.2% by 2025). It amounted to 30.5%, with 31.3% in senior management positions and 27.7% in other management positions. At the same time, it should be emphasised that the percentage of women in the entire workforce of Volkswagen Poznań is 9%. Compared to the other companies of the Group, Volkswagen Poznań is also unique, in that it has the only three-member management board in the entire Group made up exclusively of women. As of 1 July 2023, the position of CEO of VWP was taken over by Stefanie Hegels, who previously held the position of director of the production plant in Białężyce. Board members at the moment also include Agnieszka Olenderek, who is in charge of finance, purchasing, and IT, and Jolanta Musielak, who is responsible for personnel policy and organisation. The female management board is the result of implementing an equality and diversity policy pursued by the Volkswagen Group, confirmation of the high professional and personal qualifications, and at the same time, the first such board in the history of the Group and on the scale of the automotive industry in Poland.

The phenomenon of the high gender diversity rate at the Volkswagen Poznań plant (Volkswagen Group, n.d. b)

The high percentage of women in management positions at Volkswagen Poznań is essentially the result of the company's active, long-standing human resources (HR) policy. In all its activities related to HR, Volkswagen Poznań supports diversity and thus promotes work–life balance attitudes and builds a family-friendly environment. Due to its active role in building the family, such attitudes are supported primarily by ladies. At Volkswagen Poznań, several programmes and activities actively support women who want to build their professional position in conjunction with the well-being of their families. Examples of such activities include

- Future Mother programme;
- Flexitime and hybrid work opportunities;
- Offer of professional development within VWP – active encouragement of women to take up work at VWP and extension of knowledge and competencies of the women employed by the company;
- Best practice – active participation of women leaders of VWP in public discussions.

As part of the Future Mother programme, Volkswagen Poznań has introduced working time facilities for mothers-to-be. The possibility of flexible working hours has been created (six hours of work with the same payment), parking spaces have been provided in a closer and more convenient location, and the workplace has been adapted. It is possible to hire a comfortable chair for pregnant women. Special restrooms have also been prepared for pregnant women and nursing mothers. Additional benefits include free medical examinations, which mothers-to-be can have at the company outpatient clinic. The company's top management and a project group comprising representatives from various company departments were involved in implementing the programme. The project aims to encourage mothers-to-be to work as long as possible during pregnancy and create the most attractive and secure employment conditions.

The possibility of flexible and remote working, which is friendly to women who are economically active while running a household and raising children, appeared at VWP even before the COVID-19 pandemic, during which many companies in the world adopted such a solution. At Volkswagen Poznań, it had already been adopted earlier. The solution was that employees whose nature of work allowed them to do so could perform their work duties from home two days a month. This experience was put to good use when, in connection with the spread of the coronavirus, the so-called Covid Law was introduced. According to it, the employer could have the work carried out remotely. And this is what happened. At VWP, as in other companies during the pandemic, remote working was made mandatory wherever possible. Once the pandemic was called off, it was felt that the experience of hybrid working in the company was positive enough that the model could be further developed and implemented.

What does this model consist of? An employee is expected to spend 40% of his or her working time on the company's premises in a month. In practice, this means that he performs his duties at the workplace two days a week and works from home three days a week. Notably, a person employed at Volkswagen Poznań can start work between 6 a.m. and 9 a.m. This flexible solution is a considerable convenience, especially for women who, for example, drive their children to school or kindergarten. Hybrid working is a consensus solution. It allows a reasonable reconciliation of the needs of the employer and the employees with significant consideration for women. Of course, Volkswagen Poznań is a manufacturing company, so the presence of employees directly in production positions is always necessary. Therefore, hybrid working cannot apply to all employees at Volkswagen Poznań. On the other hand, those who can perform their duties at home can work in the hybrid model.

In the recruitment process, Volkswagen Poznań focuses primarily on diversity in the broad sense of the word. However, the company knows that women taking up a job in this technical, "male" environment do not always have the knowledge related to this kind of employment. Hence, VWP carried out activities to bring and show the automotive world "from behind the scenes" and to encourage ladies to work in purely technical positions. Girl's Day was an event aimed at girls completing their primary education. It aimed to increase girls' interest in education in trade schools associated with VWP. Activities like factory tours and workshops to test practical skills brought the automotive world closer to young girls. In addition, thanks to cooperation with vocational schools, the best male and female students are offered support in their development through employment, while as part of intensive cooperation with Poznań universities, female students are offered summer internships in various fields.

Volkswagen Poznań also met the expectations of women from outside the organisation by creating a Women's Day, during which women could test their predispositions to work in production positions and listen to motivational speeches of women working at Volkswagen Poznań, who combine their passion, which is at the same time their professional work, with family duties. The day dedicated to women made it possible to understand the essence of VWP work in practice as well as in theory, simultaneously an interesting experience for both parties.

Women leaders at Volkswagen Poznań have an excellent opportunity to share their knowledge and experience with others, thus encouraging other women to build their professional paths consciously. Volkswagen Poznań actively participates in many branch conferences – automotive, economic, or HR conferences, and the speakers of presentations, lectures, or discussion panel participants are often women. The best example of the high position of women at Volkswagen Poznań is the three members of the VWP Management Board who actively participate in such events.

Conclusion

Poland has rather traditional conservative (compared to many other European countries) cultural and social conditions. These are indeed due to historical aspects and the still Catholic-religious solid attitudes determining the role of women in society. At the same time, considering these conditions, it is a country that stands out in the European Union regarding women's education. According to Eurostat data for 2022, 40.5% of people aged 25–34 in Poland will have completed tertiary education. This figure is 50.1% for women and 31.2% for men. This places our country in the average of EU countries (EU average for 2022: women 48%, men 37 %), but much higher for the percentage of women than economically better developed neighbouring countries such as Germany or the Czech Republic: Germany 37.1% (Total), 39.5% (Women), 34.9% (Men); Czech Republic 34.5% (Total), 42.9 % (Women), 26.6% (Men) (European Commission, 2022).

The high percentage of women with higher education, which now significantly exceeds the percentage of men with higher education, is undoubtedly one of the main reasons for the systematic improvement of the professional position of women in Polish society (Ghosh & McLean, 2018). This is also reflected in the case of Volkswagen Poznań.

Paradoxically, despite traditionalist and religious factors, women in Poland have long since acquired a significant role in modern and postmodern Polish society. Several factors influenced this – from the present point of view, already treated as historical. First and foremost, compulsory schooling was introduced in Poland as early as the mid-nineteenth century (primarily in the Prussian partition, later also in the Russian partition), and positivist attitudes were strong then. Another factor – after Poland regained its independence – was the equal rights of women, the best emanation of which was the granting of total voting rights to women already in 1918 (as one of the first European countries) and constitutionally guaranteed access to education. Finally, the years of real socialism in Poland (1945 to 1989), during which women were promoted in the labour market (although, it must be admitted, not always in positions appropriate to a woman's physicality), while at the same time being given even more excellent opportunities for free education. Finally, one more crucial aspect of the presence of women in the labour market, the education of ladies and their functioning in the highest management structures of companies cannot be overlooked. This is the economic aspect. Despite tremendous progress – especially in the last 20 years, it is still a country with an average level of development and average family household incomes. This factor also often influences the need for women to enter the workforce.

In summary, taking into account the above factors, the phenomenon of the high percentage of female managers at Volkswagen Poznań is due, on the one hand, to effective, development-oriented and flexibility-enhancing HR programmes supporting diversity, and on the other hand, to the favourable influence of the environment and the social, cultural, and religious context in which the company is embedded (Chao, 2011; Cho & McLean, 2018; Evans, 2010; Ghosh & McLean, 2018; Heller & Gabaldon, 2018; Lyness & Grotto, 2018; Sidani et al., 2015; Van Emmerik et al., 2010). For this reason, it can be concluded that the effectiveness of the same diversity programmes will vary from country to country, characterised by different cultures, religions, or histories.

Companies may influence policymakers to adopt and strengthen sound policies and enforceable legislation to promote gender equality and the empowerment of all women and girls at all levels, as well as enhance the use of enabling technology, mainly information and communications technology, to promote women's empowerment. The presence of women in the marketplace and top managerial and leadership positions is crucial for each country's economic and societal development, as they represent half of the available human resources on the market; therefore, further in-depth research to shape the internal policies of companies and states is essential.

Bibliography

Alhadhrami, A., Goby, V.P., & Al-Ansaari, Y. (2018). Women's enactment of leadership in a heavily gender-marked Islamic context: An exploration within the United Arab Emirates. *International Journal of Organizational Analysis, 26*(4), 728–747, https://doi.org/10.1108/IJOA-08-2017-1206

Anambane, G., & Adom, K. (2018). Assessing the role of culture in female entrepreneurship in contemporary sub-Saharian society: Insights from the Nabadam district of Ghana. *Journal of Developmental Entrepreneurship*, *23*(3), https://doi.org/10.1142/S1084946718500176

Baughn, C.C., Chua, B., & Neupert, K.E. (2006). The normative context for women's participation in entrepreneurship: A multicountry study. *Entrepreneurship Theory and Practice*, *30*(5), 687–708. https://doi.org/10.1111/j.1540-6520.2006.00142.x

Bullough, A., & de Luque, M.S. (2015). Women's participation in entrepreneurial and political leadership: The importance of culturally endorsed implicit leadership theories. *Leadership*, *11*(1), 36–56. https://doi.org/10.1177/1742715013504427

Carrasco, A., Francoeur, C., Labelle, R., Laffarga, J., & Ruiz-Barbadillo, E. (2015). Appointing women to boards: Is there a cultural bias? *Journal of Business Ethics*, *129*(2), 429–444.

Catalyst. (2019). www.catalyst.org/wp-content/uploads/2019/05/

Catalyst. (2020). www.catalyst.org-/research/women-on-corporate-boards/

Chao, C.C. (2011). Climbing the Himalayas: A cross-cultural analysis of female leadership and glass ceiling effect in non-profit organizations. *Leadership & Organization Development Journal*, *32*(8), 760–781.

Cho, Y., & McLean, G.N. (2018). *Korean Women in Leadership* (1st ed.). Cham: Palgrave Macmillan.

Eagly, A.H., & Carli, L.L. (2007). *Through the Labyrinth: The Truth About How Women Become Leaders*. Boston, MA: Harvard Business School Press.

Eagly, A.H., & Sczesny, S. (2009). Stereotypes about women, men, and leaders: Have times changed? In M. Barreto, M.K. Ryan & M.T. Schmitt, M. T (Eds.), *The Glass Ceiling in the 21th Century: Understanding Barriers to Gender Equality*. Washington, DC: American Psychological Association.

Eden, L., & Forquer Gupta, S. (2017). Culture and context matter: Gender in international business and management. *Cross Cultural & Strategic Management*, *24*(2), 194–210.

European Commission: Education and Training Monitor. (2022). *Polska*. https://op.europa.eu/webpub/eac/education-and-training-monitor-2022/pl/country-reports/poland.html. https://doi.org/10.2766/354456

European Institute for Gender Equality. (2019). *Gender Equity Index*. https://eige.europa.eu/gender-equality-index/publications

Evans, D. (2010). Aspiring to leadership . . . a women's world? An example of developments in France. *Cross Cultural Management: An International Journal*, *17*(4), 347–367.
Ghosh, R., & McLean, G.N. (2018). *Indian Women in Leadership* (1st ed.). Cham: Palgrave MacMillan.
Gonzales, M. (2023). *The Bumpy Path to Leadership for Women*. www.shrm.org/resourcesandtools/hr-topics/behavioral-competencies/pages/the-bumpy-path-to-leadership-for-women.aspx
Hechavarría, D.M., & Ingram, A.E. (2019). Entrepreneurial ecosystem conditions and gendered national-level entrepreneurial activity: A 14-year panel study of GEM. *Small Business Economics*, *53*(2), 431–458. https://doi.org/10.1007/s11187-018-9994-7
Heller, L., & Gabaldon, P. (2018). Women on boards of directors in Latin America: Building a model. *Academia Revista Latinoamericana de Administración*, *31*(1), 43–72.
Hodges, J. (2017). Cracking the walls of leadership: Women in Saudi Arabia. *Gender in Management: An International Journal*, *32*(1), 34–46.
Hofstede, G. (1998). *Masculinity and Femininity: The Taboo Dimension of National Cultures*. Thousand Oaks, CA: Sage Publications.
Hofstede, G. (2001). *Culture's Consequences: Comparing Values, Behaviors, Institutions, and Organizations across Nations* (2nd ed.). Thousand Oaks, CA: Sage Publications.
Hofstede, G., & Bond, M.H. (1984). Hofstede's culture dimensions: An independent validation using Rokeach's Value Survey. *Journal of Cross-Cultural Psychology*, *15*(4), 417–433. https://doi.org/10.1177/0022002184015004003
House, R.J., Dorfman, P.W., Javidan, M., Hanges, P.J., & Sully de Luque, M.F. (2014). *Strategic Leadership across Cultures: The GLOBE Study of CEO Leadership Behavior and Effectiveness in 24 Countries* (1st ed.). Thousand Oaks, CA: Sage Publications.
Lyness, K.S., & Grotto, A.R. (2018). Women and leadership in the United States: Are we closing the gender gap? *Annual Review of Organizational Psychology and Organizational Behavior*, *5*, 227–265.
Manolova, T.S., Brush, C.G., Edelman, L.F., & Elam, A. (2020). Pivoting to stay the course: How women entrepreneurs take advantage of opportunities created by the COVID-19 pandemic. *International Small Business Journal*, *38*(6), 481–491. https://doi.org/10.1177/0266242620949136
Manzoor, S. (2015). The impact of indigenous culture on female leadership in Pakistan. *International Journal of Organizational Leadership*, *4*, 414–429.
Mielcarek, P. (2014). Metoda case study w rozwoju teorii naukowych. *Organizacja i Kierowanie*, *1*, 105–117.
Milkie, M.A., & Peltola, P. (1999). Playing all the roles: Gender and the work family balancing act. *Journal of Marriage and Family*, *61*, 476–490. https://doi.org/10.2307/353763
Northouse, P.G. (2016). *Leadership: Theory and Practice* (7th ed.). Thousand Oaks, CA: Sage Publications.
Northouse, P.G. (2018). *Leadership: Theory and Practice* (8th ed.). Thousand Oaks, CA: Sage Publications.
Palka, S. (2006). *Metodologia, badania, praktyka pedagogiczna*. Gdańsk: GWP Publications.
Quader, S.A.R., & Oplatka, I. (2008). The power of femininity: Exploring the gender and ethnic experiences of Muslim women who accessed supervisory roles in a Bedouin society. *Journal of Educational Administration*, *46*(3), 396–415.
Samo, A.H., Qazi, S.W., & Mansoor Buriro, W. (2019). Labelling them is negating them: A phenomenological study of stereotypes and followers' experiences about women leadership in Pakistan. *Management Research Review*, *42*(3), 391–411.
Sehgal, A., & Khandelwal, P. (2020). Work–Family interface of women entrepreneurs: Evidence from India. *South Asian Journal of Business Studies*, *9*(3), 411–428.

Sidani, Y.M., Konrad, A., & Karam, C.M. (2015). From female leadership advantage to female leadership deficit: A developing country perspective. *Career Development International*, *20*(3), 273–292.
Singh, V., & Vinnicombe, S. (2003). The 2002 female FTSE index and women directors. *Women in Management Review*, *18*, 349–358. http://dx.doi.org/10.1108/09649420310498975xxdxdfdxxcdxx
United Nations. (2020). www.un.org/en/sections/issues-depth/gender-equality/
United Nations. (2023, July 10). *The Sustainable Development Goals Report*. https://unstats.un.org/sdgs/report/2023/
U.S. National Center for Education Statistics. (2016). *Degrees Conferred by Race/Ethnicity and Sex*. https://nces.ed.gov/fastfacts/display.asp?id=72
Van Emmerik, H., Wendt, H., & Euwema, M.C. (2010). Gender ratio, societal culture, and male and female leadership. *Journal of Occupational and Organizational Psychology*, *83*, 895–914.
Vasile, A.C., & Nicolescu, L. (2016). Hofstede's cultural dimensions and management in corporations. *Cross-Cultural Management Journal*, *18*(1), 35–46.
Virick, M., & Greer, C.R. (2012). Gender diversity in leadership succession: Preparing for the future. *Human Resource Management*, *51*(4), 575–600.
Volkswagen Group. (n.d. a). *Mitarbeiter*. https://geschaeftsbericht2022.volkswagenag.com/konzernlagebericht/nachhaltige-wertsteigerung/mitarbeiter.html
Volkswagen Group. (n.d. b). www.vw-group.pl/
Von Alberti-Alhtaybat, L., & Aazam, S. (2018). Female leadership in the middle eastern higher education. *Journal of Economic and Administrative Sciences*, *34*(2), 90–107.

15 Culture and business

Looking ahead 2035

Małgorzata Bartosik-Purgat and Łukasz Puślecki

The relationship between culture and business is undeniably interdependent and complex. The studies presented in the particular parts of the monograph delved into the intricate ways in which culture influences various aspects of the business world and how businesses, in turn, shape and adapt to cultural contexts.

In the global market in the third decade of the twenty-first century, various trends and behaviours are observed among both individual consumers and organisations (including enterprises). On the one hand, globalisation is continuing, which contributes to the proliferation of companies' activities in various foreign markets (Aguinis & Burgi-Tian, 2023; Nakouwo et al., 2023; Qin et al., 2023). In addition, there are many similarities among the needs and preferences of buyers from different markets (Vescovi, 2022). This situation and behaviour is primarily influenced by, among other things, the development of technology and media (as well as increased access to the Internet and social media), the increased mobility of people around the world, as well as generational changes, for example, representatives of younger generations show similar characteristics regardless of where they live (de Boer & Bordoloi, 2022). Access to the boarding house and the media allows for a better understanding of the customs and behaviour of other cultures. However, the increased migration of the population due to various factors causes situations in which previously culturally homogeneous societies become culturally diverse. This allows us to get to know representatives of other cultures, their customs, needs, behaviour, etc. (Lee et al., 2023; Vescovi, 2022).

On the other hand, global market events such as wars (e.g. the war in Ukraine and the war in the Middle East) or pandemics (e.g. the COVID-19 pandemic) and the great threats and dangers arising from these are driving a return to a focus on national or regional markets (Rahbari et al., 2023; Roscoe et al., 2022). The emergence of the COVID-19 pandemic unquestionably stands out as the most significant "black swan" event of the century. Its transformative impact is groundbreaking, posing current challenges in ensuring business continuity and enhancing organisational resilience in the intercultural dimension. A direct fallout of the pandemic is the global acceleration of digital transformation. Remote work has seen a substantial surge, with IT infrastructure, VPN solutions, and

DOI: 10.4324/9781032636962-18

videoconferencing playing pivotal roles, establishing a "new normal" that will persist beyond the pandemic. A discernible trend is the drive to minimise business risks, manifesting in the diversification of office locations. Dissatisfaction with certain Asian countries' crisis management has fuelled the momentum towards nearshoring (Dziurski, 2016; Djelic, 2021; Roscoe et al., 2022; Jaklić et al., 2023; Schuh et al., 2024). Western Europe leans towards service centre locations in Central and Eastern Europe, while U.S. entities opt for locales in Central and Eastern Europe and Latin America. The service sector is undergoing profound changes, with more intercultural teams (ABSL, 2020). Adapting to emerging global trends, potential catalysts of change, and both adverse and positive "black swans" become imperative. Survival mandates a proactive readiness for change (ABSL, 2023). Moreover, the potential destabilisation of macroeconomic fundamentals, such as inflationary pressures and global stagflation, is a major threat to global business operations (ABSL, 2023). Another significant concern is a global talent shortage. Despite their adverse nature, many of these drivers of change can be viewed as opportunities. The COVID-19 pandemic, initially a shock, became a catalyst for structural changes, accelerating digital transformation and a widespread shift to new working models. Post-pandemic, remote and hybrid modes have become integral, accompanied by increasingly internationalised teams with members from different countries and cultures.

The aforementioned migration of representatives from various countries and cultures, besides its positive outcomes such as gaining insights into their behaviours, providing assistance, and augmenting the workforce in individual markets, also brings about adverse effects (Aguinis & Burgi-Tian, 2023). It can evoke fear among the native population, for example, due to increased competitiveness in the job market, the spread of a different culture, and consequently, the emergence of tensions. Besides, the political scene is witnessing the rise of political factions with far-right views seeking a strong focus on indigenous markets and cultures. The fear of many people of the dangers of world events may cause an even more significant increase in support for such views in the future, resulting in the "closure" of domestic markets.

Taking into account the trends in behaviours of companies and people concerning the world economic and political situation, the key conclusions and predictions may concern (1) the future development of the globalisation trends and related processes of convergence or divergence, (2) dilemma of companies linked with standardisation versus adaptation strategies, (3) cultural diversity management, (4) digitalisation, changes in labour market and cultural effects, (5) the significance of ethical and social responsibilities of businesses, and (6) ecological sensitivity and cultures.

While globalisation opens up opportunities, it also poses challenges. Cultural misunderstandings, misinterpretations, and clashes can arise. Businesses must invest in cultural education and training to mitigate these challenges and promote smooth operations because the globalised business landscape demands high cultural sensitivity (Kent et al., 2023; Qin et al., 2023). Organisations that recognise and respect cultural nuances gain a competitive advantage. Just as financial and legal due diligence are critical in business, cultural due diligence is equally important. Cross-cultural understanding fosters better communication, trust, and collaboration, leading to more successful partnerships and ventures (Gao et al., 2022; Kent et al., 2023). Before entering new markets or collaborations, businesses should invest time in researching and comprehending the cultural landscape to make informed decisions.

In conclusion, the future development of globalisation trends and their associated processes of convergence or divergence remain complex and dynamic phenomena (Aguinis & Burgi-Tian, 2023). As the world becomes more interconnected through advancements in technology, communication, and trade, the trajectory of globalisation will likely continue. However, whether this will result in greater convergence or divergence among different cultures, economies, and societies is a subject of ongoing debate (Vescovi, 2022). Proponents of convergence argue that globalisation will lead to increased cultural exchange, the spread of shared values, and a more interconnected global economy (Guedes et al., 2023). This could result in greater standardisation, improved cross-cultural understanding, and the potential for solving global challenges collectively (Lee et al., 2023). On the other hand, advocates of divergence suggest that as cultures and nations interact more extensively, there is a heightened emphasis on preserving and promoting distinct identities. Economic disparities could persist or even widen, leading to potential conflicts and inequalities (Nakouwo et al., 2023). Local cultures might resist homogenisation, striving to maintain uniqueness despite global influences. This phenomenon may be developed because of the by-world events that evoke fear and threat in people (presented in the above paragraphs). The ultimate outcome will likely be a combination of convergence and divergence. Certain aspects of life may become more standardised and globally interconnected, while others remain distinct and regionally rooted. The balance between these forces will depend on factors such as government policies, technological advancements, social dynamics, and individual choices. To predict the exact direction of these trends would be challenging, as a myriad of unpredictable factors shapes the future development of globalisation. However, continued dialogue and cooperation on a global scale will be crucial in navigating the complexities of this ongoing process.

Convergence and divergence processes cause the companies to be constantly faced with a dilemma regarding the degree of application of standardisation and adaptation strategies (Liu & Shi, 2020). In other words, businesses have a perpetual dilemma of adapting to local cultures or standardising operations. Striking the right balance is crucial. Successful companies often tailor their products, services, and marketing strategies according to cultural conditions while maintaining their core values and brand identity. This is an intermediate solution, often referred to as semi-standardisation in the literature (Liu & Shi, 2020). It commonly involves standardising feasible strategic elements and adapting those elements necessary for the company's smooth operation in foreign markets (Vrontis et al., 2009). It combines the benefits of standardisation (such as economies of scale) with adaptation (such as customer approval due to adjusting some aspects to their tastes and preferences) (Gao et al., 2022; Guedes et al., 2023).

The activities of companies and other institutions internationally contribute to the involvement of employees from different countries and, thus, different cultures. This will certainly be a development trend in the future due to a number of circumstances. One of the reasons for the differentiation of the origin of employees in companies is also the migration of the population associated with many different situations such as wars, natural disasters, political and economic problems, ethnic and religious conflicts, and many others (Caputo et al., 2023; Ozkazanc-Pan, 2019). In addition, the development of technology or increased access to high-speed Internet (an increasing number of countries around the world on access to fixed Internet connections) contributes to the increasing formation of culturally diverse virtual teams carrying out projects within the framework of work in a specific company (Caputo et al., 2023; Chang et al., 2023; Orsini & Magnier-Watanabe, 2023).

The circumstances mentioned earlier imply the need to manage cultural diversity, which is associated with many benefits but challenges (Aytemiz Seymen, 2006; Orsini & Magnier-Watanabe, 2023). Culturally diverse teams foster creativity and innovation (Yeganeh, 2023). Businesses can access a broader range of perspectives, ideas, and problem-solving approaches by integrating individuals from different cultural backgrounds. This diversity can lead to breakthroughs and the development of products that cater to a broader customer base. In addition, the presence of cultural diversity in a company contributes to improving its image and reputation internationally, which also affects relations with business partners. However, diversity management also involves many barriers and challenges due to the individual characteristics of the employee, the specifics of the employee team, and the organisation itself (Caputo et al., 2023). These issues are multifaceted and range from problems of communication, values, and religion to stereotypes and prejudices (Chang et al., 2023; Wolfgruber et al., 2022).

In the realm of labour market and talent pool dynamics, shaped by the transformative impact of the COVID-19 pandemic (mainly due to the digitalisation process), companies in the future will grapple with challenges in building effective, multicultural teams. While there are new opportunities to evolve talent strategies and adapt to the current landscape, the scarcity of talent remains a major global challenge for the business services sector and other industries. Recruitment patterns have shifted due to the pandemic, with a rise in hiring from anywhere (employees from different countries and cultures). Specific locations are still valued for their unique competencies tied to local business culture and organisational knowledge. Simultaneously, the sector's growth and talent demand force organisations to source employees globally. According to

Randstad (ABSL, 2023), retaining employees with the right skills poses a growing challenge. To address this, companies increasingly offer extended benefits and prioritise employee well-being, including remote work incentives. The future of talent management pivots away from specific qualifications and positional hiring, focusing instead on skill groups. Grouping roles based on skills clusters, rather than narrow specialisations, not only enhances job opportunities but also provides flexibility for employees (especially those operating in international teams) to transition smoothly between roles within the same skill cluster. This approach aligns with neuroscience, making it easier for employees to adapt when their role undergoes redefinition (Digital University, 2020). As the concept of work evolves in the era of digitalisation, a philosophy of smarter working has emerged, granting employees the freedom to choose where and when they work, contingent on achieving results. Employers embracing Activity-Based Working will provide varied spaces for individual or teamwork, allowing employees to choose where they can most effectively complete their assigned tasks.

On the other hand, the pervasive nature of technology enables work from anywhere, presenting a challenge in maintaining face-to-face communication. Managing dispersed teams across continents demands new skills, competencies, and behaviours. Empathic leadership becomes crucial, fostering understanding, recruitment, and retention of talent within an organisation. Empathy, a vital leadership tool, helps companies stay attuned to the market and societal changes. As technology's impact on societies and communities evolves, careful and empathetic analysis of its effects on people is imperative before implementing solutions. Companies must be attuned to the ongoing digital transformation, moving beyond the optimisation of existing solutions to genuine innovation. This requires questioning assumptions, developing new perspectives, and identifying future potential beyond current trends (Diamandis & Kotler, 2012, 2020; Śliwiński & Puślecki, 2022a, 2022b). Organisations aspiring to foster innovation and change, positioning them as "Enabling Spaces", need committed leadership and an open approach to the future. Innovation demands a change in mindset, questioning existing frameworks, and being sensitive to changes in the market, social value systems, culture, environment, and technology (Digital University, 2020). In navigating the future, the workforce must possess the ability to reflect deeply, a crucial skill in a technology-driven environment that tends to flatten curiosity. Developing epistemic curiosity, a desire for knowledge for its own sake, becomes essential for navigating complex questions in a rapidly changing reality.

It is also important to mention that the sustainability and ESG (Environmental, Social, and Governance) principles are gaining prominence, becoming integral to everyday business practice. These principles address environmental and social challenges, influencing long-term value creation in companies. Climate change, net-zero emission targets, the circular economy, gender pay gaps, talent shortages, diversity and inclusion, human rights in global value chains, data security, and employee well-being are now crucial components of business reality and transformation (ABSL, 2023), and for sure should be taken into account in the future development of the relationship between culture and business.

In conclusion, the intricate relationship between culture and business continues to evolve, driven by a multitude of factors in the dynamic global landscape. In this ever-changing landscape, ongoing dialogue and cooperation on a global scale remain vital for successfully navigating the complexities of the intertwined realms of culture and business.

Bibliography

ABSL. (2020). *Sektor nowoczesnych usług biznesowych w Polsce 2020, Związek Liderów Sektora Usług Biznesowych (ABSL – Association of Business Service Leaders)*. https://shop-absl.pl/Sektor-Nowoczesnych-Uslug-Biznesowych-w-Polsce-2020-p72

ABSL. (2023). *Sektor nowoczesnych usług biznesowych w Polsce 2023, Związek Liderów Sektora Usług Biznesowych (ABSL – Association of Business Service Leaders)*. https://shop-absl.pl/Sektor-Nowoczesnych-Uslug-Biznesowych-w-Polsce-2023-p124

Aguinis, H., & Burgi-Tian, J. (2023). Performance management around the world: Solving the standardization vs adaptation dilemma. *IIM Ranchi Journal of Management Studies, ahead-of-print* (ahead-of-print). https://doi.org/10.1108/IRJMS-09-2022-0091

Aytemiz Seymen, O. (2006). The cultural diversity phenomenon in organisations and different approaches for effective cultural diversity management: A literary review. *Cross Cultural Management: An International Journal*, *13*(4), 296–315. https://doi.org/10.1108/13527600610713404

Caputo, A., Kargina, M., & Pellegrini, M.M. (2023). Conflict in virtual teams: A bibliometric analysis, systematic review, and research agenda. *International Journal of Conflict Management*, *34*(1), 1–31. https://doi.org/10.1108/IJCMA-07-2021-0117

Chang, R.X., Carvalho, M.M., & Sbragia, R. (2023). Towards a comprehensive conceptual framework for multicultural virtual teams: A multilevel perspective exploring the relationship between multiculturalism and performance. *International Journal of Managing Projects in Business*, *16*(2), 325–354. https://doi.org/10.1108/IJMPB-09-2021-0252

de Boer, P., & Bordoloi, P. (2022). Nationality differences in Gen Z work values: An exploratory study. *Journal of International Education in Business*, *15*(2), 373–392. https://doi.org/10.1108/JIEB-09-2021-0088

Diamandis, P.H., & Kotler, S. (2012). *Abundance: The Future is Better Than You Think*. London: Free Press.

Diamandis, P.H., & Kotler, S. (2020). *The Future is Faster Than You Think: How Converging Technologies Are Transforming Business, Industries and Our Lives*. London: Simon and Schuster Ltd.

Digital University. (2020). *Beyond 2030*. https://newsletter.digitaluniversity.pl/landing/beyond2030-e4b5

Djelic, B. (2021, April). From smart followership to bold leadership: The economic future of Central and Eastern Europe. *Lazard Financial Advisory*.

Dziurski, P. (2016). CEE countries as a business outsourcing destination. In P. Trąpczyński, Ł. Puślecki & M. Jarosiński (Eds.), *Competitiveness of CEE Economies and Businesses – Multidisciplinary Perspectives on Challenges and Opportunities* (pp. 115–129). Switzerland: Springer International Publishing.

Gao, J., Wang, T., Jia, Y., & Wang, C.L. (2022). How and when do exporters benefit from an international adaptation strategy? The moderating effect of formal and informal institutional distance. *International Marketing Review*, *39*(6), 1390–1416. https://doi.org/10.1108/IMR-01-2021-0007

Guedes, M.J., Fernandes Crespo, N., & Patel, P.C. (2023). When in Rome, do as the Romans do: Can international marketing adaptation improve the association between servitization and profitability? *Journal of Business & Industrial Marketing, ahead-of-print* (ahead-of-print). https://doi.org/10.1108/JBIM-03-2022-0145

Jaklič, A., Puślecki, Ł., & Trąpczyński, P. (2023). The CEE region on a new wave of transition: Towards value chain reconfiguration and innovation cooperation amidst Turbulent Times. *Journal of East European Management Studies*. (Special Issue 2023).

Kent, P., Siemsen, E., & Shao, X. (2023). The impact of co-location on production knowledge transfer in collectivist and individualist cultures. *International Journal of Operations & Production Management, ahead-of-print* (ahead-of-print). https://doi.org/10.1108/IJOPM-06-2022-0354

Lee, J.A., Usunier, J.C., & Taras, V. (2023). *Business & Marketing across Cultures*. London: Sage Publications.

Liu, Y., & Shi, Y. (2020). Behind the scenes: Addressing dual pressures for product standardization and adaptation in new product development in multinational corporations. *European Journal of Marketing, 54*(5), 1061–1085. https://doi.org/10.1108/EJM-02-2018-0153

Nakouwo, S.N., Ofori-Sasu, D., & Kusi, B.A. (2023). Natural resources and national productivity in Africa: Are there differences in high and low globalized economies? *Critical Perspectives on International Business, 19*(2), 299–318. https://doi.org/10.1108/cpoib-12-2021-0103

Orsini, P., & Magnier-Watanabe, R. (2023). Foreign coworker nationality, cultural distance, and perception of cultural diversity in the workplace. *Journal of Asia Business Studies, 17*(2), 256–278. https://doi.org/10.1108/JABS-10-2021-0413

Ozkazanc-Pan, B. (2019). Superdiversity: A new paradigm for inclusion in a transnational world. *Equality, Diversity and Inclusion, 38*(4), 477–490. https://doi.org/10.1108/EDI-07-2018-0134

Qin, Y., Wang, X., Xu, Z., & Skare, M. (2023). The effects of globalization on family firms' business model in Europe. *International Journal of Entrepreneurial Behavior & Research, 29*(1), 27–48. https://doi.org/10.1108/IJEBR-12-2021-0994

Rahbari, M., Arshadi Khamseh, A., & Sadati-Keneti, Y. (2023). Resilience strategies in coping to disruptions of wheat supply chain caused by the Russia – Ukraine war crisis: Case study from an emerging economy. *Kybernetes, ahead-of-print* (ahead-of-print). https://doi.org/10.1108/K-12-2022-1728

Roscoe, S., Aktas, E., Petersen, K.J., Skipworth, H.D., Handfield, R.B., & Habib, F. (2022). Redesigning global supply chains during compounding geopolitical disruptions: The role of supply chain logics. *International Journal of Operations & Production Management, 42*(9), 1407–1434. https://doi.org/10.1108/IJOPM-12-2021-0777

Schuh, A., Trąpczyński, P., & Puślecki, Ł. (2024). Multinational companies in central and Eastern Europe. In T. Steger, I. Rybnikova & R. Lang (Eds.), *Handbook of Central and East European Management and Organizations*. Oxford: Oxford University Press. (In Press).

Śliwiński, R., & Puślecki, Ł. (2022a). *Competition, Strategy, and Innovation: The Impact of Trends in Business and the Consumer World*. New York: Routledge.

Śliwiński, R., & Puślecki, Ł. (2022b). Looking ahead 2030. In R. Śliwiński & Ł. Puślecki (Eds.), *Competition, Strategy, and Innovation: The Impact of Trends in Business and the Consumer World* (s. 223–237). New York: Routledge.

Vescovi, T. (2022). *Cross-Cultural Marketing: European Perspectives*. Camberley: Edward Elgar Publications.

Vrontis, D., Thrassou, A., & Lamprianou, I. (2009). International marketing adaptation versus standardisation of multinational companies. *International Marketing Review, 26*(4/5), 477–500.

Wolfgruber, D., Stürmer, L., & Einwiller, S. (2022). Talking inclusion into being: Communication as a facilitator and obstructor of an inclusive work environment. *Personnel Review*, *51*(7), 1841–1860. https://doi.org/10.1108/PR-01-2021-0013

Yeganeh, H. (2023). Culture and innovation: A human emancipation perspective. *International Journal of Sociology and Social Policy*, *ahead-of-print* (ahead-of-print). https://doi.org/10.1108/IJSSP-07-2022-0185

Index

Note: Page numbers in *italics* indicate a figure and page numbers in **bold** indicate a table on the corresponding page.